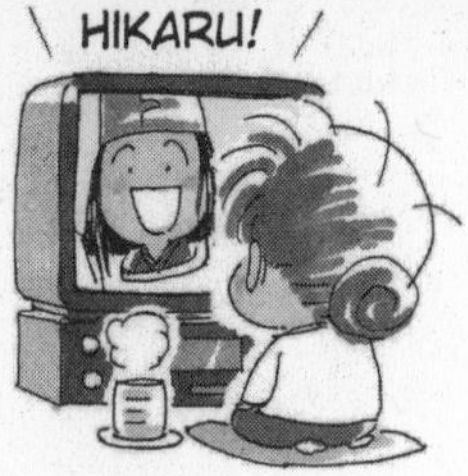
HIKARU!

Yumi Hotta

I don't think I've watched a TV anime show since *Combattler V*!

—Yumi Hotta

It all began when Yumi Hotta played a pick-up game of go with her father-in-law. As she was learning how to play, Ms. Hotta thought it might be fun to create a story around the traditional board game. More confident in her storytelling abilities than her drawing skills, she submitted the beginnings of **Hikaru no Go** to **Weekly Shonen Jump**'s Story King Award. The Story King Award is an award that picks the best story, manga, character design and youth (under 15) manga submissions every year in Japan. As fate would have it, Ms. Hotta's story (originally named, "***Kokonotsu no Hoshi***"), was a runner-up in the "Story" category of the Story King Award. Many years earlier, Takeshi Obata was a runner-up for the Tezuka Award, another Japanese manga contest sponsored by **Weekly Shonen Jump** and **Monthly Shonen Jump**. An editor assigned to Mr. Obata's artwork came upon Ms. Hotta's story and paired the two for a full-fledged manga about go. The rest is modern go history.

HIKARU NO GO VOL. 15
The SHONEN JUMP Manga Edition

STORY BY YUMI HOTTA
ART BY TAKESHI OBATA
Supervised by YUKARI UMEZAWA (5 Dan)

Translation & English Adaptation/Naoko Amemiya
English Script Consultant/Janice Kim (3 Dan)
Touch-up Art & Lettering/Inori Fukuda Trant
Design/Julie Behn
Additional Touch-up/Rachel Lightfoot
Editor/Annette Roman

Editor in Chief, Books/Alvin Lu
Editor in Chief, Magazines/Marc Weidenbaum
VP, Publishing Licensing/Rika Inouye
VP, Sales & Product Marketing/Gonzalo Ferreyra
VP, Creative/Linda Espinosa
Publisher/Hyoe Narita

Printed in Canada

Published by VIZ Media, LLC
P.O. Box 77010
San Francisco, CA 94107

SHONEN JUMP Manga Edition
10 9 8 7 6 5 4 3 2 1
First printing, May 2009

www.viz.com

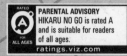

THE WORLD'S
MOST POPULAR MANGA

SHONEN JUMP

www.shonenjump.com

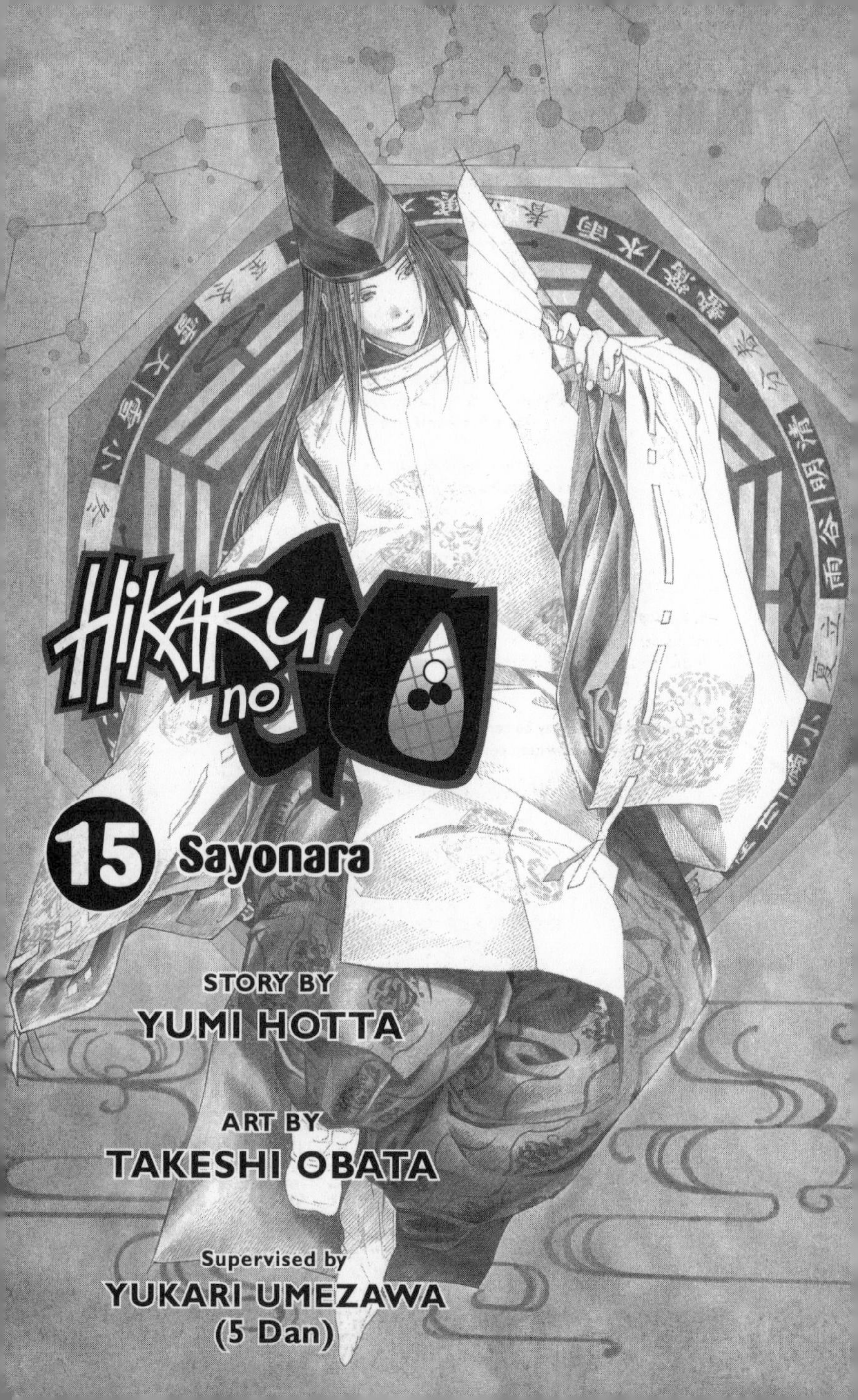
HIKARU no GO
15 Sayonara
STORY BY
YUMI HOTTA
ART BY
TAKESHI OBATA
Supervised by
YUKARI UMEZAWA
(5 Dan)

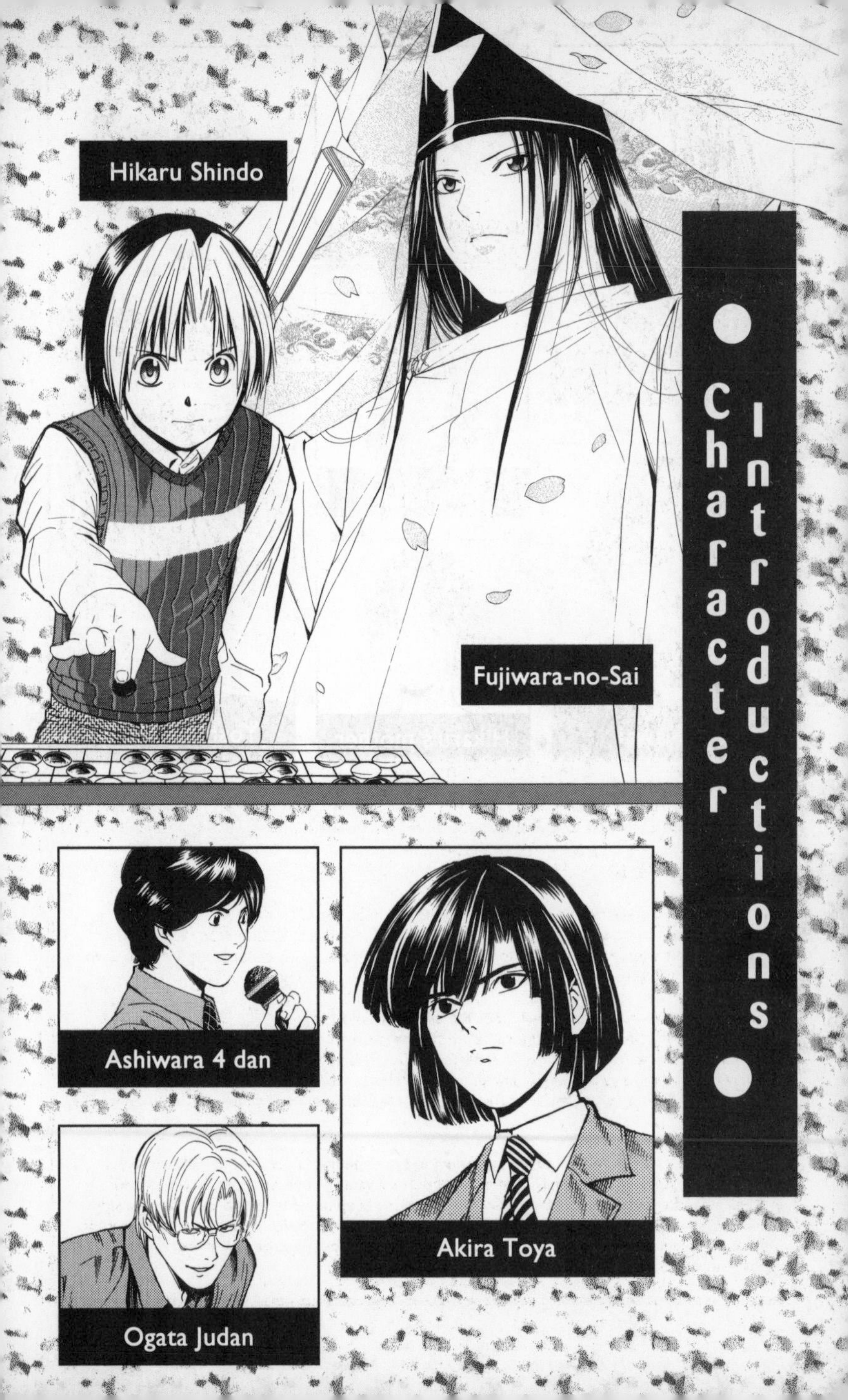
Character Introductions
Fujiwara-no-Sai
Hikaru Shindo
Akira Toya
Ashiwara 4 dan
Ogata Judan

Akari Fujisaki

Tomonori Honda

Isumi Shinichiro

Asumi Nase

Mr. Kawai

Hikaru's mother

Yoshitaka Waya

Story Thus Far

Hikaru Shindo discovers an old go board one day up in his grandfather's attic. The moment Hikaru touches the board, the spirit of Fujiwara-no-Sai, a genius go player from Japan's Heian Era, enters his consciousness. Sai's love of go inspires Hikaru, as does a meeting with the child prodigy Akira Toya—son of go master Toya Meijin.

Partway through an intense online go match between Toya Meijin and Sai, Sai makes a clever move that shifts the balance of the game. In the end, the meijin resigns, Sai wins, and the meijin makes good on his promise to retire if beaten by Sai. Afterwards, Ogata 9 dan hounds Hikaru, demanding a chance to play the online entity "sai." Ogata attempts to pry out the truth about Hikaru's relationship with "sai," but the secret remains safe and "sai" vanishes from the Internet once more.

One day after school, Hikaru runs into Kurata 6 dan. Wanting to test himself, Hikaru asks Kurata for a game. Kurata finally agrees but chooses a game of one-color go, in which both players use the same color stones! Hikaru manages to keep up with Kurata, who acknowledges Hikaru's strength. As the world of go reels in shock over Toya Meijin's unexpected retirement, Hikaru concentrates on the next game on his path to go fame. Thus occupied, he remains oblivious to Sai's growing apprehensions...

CONTENTS

15

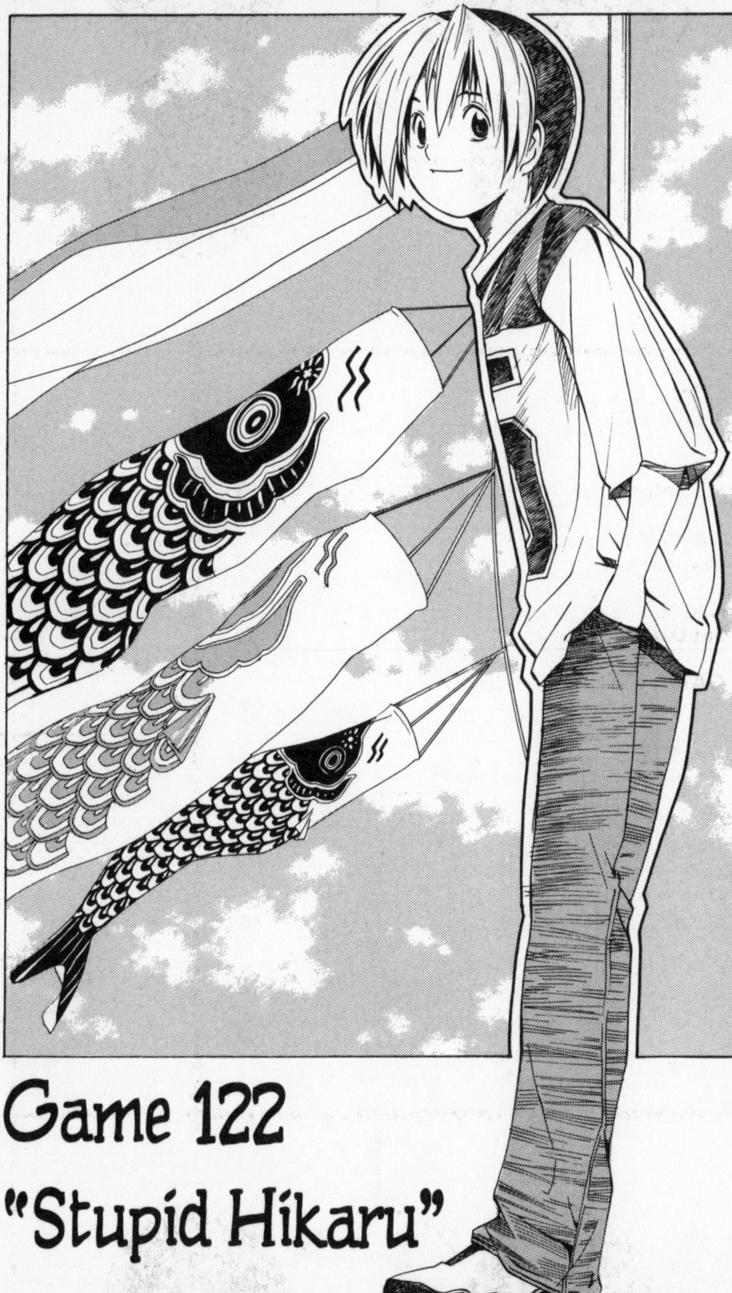

Game 122
"Stupid Hikaru"

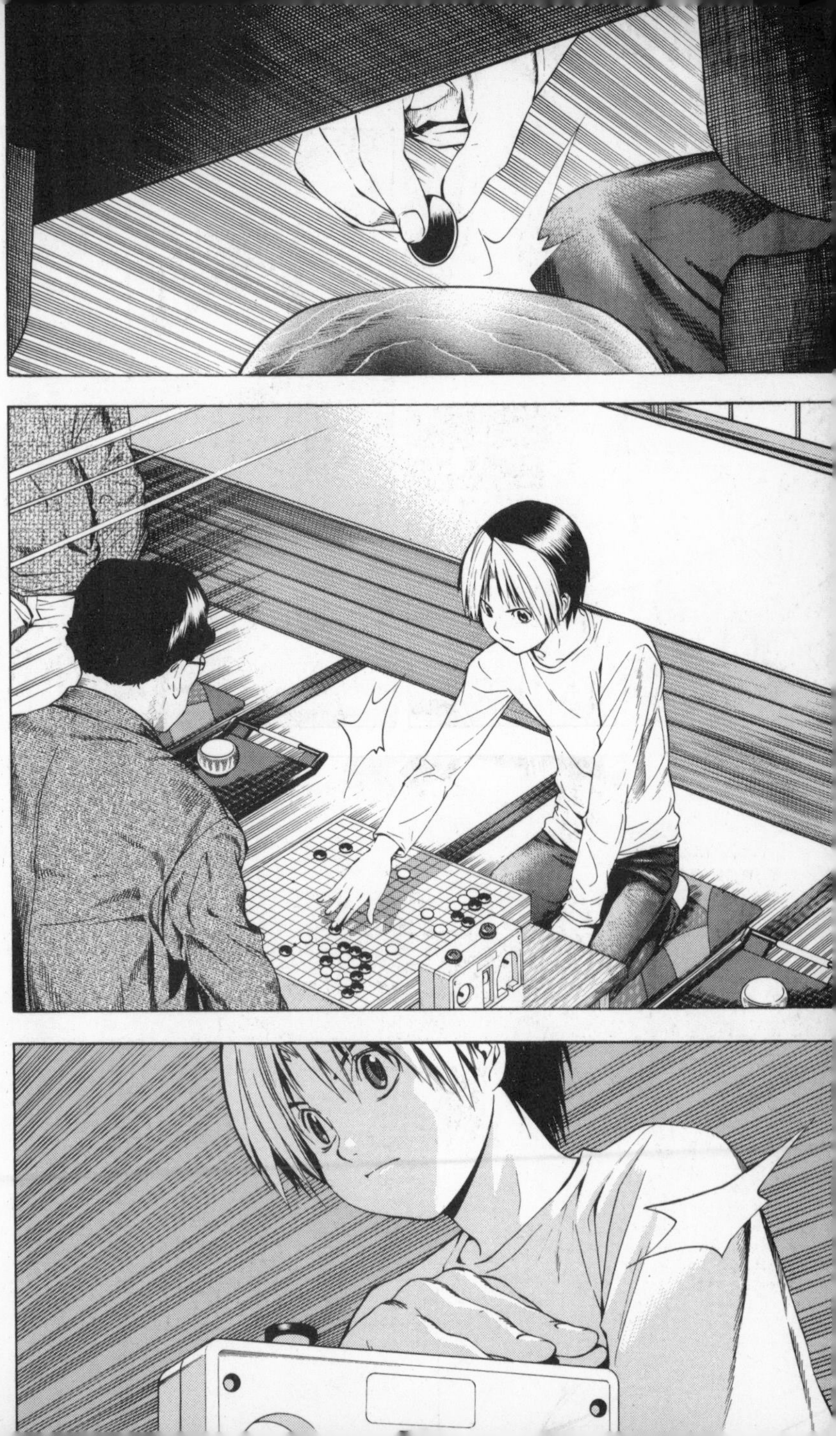

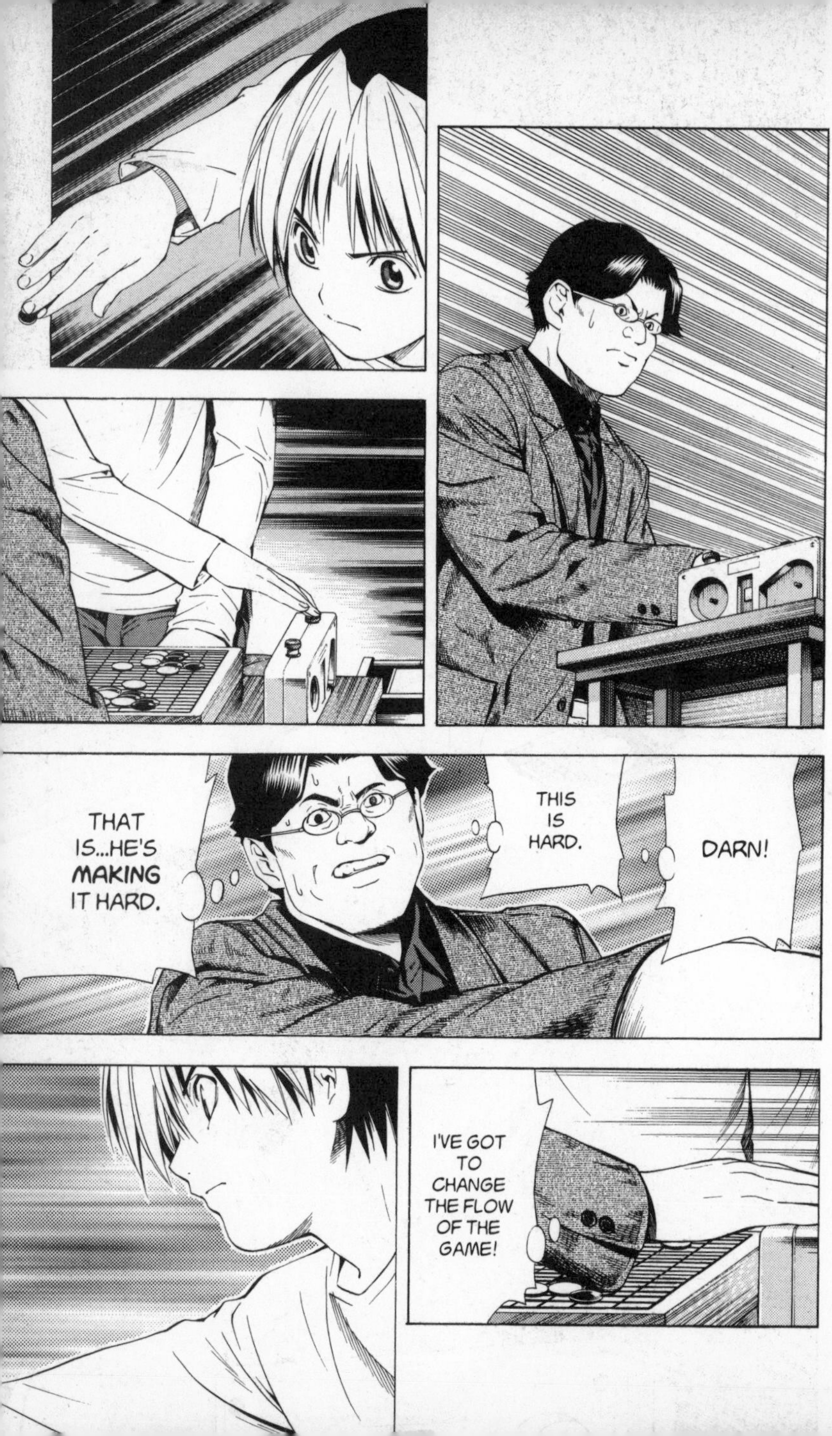
DARN!
THIS IS HARD.
THAT IS...HE'S MAKING IT HARD.
I'VE GOT TO CHANGE THE FLOW OF THE GAME!

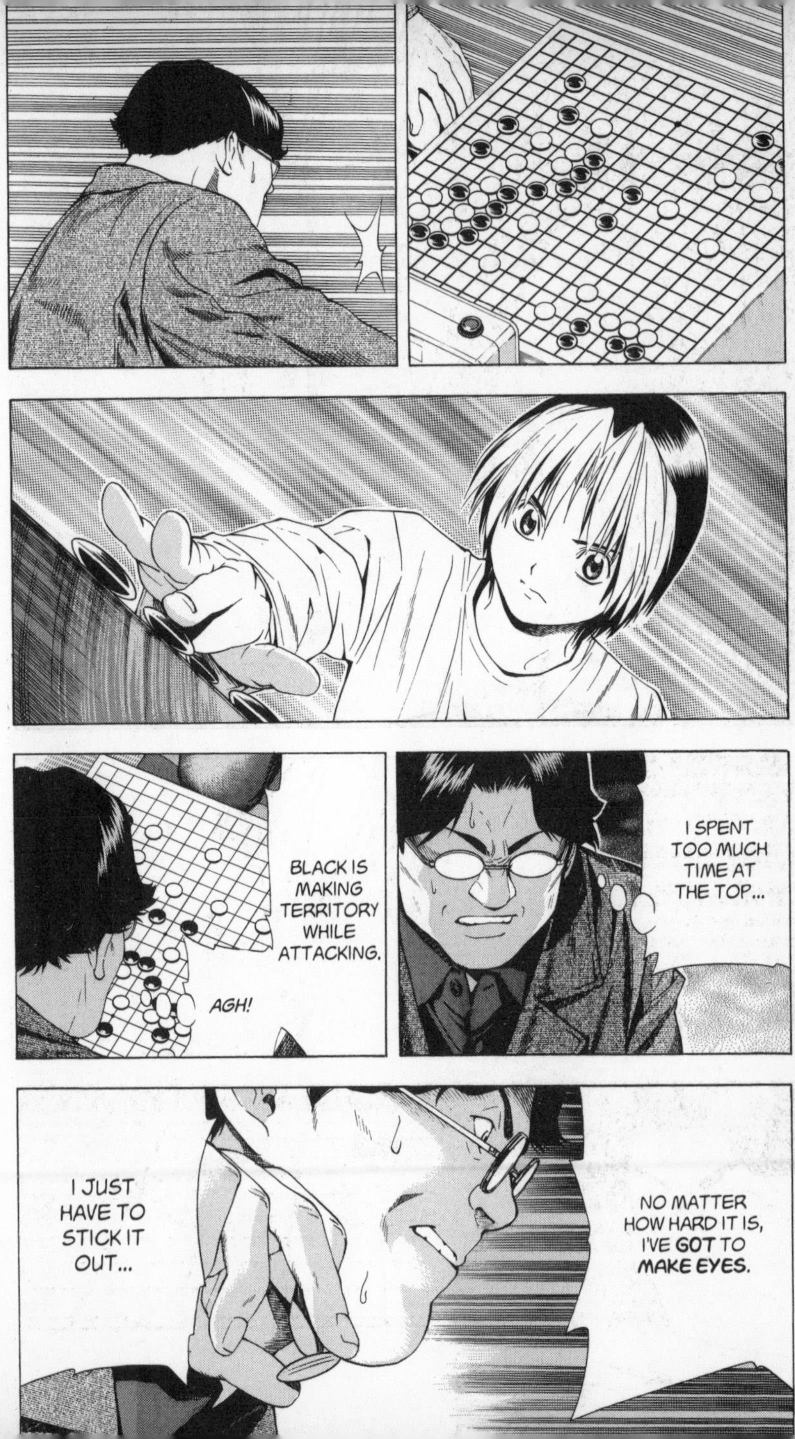
I SPENT TOO MUCH TIME AT THE TOP...
BLACK IS MAKING TERRITORY WHILE ATTACKING.
AGH!
NO MATTER HOW HARD IT IS, I'VE **GOT** TO **MAKE EYES.**
I JUST HAVE TO STICK IT OUT...

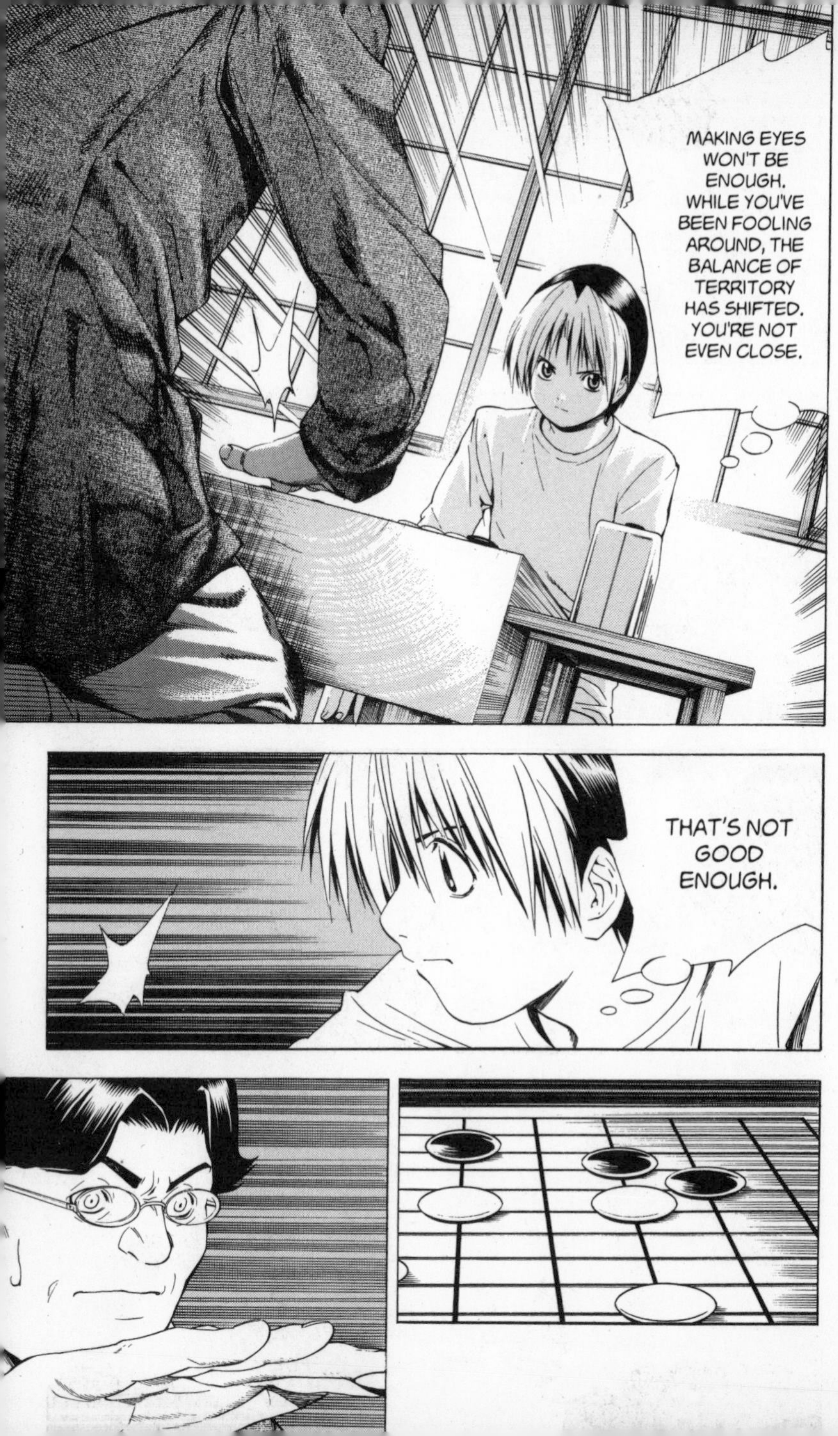
MAKING EYES WON'T BE ENOUGH. WHILE YOU'VE BEEN FOOLING AROUND, THE BALANCE OF TERRITORY HAS SHIFTED. YOU'RE NOT EVEN CLOSE.
THAT'S NOT GOOD ENOUGH.

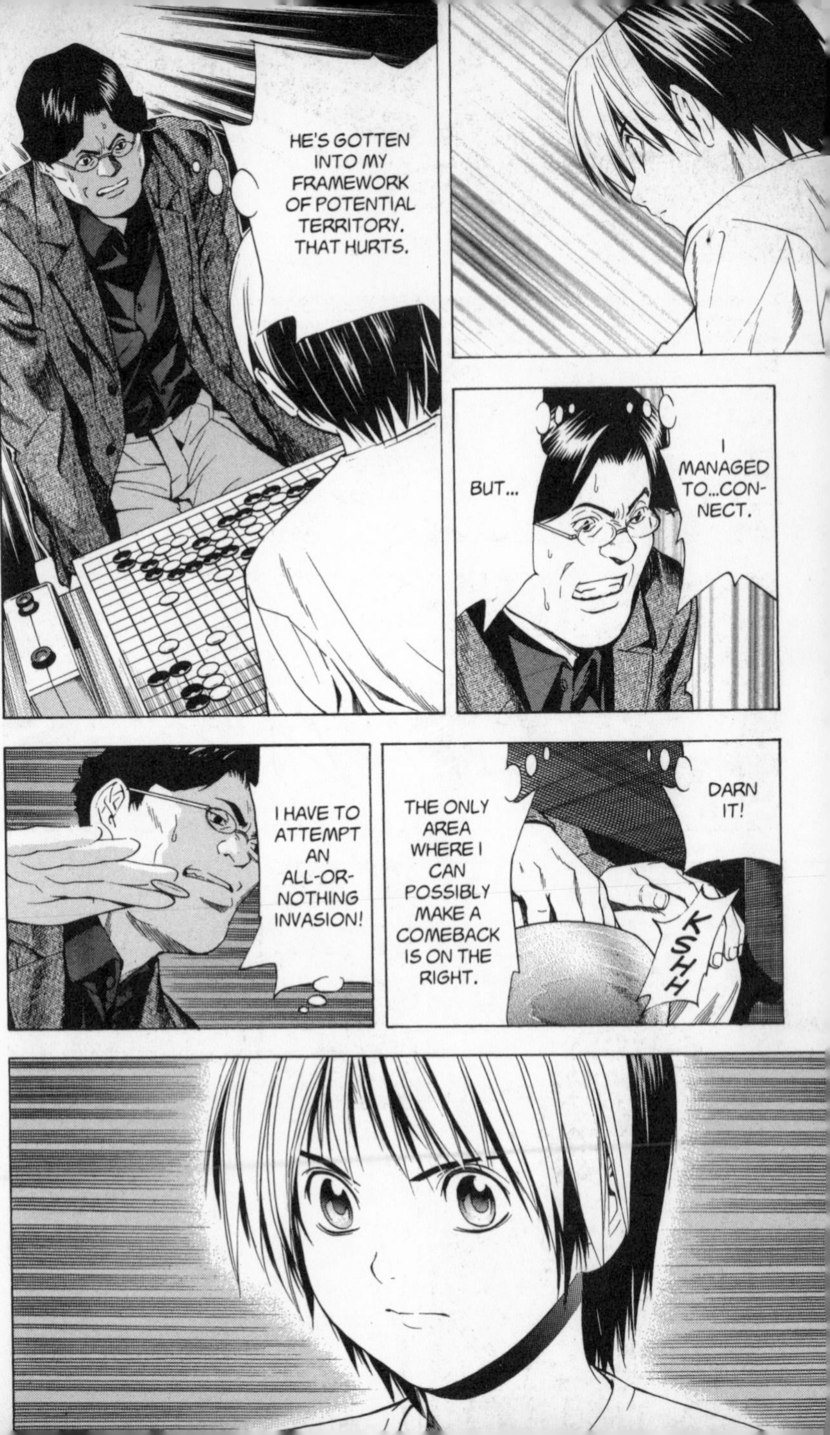
I MANAGED TO...CON-NECT.
BUT...
HE'S GOTTEN INTO MY FRAMEWORK OF POTENTIAL TERRITORY. THAT HURTS.
DARN IT!
KSHH
THE ONLY AREA WHERE I CAN POSSIBLY MAKE A COMEBACK IS ON THE RIGHT.
I HAVE TO ATTEMPT AN ALL-OR-NOTHING INVASION!

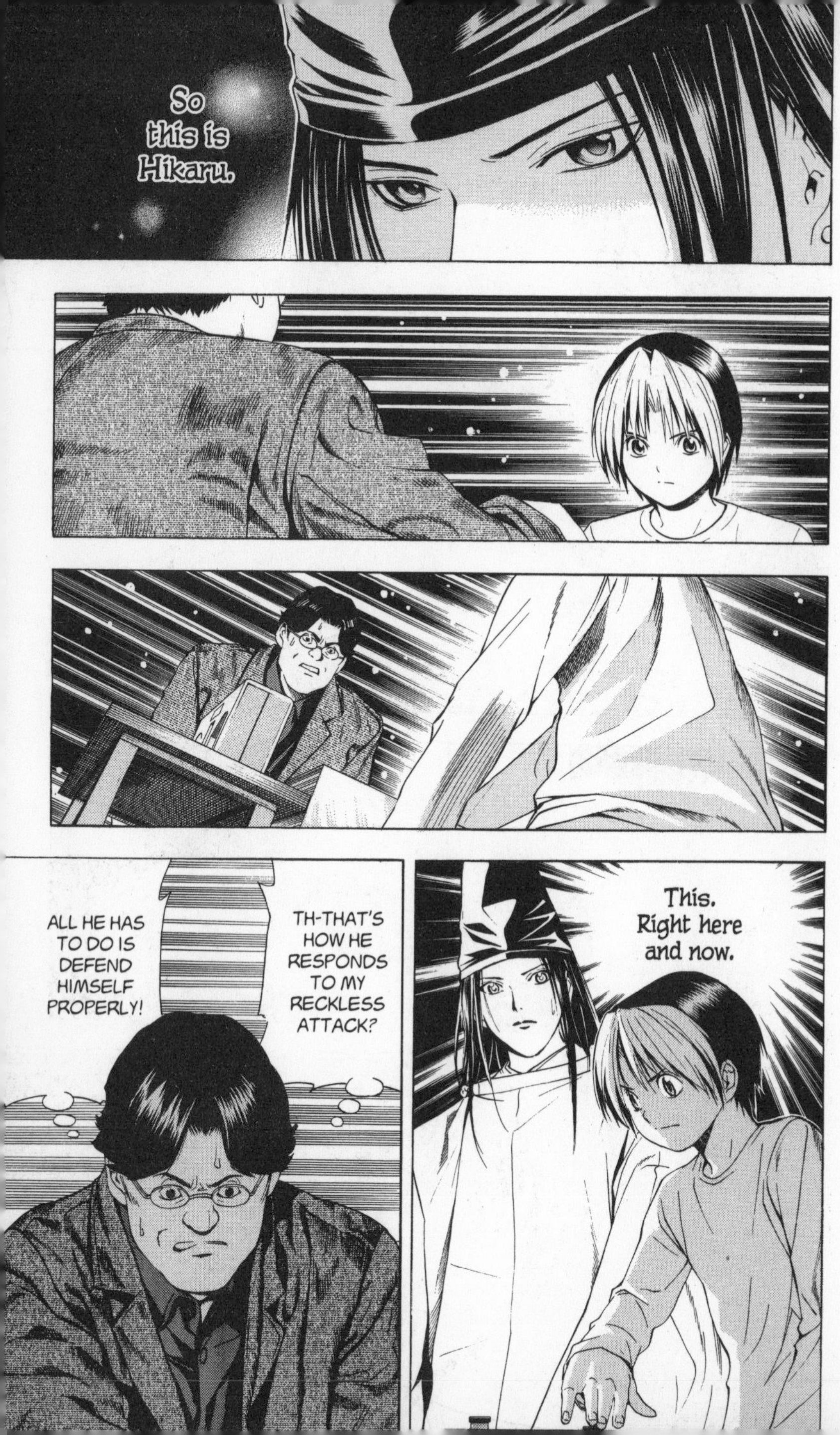
So this is Hikaru.
This. Right here and now.
TH-THAT'S HOW HE RESPONDS TO MY RECKLESS ATTACK?
ALL HE HAS TO DO IS DEFEND HIMSELF PROPERLY!

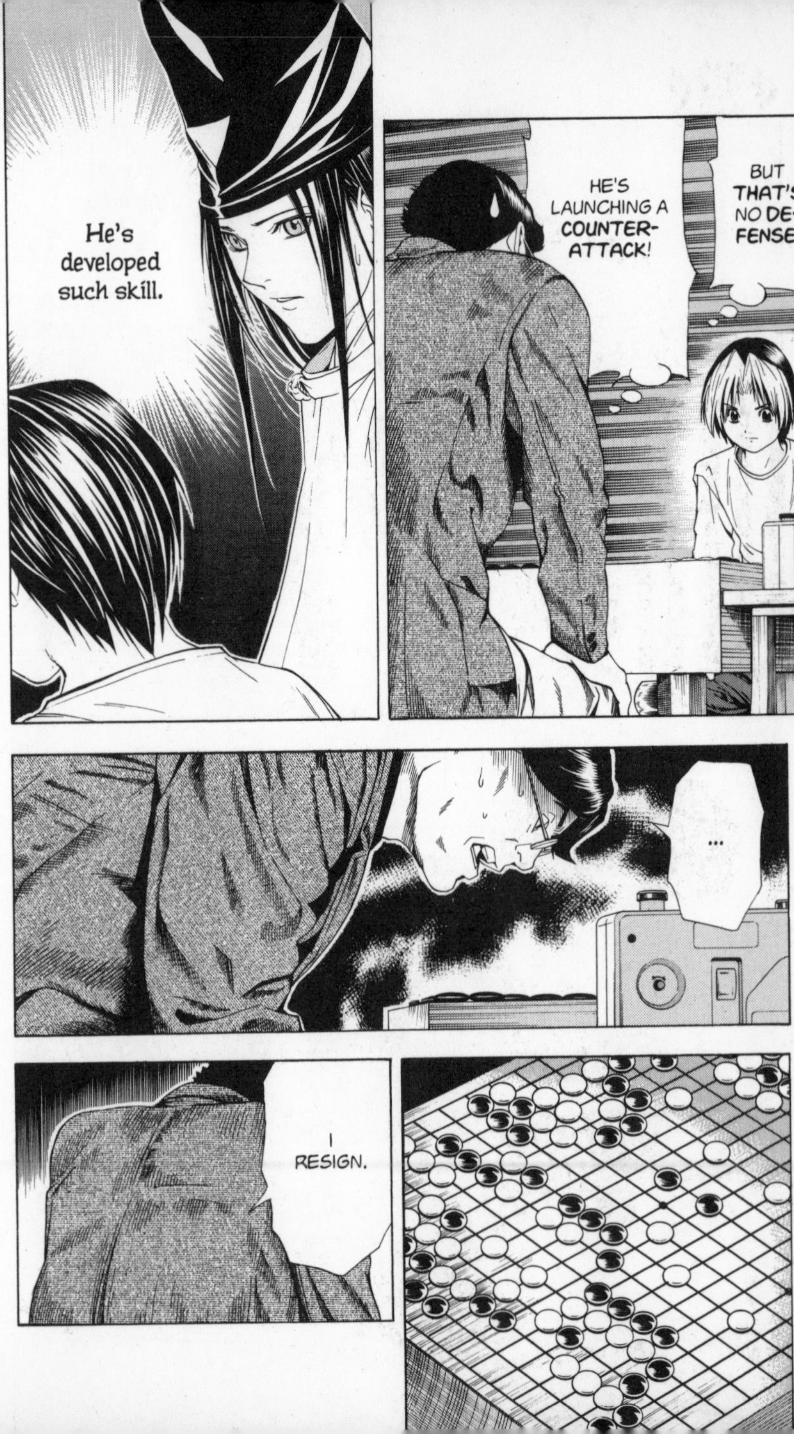
HE'S LAUNCHING A COUNTER-ATTACK!
BUT THAT'S NO DEFENSE.
He's developed such skill.
...
I RESIGN.

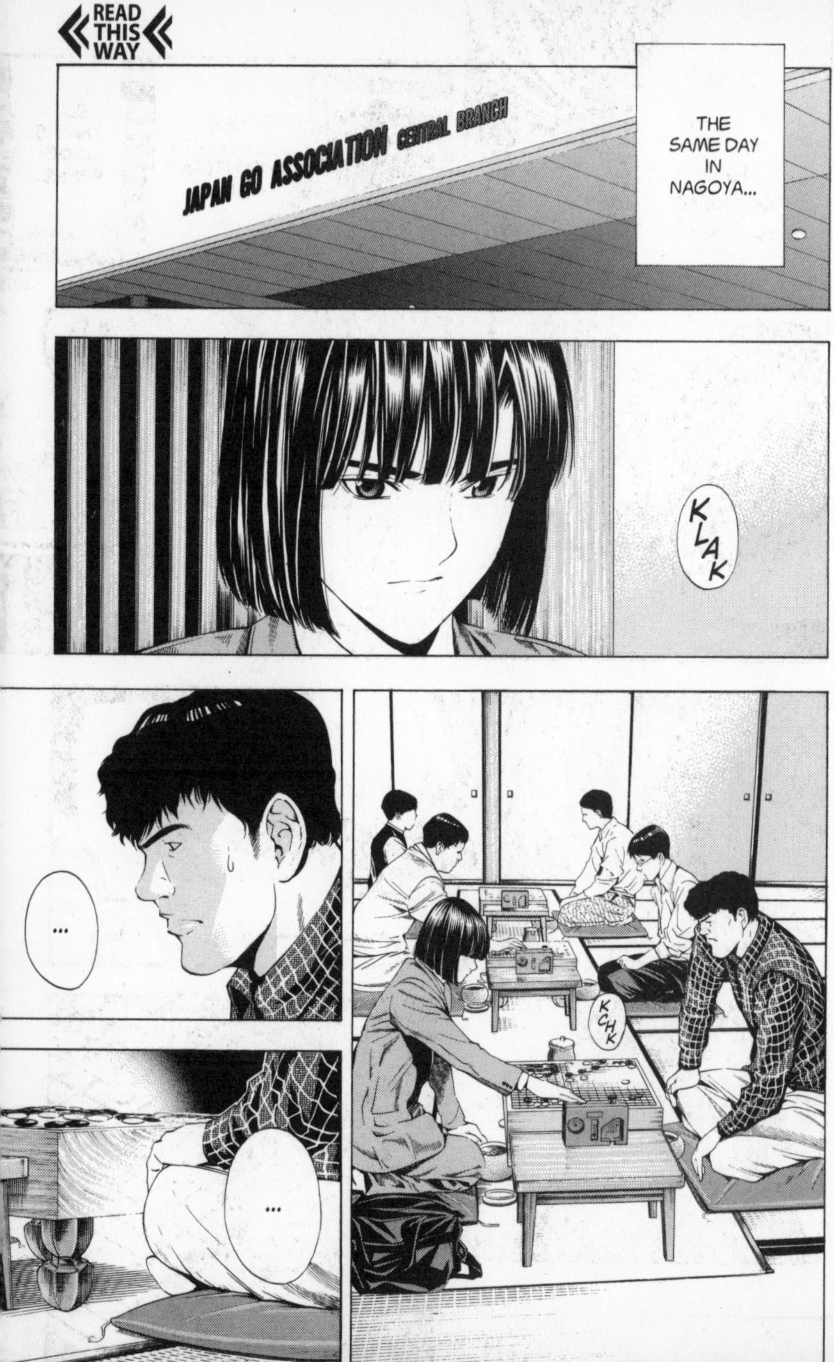
READ THIS WAY
THE SAME DAY IN NAGOYA...
JAPAN GO ASSOCIATION CENTRAL BRANCH
KLAK
KCHK
...
...

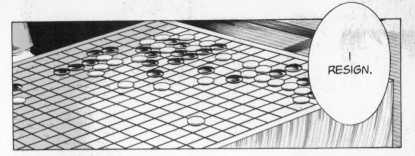

I RESIGN.

I WONDER HOW SHINDO'S GAME WENT...

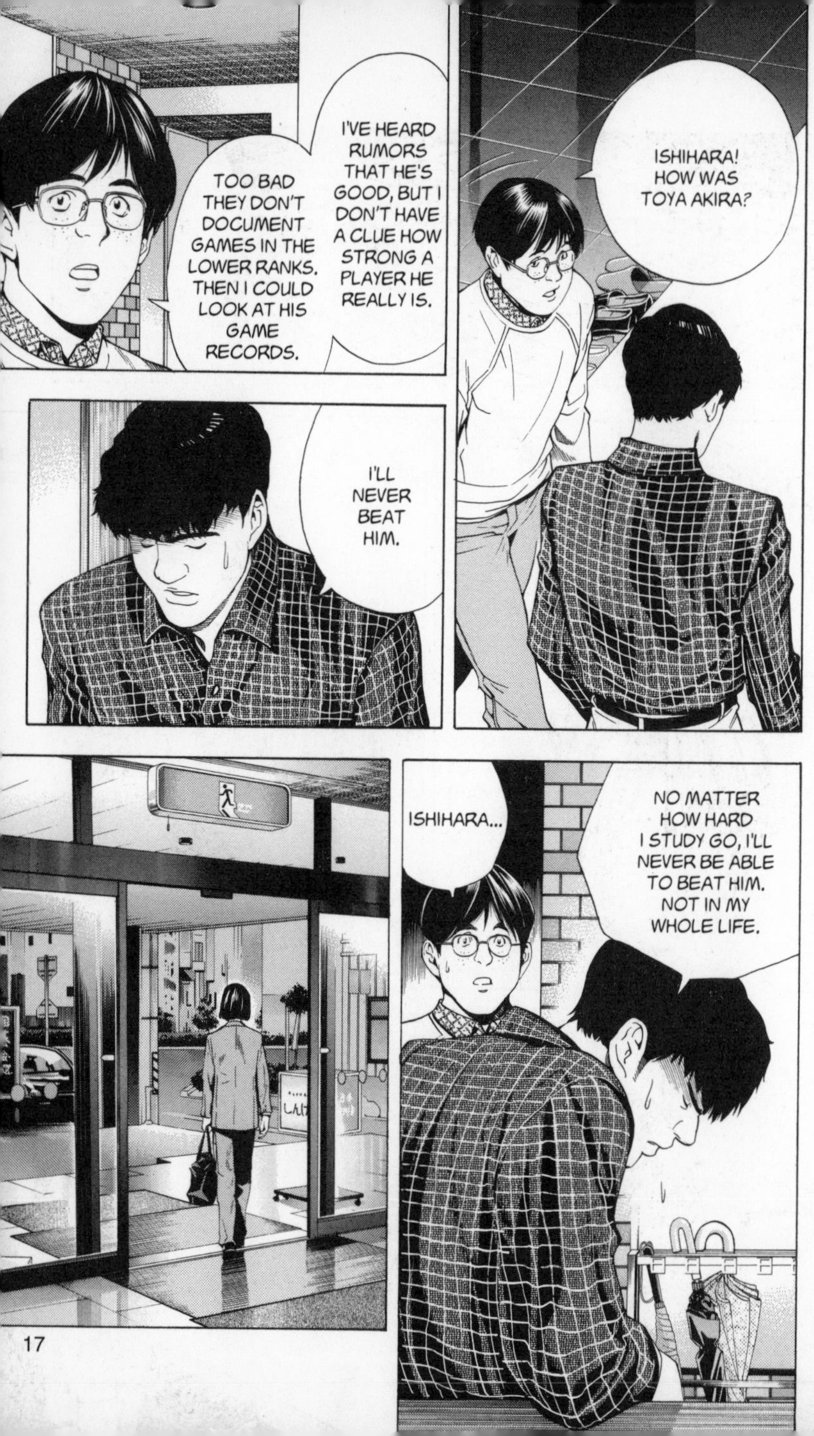
ISHIHARA! HOW WAS TOYA AKIRA?
I'VE HEARD RUMORS THAT HE'S GOOD, BUT I DON'T HAVE A CLUE HOW STRONG A PLAYER HE REALLY IS.
TOO BAD THEY DON'T DOCUMENT GAMES IN THE LOWER RANKS. THEN I COULD LOOK AT HIS GAME RECORDS.
I'LL NEVER BEAT HIM.
NO MATTER HOW HARD I STUDY GO, I'LL NEVER BE ABLE TO BEAT HIM. NOT IN MY WHOLE LIFE.
ISHIHARA...

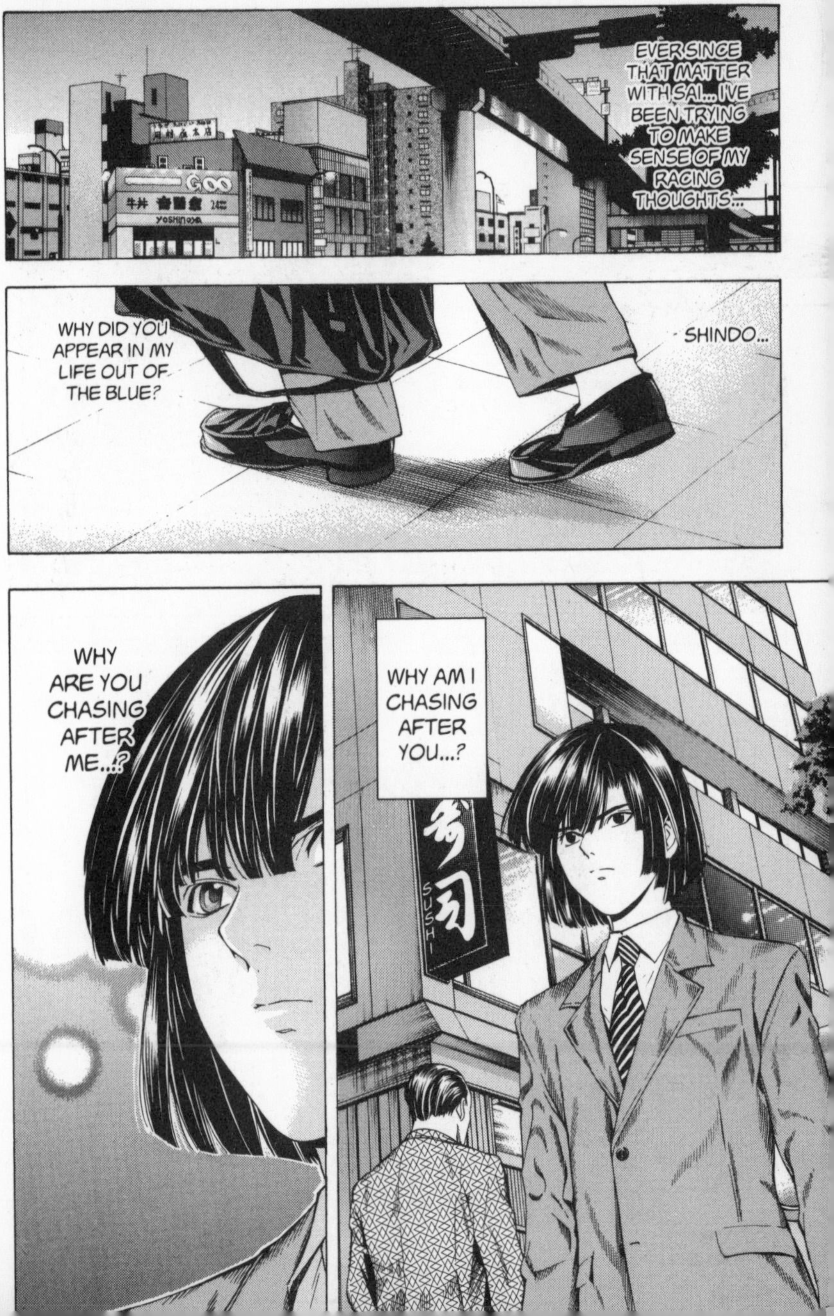
EVER SINCE THAT MATTER WITH SAI... I'VE BEEN TRYING TO MAKE SENSE OF MY RACING THOUGHTS...
SHINDO...
WHY DID YOU APPEAR IN MY LIFE OUT OF THE BLUE?
WHY AM I CHASING AFTER YOU...?
SUSHI
WHY ARE YOU CHASING AFTER ME...?

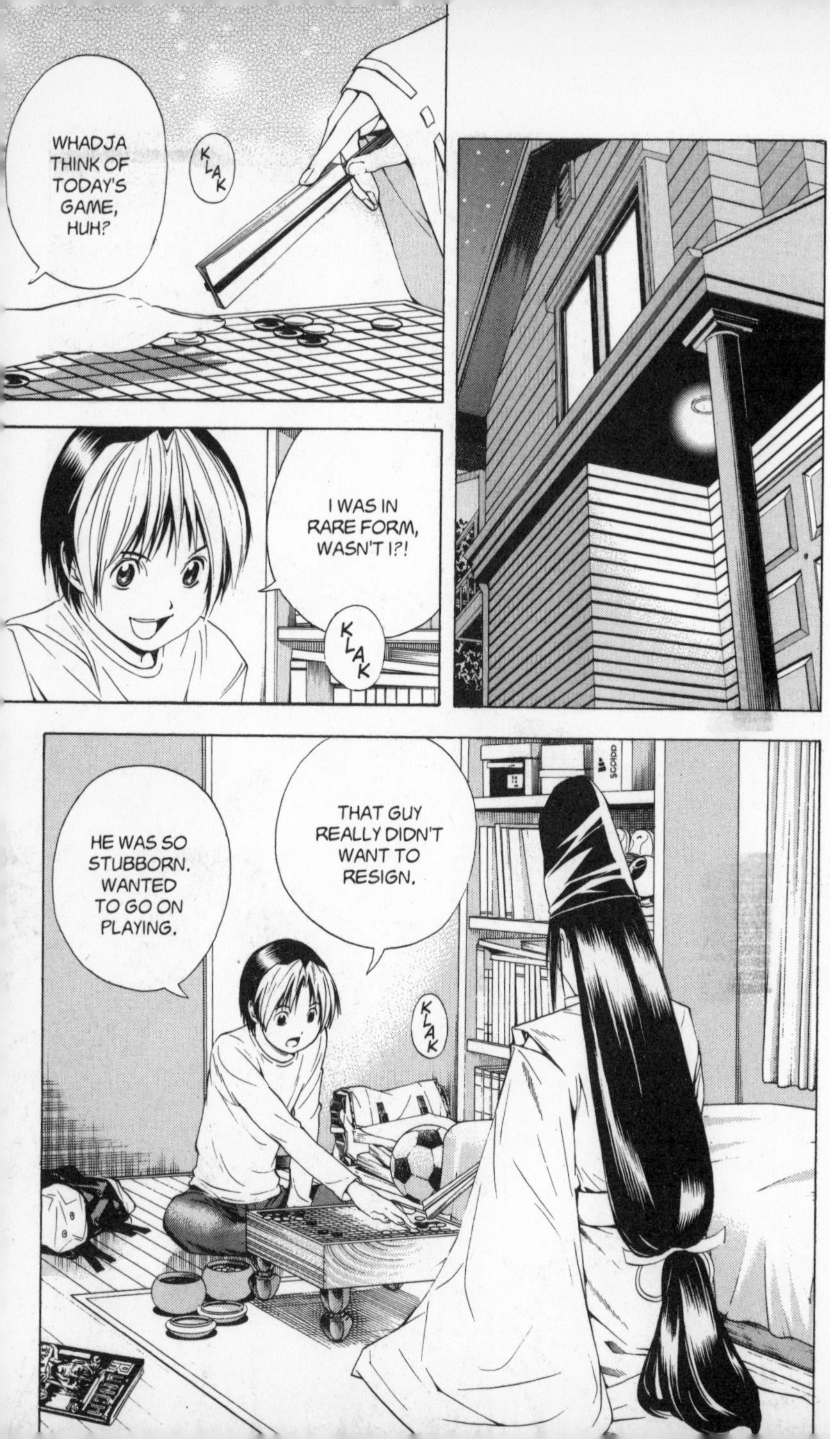
KLAK
WHADJA THINK OF TODAY'S GAME, HUH?
I WAS IN RARE FORM, WASN'T I?!
KLAK
THAT GUY REALLY DIDN'T WANT TO RESIGN.
HE WAS SO STUBBORN. WANTED TO GO ON PLAYING.
KLAK

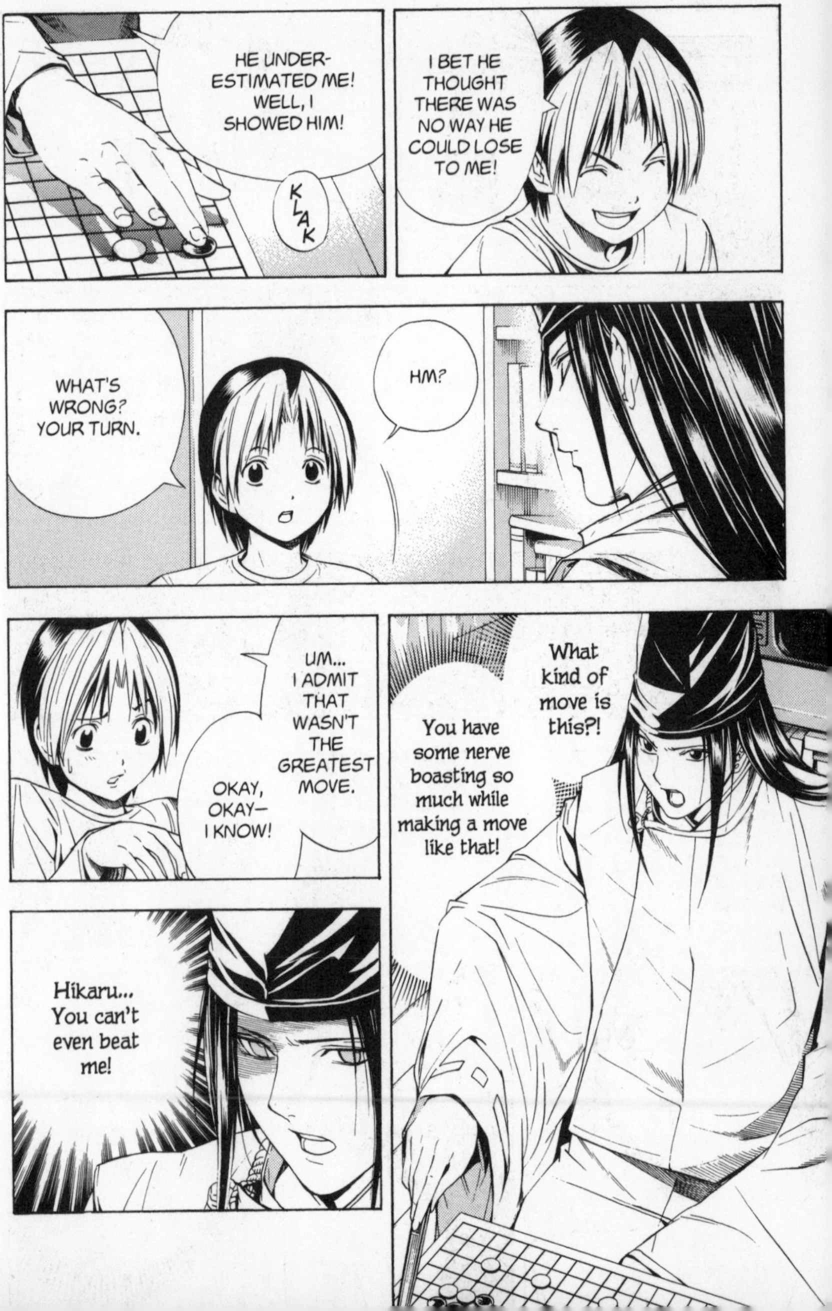
I BET HE THOUGHT THERE WAS NO WAY HE COULD LOSE TO ME!
HE UNDER-ESTIMATED ME! WELL, I SHOWED HIM!
KLAK
HM?
WHAT'S WRONG? YOUR TURN.
What kind of move is this?!
You have some nerve boasting so much while making a move like that!
UM... I ADMIT THAT WASN'T THE GREATEST MOVE.
OKAY, OKAY— I KNOW!
Hikaru... You can't even beat me!

READ THIS WAY

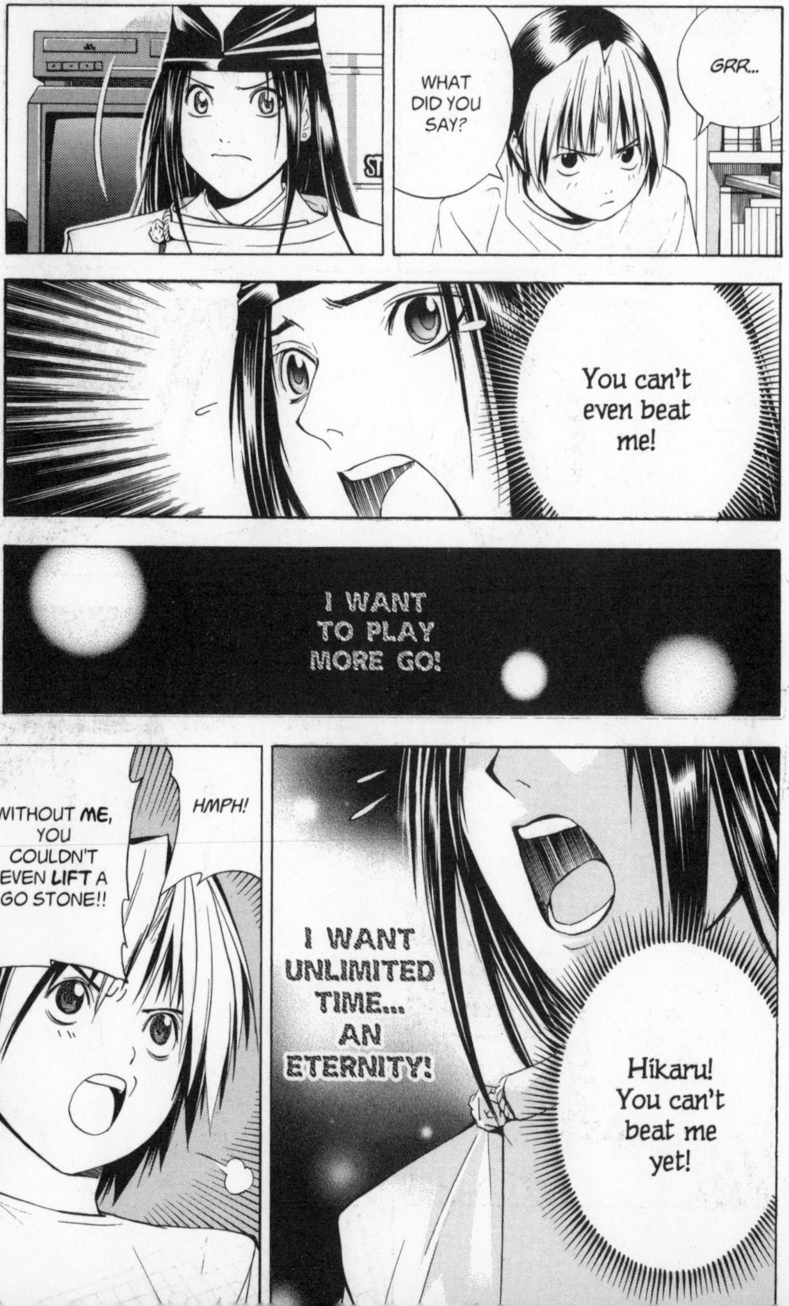
GRR...
WHAT DID YOU SAY?
You can't even beat me!
I WANT TO PLAY MORE GO!
I WANT UNLIMITED TIME... AN ETERNITY!
Hikaru! You can't beat me yet!
HMPH!
WITHOUT ME, YOU COULDN'T EVEN LIFT A GO STONE!!

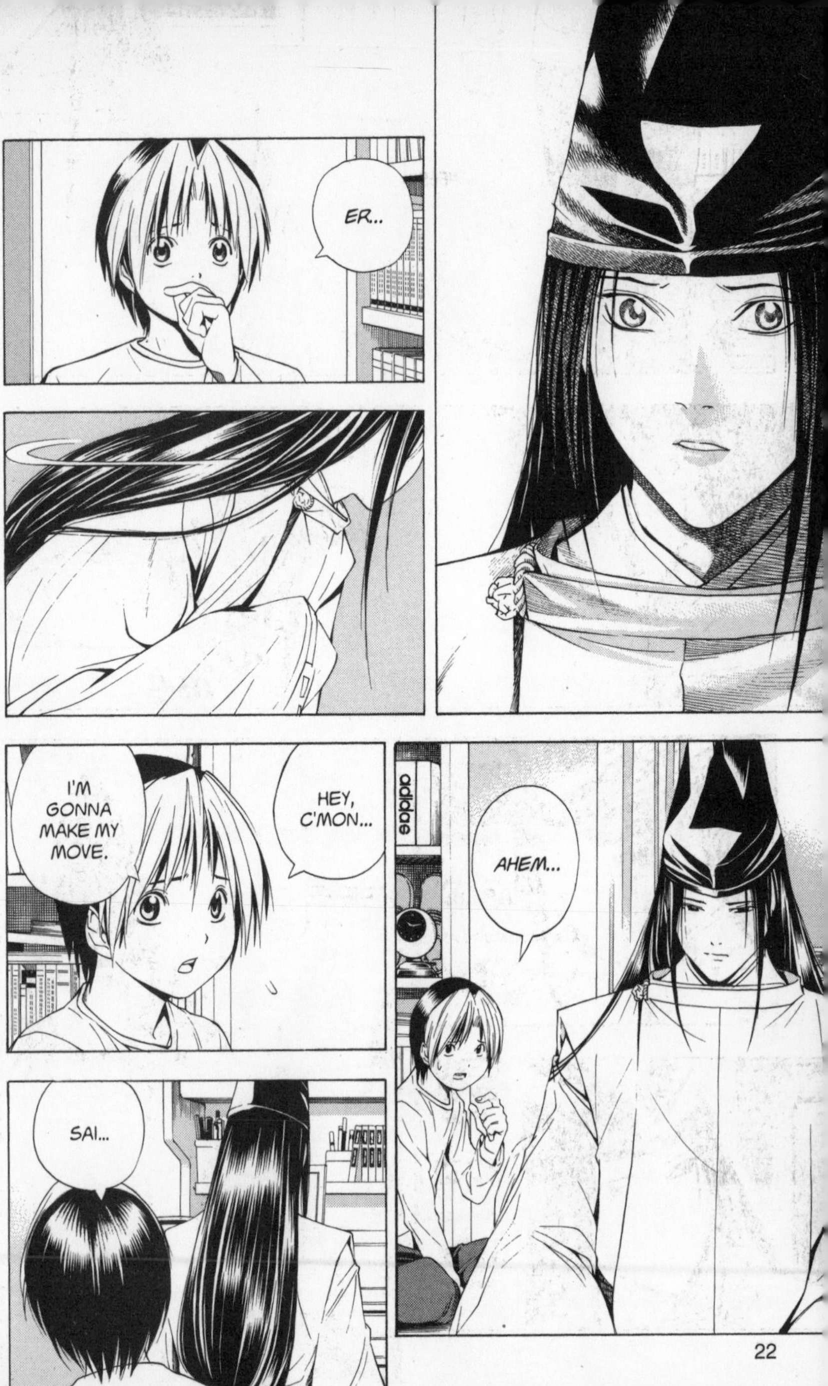
ER...
AHEM...
HEY, C'MON...
I'M GONNA MAKE MY MOVE.
SAI...

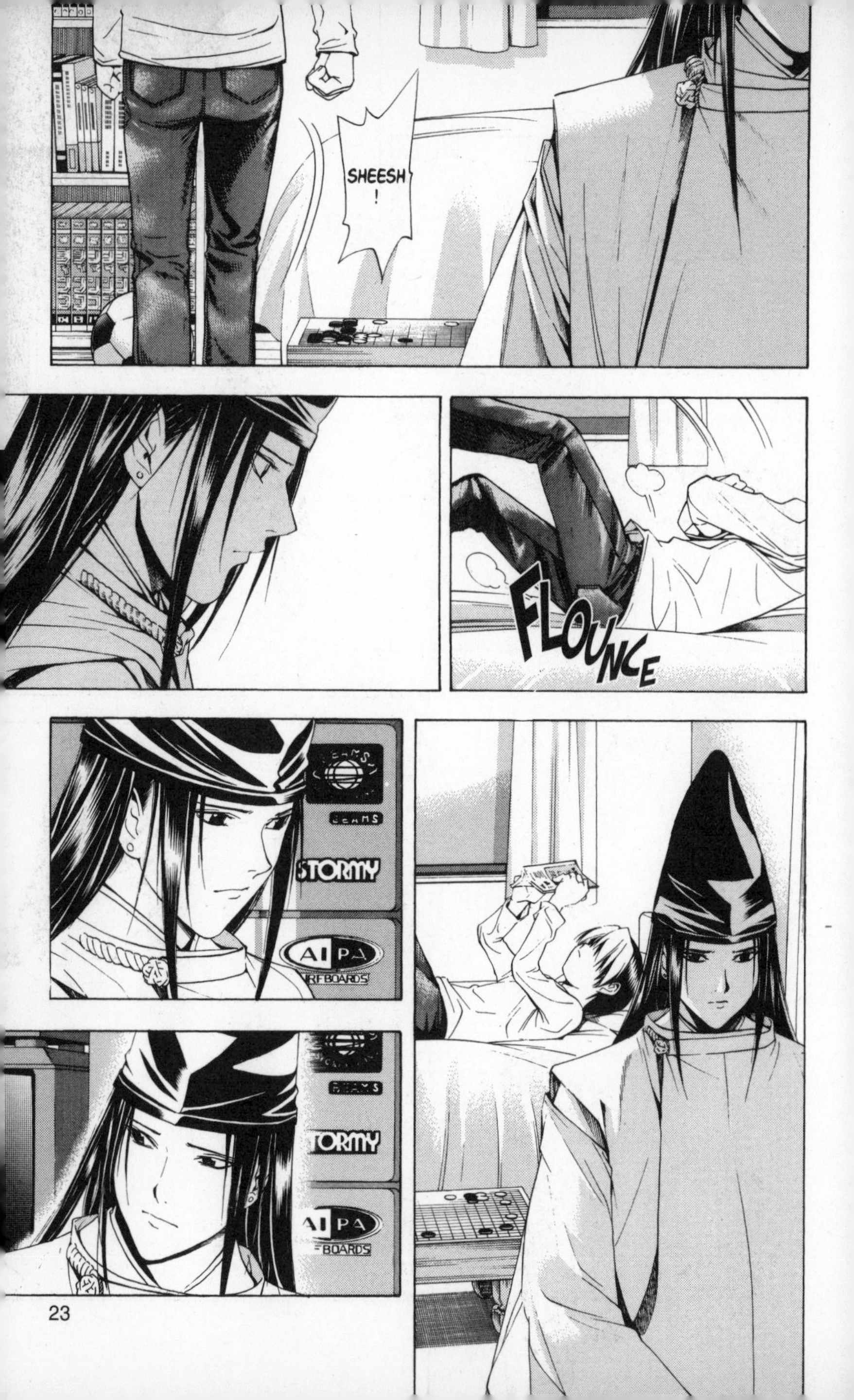
SHEESH!
FLOUNCE
STORMY
AIPA
STORMY
AIPA

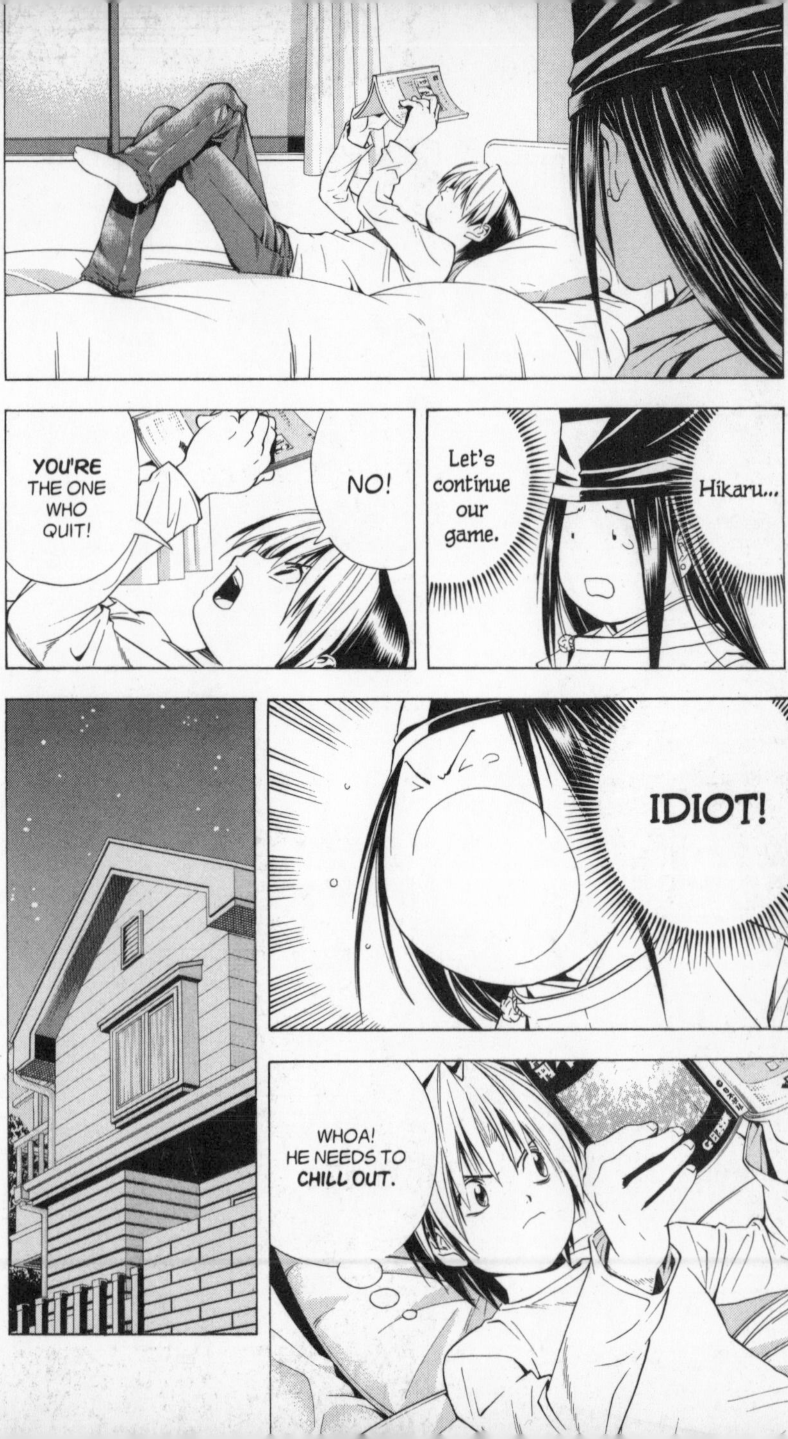
Hikaru...
Let's continue our game.
NO!
YOU'RE THE ONE WHO QUIT!
IDIOT!
WHOA! HE NEEDS TO CHILL OUT.

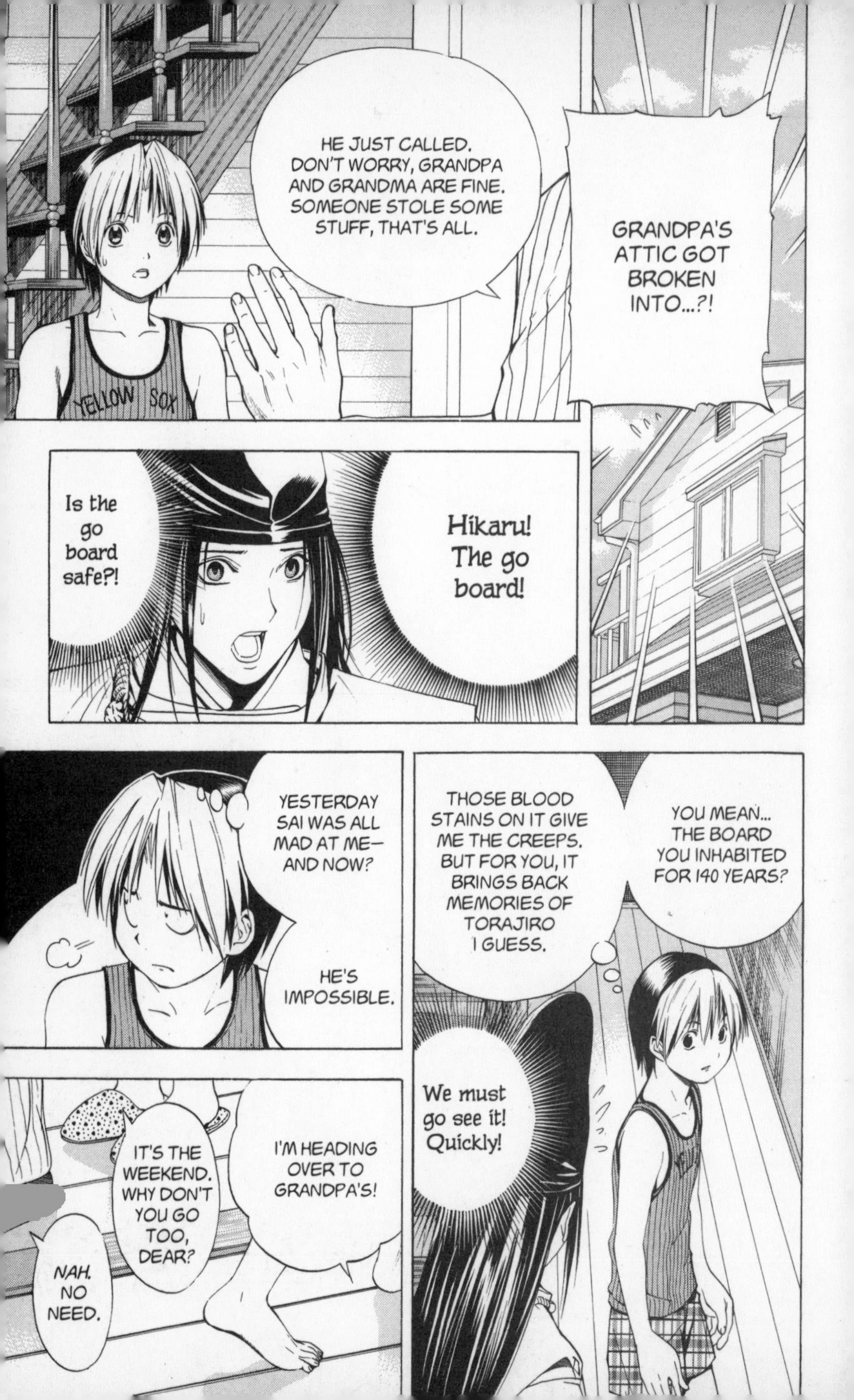
GRANDPA'S ATTIC GOT BROKEN INTO...?!
HE JUST CALLED. DON'T WORRY, GRANDPA AND GRANDMA ARE FINE. SOMEONE STOLE SOME STUFF, THAT'S ALL.
Hikaru! The go board!
Is the go board safe?!
YOU MEAN... THE BOARD YOU INHABITED FOR 140 YEARS?
THOSE BLOOD STAINS ON IT GIVE ME THE CREEPS. BUT FOR YOU, IT BRINGS BACK MEMORIES OF TORAJIRO I GUESS.
We must go see it! Quickly!
YESTERDAY SAI WAS ALL MAD AT ME— AND NOW?
HE'S IMPOSSIBLE.
I'M HEADING OVER TO GRANDPA'S!
IT'S THE WEEKEND. WHY DON'T YOU GO TOO, DEAR?
NAH. NO NEED.

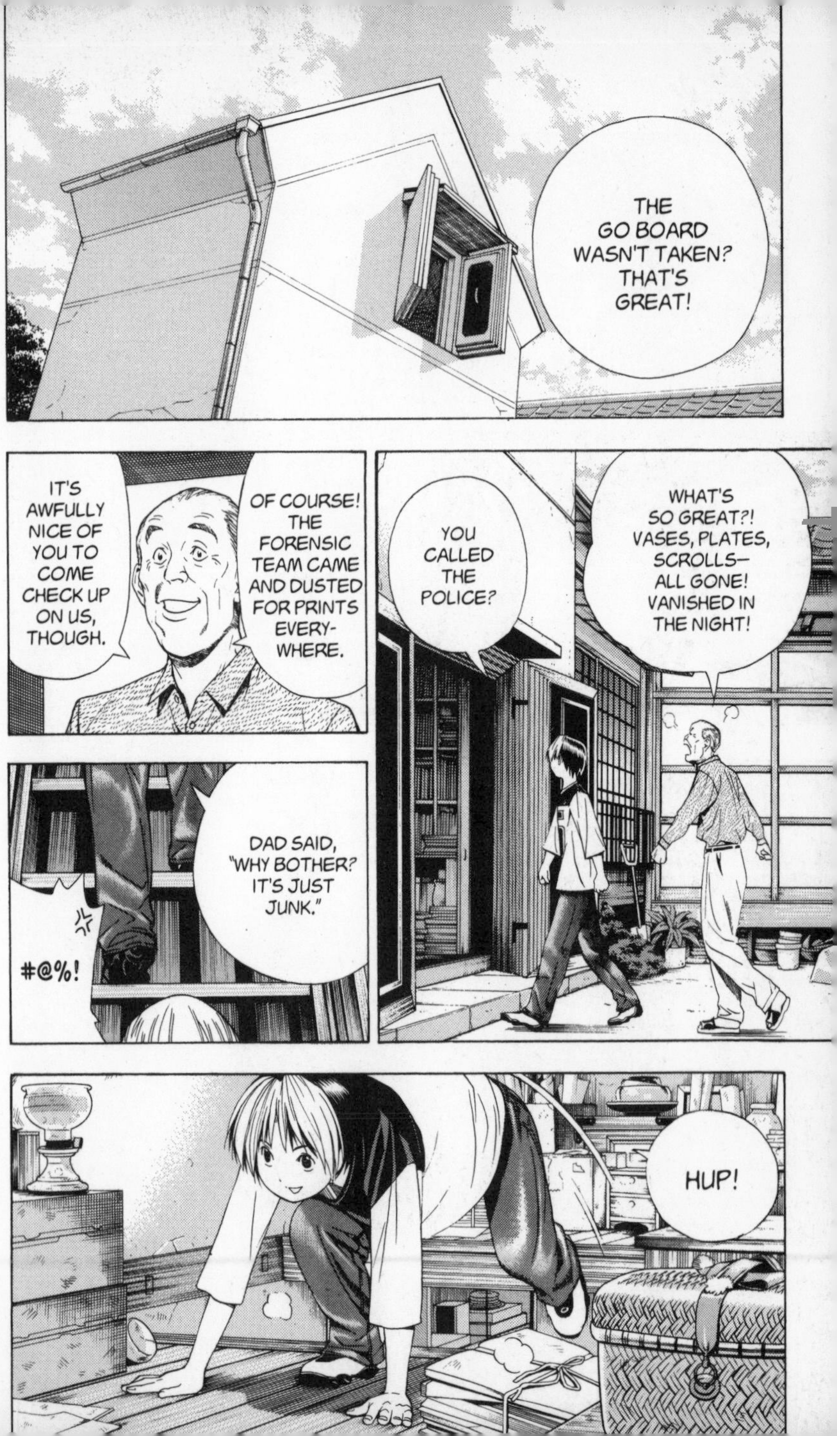
THE GO BOARD WASN'T TAKEN? THAT'S GREAT!
WHAT'S SO GREAT?! VASES, PLATES, SCROLLS— ALL GONE! VANISHED IN THE NIGHT!
YOU CALLED THE POLICE?
OF COURSE! THE FORENSIC TEAM CAME AND DUSTED FOR PRINTS EVERY-WHERE.
IT'S AWFULLY NICE OF YOU TO COME CHECK UP ON US, THOUGH.
DAD SAID, "WHY BOTHER? IT'S JUST JUNK."
#@%!
HUP!

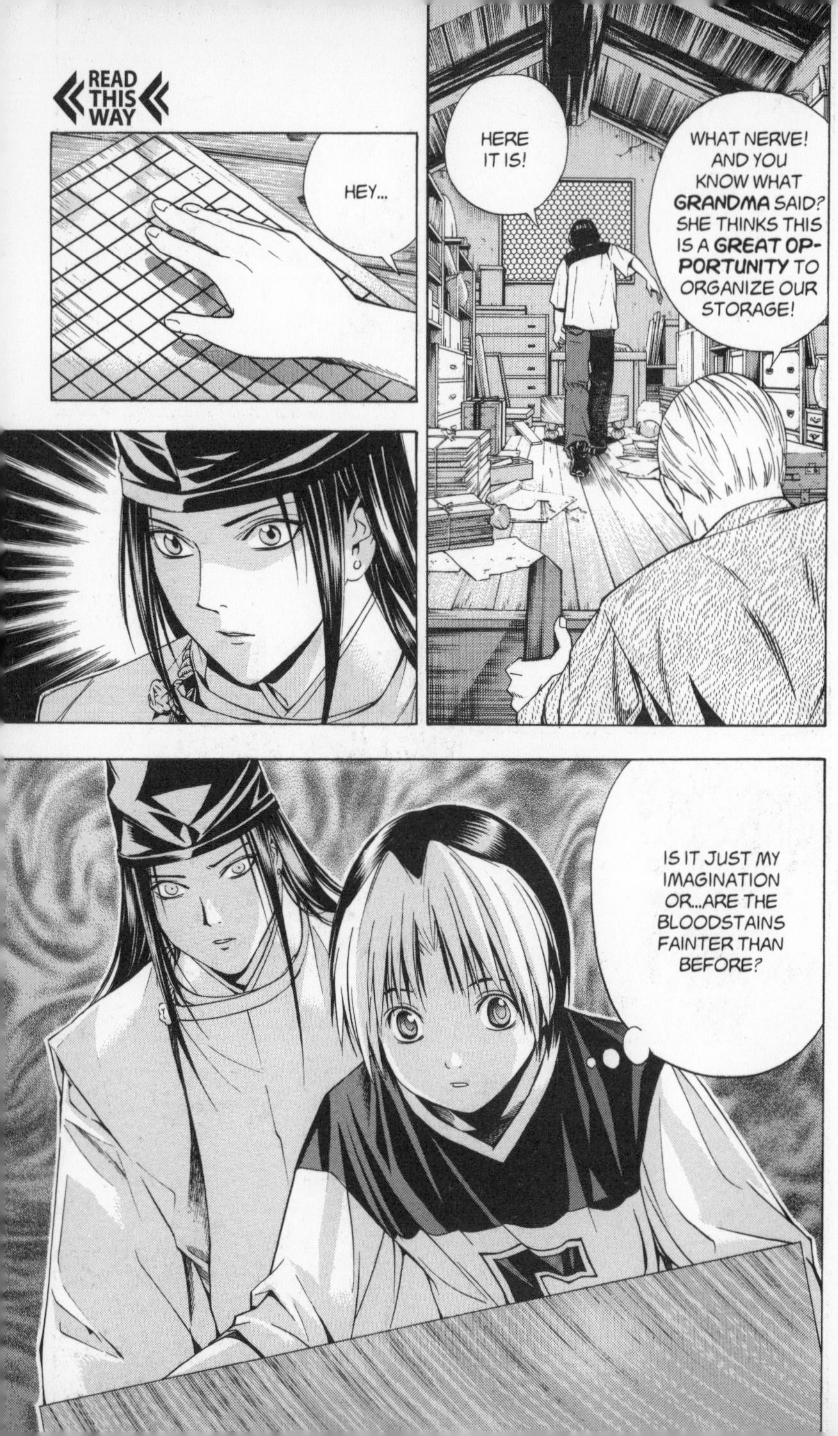
READ THIS WAY
WHAT NERVE! AND YOU KNOW WHAT GRANDMA SAID? SHE THINKS THIS IS A GREAT OP-PORTUNITY TO ORGANIZE OUR STORAGE!
HERE IT IS!
HEY...
IS IT JUST MY IMAGINATION OR...ARE THE BLOODSTAINS FAINTER THAN BEFORE?

HIKARU NO GO STORYBOARDS

39

YUMI HOTTA

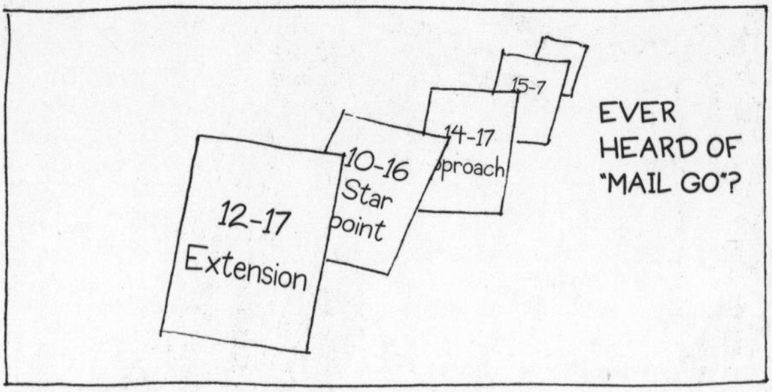
EVER HEARD OF "MAIL GO"?
15-7
14-17
10-16 Star
12-17 Extension

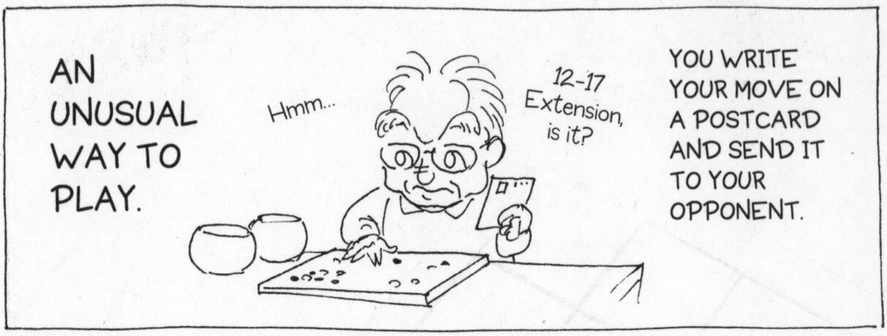
YOU WRITE YOUR MOVE ON A POSTCARD AND SEND IT TO YOUR OPPONENT.
12-17 Extension, is it?
Hmm...
AN UNUSUAL WAY TO PLAY.

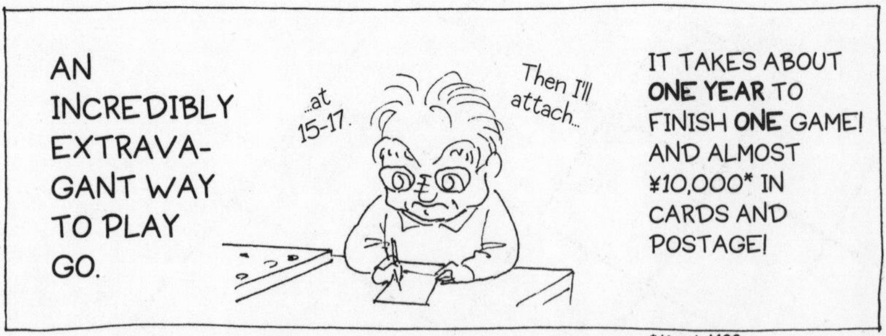
IT TAKES ABOUT **ONE YEAR** TO FINISH **ONE** GAME! AND ALMOST ¥10,000* IN CARDS AND POSTAGE!
Then I'll attach...
...at 15-17.
AN INCREDIBLY EXTRAVAGANT WAY TO PLAY GO.

*About $100

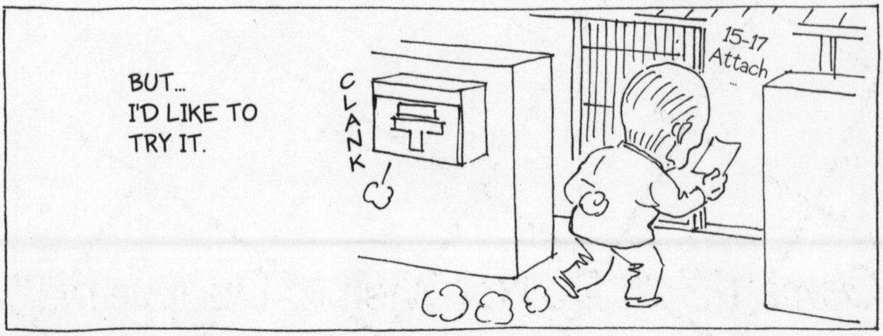
15-17 Attach ...
CLANK
BUT... I'D LIKE TO TRY IT.

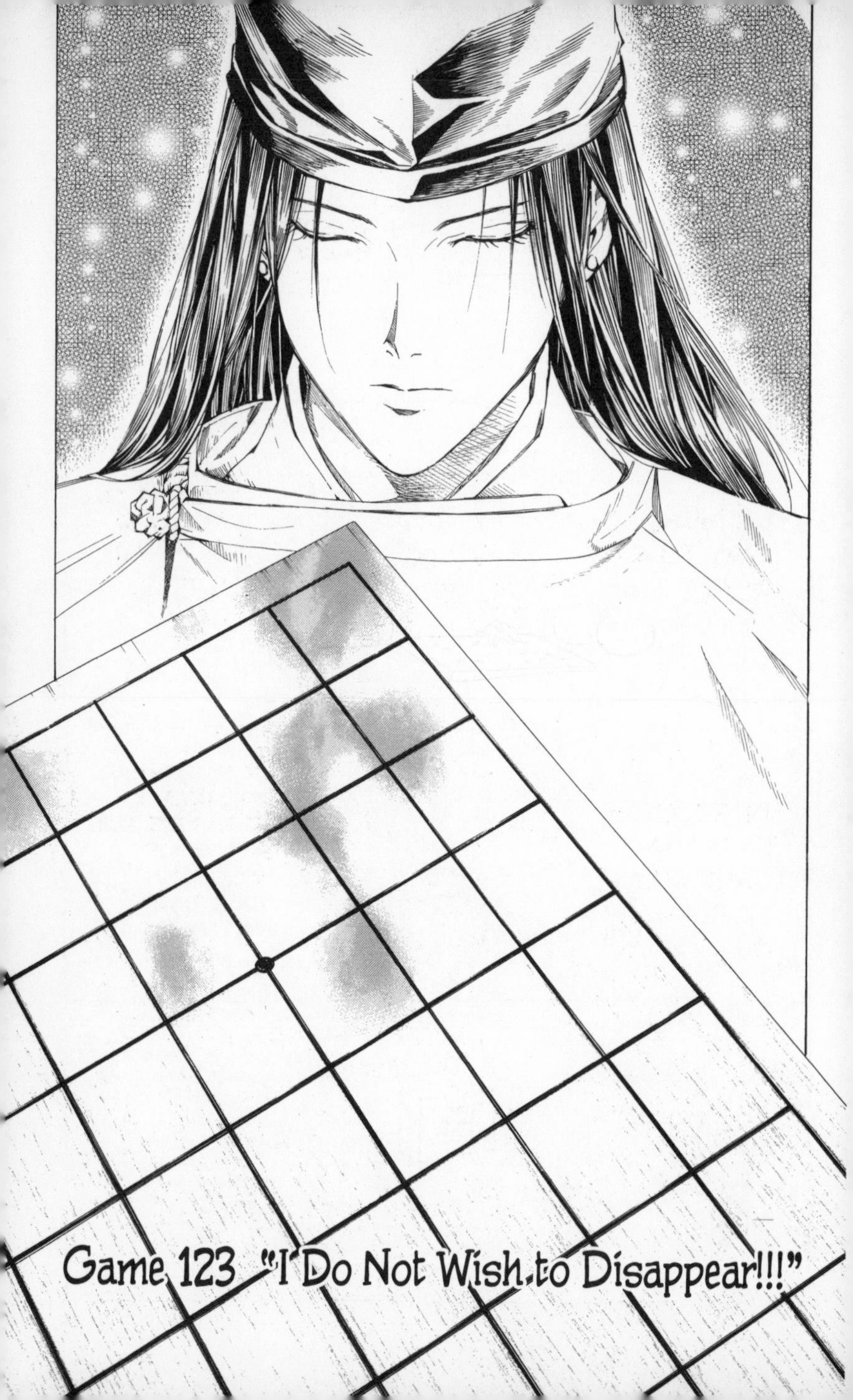
Game 123 "I Do Not Wish to Disappear!!!"

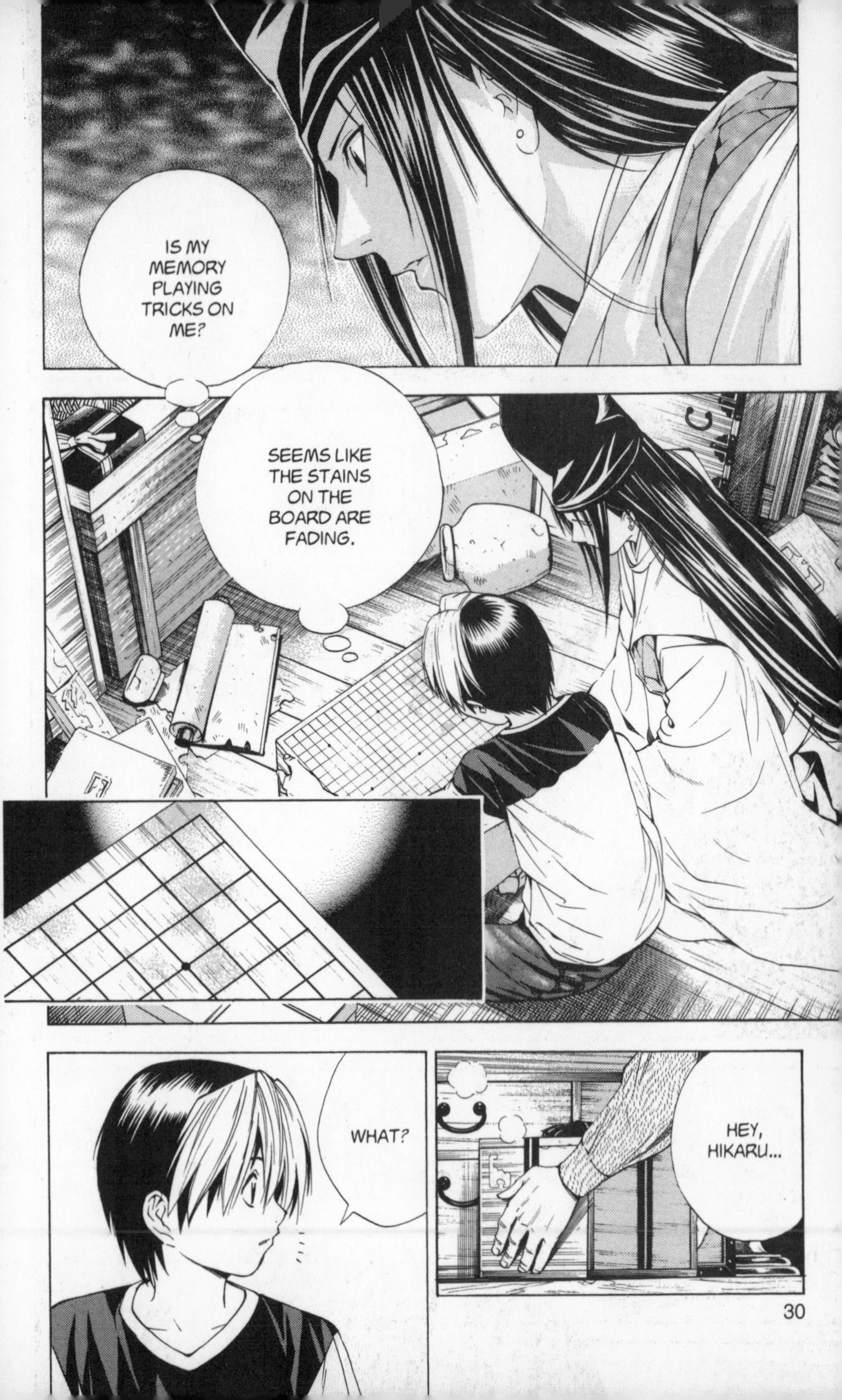
IS MY MEMORY PLAYING TRICKS ON ME?
SEEMS LIKE THE STAINS ON THE BOARD ARE FADING.
HEY, HIKARU...
WHAT?

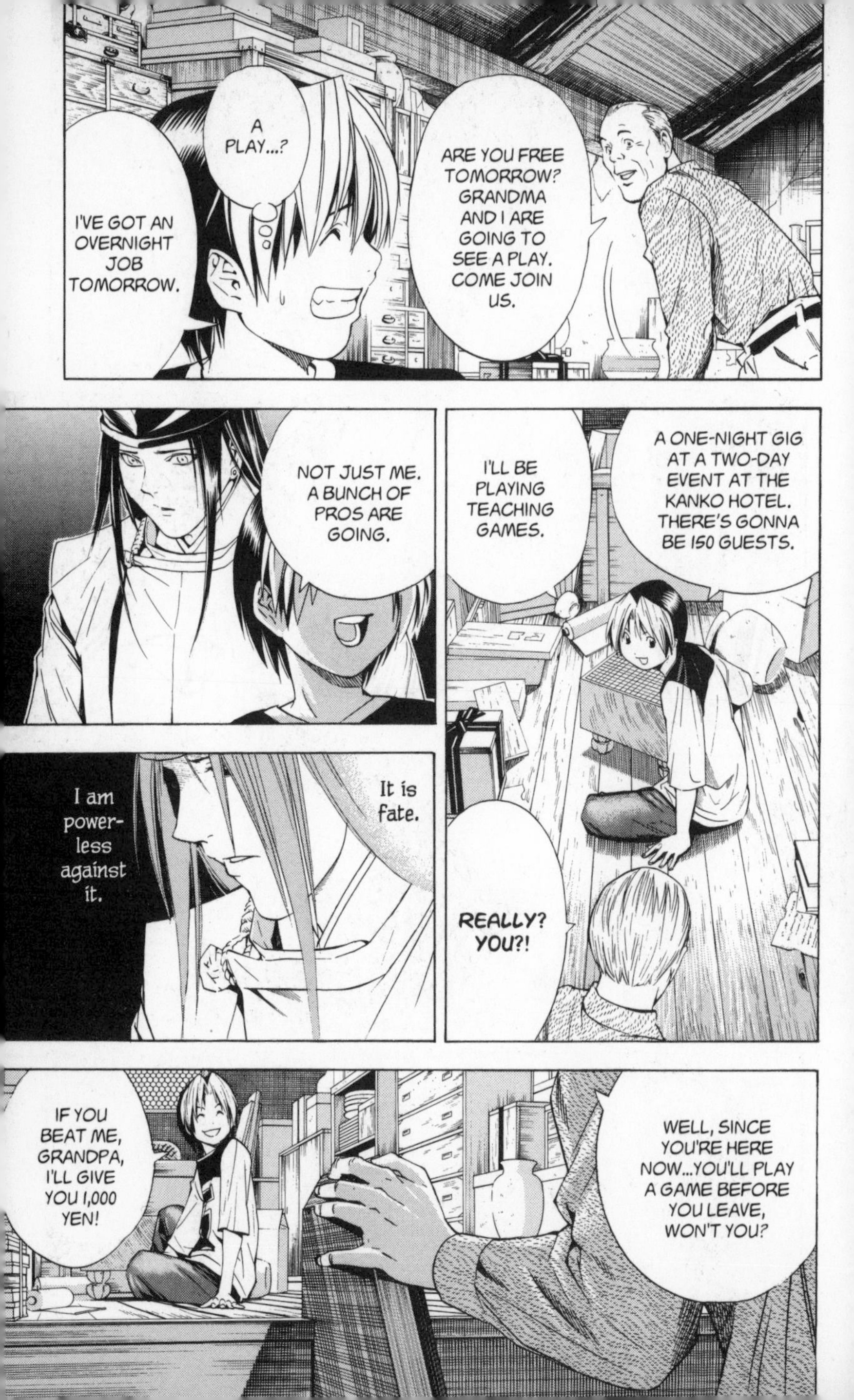
ARE YOU FREE TOMORROW? GRANDMA AND I ARE GOING TO SEE A PLAY. COME JOIN US.
A PLAY...?
I'VE GOT AN OVERNIGHT JOB TOMORROW.
A ONE-NIGHT GIG AT A TWO-DAY EVENT AT THE KANKO HOTEL. THERE'S GONNA BE 150 GUESTS.
I'LL BE PLAYING TEACHING GAMES.
REALLY? YOU?!
NOT JUST ME. A BUNCH OF PROS ARE GOING.
It is fate.
I am power-less against it.
WELL, SINCE YOU'RE HERE NOW...YOU'LL PLAY A GAME BEFORE YOU LEAVE, WON'T YOU?
IF YOU BEAT ME, GRANDPA, I'LL GIVE YOU 1,000 YEN!

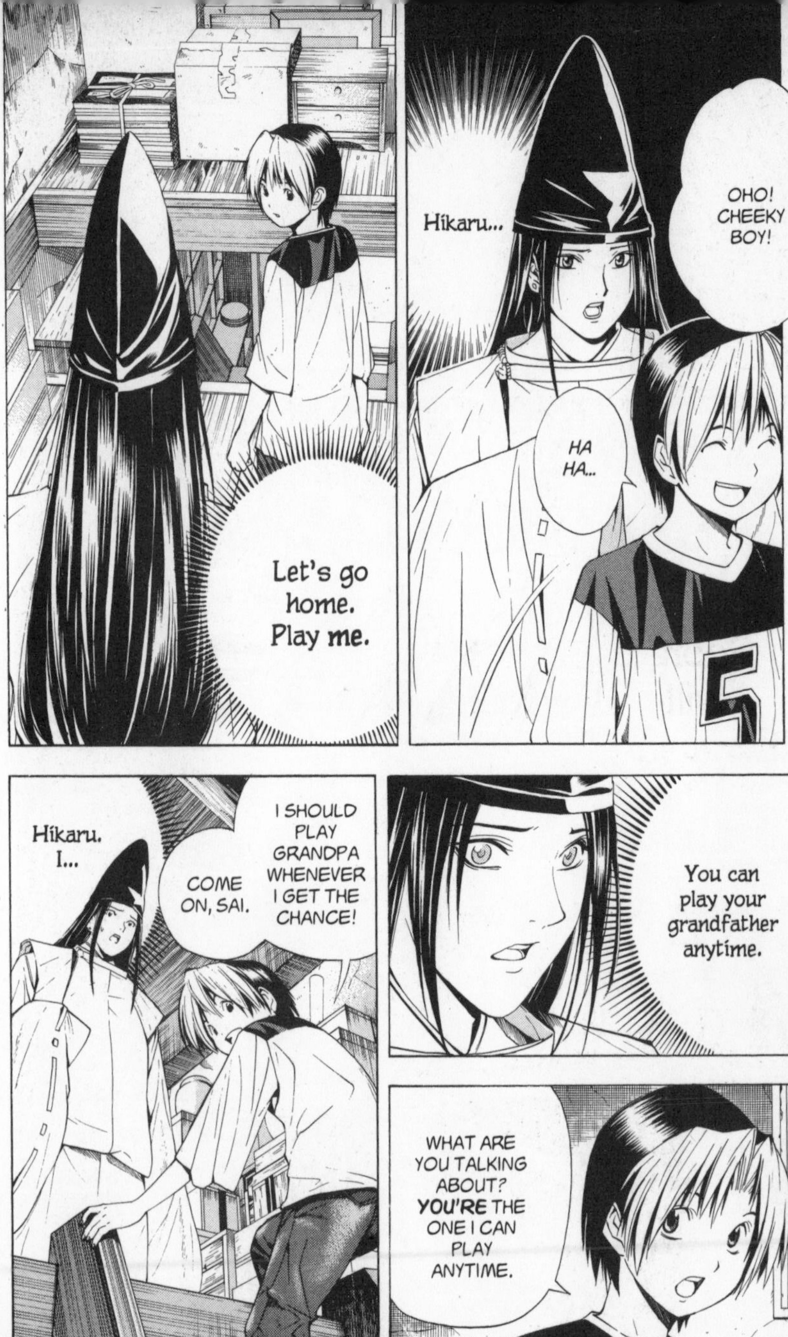

OHO! CHEEKY BOY!
Hikaru...
HA HA...
Let's go home. Play me.
You can play your grandfather anytime.
WHAT ARE YOU TALKING ABOUT? **YOU'RE** THE ONE I CAN PLAY ANYTIME.
I SHOULD PLAY GRANDPA WHENEVER I GET THE CHANCE!
COME ON, SAI.
Hikaru. I...

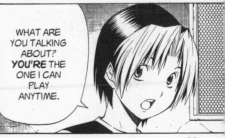

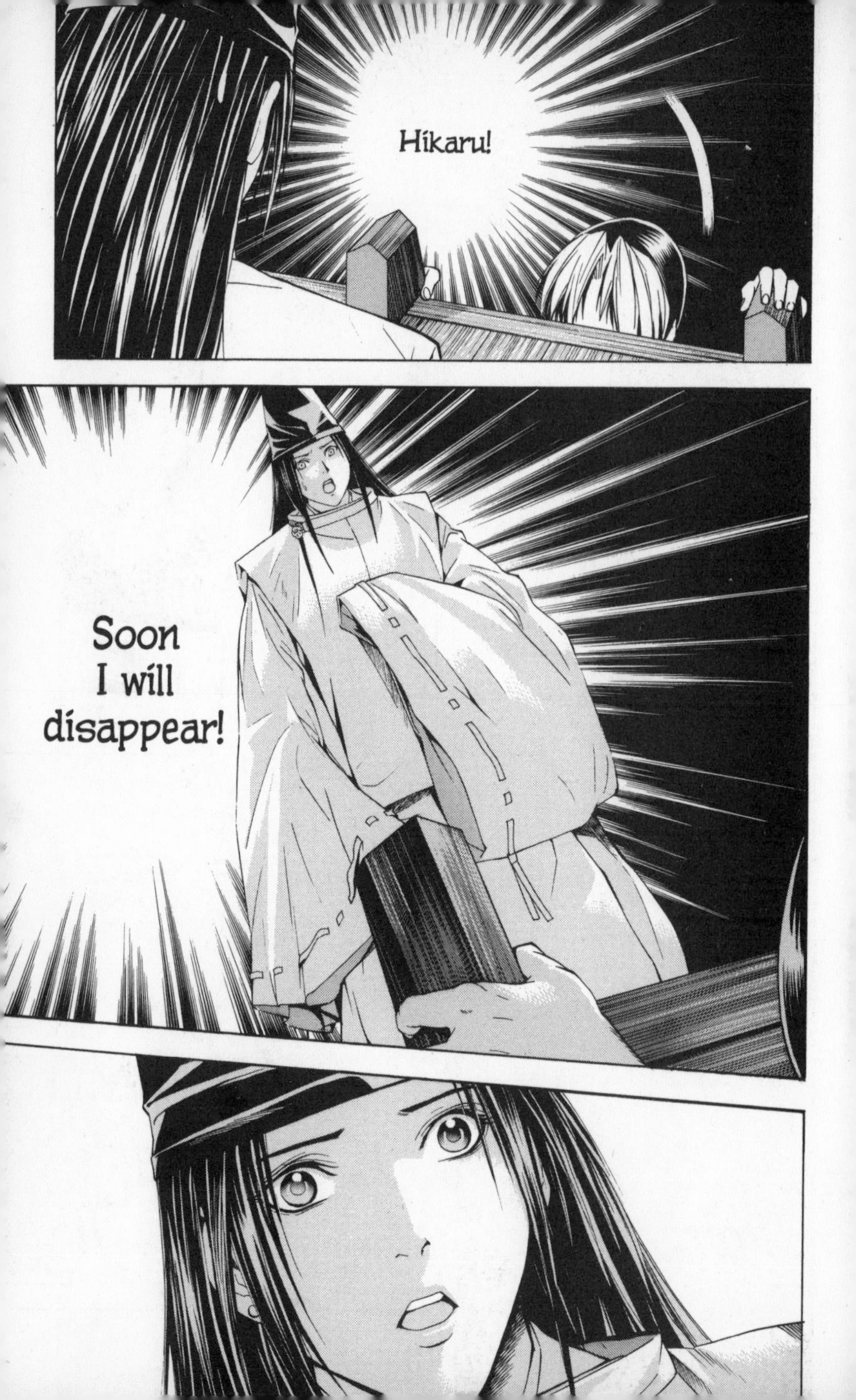
Hikaru!
Soon I will disappear!

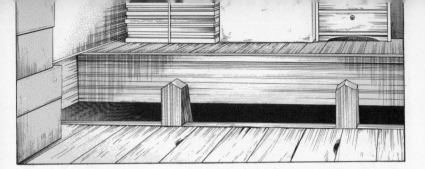

YOU'RE SUCH A WORRYWART!

POINK

DON'T BE STUPID. YOU'VE BEEN AROUND FOR **A THOUSAND YEARS!**

IF YOU THINK I'M GONNA DO **WHATEVER** YOU WANT **WHENEVER** YOU WANT JUST BECAUSE OF SOME SOB STORY, YOU'RE OUTTA LUCK.

YOU'RE SO CRITICAL AND DEMANDING LATELY!

READ THIS WAY

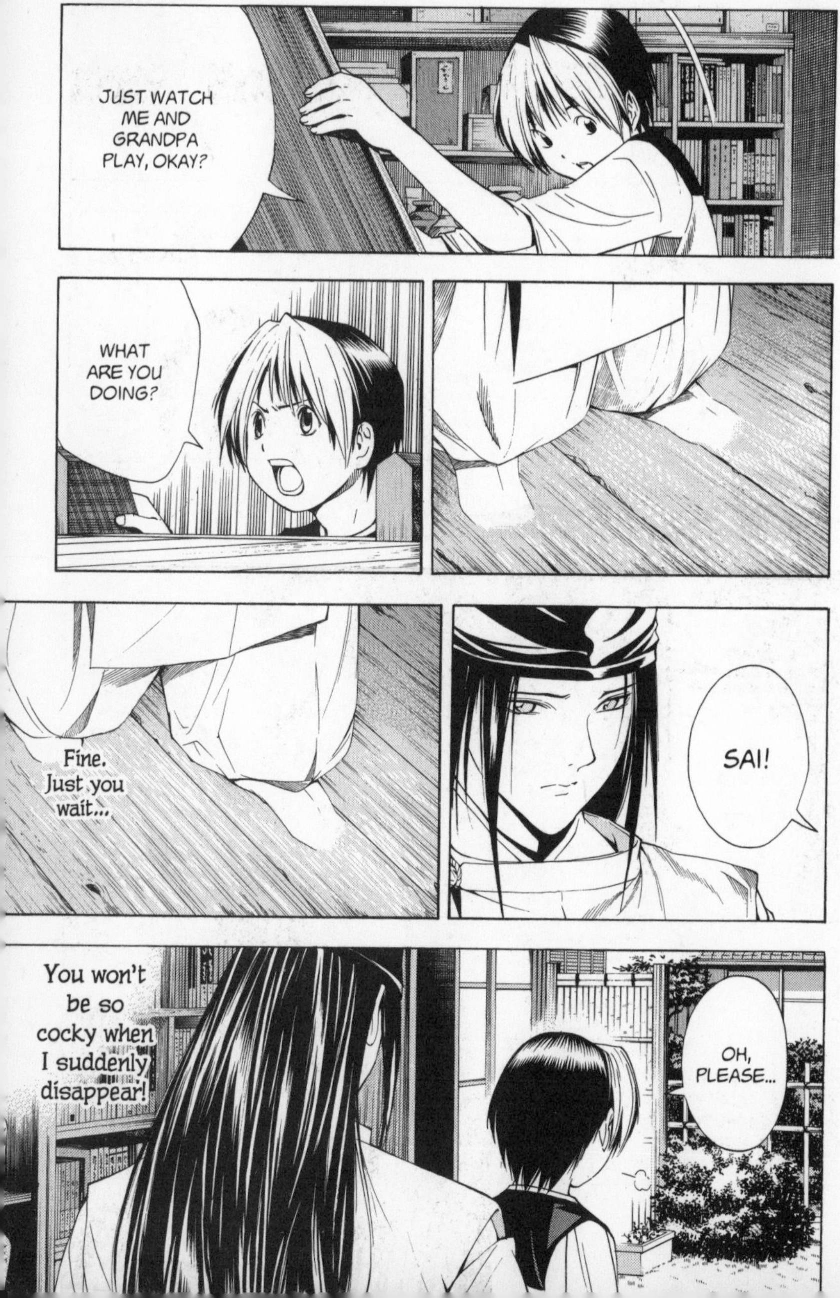
JUST WATCH ME AND GRANDPA PLAY, OKAY?
WHAT ARE YOU DOING?
SAI!
Fine. Just you wait...
OH, PLEASE...
You won't be so cocky when I suddenly disappear!

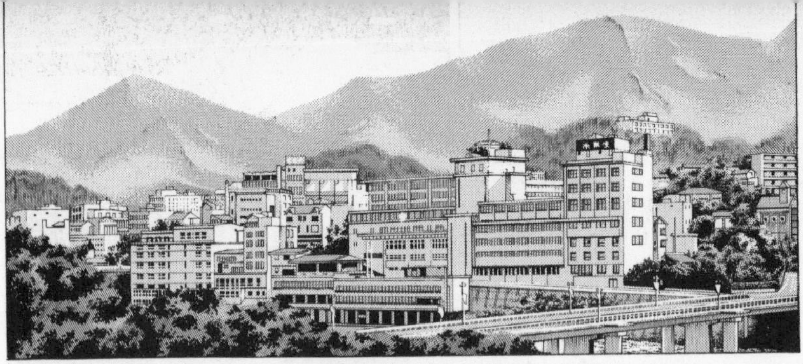

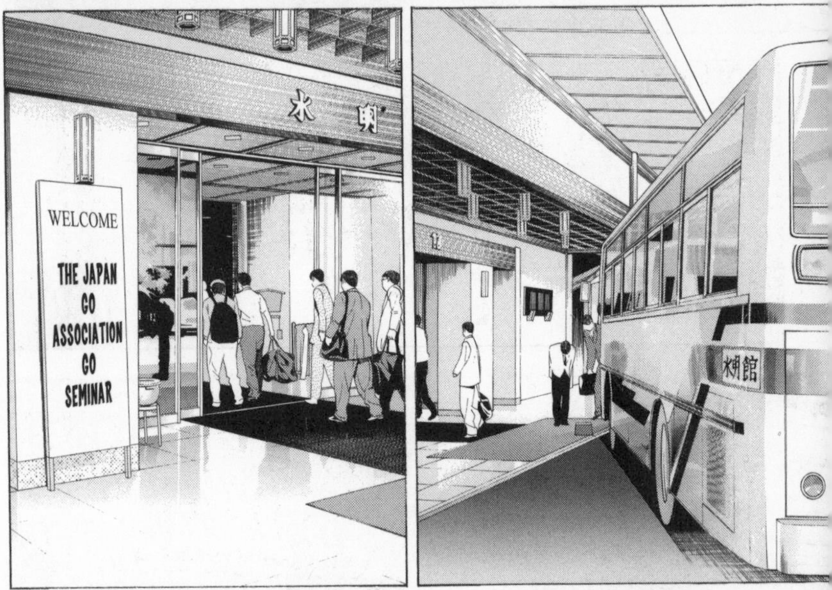
水明館
水明
WELCOME
THE JAPAN GO ASSOCIATION GO SEMINAR

*Suimeikan Hotel

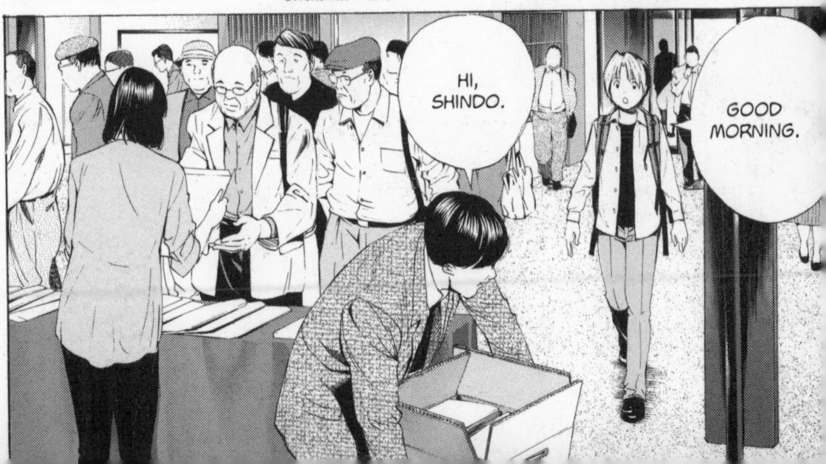
GOOD MORNING.
HI, SHINDO.

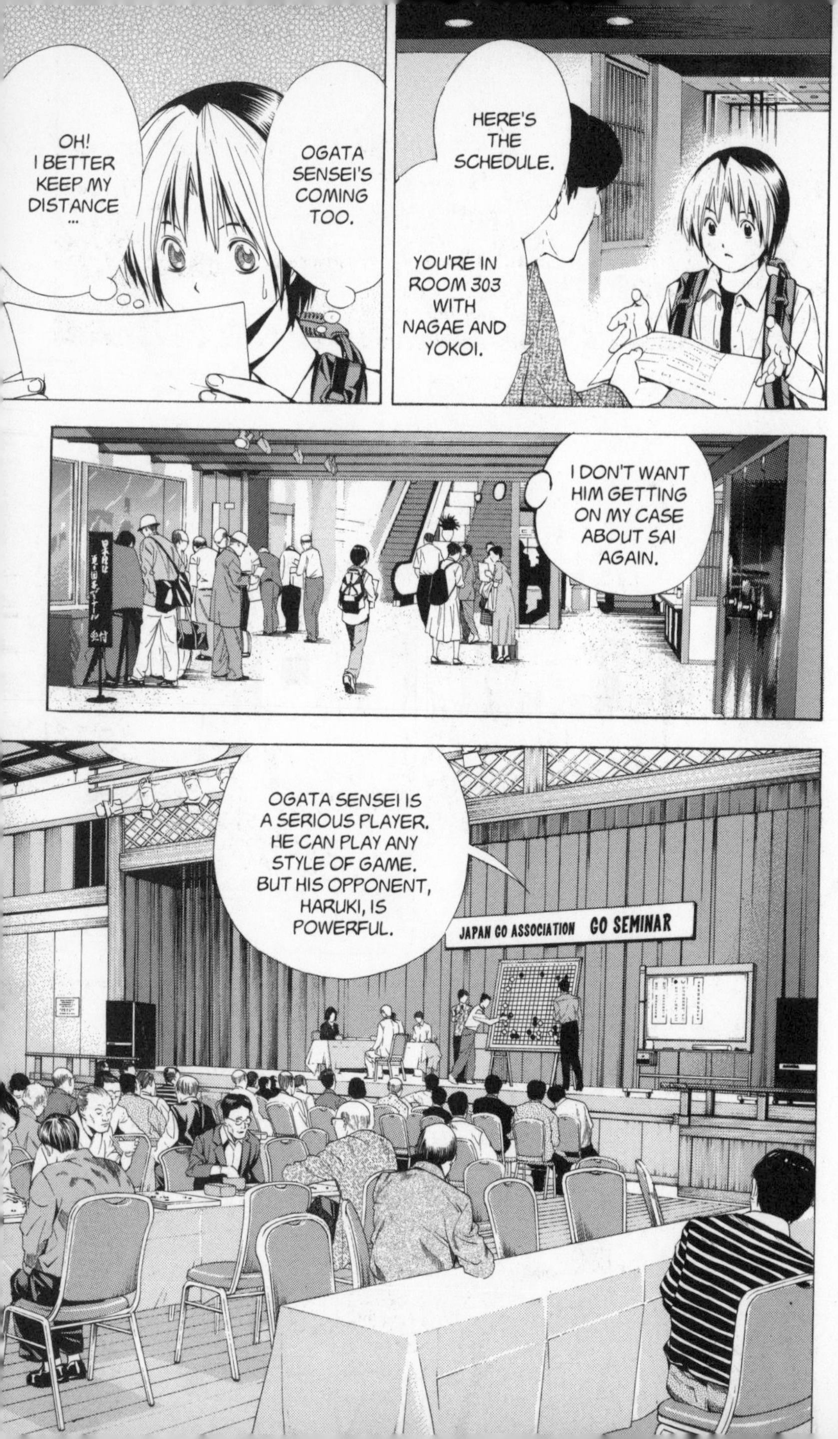
HERE'S THE SCHEDULE.
YOU'RE IN ROOM 303 WITH NAGAE AND YOKOI.
OGATA SENSEI'S COMING TOO.
OH! I BETTER KEEP MY DISTANCE ...
I DON'T WANT HIM GETTING ON MY CASE ABOUT SAI AGAIN.
OGATA SENSEI IS A SERIOUS PLAYER. HE CAN PLAY ANY STYLE OF GAME. BUT HIS OPPONENT, HARUKI, IS POWERFUL.
JAPAN GO ASSOCIATION GO SEMINAR

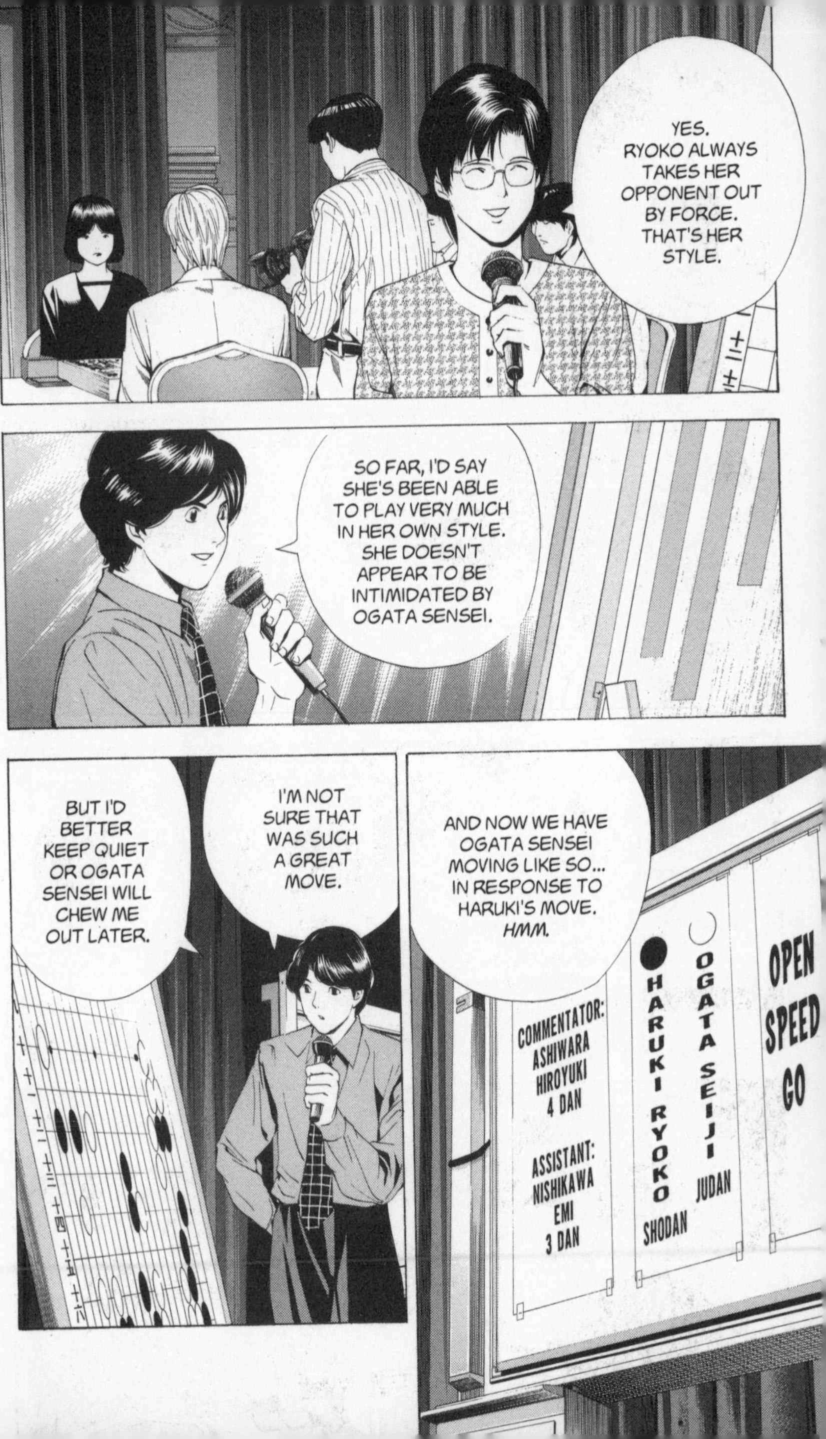
YES. RYOKO ALWAYS TAKES HER OPPONENT OUT BY FORCE. THAT'S HER STYLE.
SO FAR, I'D SAY SHE'S BEEN ABLE TO PLAY VERY MUCH IN HER OWN STYLE. SHE DOESN'T APPEAR TO BE INTIMIDATED BY OGATA SENSEI.
AND NOW WE HAVE OGATA SENSEI MOVING LIKE SO... IN RESPONSE TO HARUKI'S MOVE. *HMM.*
OPEN SPEED GO
OGATA SEIJI JUDAN
HARUKI RYOKO SHODAN
COMMENTATOR: ASHIWARA HIROYUKI 4 DAN
ASSISTANT: NISHIKAWA EMI 3 DAN
I'M NOT SURE THAT WAS SUCH A GREAT MOVE.
BUT I'D BETTER KEEP QUIET OR OGATA SENSEI WILL CHEW ME OUT LATER.

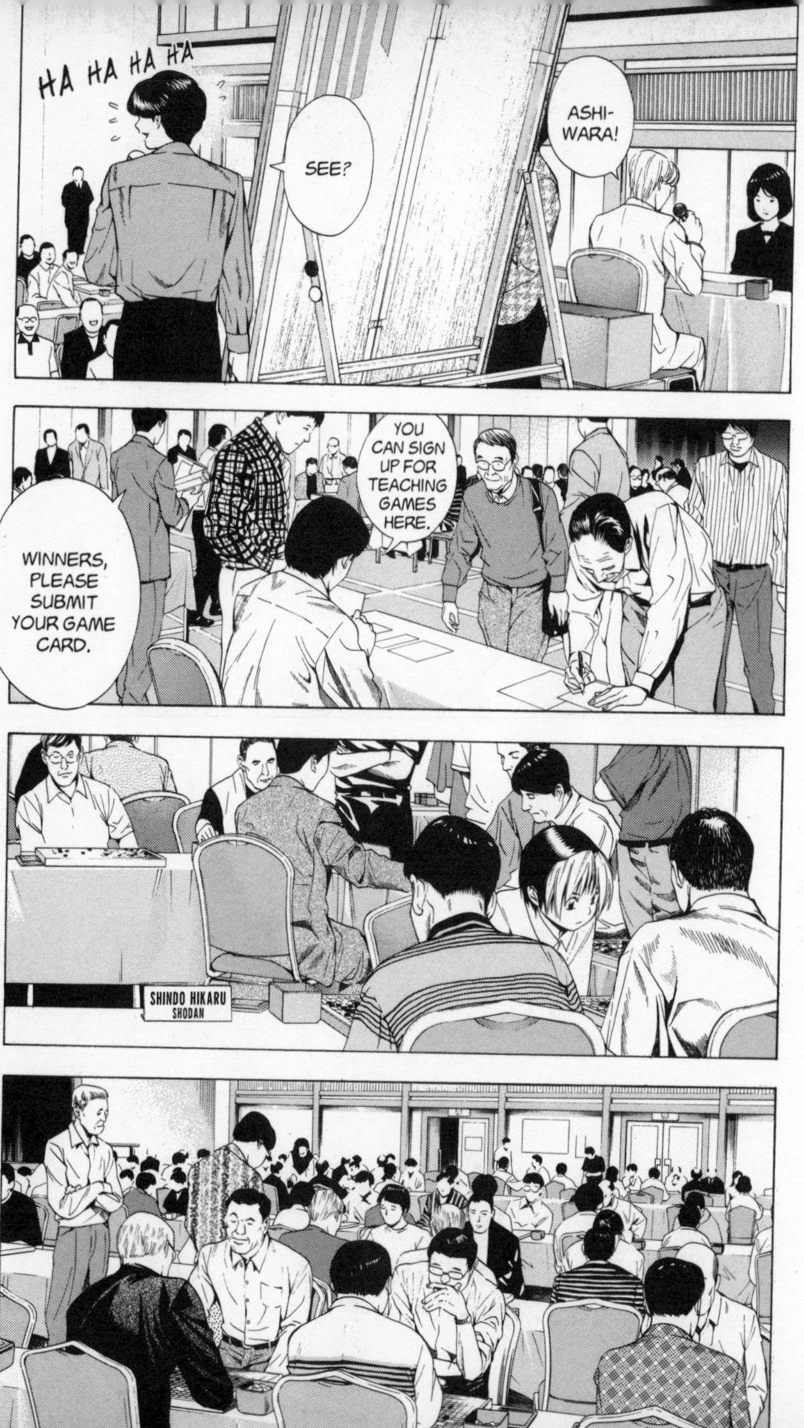
ASHI-WARA!
SEE?
HA HA HA HA
YOU CAN SIGN UP FOR TEACHING GAMES HERE.
WINNERS, PLEASE SUBMIT YOUR GAME CARD.
SHINDO HIKARU
SHODAN

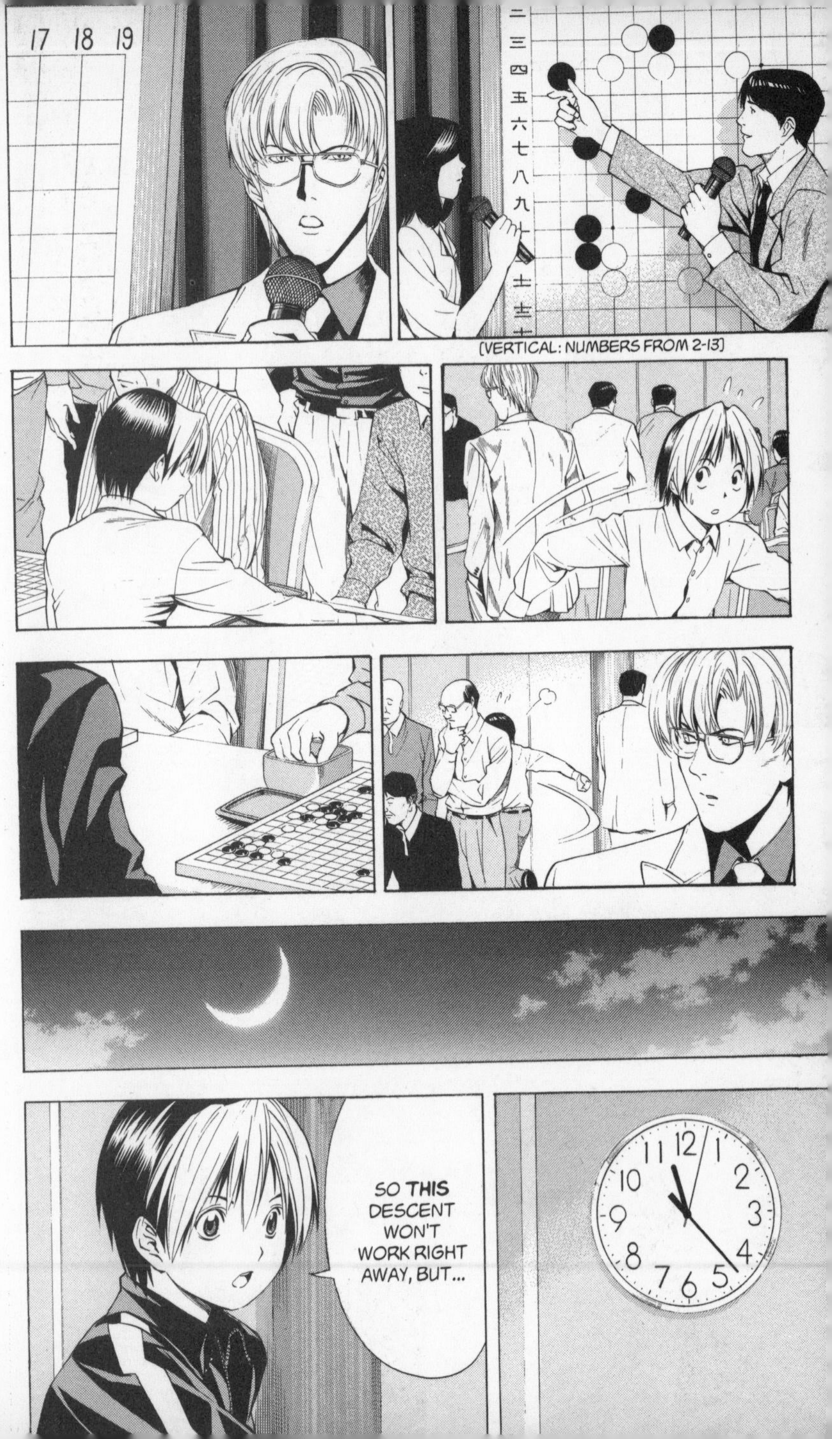
[VERTICAL: NUMBERS FROM 2-13]
17 18 19
SO THIS DESCENT WON'T WORK RIGHT AWAY, BUT...

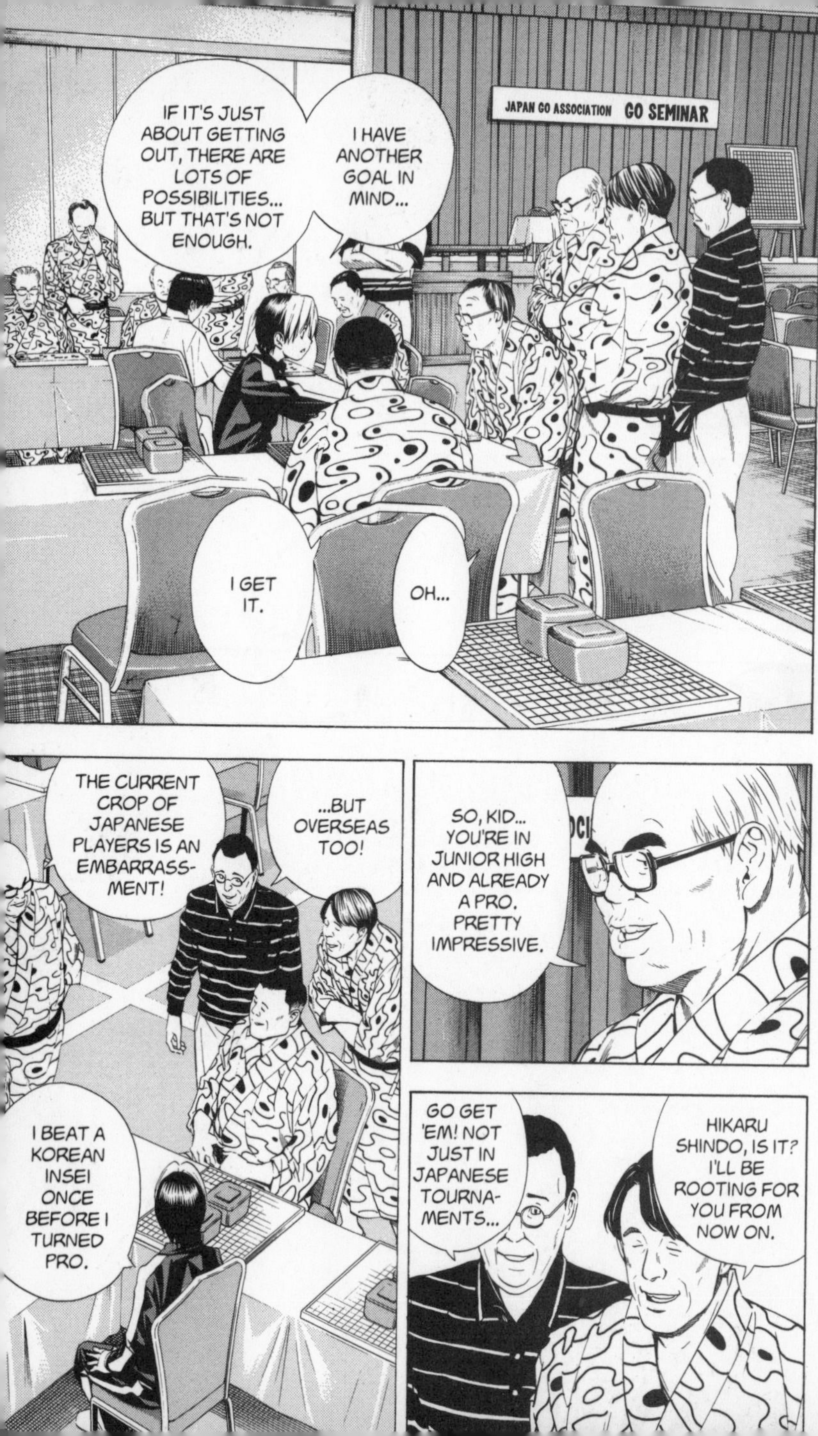
JAPAN GO ASSOCIATION GO SEMINAR
I HAVE ANOTHER GOAL IN MIND...
IF IT'S JUST ABOUT GETTING OUT, THERE ARE LOTS OF POSSIBILITIES... BUT THAT'S NOT ENOUGH.
OH...
I GET IT.
SO, KID... YOU'RE IN JUNIOR HIGH AND ALREADY A PRO. PRETTY IMPRESSIVE.
HIKARU SHINDO, IS IT? I'LL BE ROOTING FOR YOU FROM NOW ON.
GO GET 'EM! NOT JUST IN JAPANESE TOURNA-MENTS...
...BUT OVERSEAS TOO!
THE CURRENT CROP OF JAPANESE PLAYERS IS AN EMBARRASS-MENT!
I BEAT A KOREAN INSEI ONCE BEFORE I TURNED PRO.

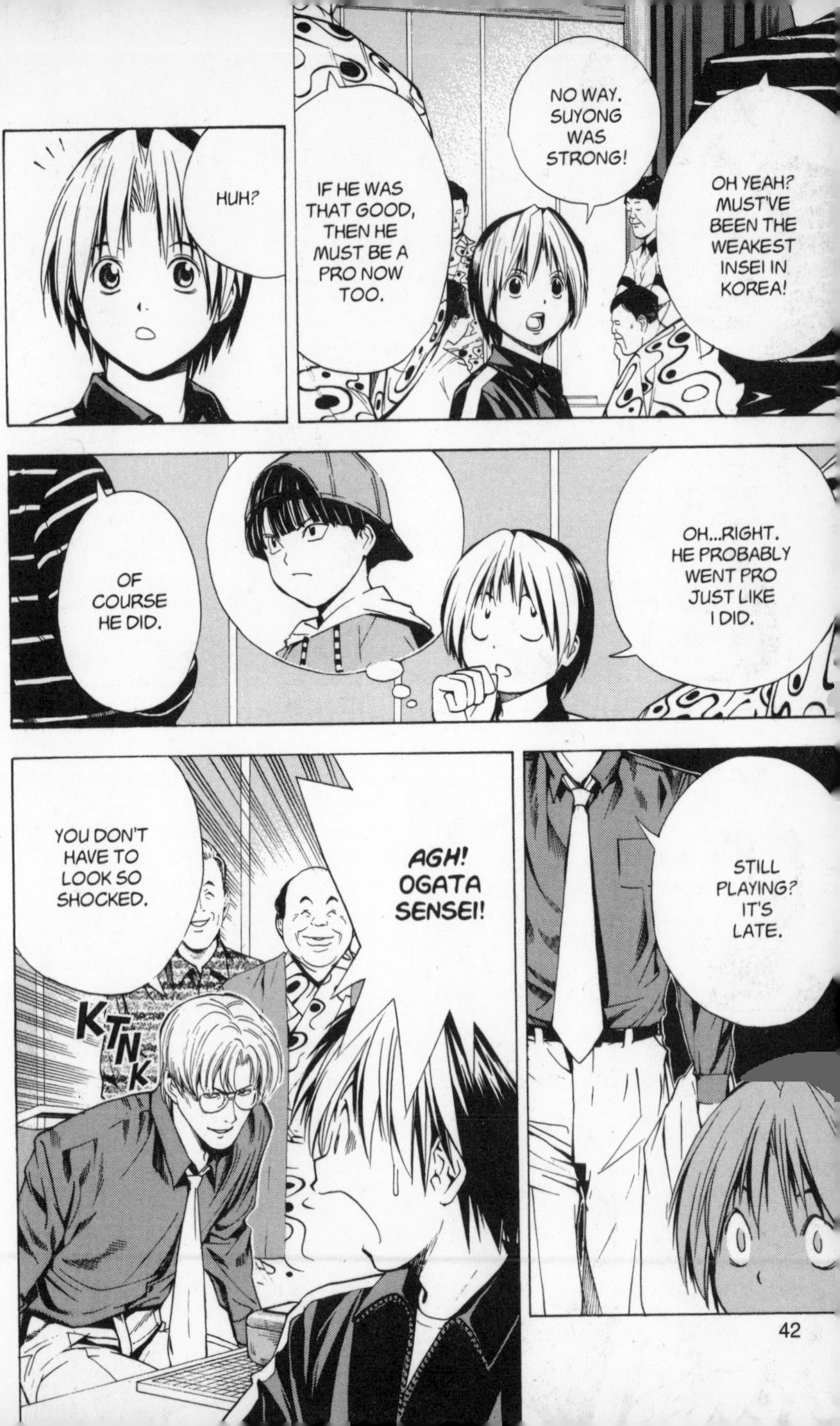
NO WAY. SUYONG WAS STRONG!
OH YEAH? MUST'VE BEEN THE WEAKEST INSEI IN KOREA!
IF HE WAS THAT GOOD, THEN HE MUST BE A PRO NOW TOO.
HUH?
OH...RIGHT. HE PROBABLY WENT PRO JUST LIKE I DID.
OF COURSE HE DID.
STILL PLAYING? IT'S LATE.
AGH! OGATA SENSEI!
YOU DON'T HAVE TO LOOK SO SHOCKED.
KTNK

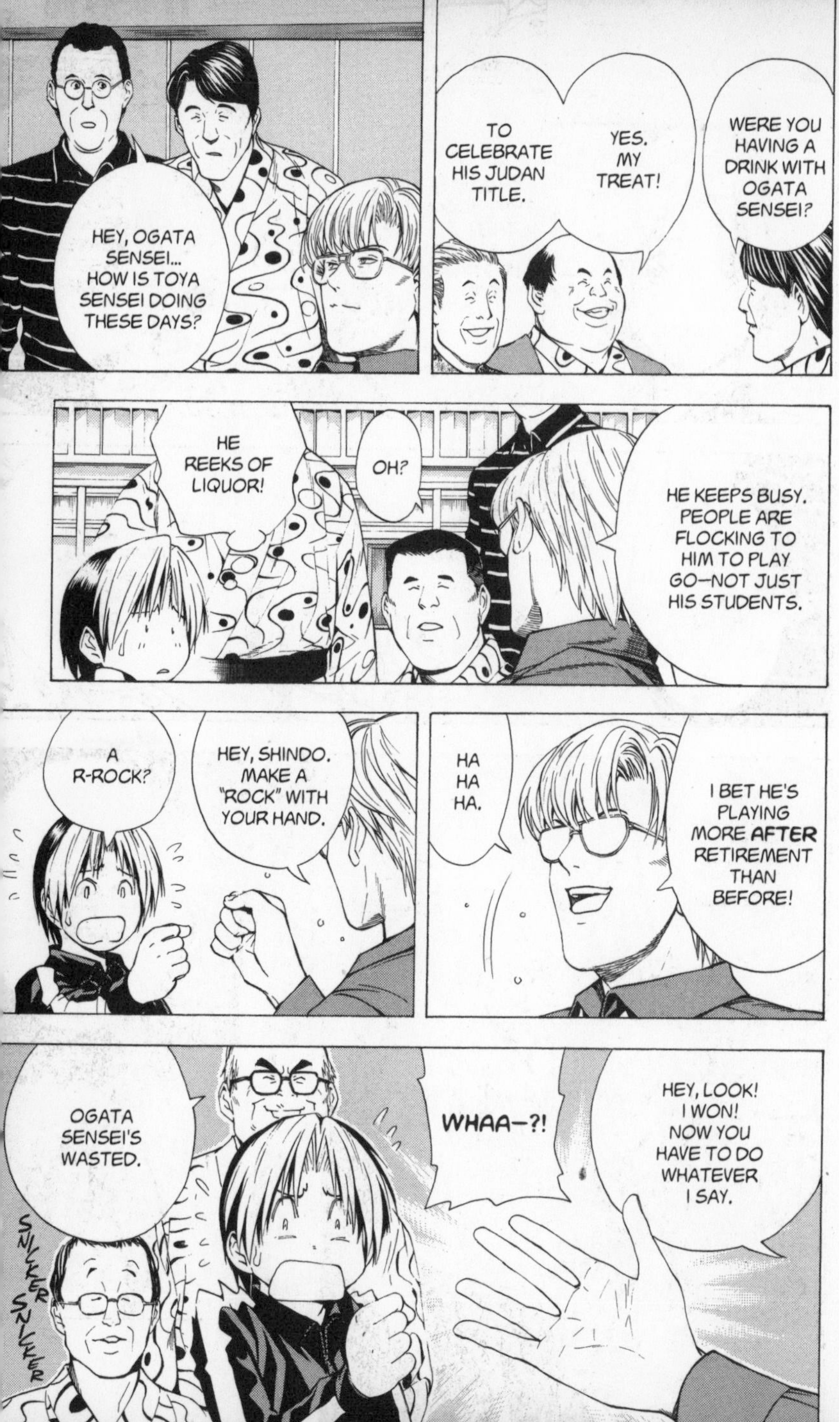
WERE YOU HAVING A DRINK WITH OGATA SENSEI?
YES. MY TREAT!
TO CELEBRATE HIS JUDAN TITLE.
HEY, OGATA SENSEI... HOW IS TOYA SENSEI DOING THESE DAYS?
HE KEEPS BUSY. PEOPLE ARE FLOCKING TO HIM TO PLAY GO—NOT JUST HIS STUDENTS.
OH?
HE REEKS OF LIQUOR!
I BET HE'S PLAYING MORE **AFTER** RETIREMENT THAN BEFORE!
HA HA HA.
HEY, SHINDO. MAKE A "ROCK" WITH YOUR HAND.
A R-ROCK?
HEY, LOOK! I WON! NOW YOU HAVE TO DO WHATEVER I SAY.
WHAA—?!
OGATA SENSEI'S WASTED.
SNICKER SNICKER

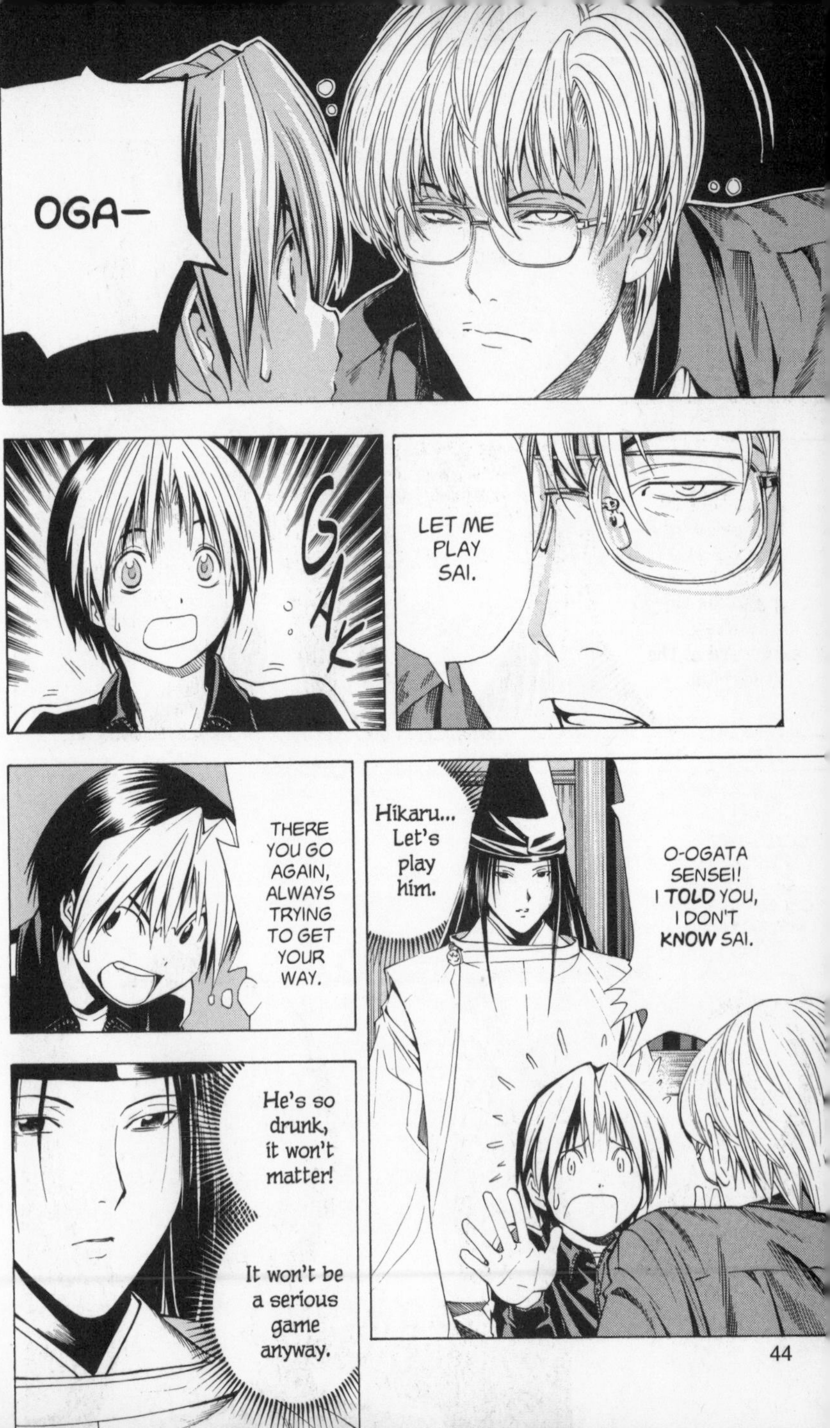
OGA—
LET ME PLAY SAI.
GAK
O-OGATA SENSEI! I **TOLD** YOU, I DON'T **KNOW** SAI.
Hikaru... Let's play him.
THERE YOU GO AGAIN, ALWAYS TRYING TO GET YOUR WAY.
He's so drunk, it won't matter!
It won't be a serious game anyway.

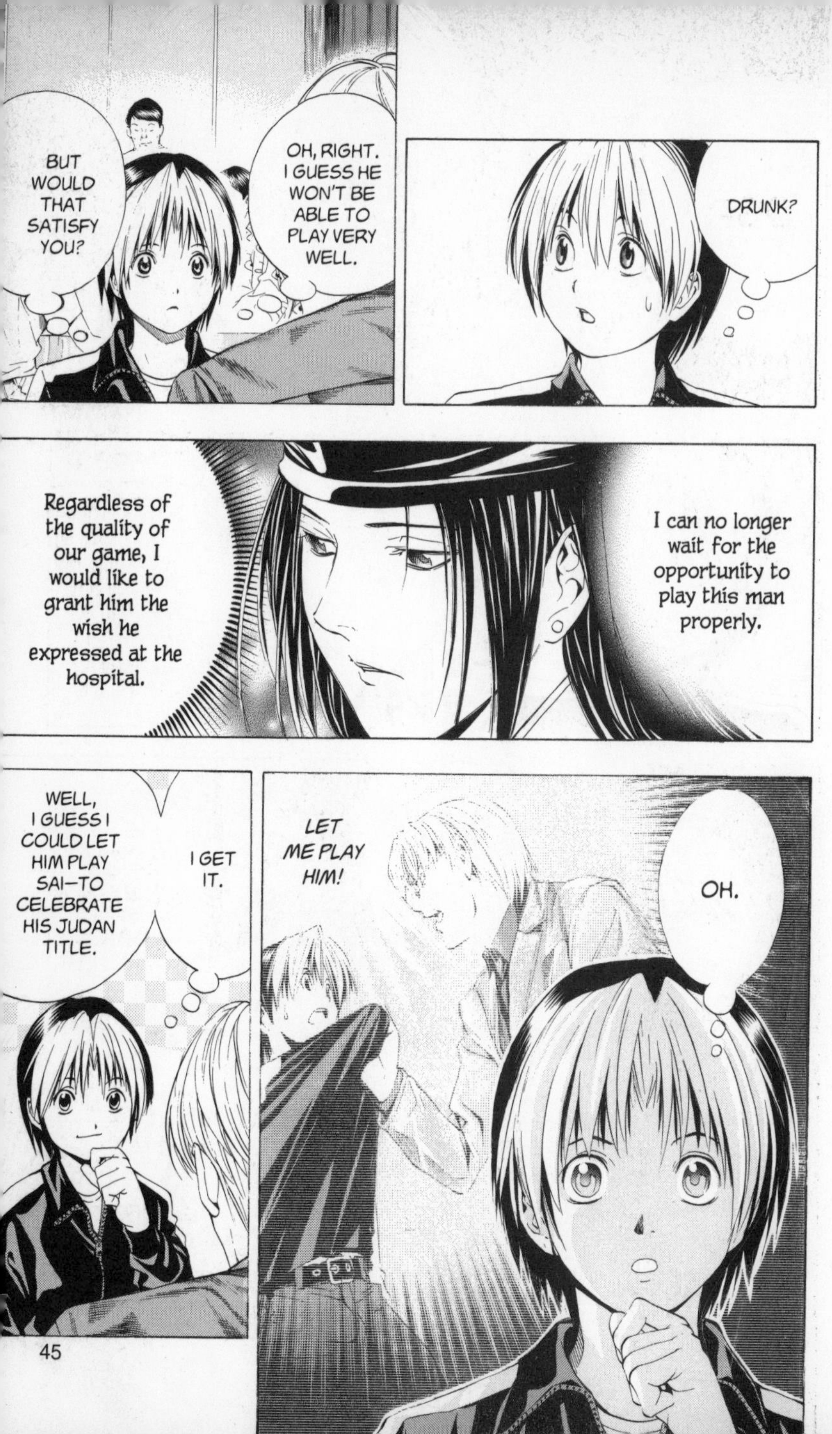
DRUNK?
OH, RIGHT. I GUESS HE WON'T BE ABLE TO PLAY VERY WELL.
BUT WOULD THAT SATISFY YOU?
I can no longer wait for the opportunity to play this man properly.
Regardless of the quality of our game, I would like to grant him the wish he expressed at the hospital.
OH.
LET ME PLAY HIM!
I GET IT.
WELL, I GUESS I COULD LET HIM PLAY SAI—TO CELEBRATE HIS JUDAN TITLE.

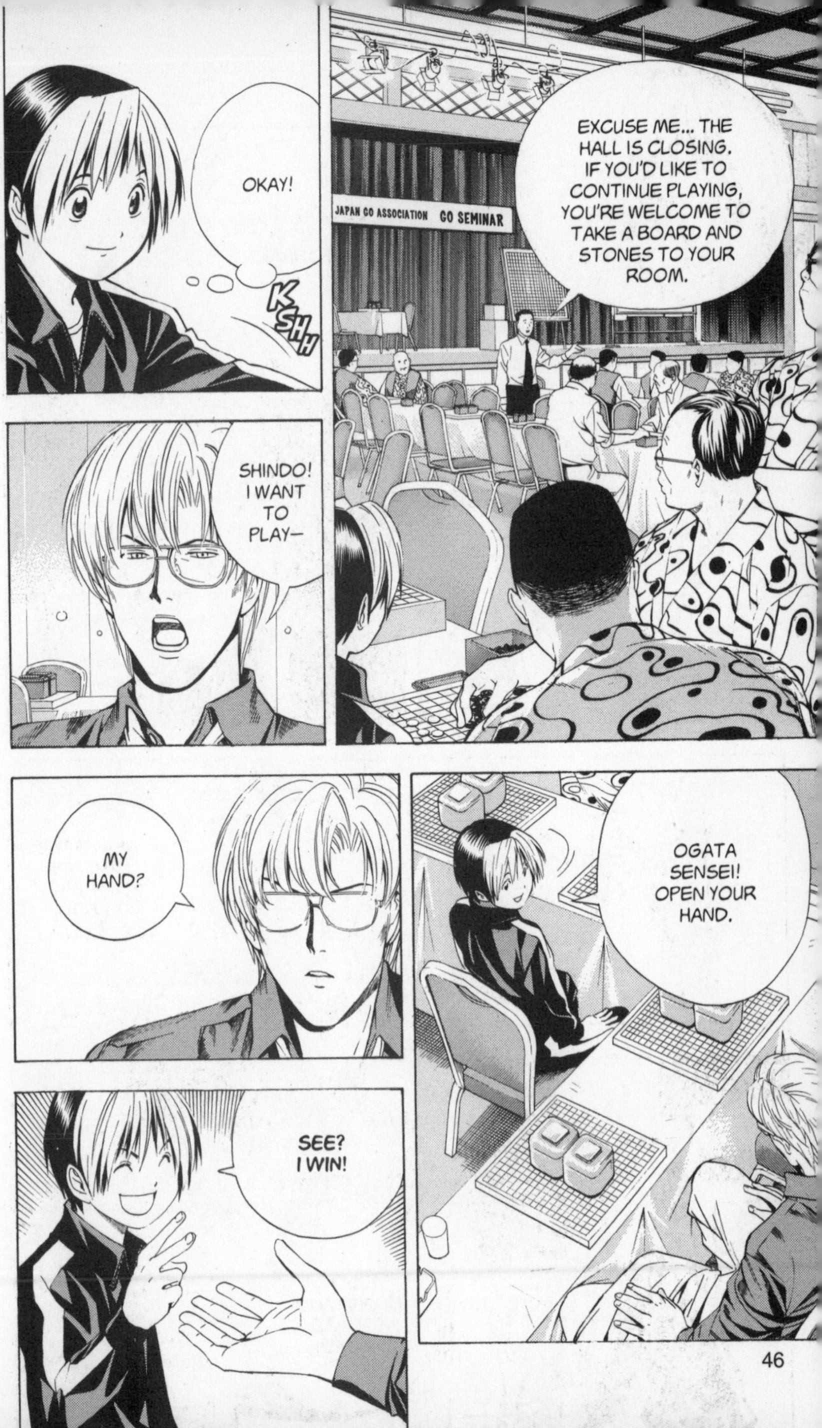
JAPAN GO ASSOCIATION GO SEMINAR
EXCUSE ME... THE HALL IS CLOSING. IF YOU'D LIKE TO CONTINUE PLAYING, YOU'RE WELCOME TO TAKE A BOARD AND STONES TO YOUR ROOM.
OKAY!
KSHH
SHINDO! I WANT TO PLAY—
OGATA SENSEI! OPEN YOUR HAND.
MY HAND?
SEE? I WIN!

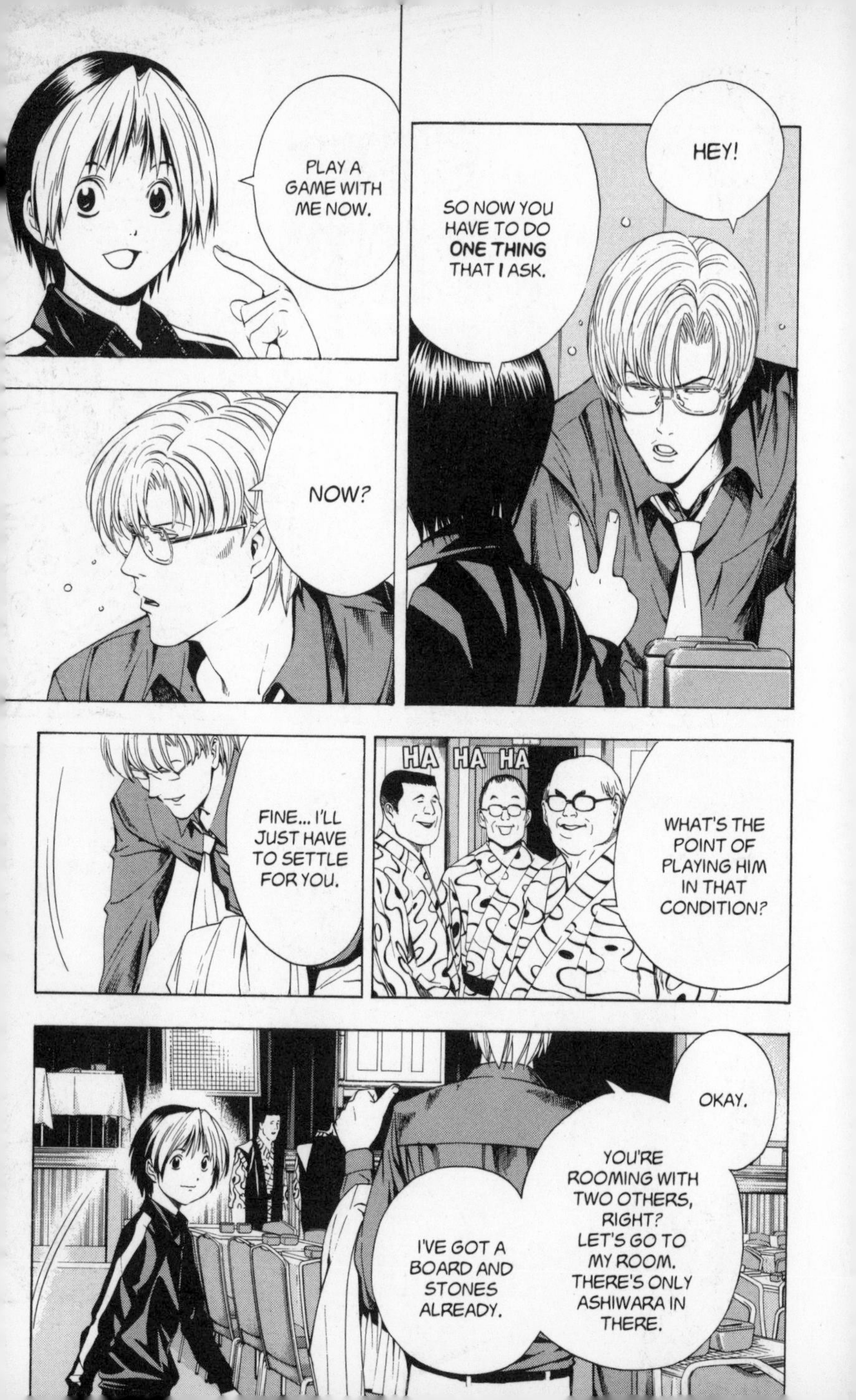
HEY!
SO NOW YOU HAVE TO DO **ONE THING** THAT I ASK.
PLAY A GAME WITH ME NOW.
NOW?
HA HA HA
WHAT'S THE POINT OF PLAYING HIM IN THAT CONDITION?
FINE... I'LL JUST HAVE TO SETTLE FOR YOU.
OKAY.
YOU'RE ROOMING WITH TWO OTHERS, RIGHT? LET'S GO TO MY ROOM. THERE'S ONLY ASHIWARA IN THERE.
I'VE GOT A BOARD AND STONES ALREADY.

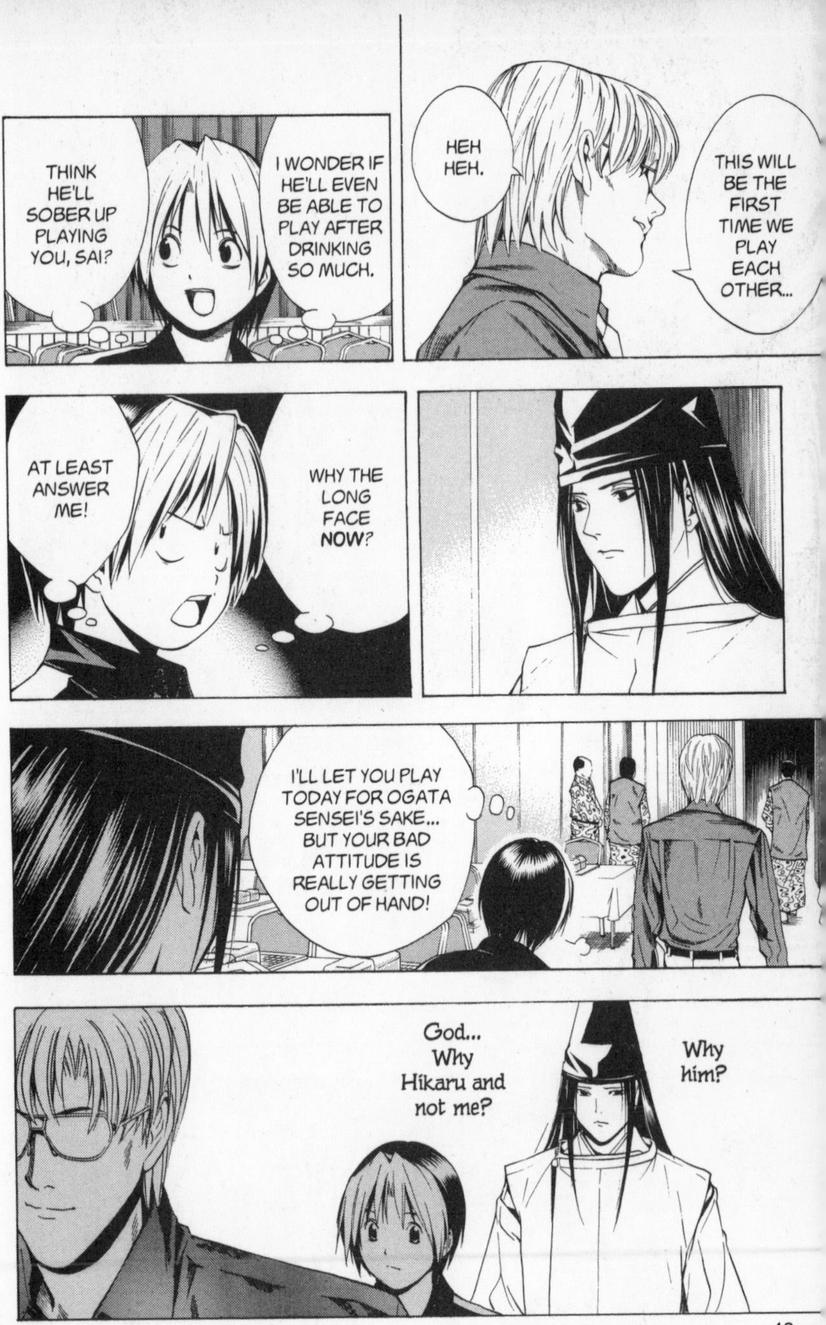
HEH HEH.
THIS WILL BE THE FIRST TIME WE PLAY EACH OTHER...
I WONDER IF HE'LL EVEN BE ABLE TO PLAY AFTER DRINKING SO MUCH.
THINK HE'LL SOBER UP PLAYING YOU, SAI?
WHY THE LONG FACE NOW?
AT LEAST ANSWER ME!
I'LL LET YOU PLAY TODAY FOR OGATA SENSEI'S SAKE... BUT YOUR BAD ATTITUDE IS REALLY GETTING OUT OF HAND!
Why him?
God... Why Hikaru and not me?

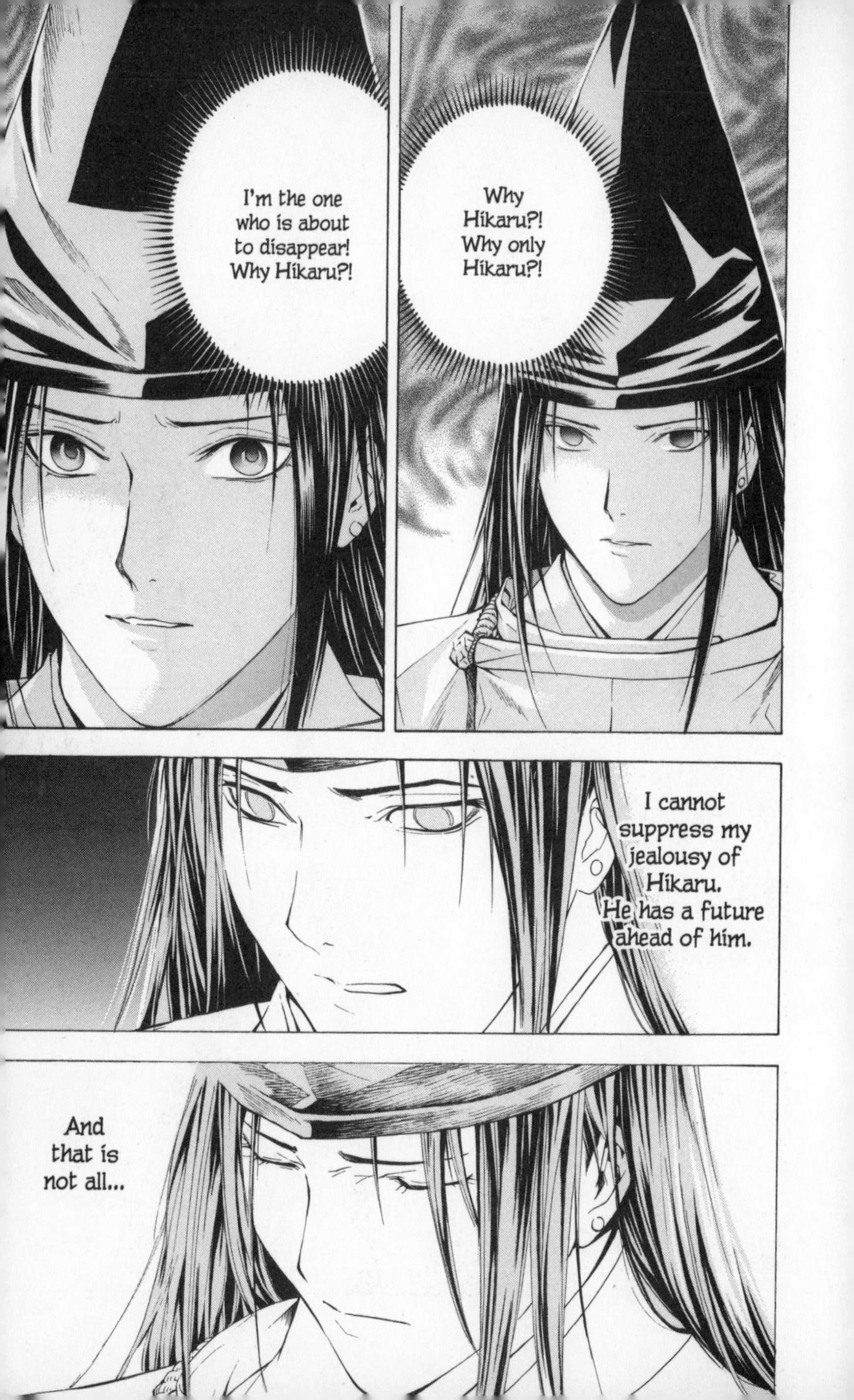
Why Hikaru?! Why only Hikaru?!
I'm the one who is about to disappear! Why Hikaru?!
I cannot suppress my jealousy of Hikaru. He has a future ahead of him.
And that is not all...

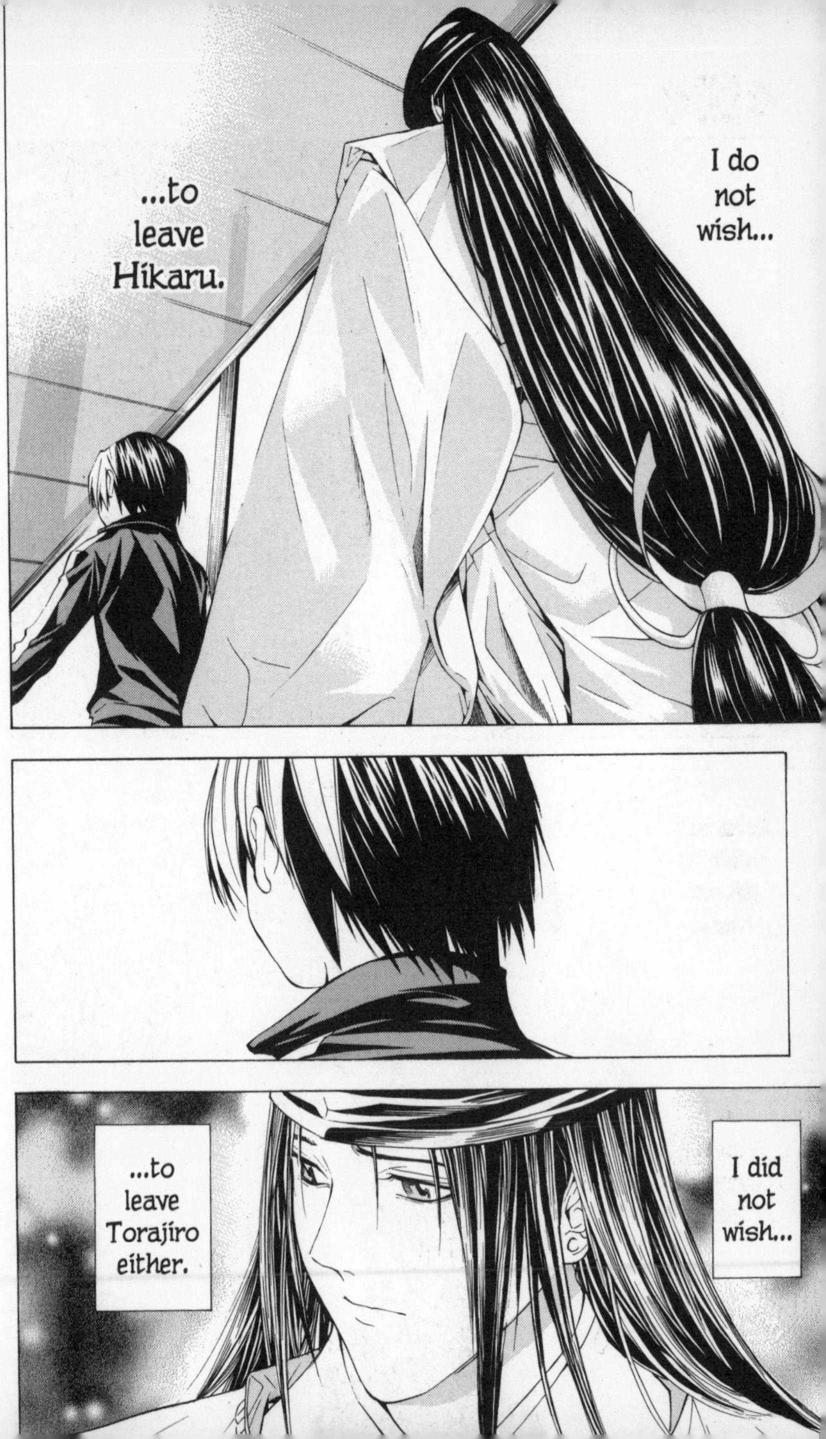
I do not wish...
...to leave Hikaru.
I did not wish...
...to leave Torajiro either.

READ THIS WAY

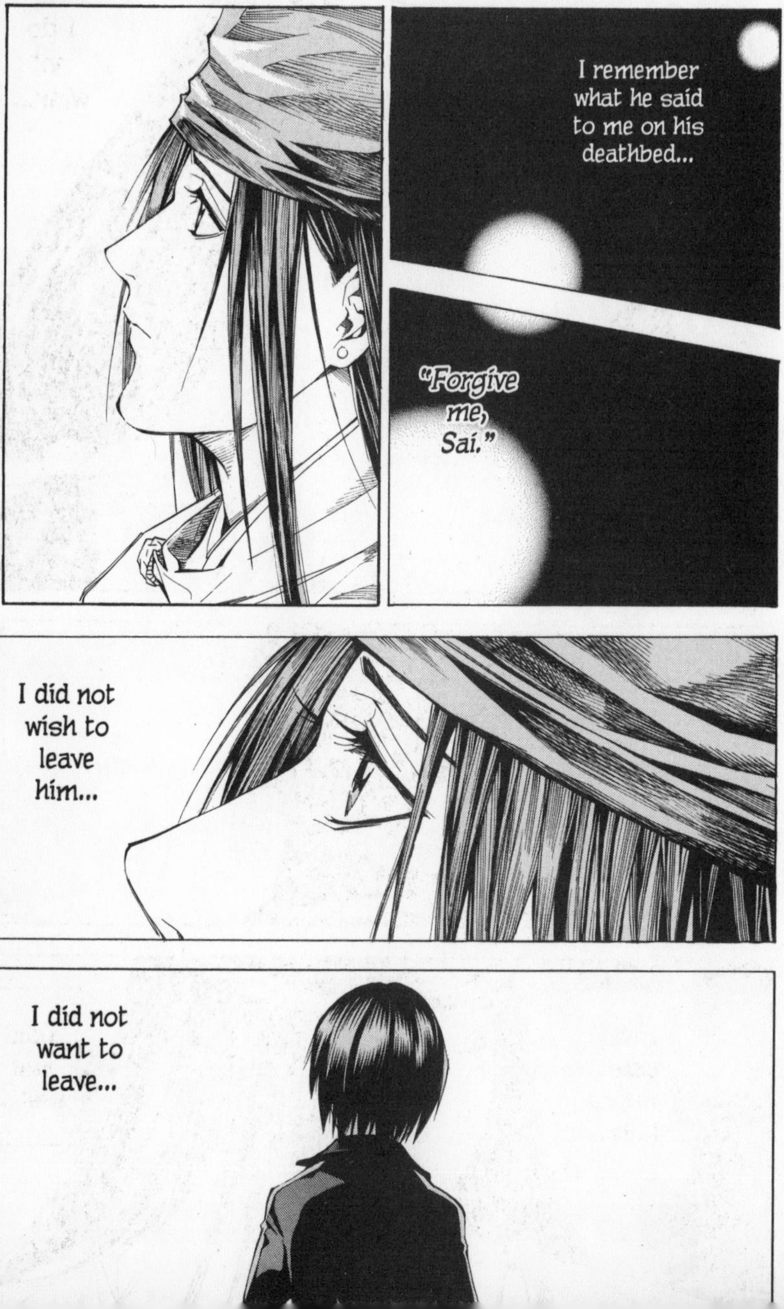
I remember what he said to me on his deathbed...
"Forgive me, Sai."
I did not wish to leave him...
I did not want to leave...

A WORD ABOUT HIKARU NO GO

GO SEMINAR

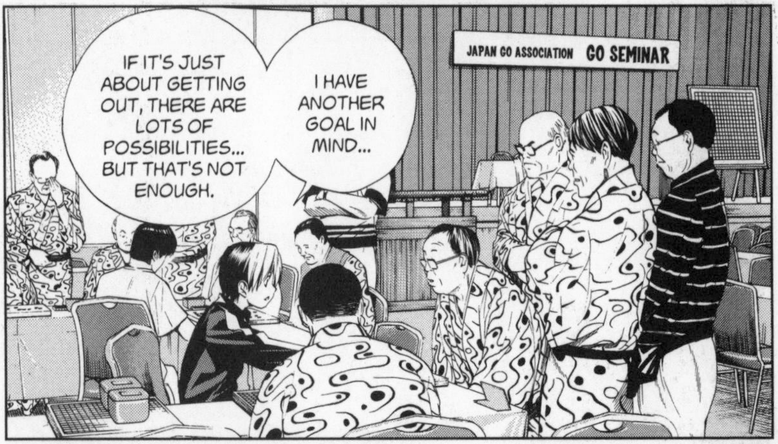
JAPAN GO ASSOCIATION GO SEMINAR
I HAVE ANOTHER GOAL IN MIND...
IF IT'S JUST ABOUT GETTING OUT, THERE ARE LOTS OF POSSIBILITIES... BUT THAT'S NOT ENOUGH.

GO SEMINARS ARE GO GETAWAYS THAT HAPPEN A FEW TIMES A YEAR AND ARE ATTENDED BY GO FANS. THERE ARE MANY KINDS, RANGING FROM ONE NIGHT AT A NEARBY ONSEN SPA TO A WEEK IN EUROPE OR CHINA.

THEY ARE OPPORTUNITIES TO HANG OUT WITH PROS AND DO NOTHING BUT PLAY GO.

YOU CAN FIND BOTH TIPSY TITLE HOLDERS AND TENDER YOUNG PROS IN THEIR TEENS AT THESE EVENTS... REALLY! IT'S TRUE!

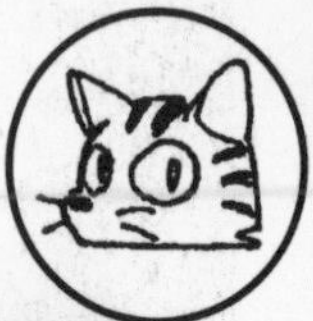

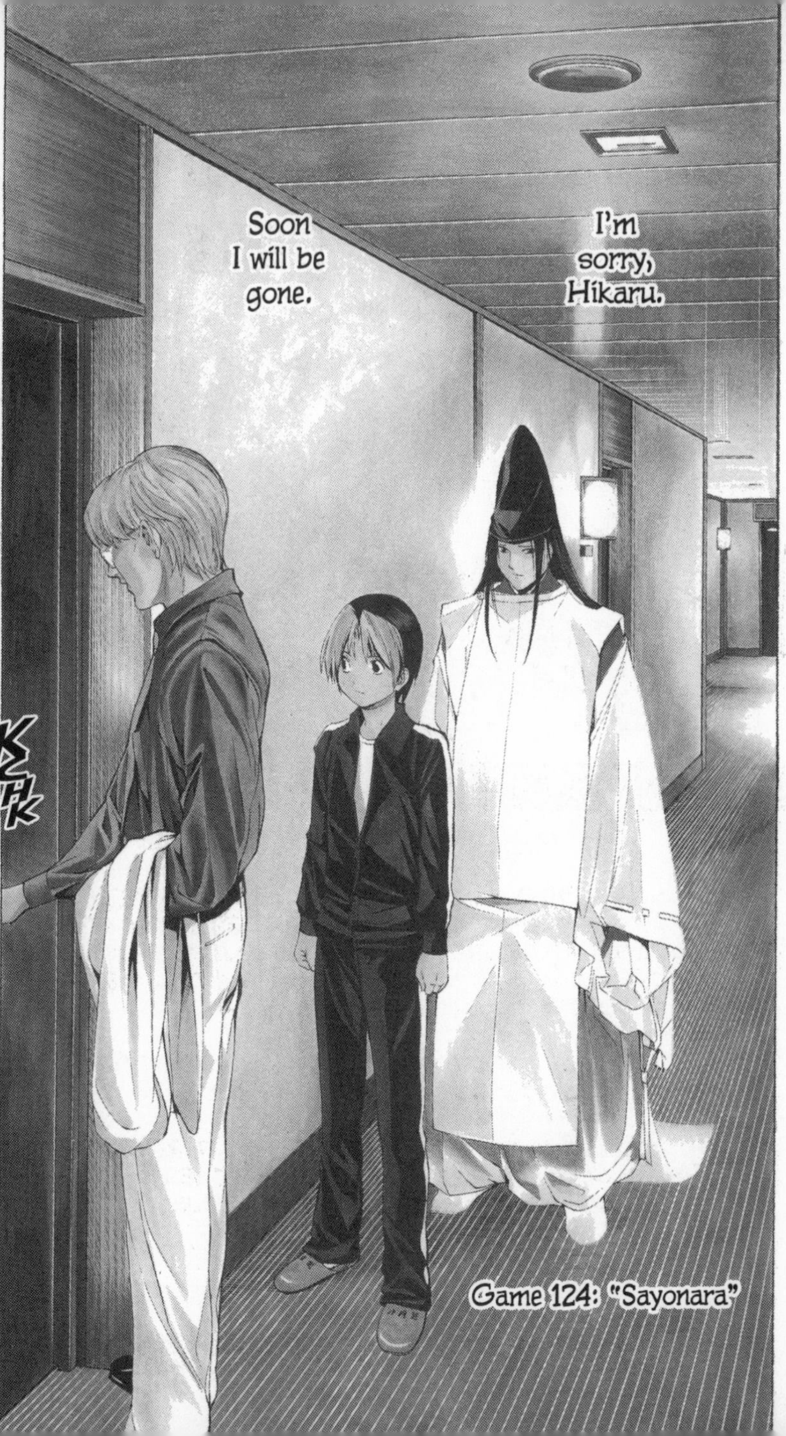
I'm sorry, Hikaru.
Soon I will be gone.
KCHK
Game 124: "Sayonara"

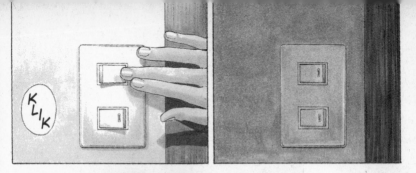

KLIK

NNGH.

OH, YOU WERE ASLEEP? SORRY ABOUT THE LIGHT.

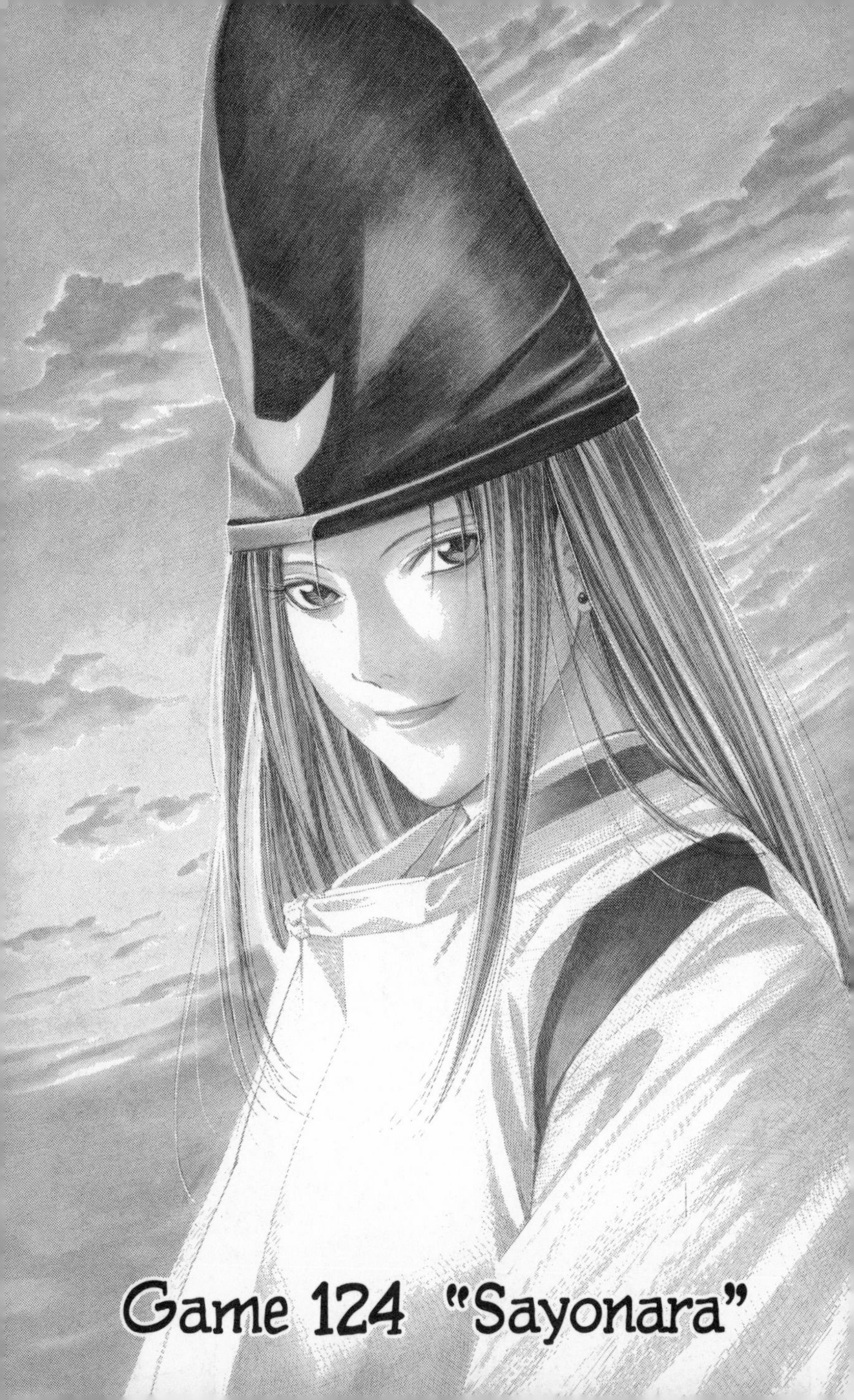
Game 124 "Sayonara"

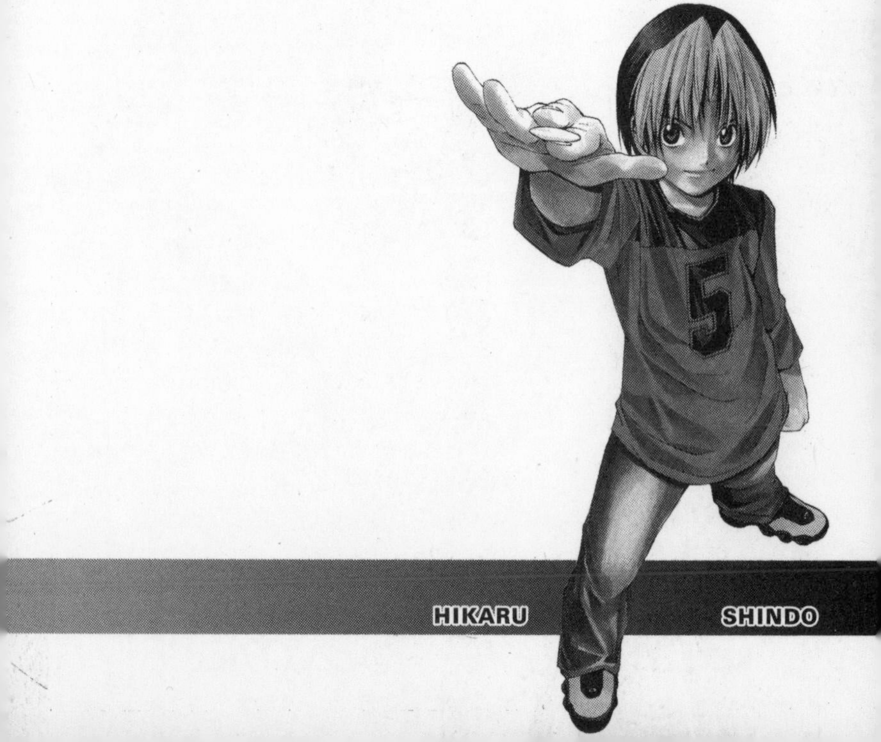

HIKARU
SHINDO

READ THIS WAY

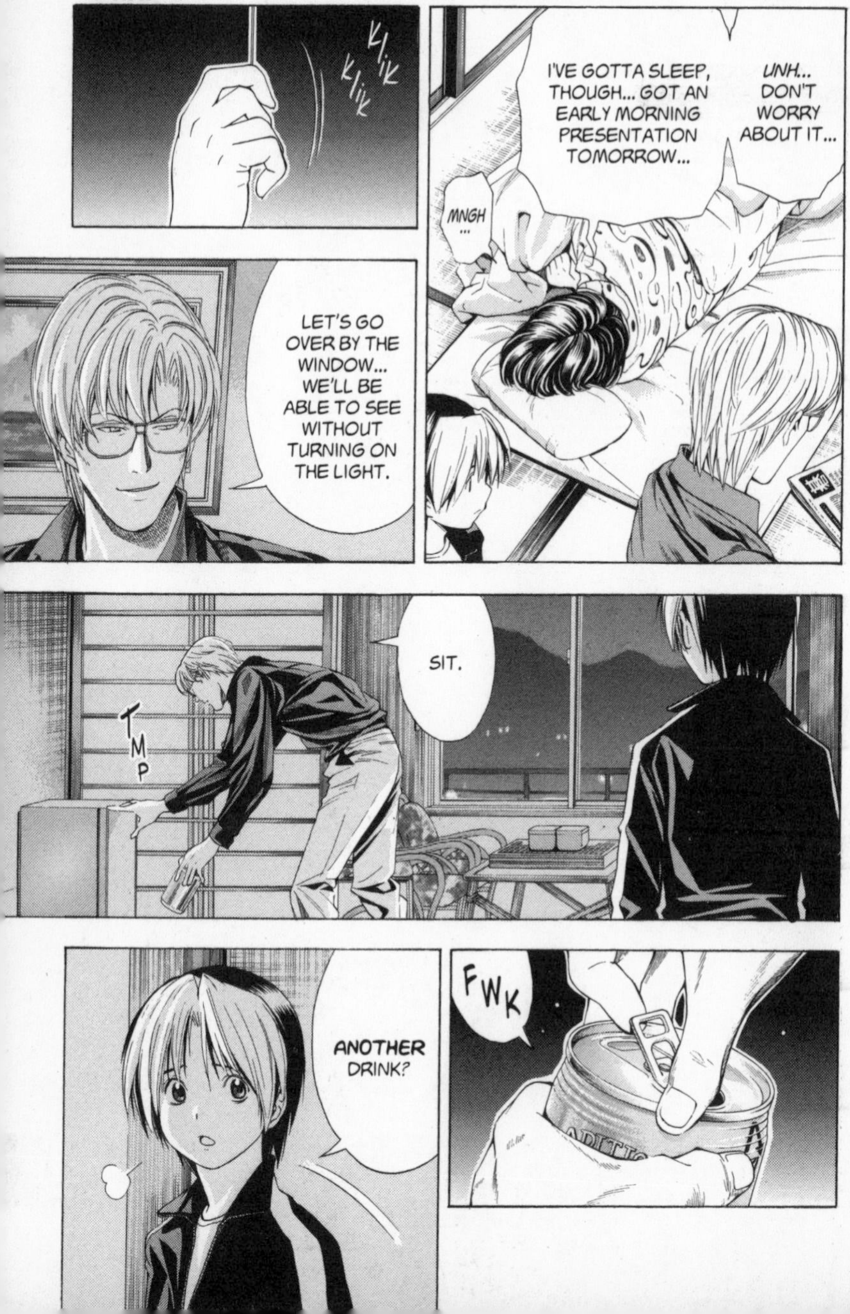
UNH... DON'T WORRY ABOUT IT...
I'VE GOTTA SLEEP, THOUGH... GOT AN EARLY MORNING PRESENTATION TOMORROW...
MNGH...
KLIK KLIK
LET'S GO OVER BY THE WINDOW... WE'LL BE ABLE TO SEE WITHOUT TURNING ON THE LIGHT.
SIT.
TMP
FWK
ANOTHER DRINK?

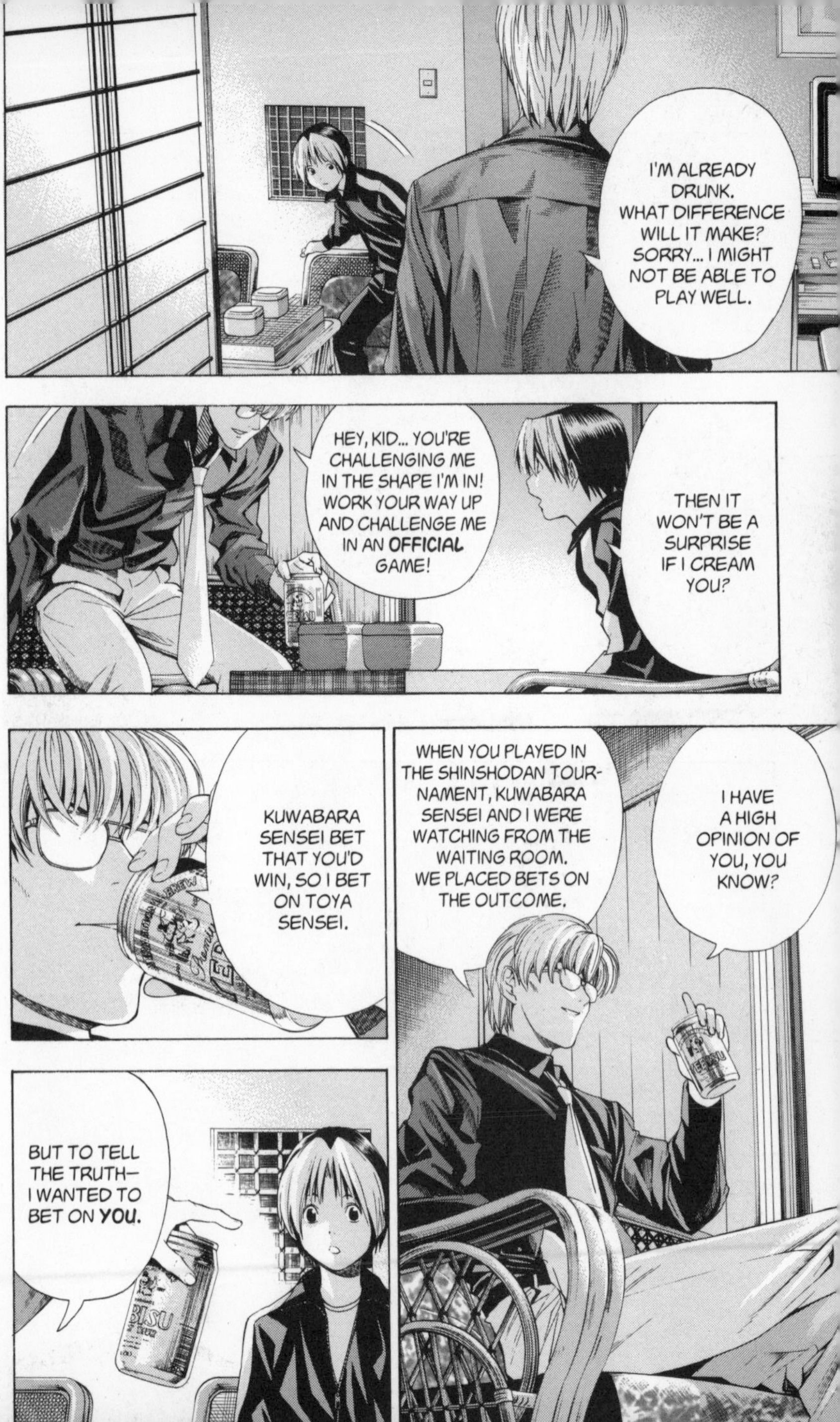

I'M ALREADY DRUNK. WHAT DIFFERENCE WILL IT MAKE? SORRY... I MIGHT NOT BE ABLE TO PLAY WELL.
THEN IT WON'T BE A SURPRISE IF I CREAM YOU?
HEY, KID... YOU'RE CHALLENGING ME IN THE SHAPE I'M IN! WORK YOUR WAY UP AND CHALLENGE ME IN AN **OFFICIAL** GAME!
I HAVE A HIGH OPINION OF YOU, YOU KNOW?
WHEN YOU PLAYED IN THE SHINSHODAN TOURNAMENT, KUWABARA SENSEI AND I WERE WATCHING FROM THE WAITING ROOM. WE PLACED BETS ON THE OUTCOME.
KUWABARA SENSEI BET THAT YOU'D WIN, SO I BET ON TOYA SENSEI.
BUT TO TELL THE TRUTH— I WANTED TO BET ON **YOU**.

READ THIS WAY

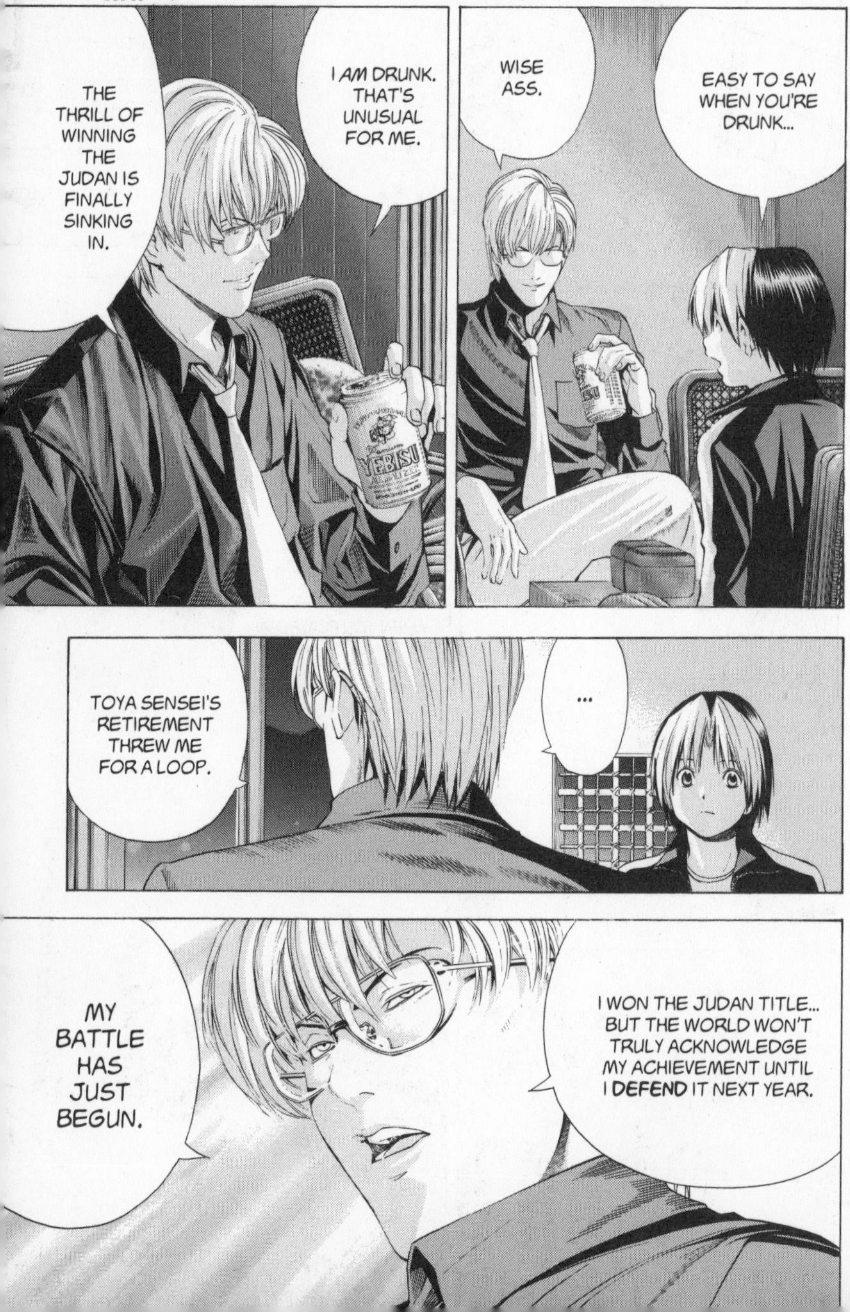
EASY TO SAY WHEN YOU'RE DRUNK...
WISE ASS.
I *AM* DRUNK. THAT'S UNUSUAL FOR ME.
THE THRILL OF WINNING THE JUDAN IS FINALLY SINKING IN.
...
TOYA SENSEI'S RETIREMENT THREW ME FOR A LOOP.
I WON THE JUDAN TITLE... BUT THE WORLD WON'T TRULY ACKNOWLEDGE MY ACHIEVEMENT UNTIL I **DEFEND** IT NEXT YEAR.
MY BATTLE HAS JUST BEGUN.

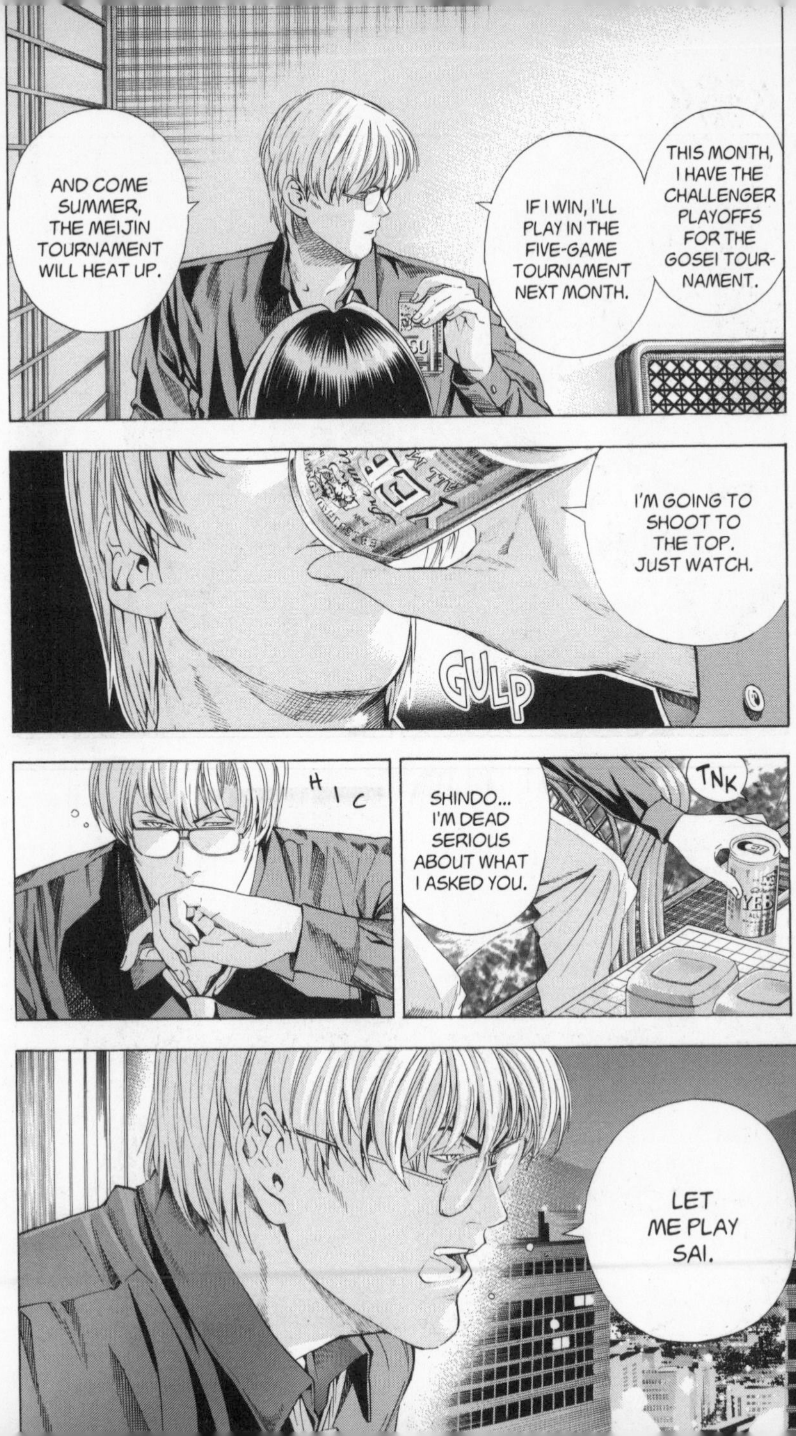
THIS MONTH, I HAVE THE CHALLENGER PLAYOFFS FOR THE GOSEI TOUR-NAMENT.
IF I WIN, I'LL PLAY IN THE FIVE-GAME TOURNAMENT NEXT MONTH.
AND COME SUMMER, THE MEIJIN TOURNAMENT WILL HEAT UP.
I'M GOING TO SHOOT TO THE TOP. JUST WATCH.
GULP
TNK
SHINDO... I'M DEAD SERIOUS ABOUT WHAT I ASKED YOU.
HIC
LET ME PLAY SAI.

READ THIS WAY

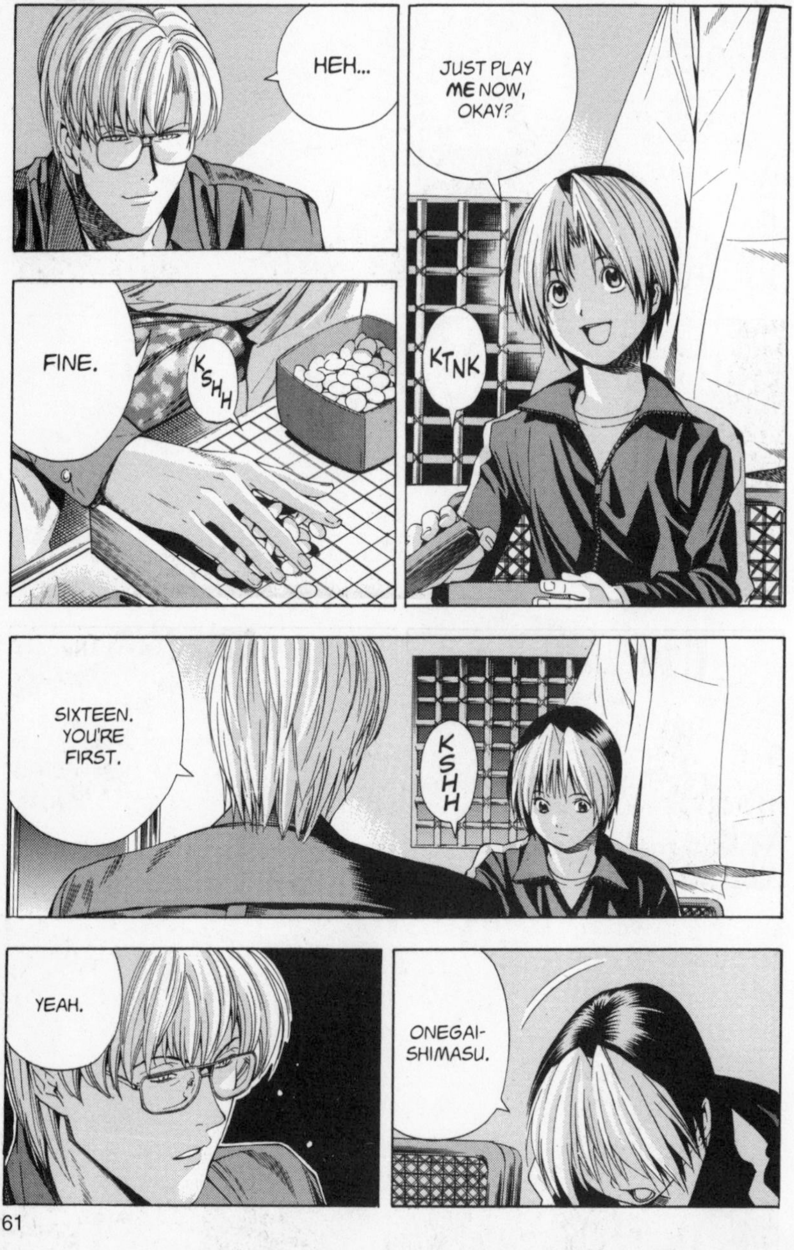
JUST PLAY ME NOW, OKAY?
HEH...
KTNK
KSHH
FINE.
KSHH
SIXTEEN. YOU'RE FIRST.
ONEGAI-SHIMASU.
YEAH.

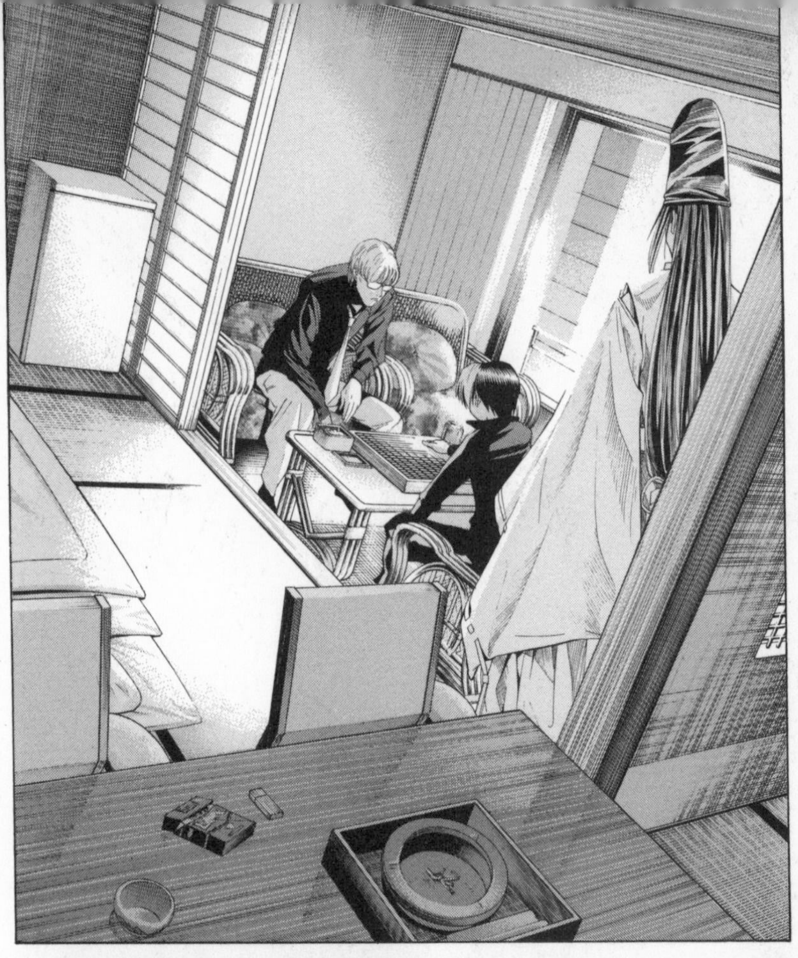
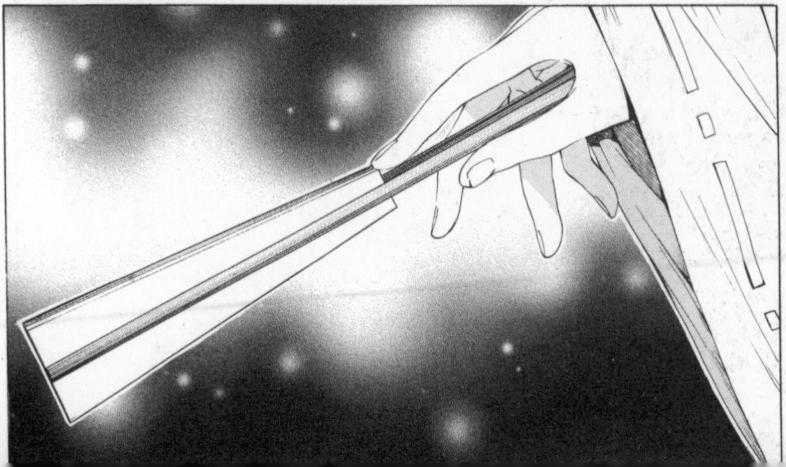

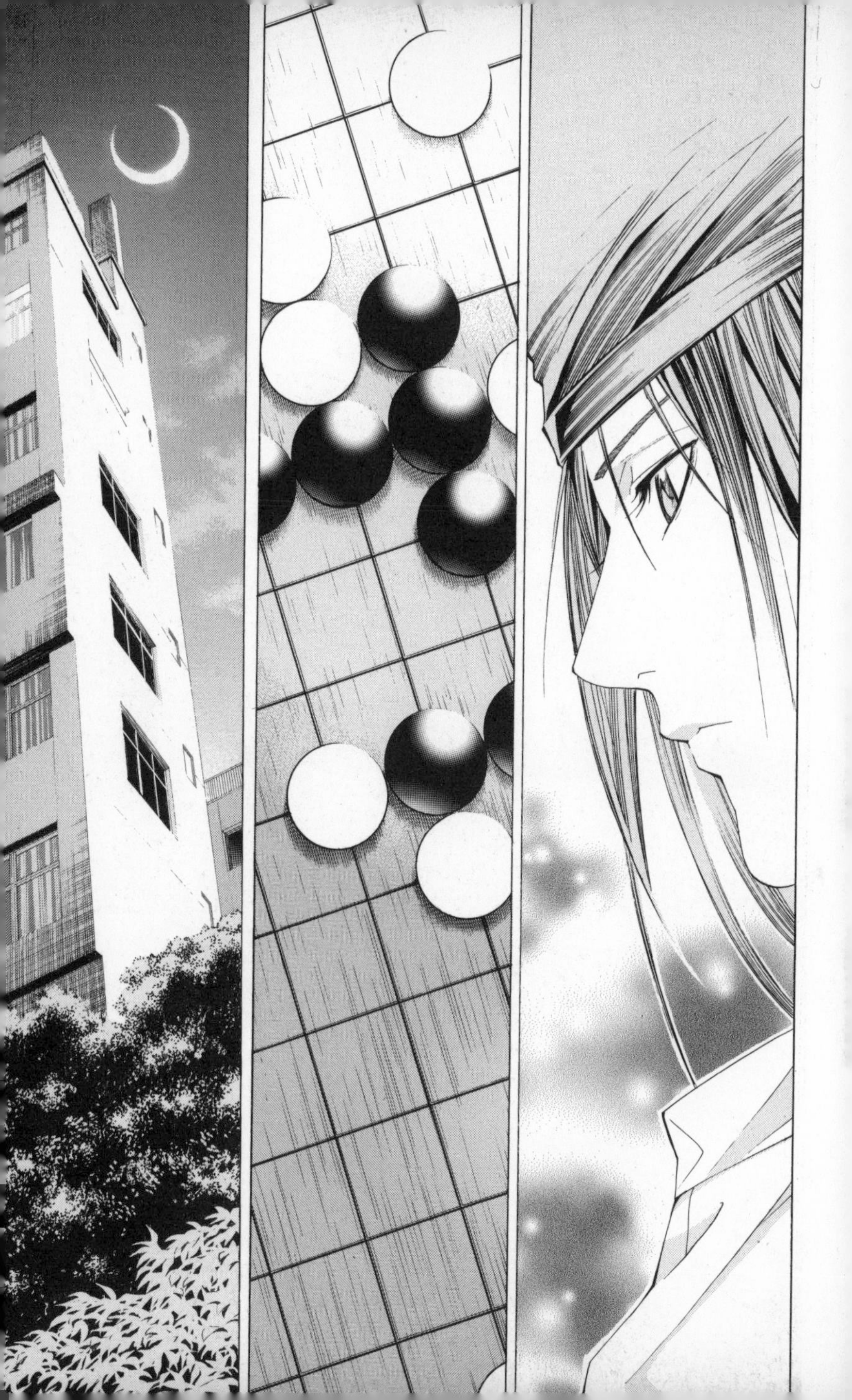

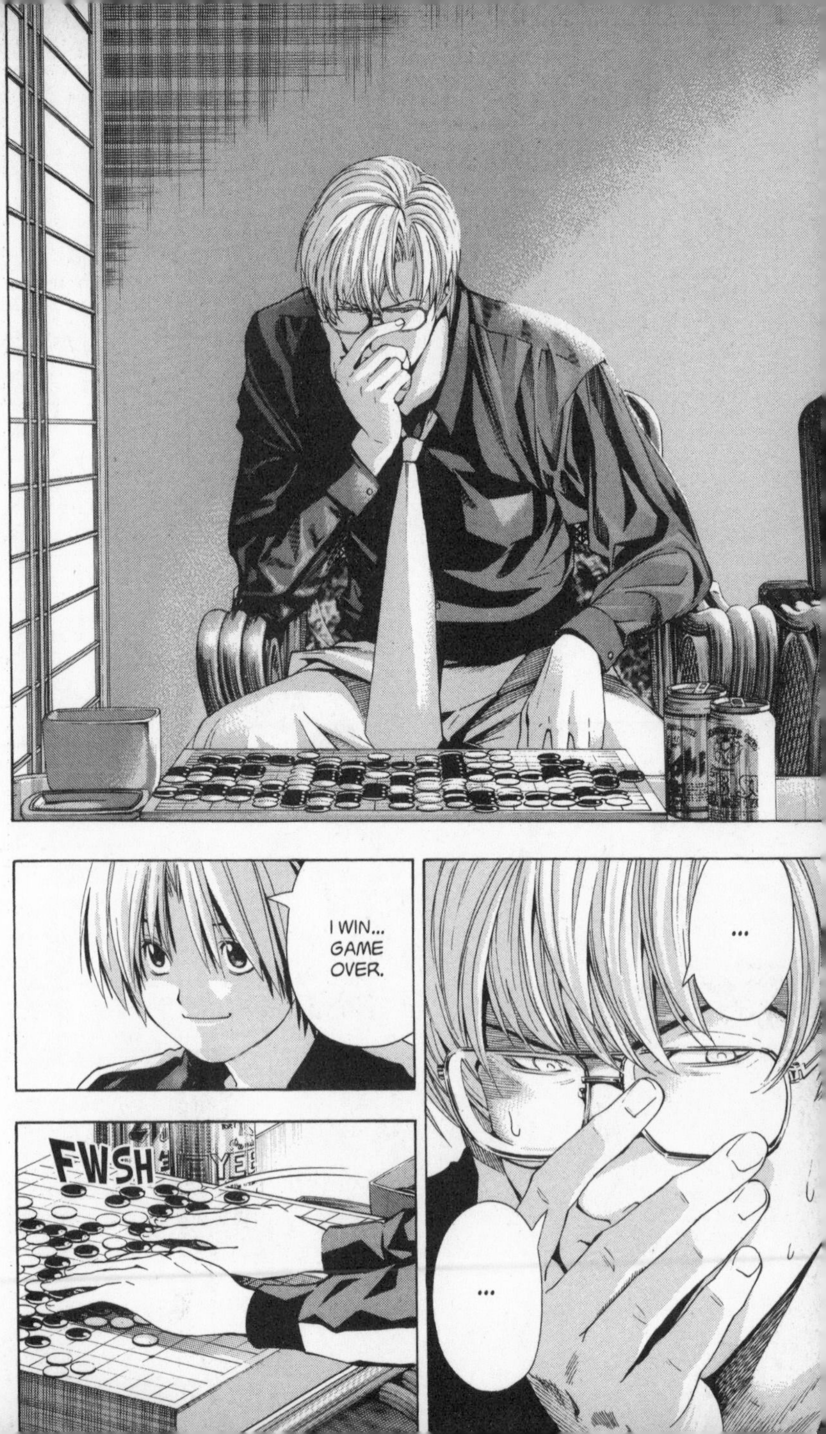
...
...
I WIN... GAME OVER.
FWSH

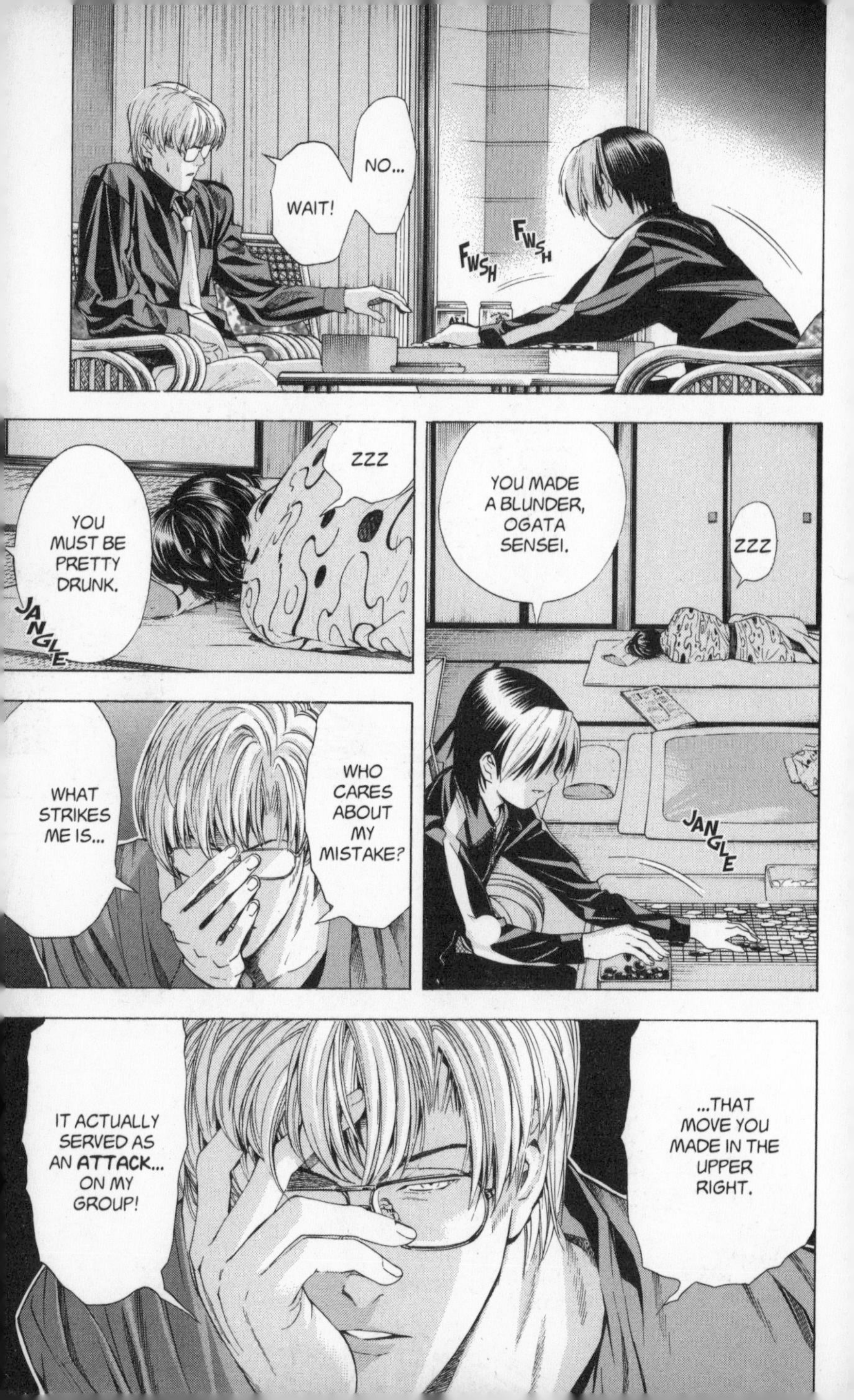
NO... WAIT!
FWSH
FWSH
YOU MADE A BLUNDER, OGATA SENSEI.
ZZZ
JANGLE
ZZZ
YOU MUST BE PRETTY DRUNK.
JANGLE
WHO CARES ABOUT MY MISTAKE?
WHAT STRIKES ME IS...
...THAT MOVE YOU MADE IN THE UPPER RIGHT.
IT ACTUALLY SERVED AS AN **ATTACK**... ON MY GROUP!

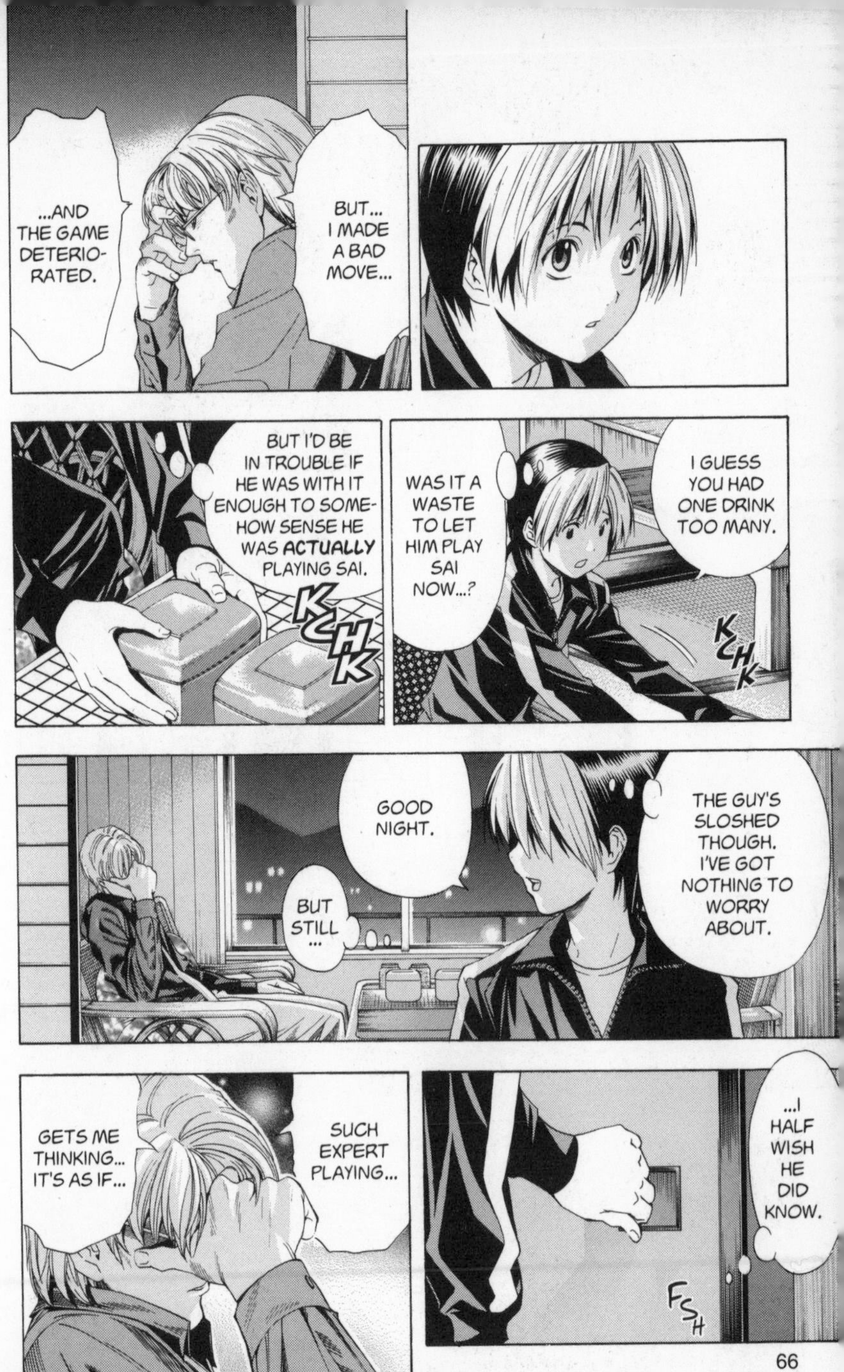
BUT... I MADE A BAD MOVE...
...AND THE GAME DETERIORATED.
I GUESS YOU HAD ONE DRINK TOO MANY.
WAS IT A WASTE TO LET HIM PLAY SAI NOW...?
KCHK
BUT I'D BE IN TROUBLE IF HE WAS WITH IT ENOUGH TO SOMEHOW SENSE HE WAS **ACTUALLY** PLAYING SAI.
KCHK
THE GUY'S SLOSHED THOUGH. I'VE GOT NOTHING TO WORRY ABOUT.
GOOD NIGHT.
BUT STILL ...
...I HALF WISH HE DID KNOW.
FSH
SUCH EXPERT PLAYING...
GETS ME THINKING... IT'S AS IF...

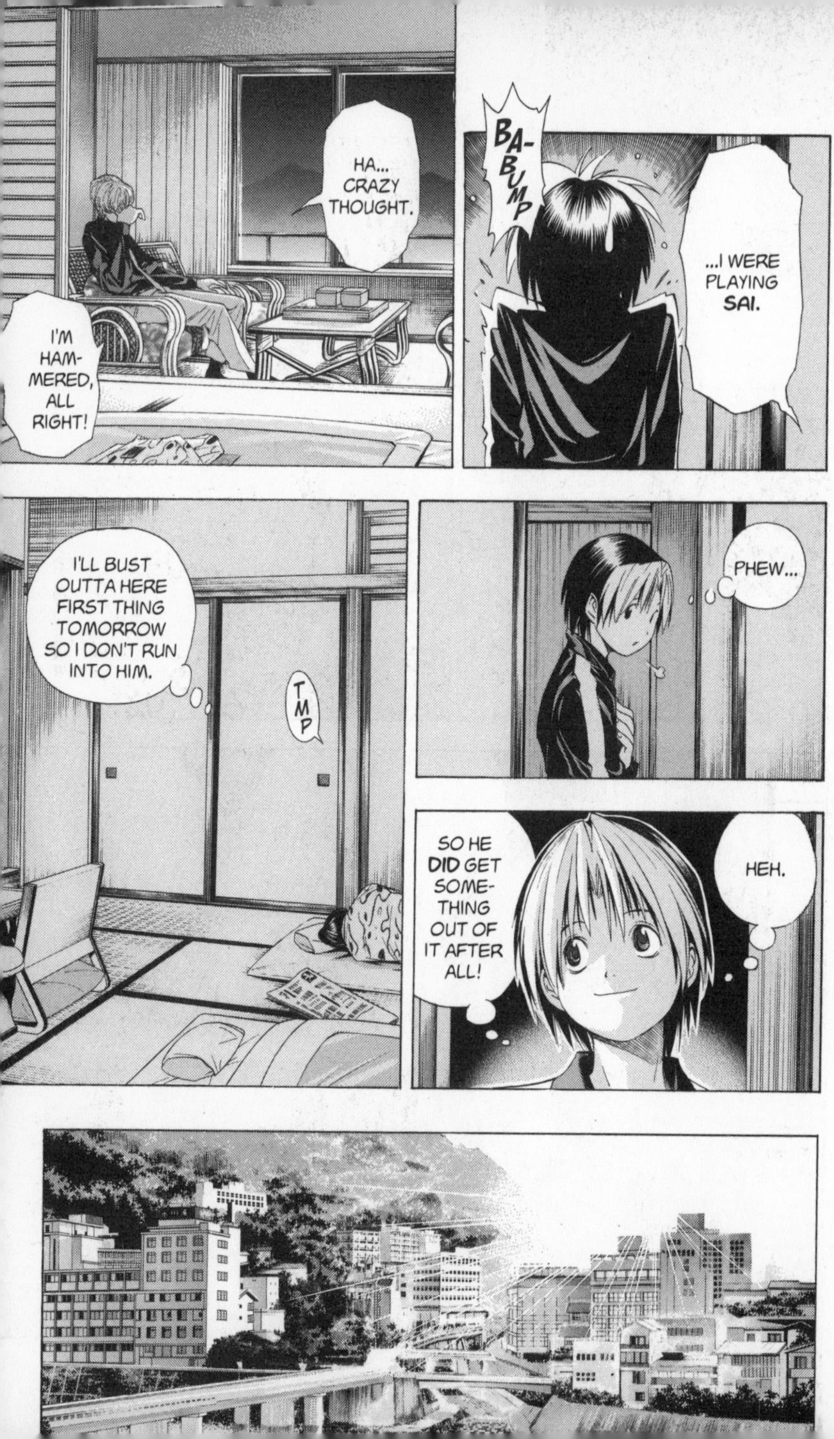
BA-BUMP
...I WERE PLAYING SAI.
HA... CRAZY THOUGHT.
I'M HAM-MERED, ALL RIGHT!
PHEW...
HEH.
SO HE DID GET SOME-THING OUT OF IT AFTER ALL!
I'LL BUST OUTTA HERE FIRST THING TOMORROW SO I DON'T RUN INTO HIM.
TMP

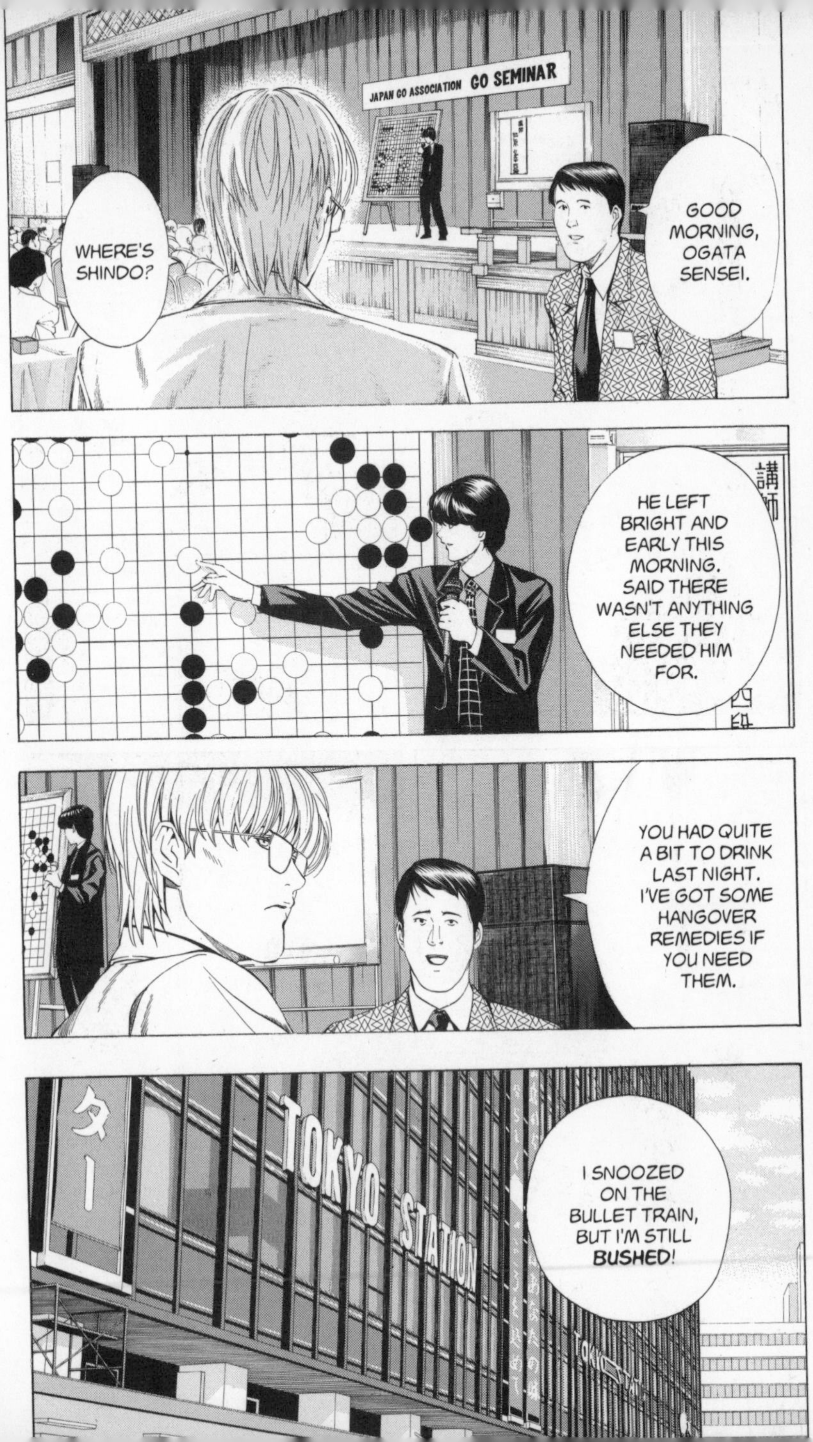
JAPAN GO ASSOCIATION GO SEMINAR
GOOD MORNING, OGATA SENSEI.
WHERE'S SHINDO?
HE LEFT BRIGHT AND EARLY THIS MORNING. SAID THERE WASN'T ANYTHING ELSE THEY NEEDED HIM FOR.
YOU HAD QUITE A BIT TO DRINK LAST NIGHT. I'VE GOT SOME HANGOVER REMEDIES IF YOU NEED THEM.
TOKYO STATION
I SNOOZED ON THE BULLET TRAIN, BUT I'M STILL **BUSHED!**

READ THIS WAY

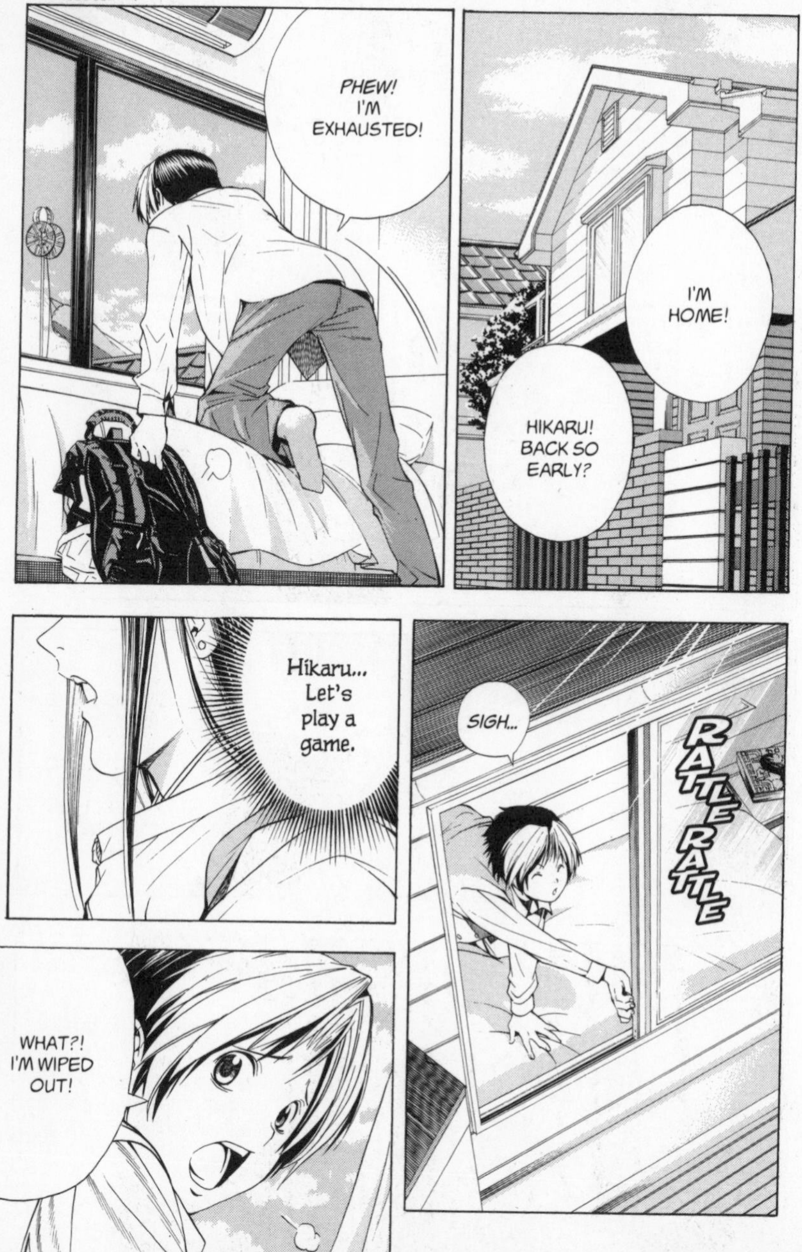
I'M HOME!
HIKARU! BACK SO EARLY?
PHEW! I'M EXHAUSTED!
SIGH...
RATTLE RATTLE
Hikaru... Let's play a game.
WHAT?! I'M WIPED OUT!

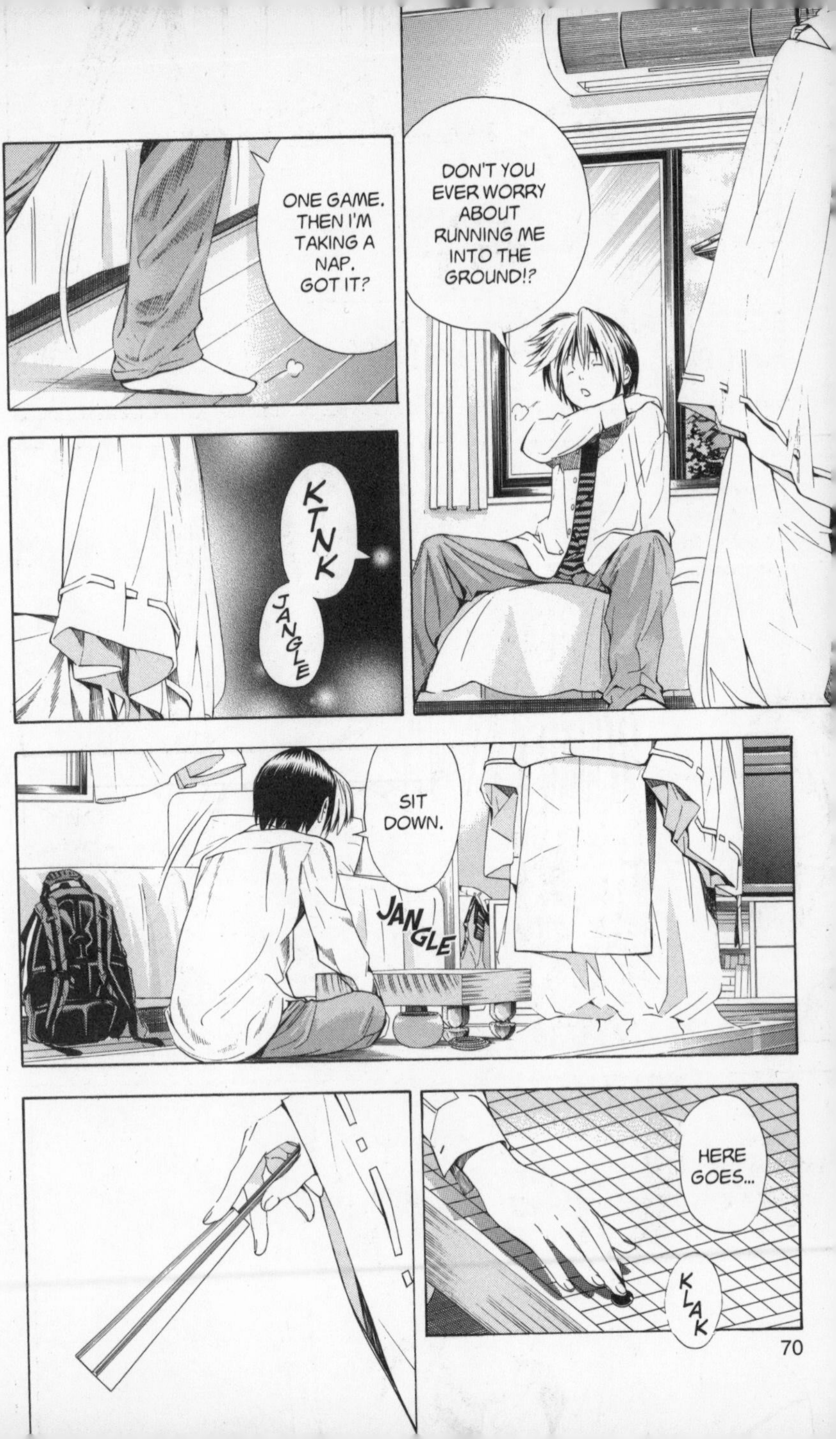
DON'T YOU EVER WORRY ABOUT RUNNING ME INTO THE GROUND!?
ONE GAME. THEN I'M TAKING A NAP. GOT IT?
KTNK
JANGLE
SIT DOWN.
JANGLE
HERE GOES...
KLAK

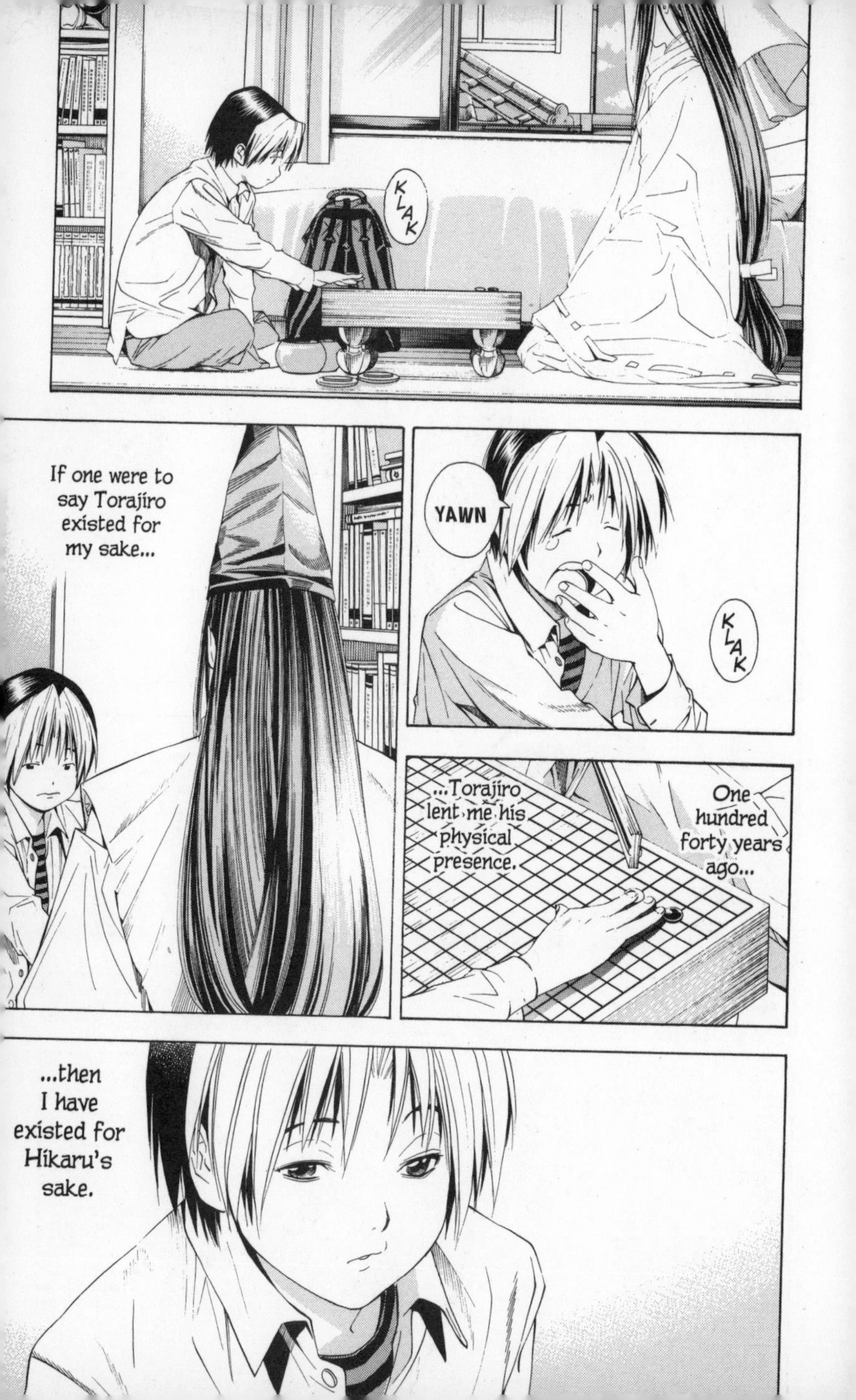
KLAK
YAWN
KLAK
One hundred forty years ago...
...Torajiro lent me his physical presence.
If one were to say Torajiro existed for my sake...
...then I have existed for Hikaru's sake.

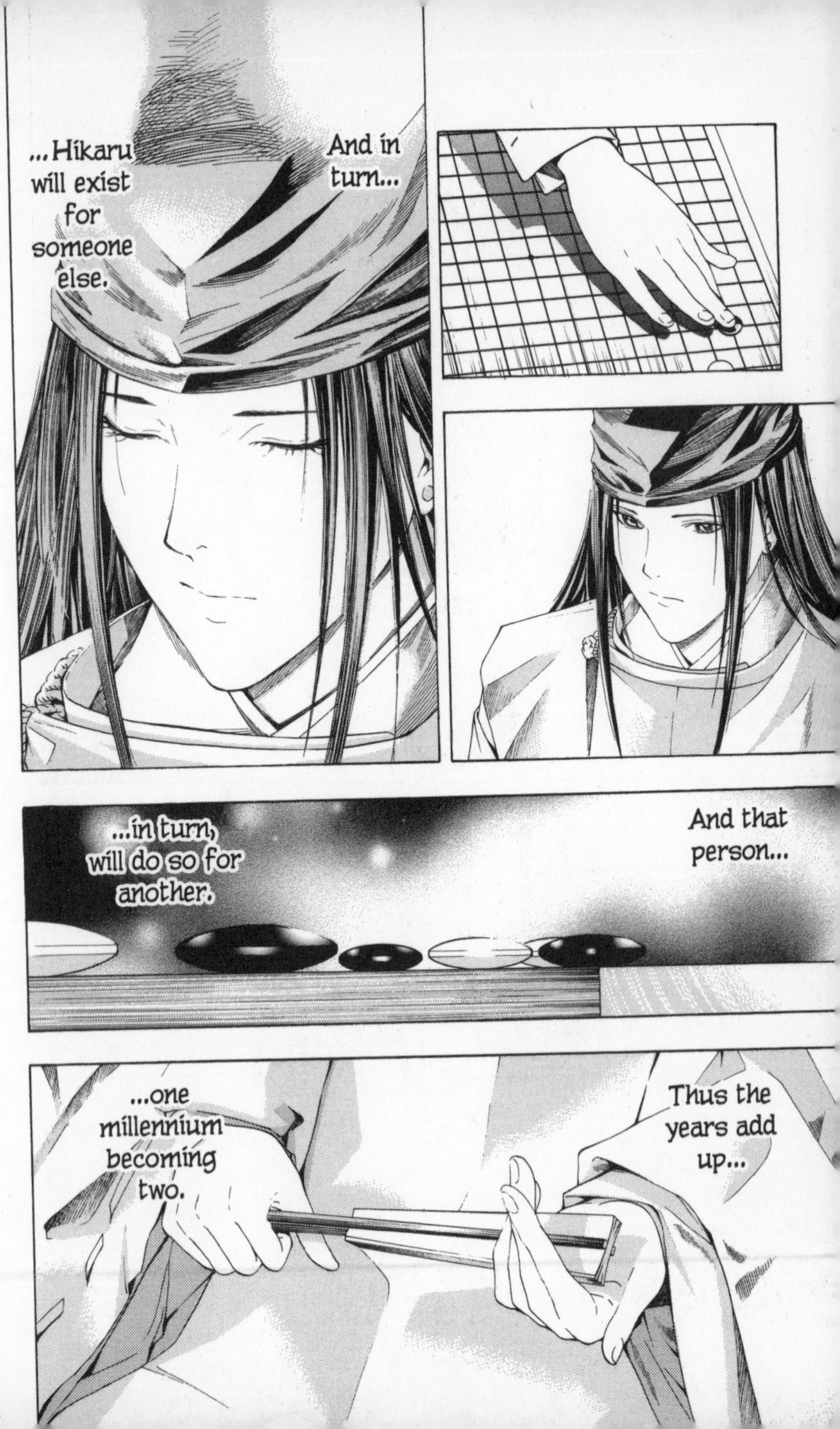
And in turn...
...Hikaru will exist for someone else.
And that person...
...in turn, will do so for another.
Thus the years add up...
...one millennium becoming two.

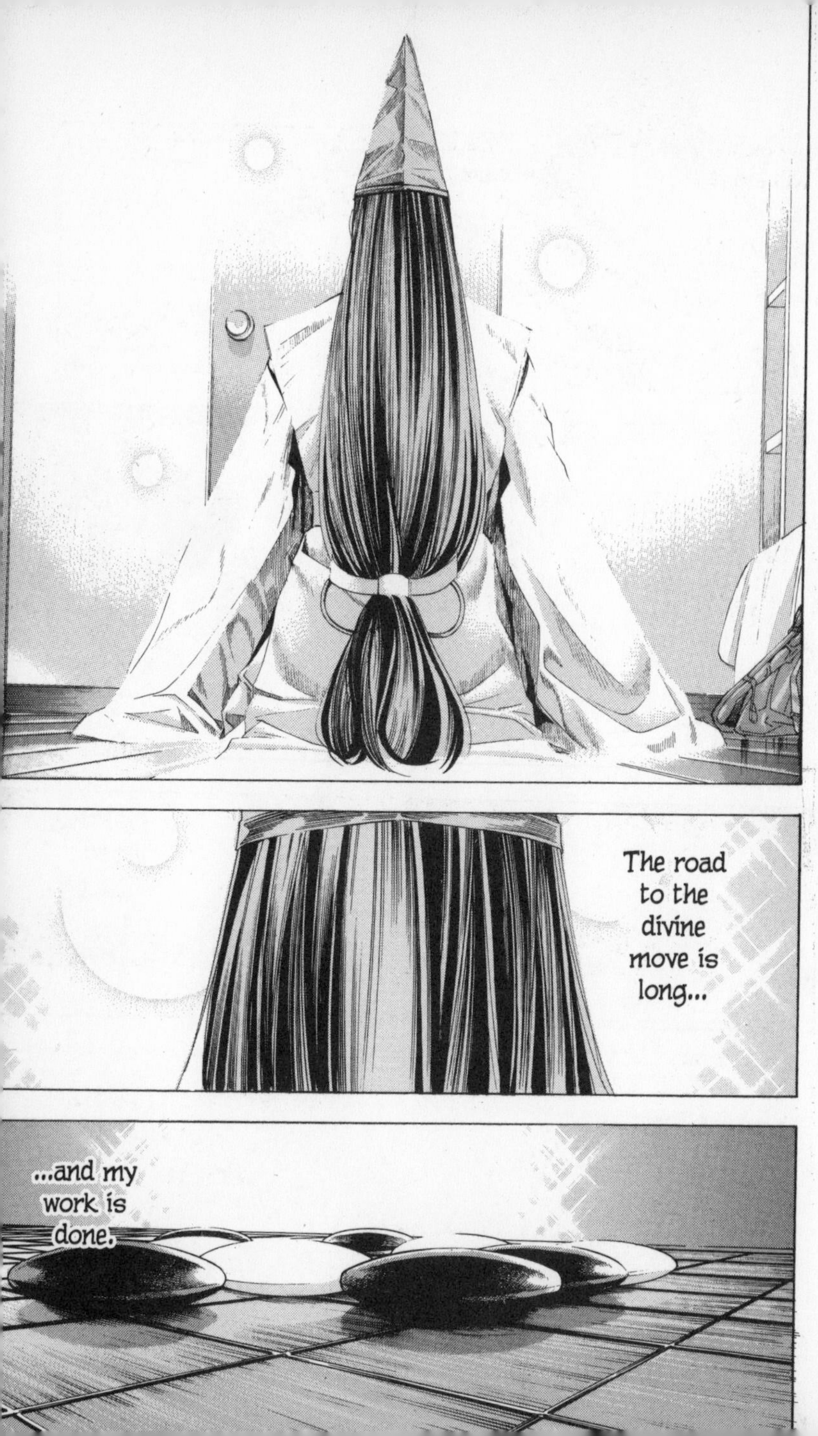
The road to the divine move is long...
...and my work is done.

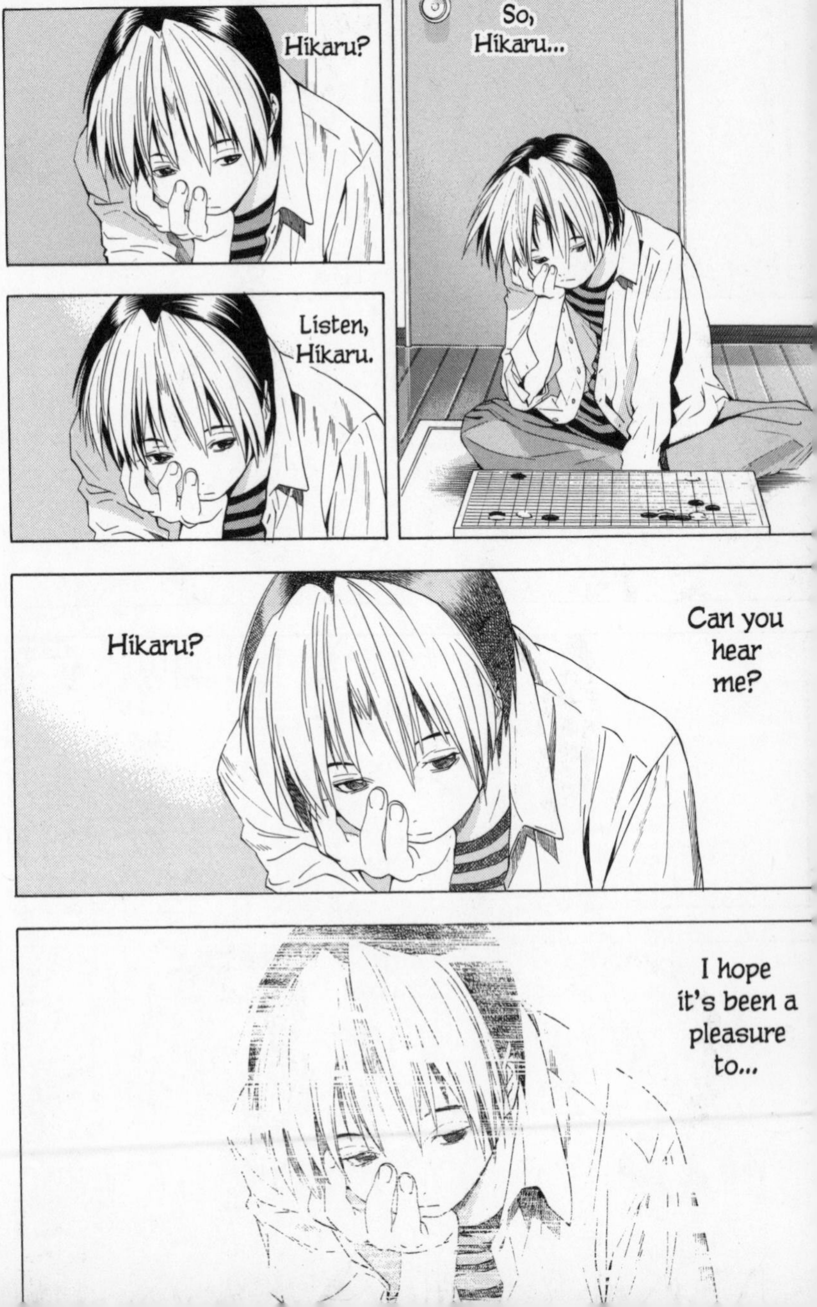
So, Hikaru...
Hikaru?
Listen, Hikaru.
Can you hear me?
Hikaru?
I hope it's been a pleasure to...

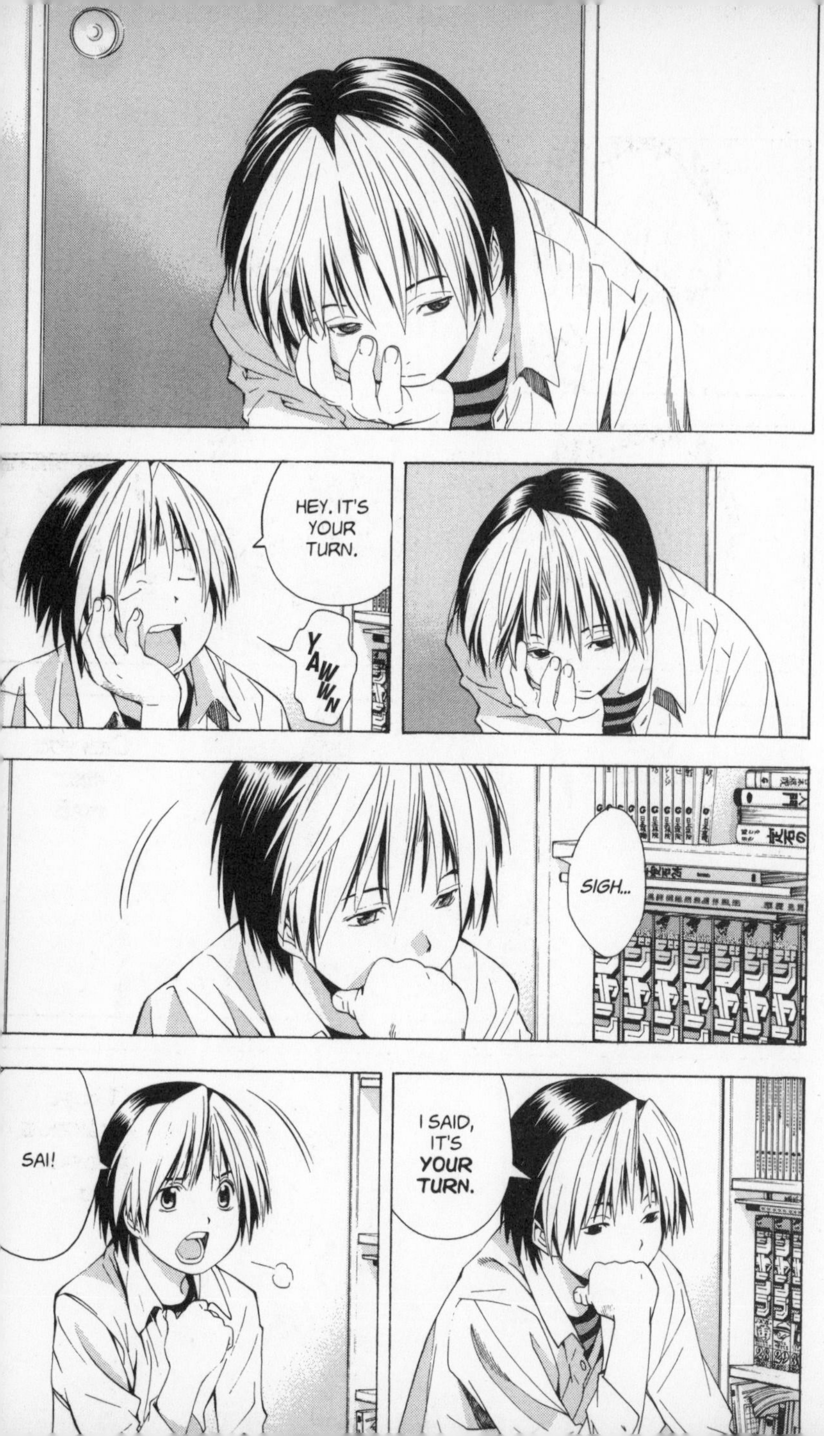
HEY. IT'S YOUR TURN.
YAWWN
SIGH...
I SAID, IT'S **YOUR TURN.**
SAI!

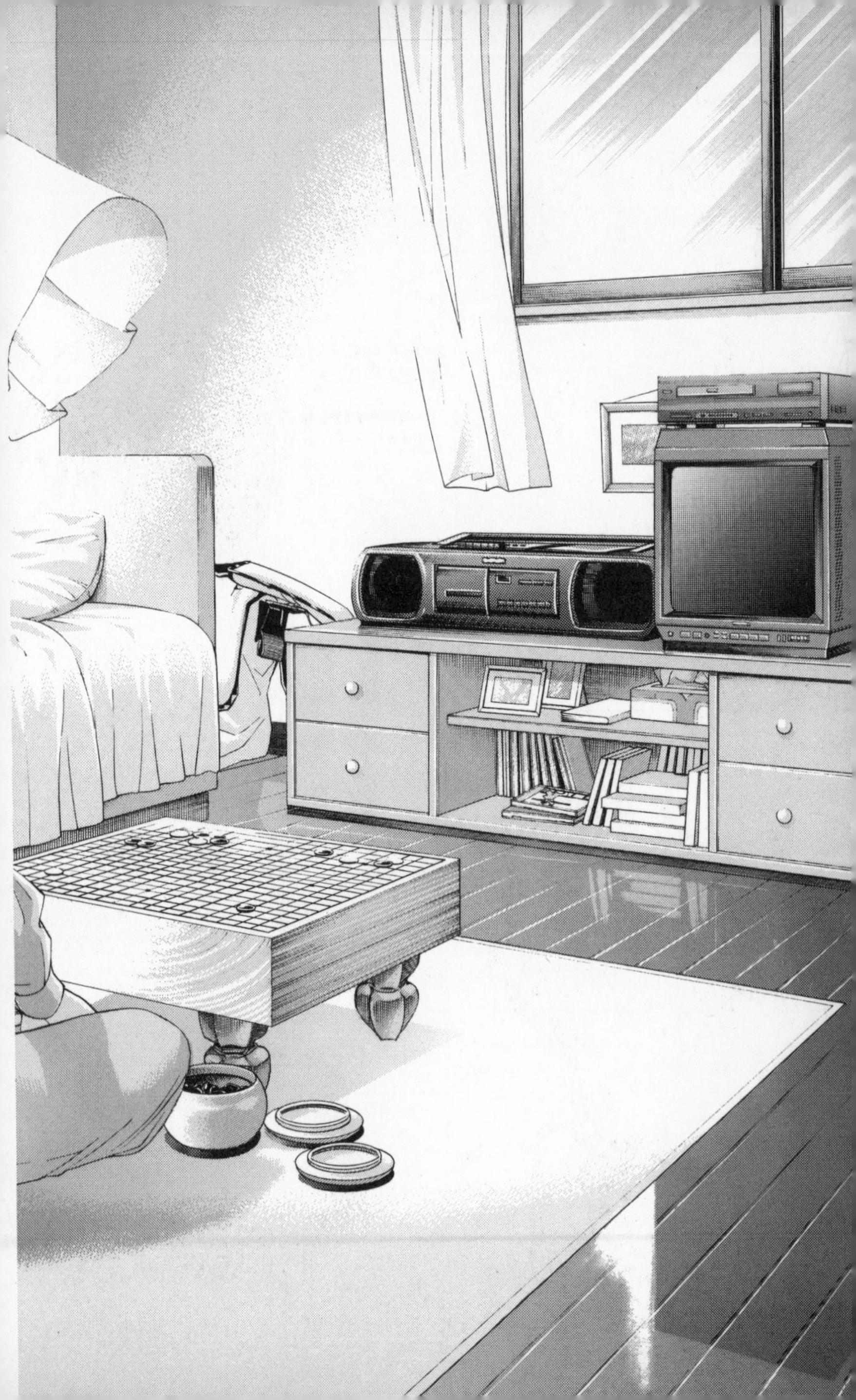

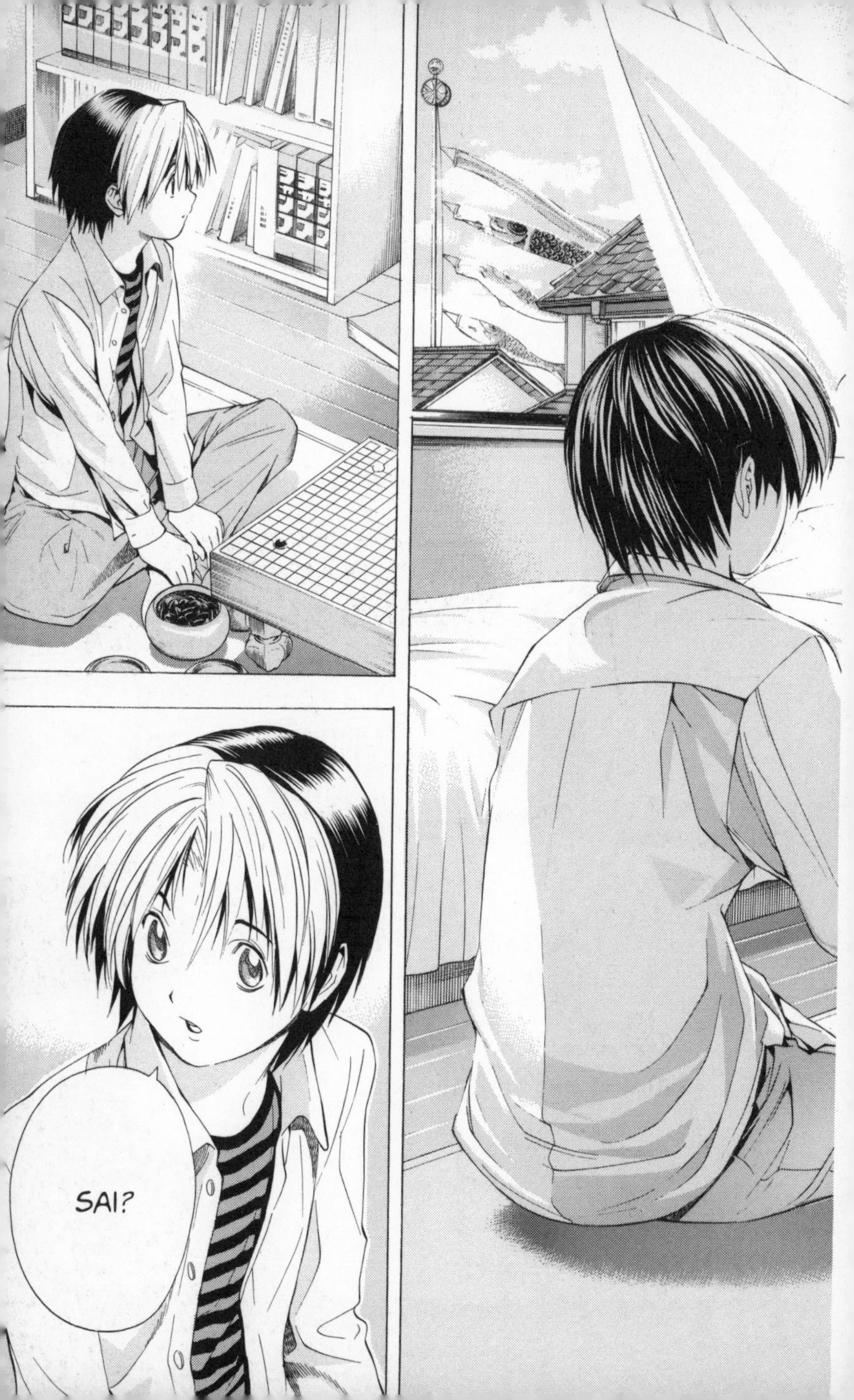
SAI?

A WORD ABOUT HIKARU NO GO

MAY 5TH

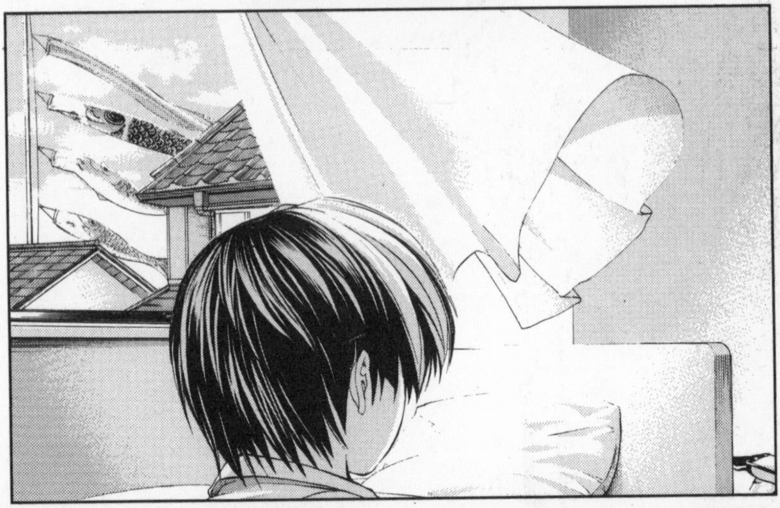

SAI DISAPPEARS ON MAY 5TH. YOU CAN SEE THE CHILDREN'S DAY CARP STREAMERS THROUGH HIKARU'S WINDOW.

AFTER CREATING THE STORYBOARDS FOR GAME 124, I REALIZED THAT SHUSAKU WAS BORN ON MAY 5TH (ON THE OLD CALENDAR).

MAYBE THE 5TH DAY OF THE 5TH MONTH SHOULD BE DESIGNATED "HIKARU NO GO DAY."*

*THE NUMBER 5 IS PRONOUNCED "GO" IN JAPANESE.

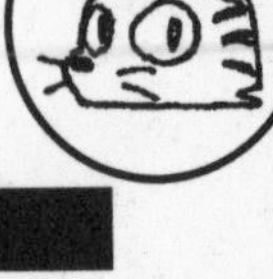

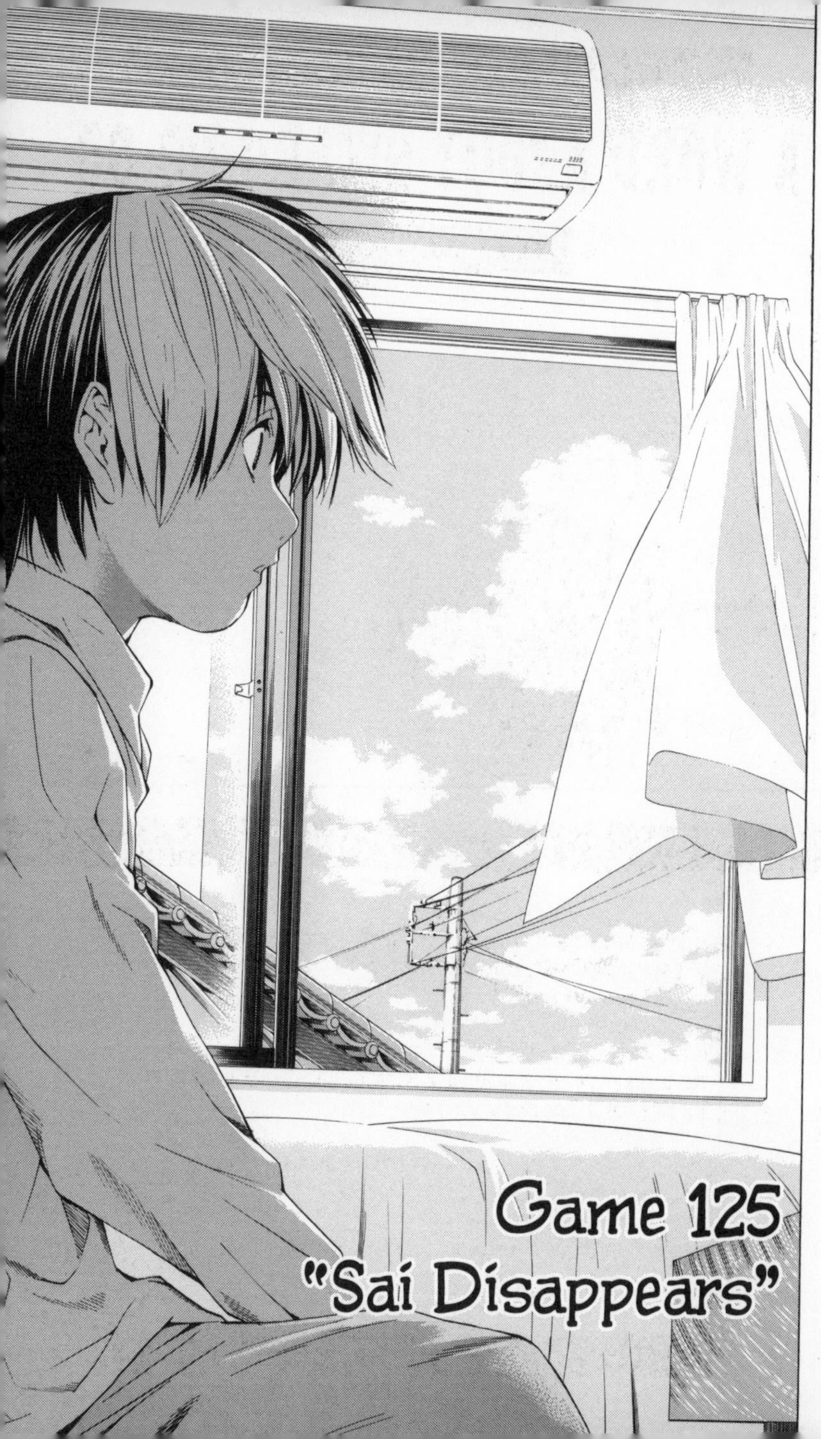
Game 125
"Sai Disappears"

HEY...

SAI?

WHY ARE YOU HIDING? DON'T TICK ME OFF!

YOU'RE THE ONE WHO WANTED TO PLAY!

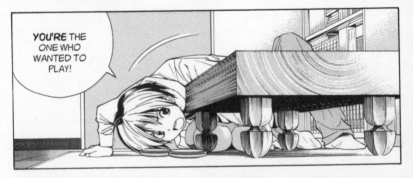

FORGET IT THEN! I'M TAKING A NAP!

FLUMP

SAI!

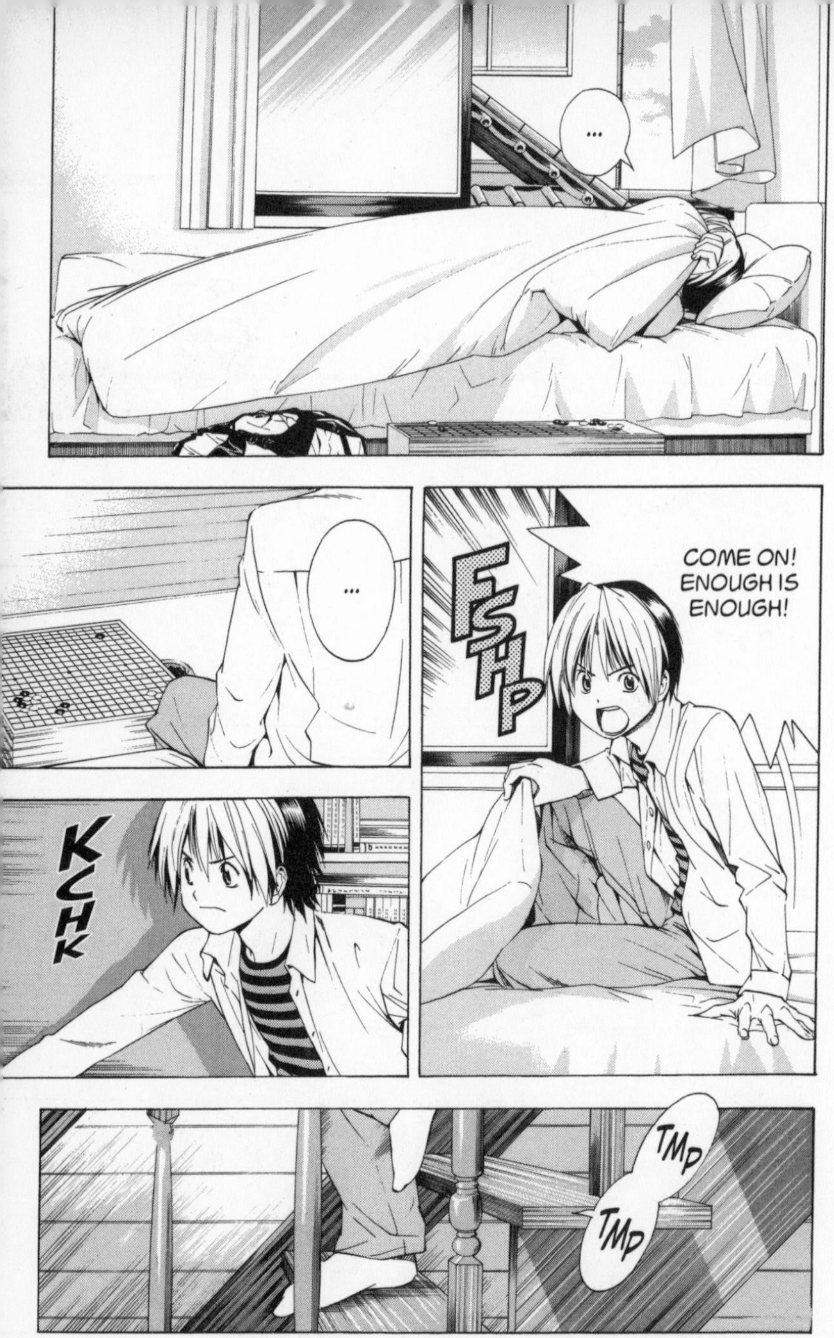
...
FSHP
COME ON! ENOUGH IS ENOUGH!
...
KCHK
TMP
TMP

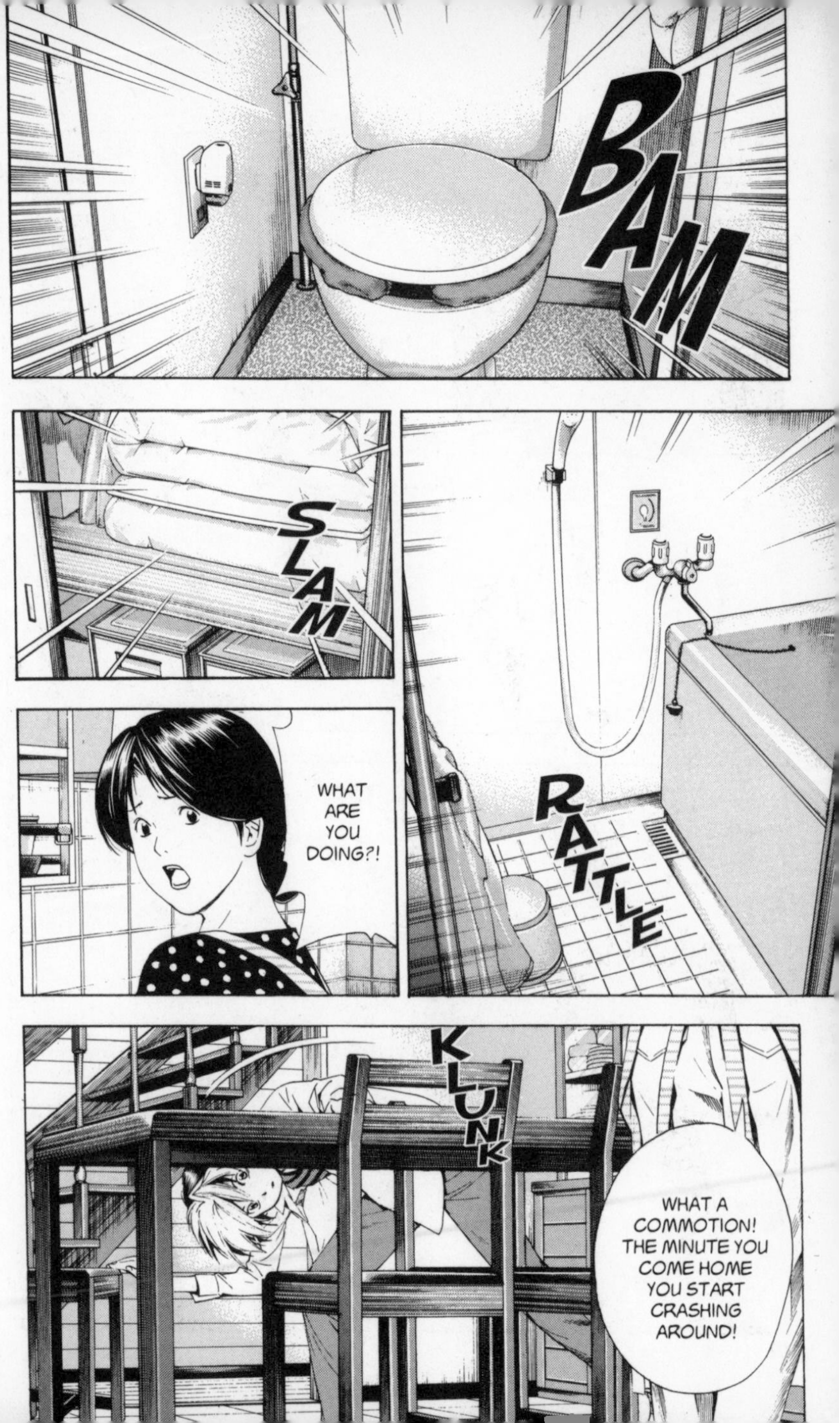
BAM
RATTLE
SLAM
WHAT ARE YOU DOING?!
KLUNK
WHAT A COMMOTION! THE MINUTE YOU COME HOME YOU START CRASHING AROUND!

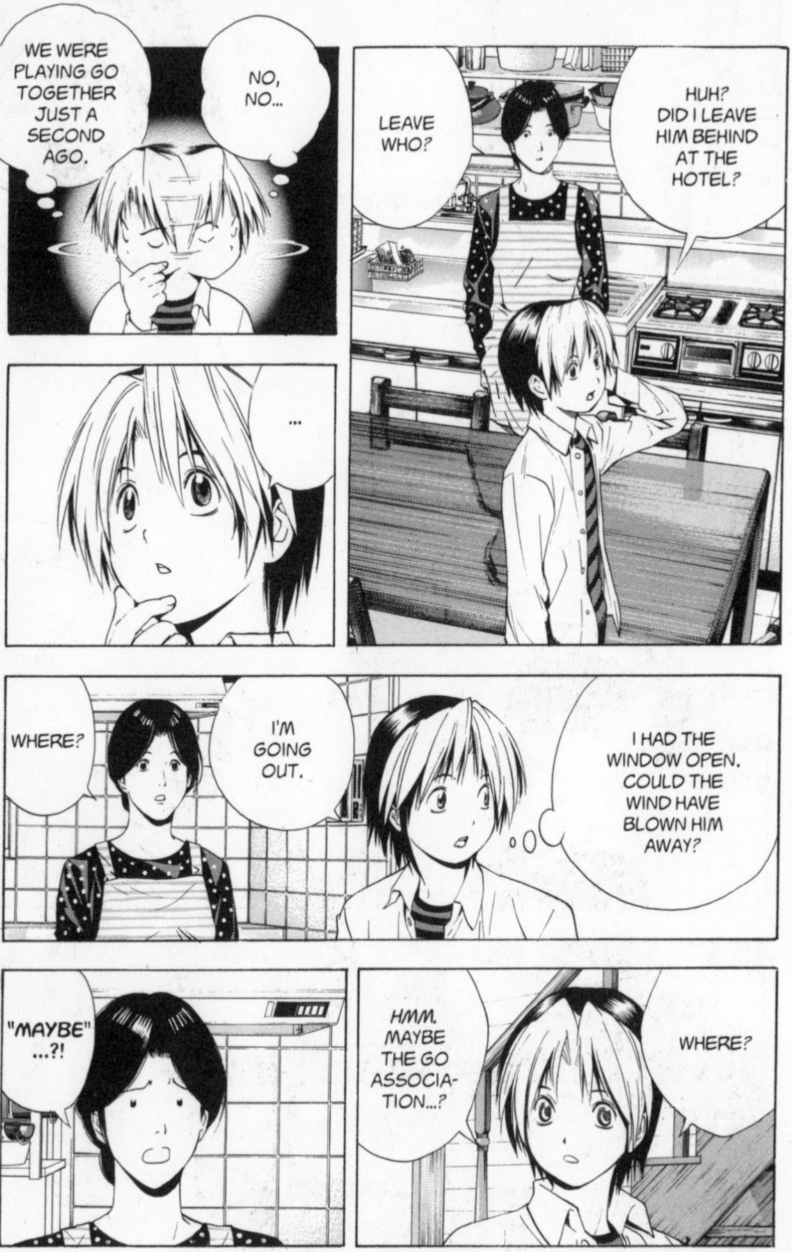
HUH? DID I LEAVE HIM BEHIND AT THE HOTEL?
LEAVE WHO?
NO, NO...
WE WERE PLAYING GO TOGETHER JUST A SECOND AGO.
...
I HAD THE WINDOW OPEN. COULD THE WIND HAVE BLOWN HIM AWAY?
I'M GOING OUT.
WHERE?
WHERE?
HMM. MAYBE THE GO ASSOCIATION...?
"MAYBE" ...?!

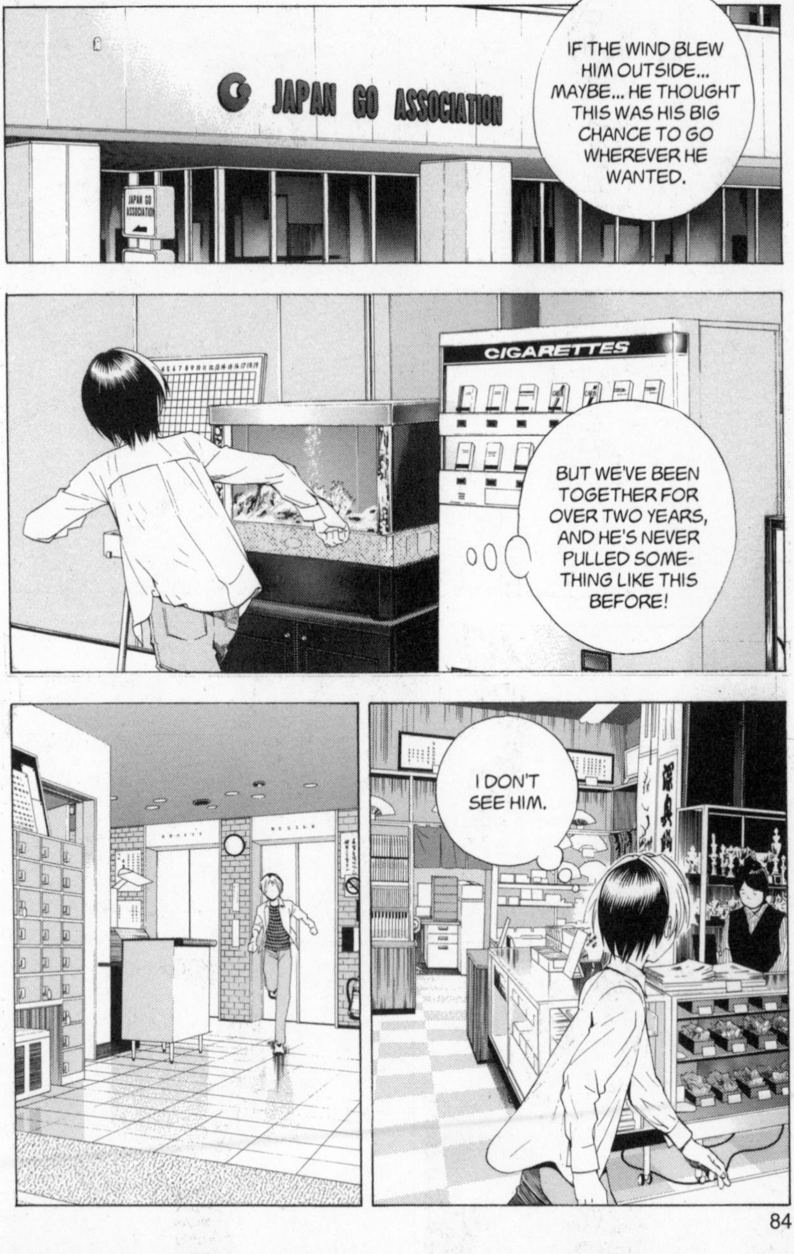
JAPAN GO ASSOCIATION
IF THE WIND BLEW HIM OUTSIDE... MAYBE... HE THOUGHT THIS WAS HIS BIG CHANCE TO GO WHEREVER HE WANTED.
CIGARETTES
BUT WE'VE BEEN TOGETHER FOR OVER TWO YEARS, AND HE'S NEVER PULLED SOME-THING LIKE THIS BEFORE!
I DON'T SEE HIM.

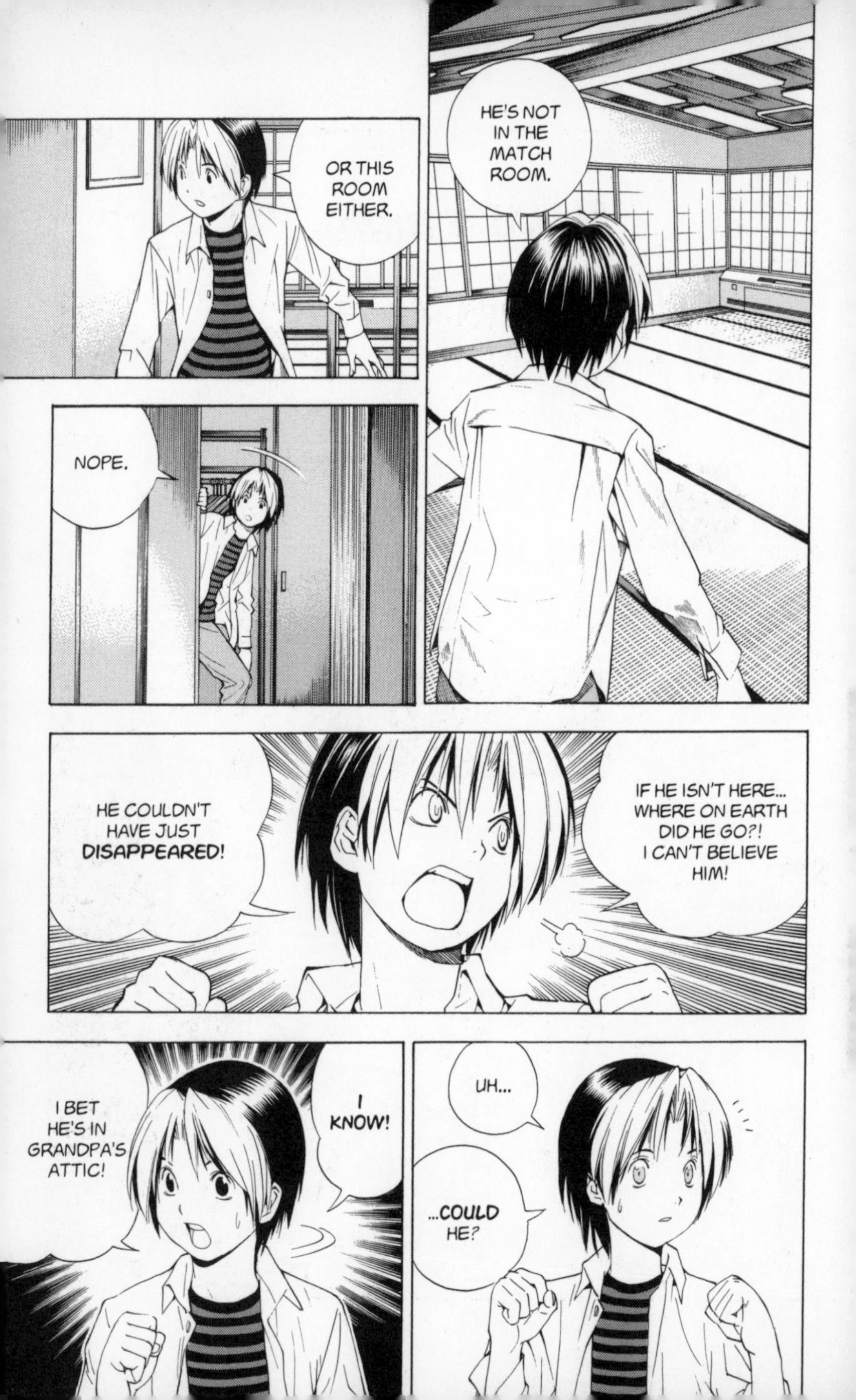
HE'S NOT IN THE MATCH ROOM.
OR THIS ROOM EITHER.
NOPE.
IF HE ISN'T HERE... WHERE ON EARTH DID HE GO?! I CAN'T BELIEVE HIM!
HE COULDN'T HAVE JUST DISAPPEARED!
UH...
...COULD HE?
I KNOW!
I BET HE'S IN GRANDPA'S ATTIC!

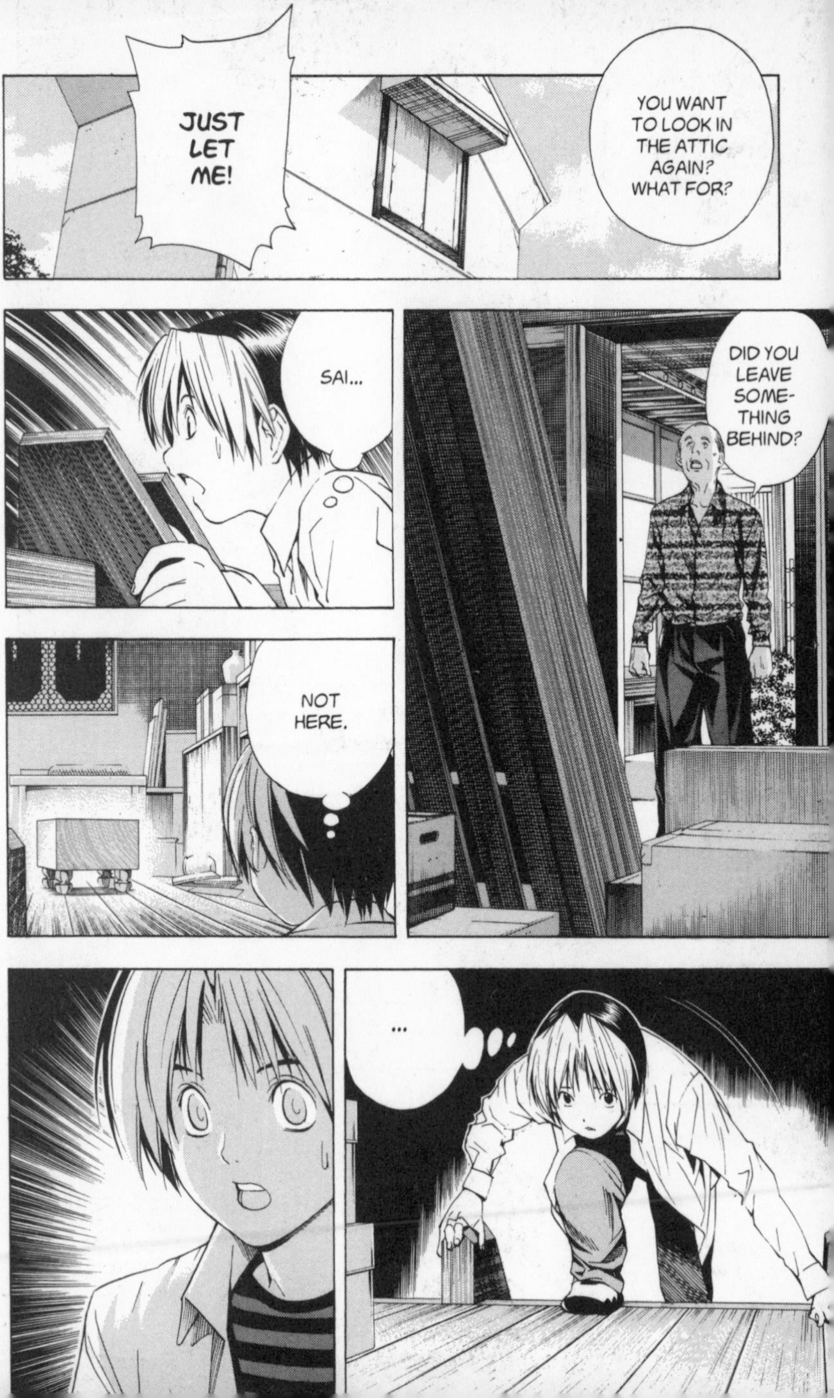
YOU WANT TO LOOK IN THE ATTIC AGAIN? WHAT FOR?
JUST LET ME!
DID YOU LEAVE SOME-THING BEHIND?
SAI...
NOT HERE.
...

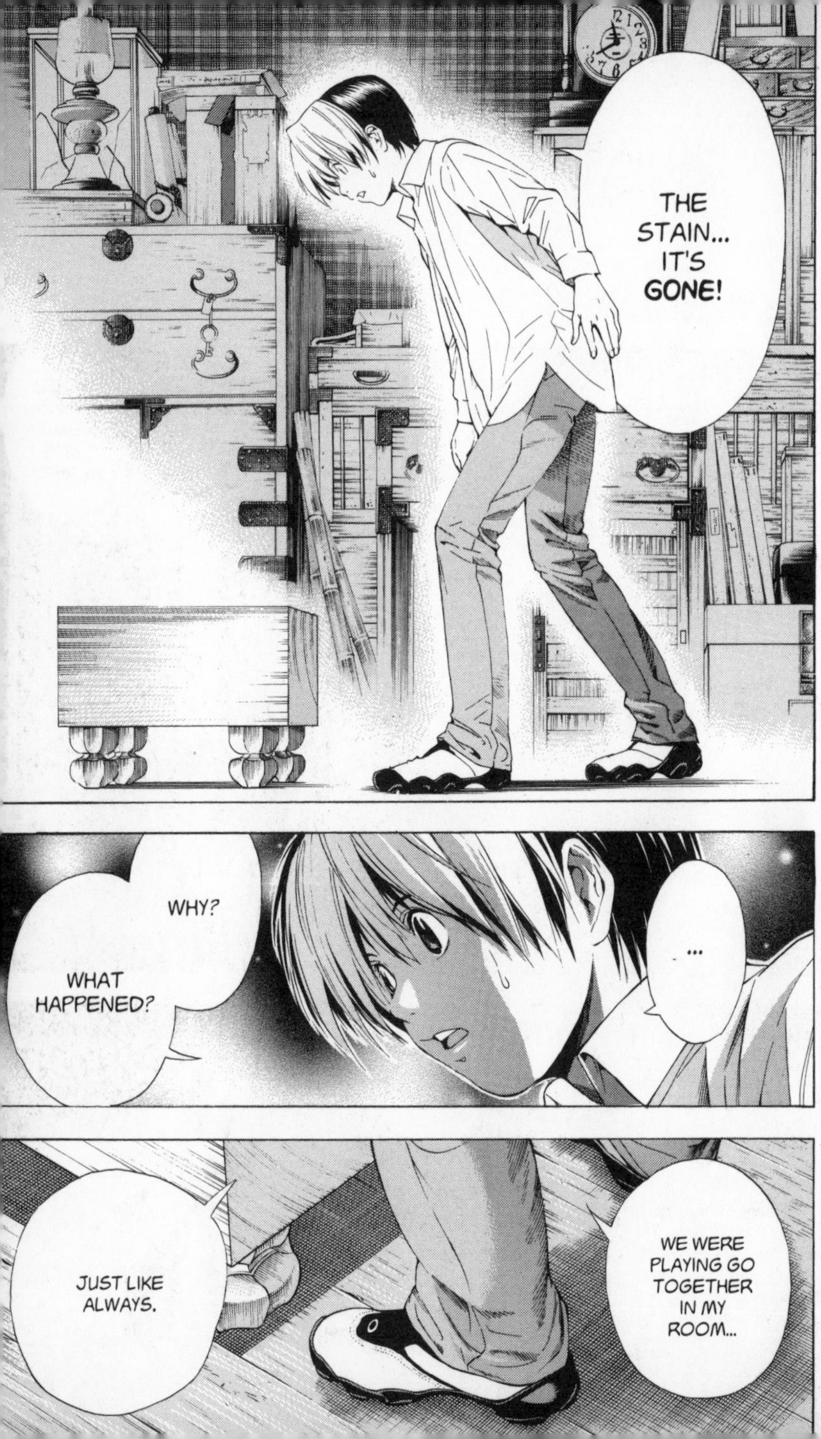
THE STAIN... IT'S GONE!
...
WHY?
WHAT HAPPENED?
WE WERE PLAYING GO TOGETHER IN MY ROOM...
JUST LIKE ALWAYS.

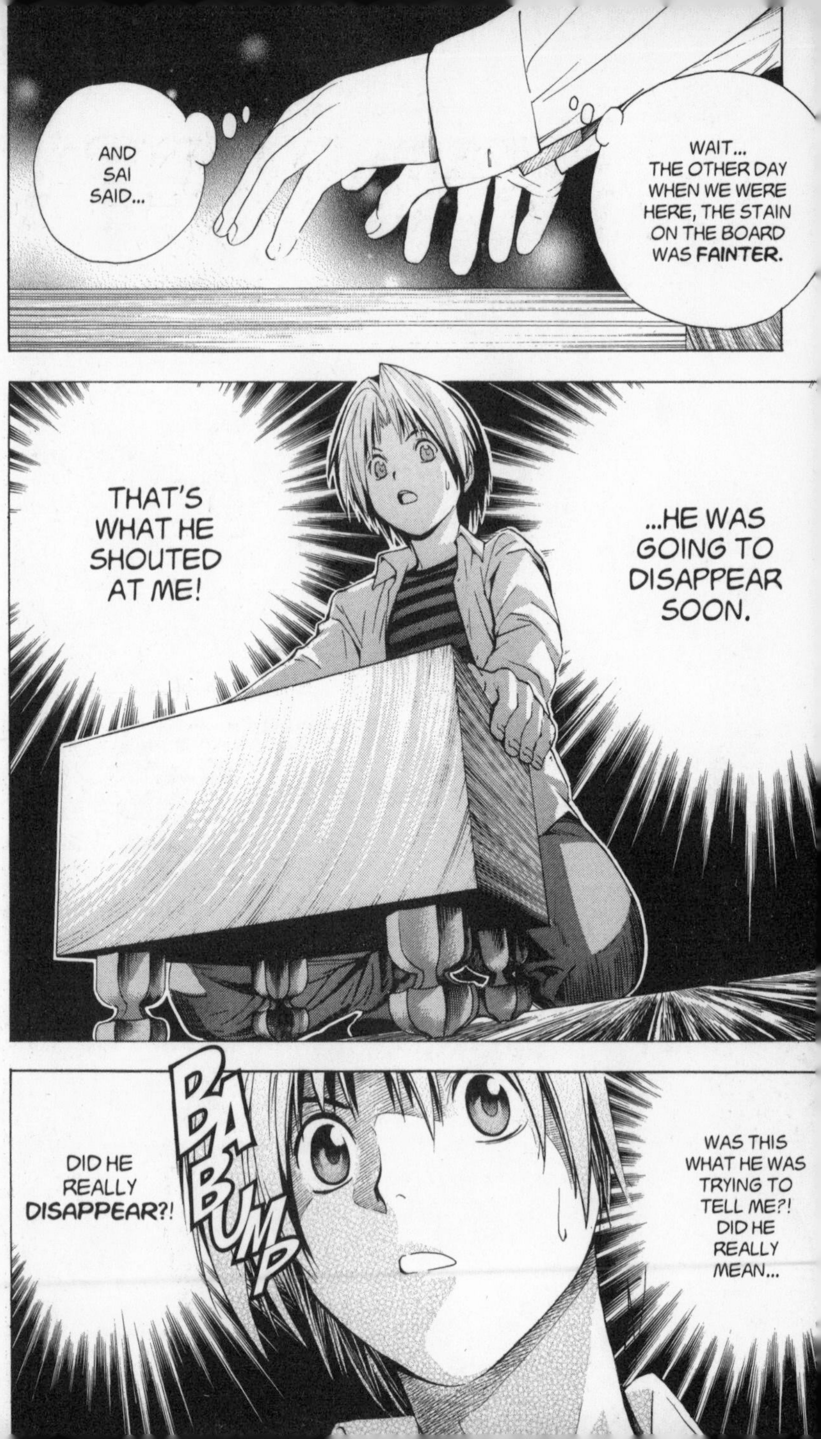
WAIT... THE OTHER DAY WHEN WE WERE HERE, THE STAIN ON THE BOARD WAS **FAINTER.**
AND SAI SAID...
...HE WAS GOING TO DISAPPEAR SOON.
THAT'S WHAT HE SHOUTED AT ME!
WAS THIS WHAT HE WAS TRYING TO TELL ME?! DID HE REALLY MEAN...
BA-BUMP
DID HE REALLY **DISAPPEAR?!**

READ THIS WAY

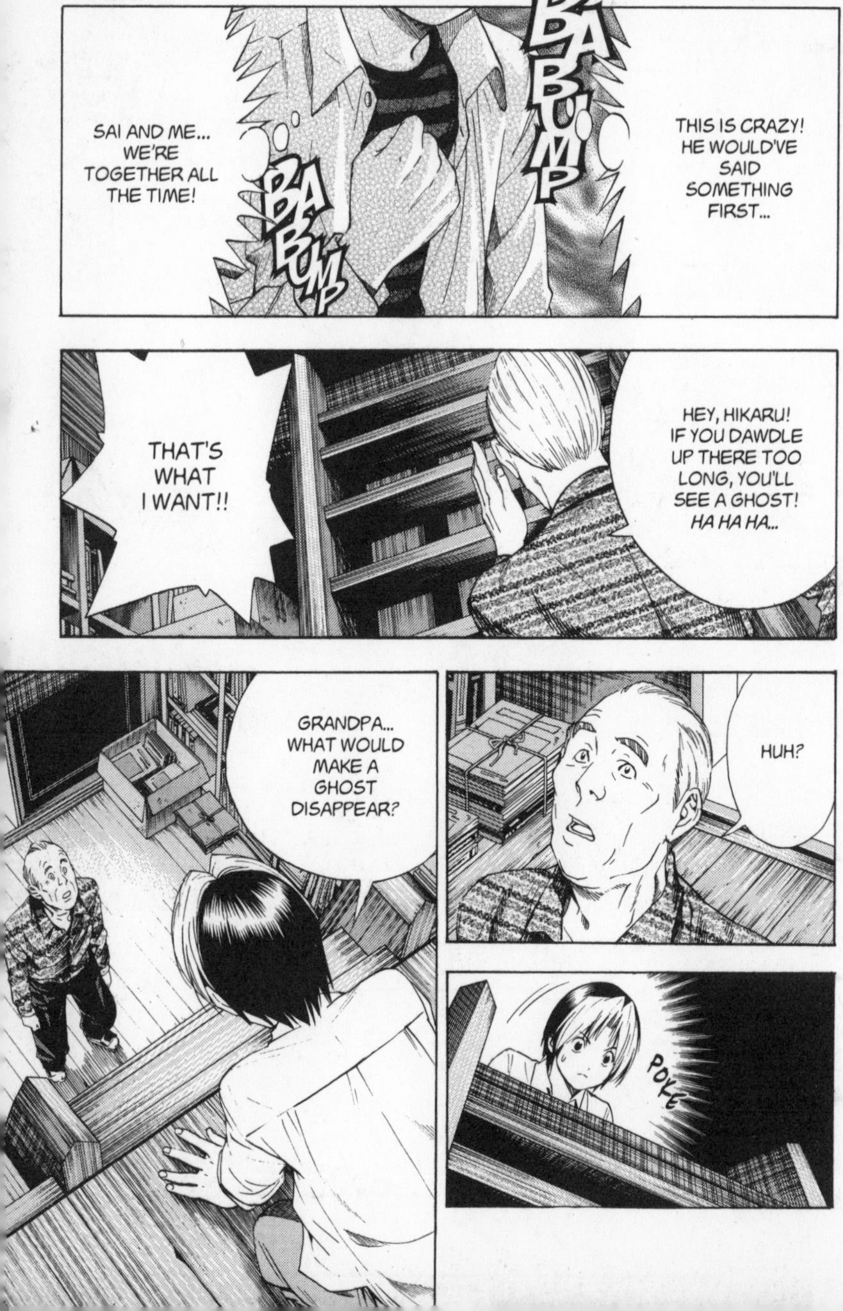
BABUMP
THIS IS CRAZY! HE WOULD'VE SAID SOMETHING FIRST...
BABUMP
SAI AND ME... WE'RE TOGETHER ALL THE TIME!
HEY, HIKARU! IF YOU DAWDLE UP THERE TOO LONG, YOU'LL SEE A GHOST! HA HA HA...
THAT'S WHAT I WANT!!
HUH?
POKE
GRANDPA... WHAT WOULD MAKE A GHOST DISAPPEAR?

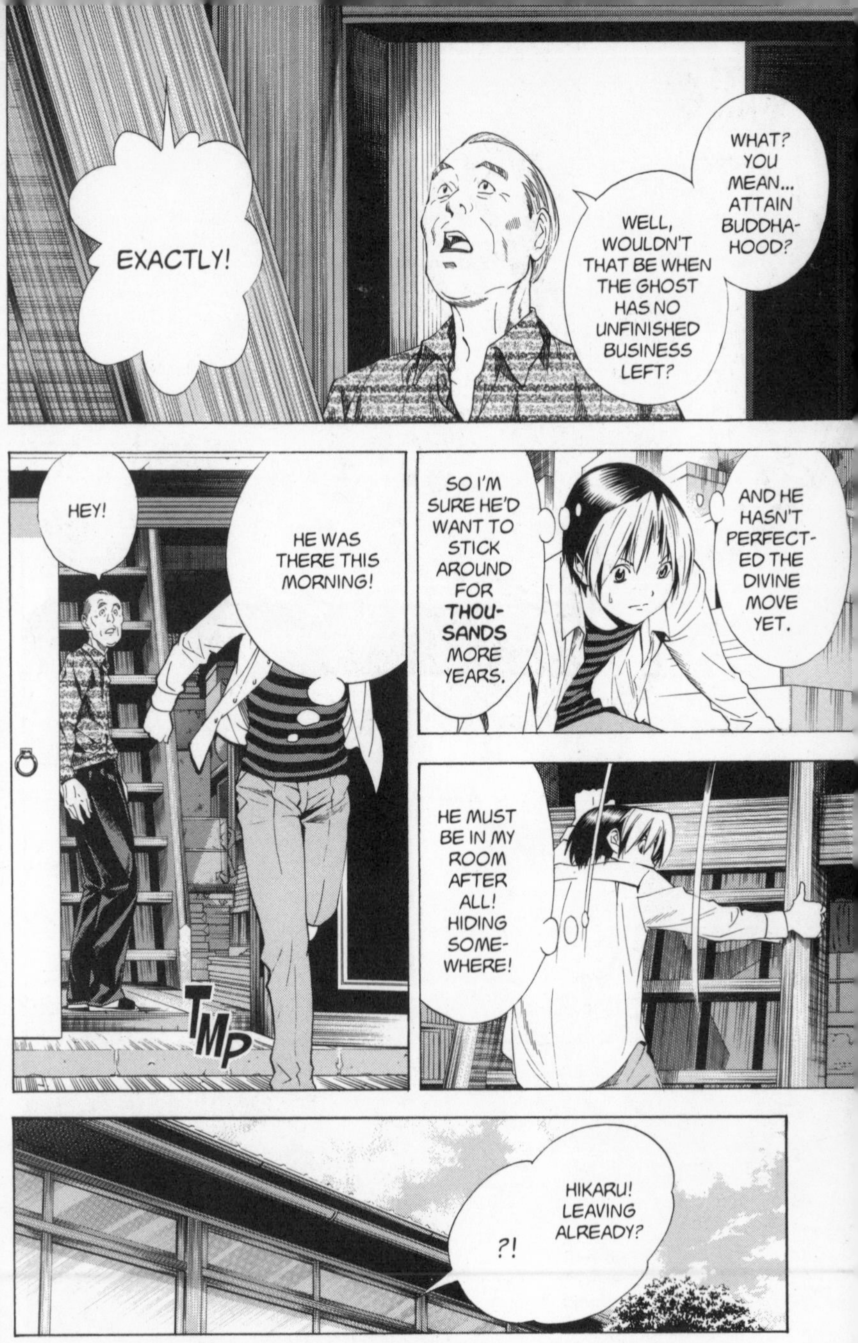
WHAT? YOU MEAN... ATTAIN BUDDHA-HOOD?
WELL, WOULDN'T THAT BE WHEN THE GHOST HAS NO UNFINISHED BUSINESS LEFT?
EXACTLY!
AND HE HASN'T PERFECT-ED THE DIVINE MOVE YET.
SO I'M SURE HE'D WANT TO STICK AROUND FOR **THOU-SANDS** MORE YEARS.
HE MUST BE IN MY ROOM AFTER ALL! HIDING SOME-WHERE!
HE WAS THERE THIS MORNING!
HEY!
TMP
HIKARU! LEAVING ALREADY?
?!

READ THIS WAY

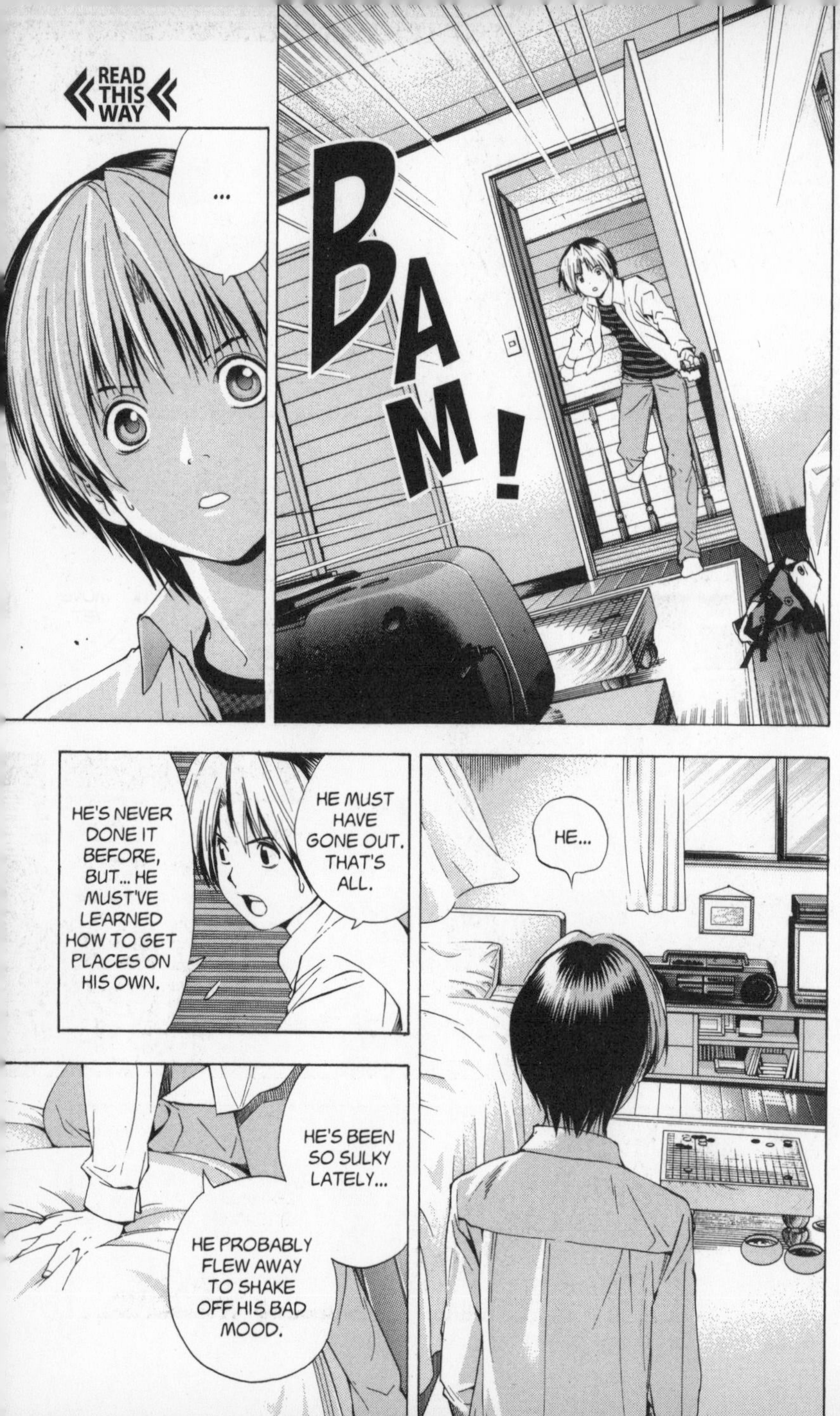
BAM!
...
HE...
HE MUST HAVE GONE OUT. THAT'S ALL.
HE'S NEVER DONE IT BEFORE, BUT... HE MUST'VE LEARNED HOW TO GET PLACES ON HIS OWN.
HE'S BEEN SO SULKY LATELY...
HE PROBABLY FLEW AWAY TO SHAKE OFF HIS BAD MOOD.

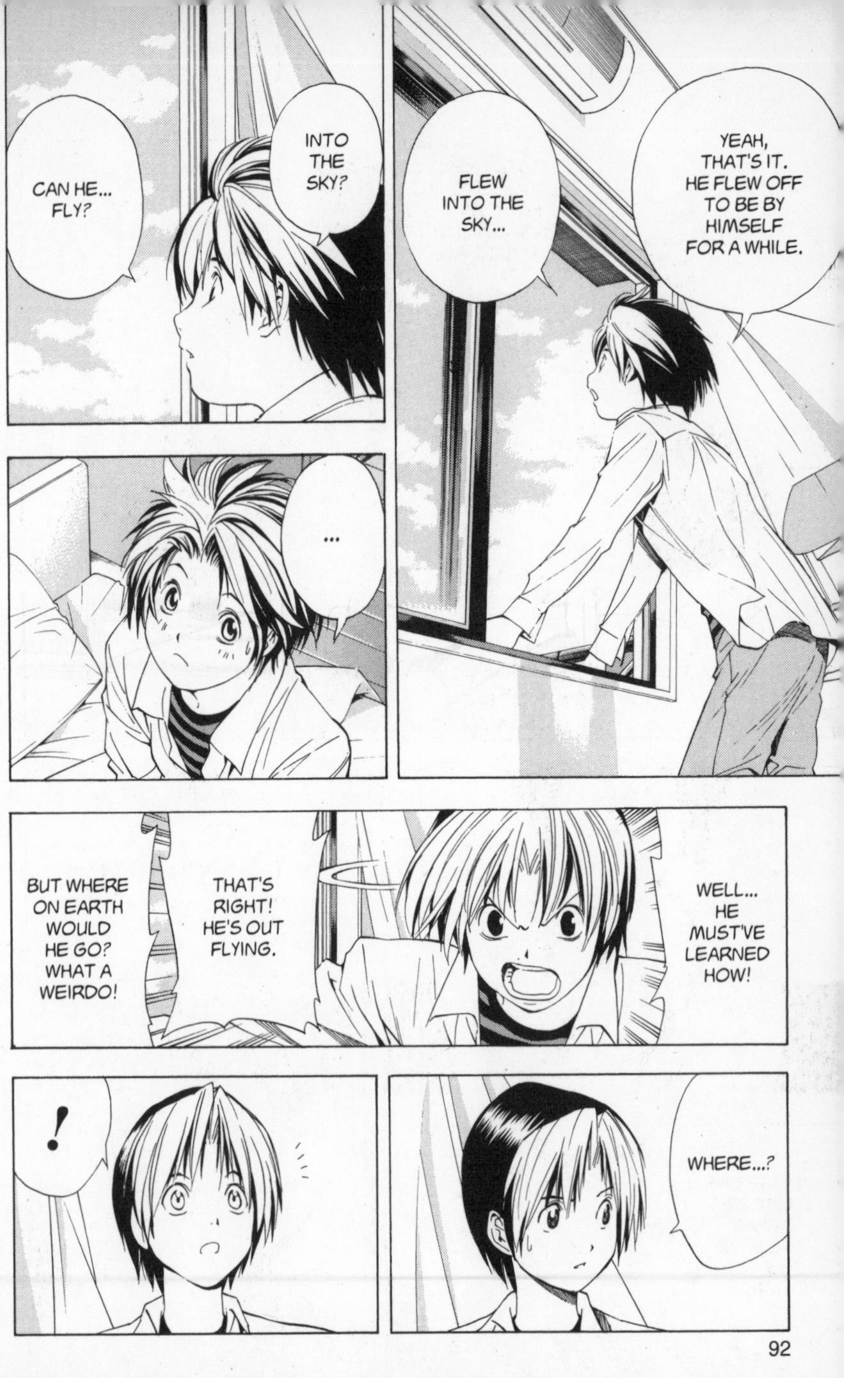
YEAH, THAT'S IT. HE FLEW OFF TO BE BY HIMSELF FOR A WHILE.
FLEW INTO THE SKY...
INTO THE SKY?
CAN HE... FLY?
...
WELL... HE MUST'VE LEARNED HOW!
THAT'S RIGHT! HE'S OUT FLYING.
BUT WHERE ON EARTH WOULD HE GO? WHAT A WEIRDO!
WHERE...?
!

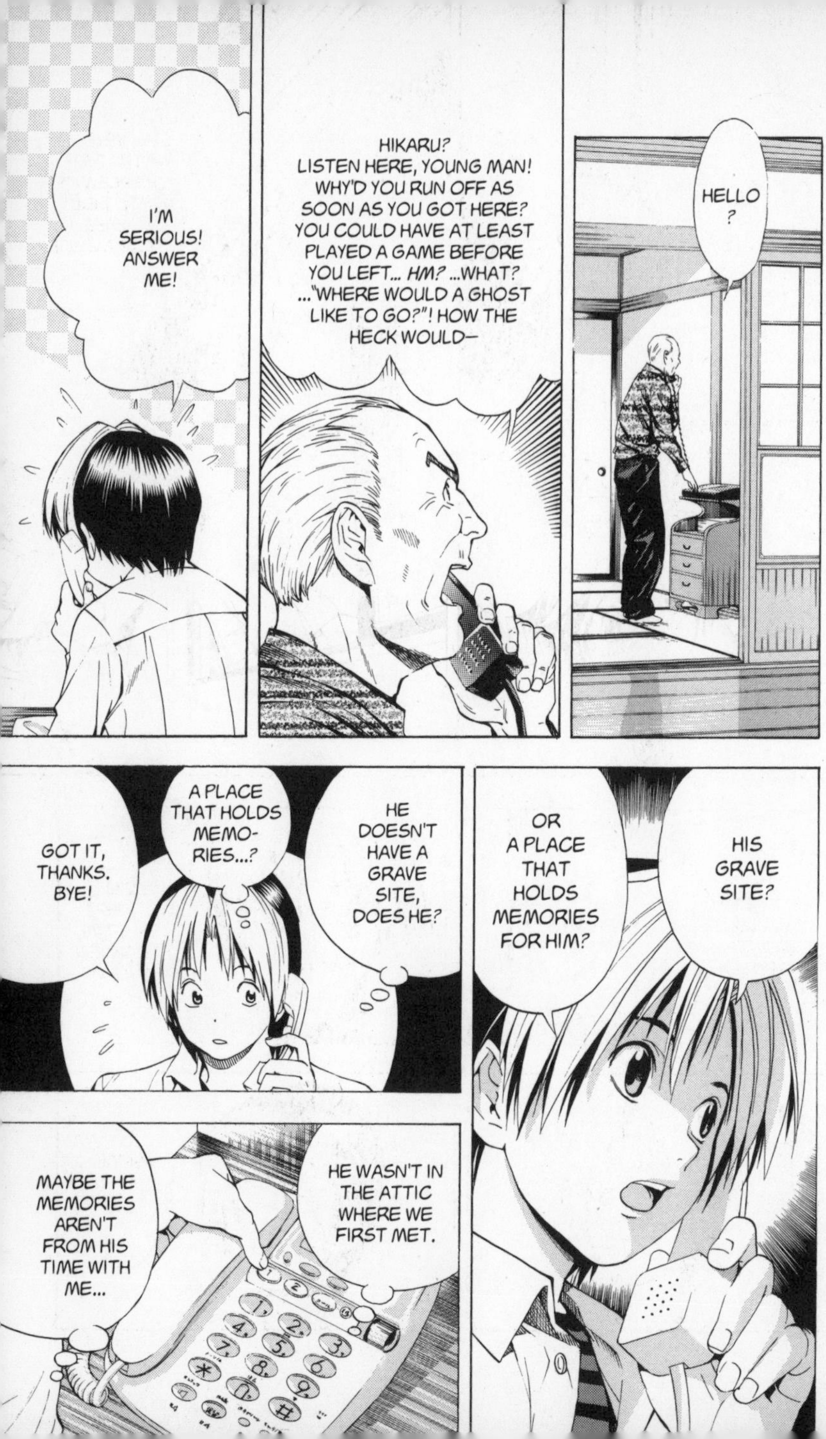
HELLO?
HIKARU? LISTEN HERE, YOUNG MAN! WHY'D YOU RUN OFF AS SOON AS YOU GOT HERE? YOU COULD HAVE AT LEAST PLAYED A GAME BEFORE YOU LEFT... *HM?* ...WHAT? ..."WHERE WOULD A GHOST LIKE TO GO?"! HOW THE HECK WOULD—
I'M SERIOUS! ANSWER ME!
HIS GRAVE SITE?
OR A PLACE THAT HOLDS MEMORIES FOR HIM?
HE DOESN'T HAVE A GRAVE SITE, DOES HE?
A PLACE THAT HOLDS MEMO-RIES...?
GOT IT, THANKS. BYE!
HE WASN'T IN THE ATTIC WHERE WE FIRST MET.
MAYBE THE MEMORIES AREN'T FROM HIS TIME WITH ME...

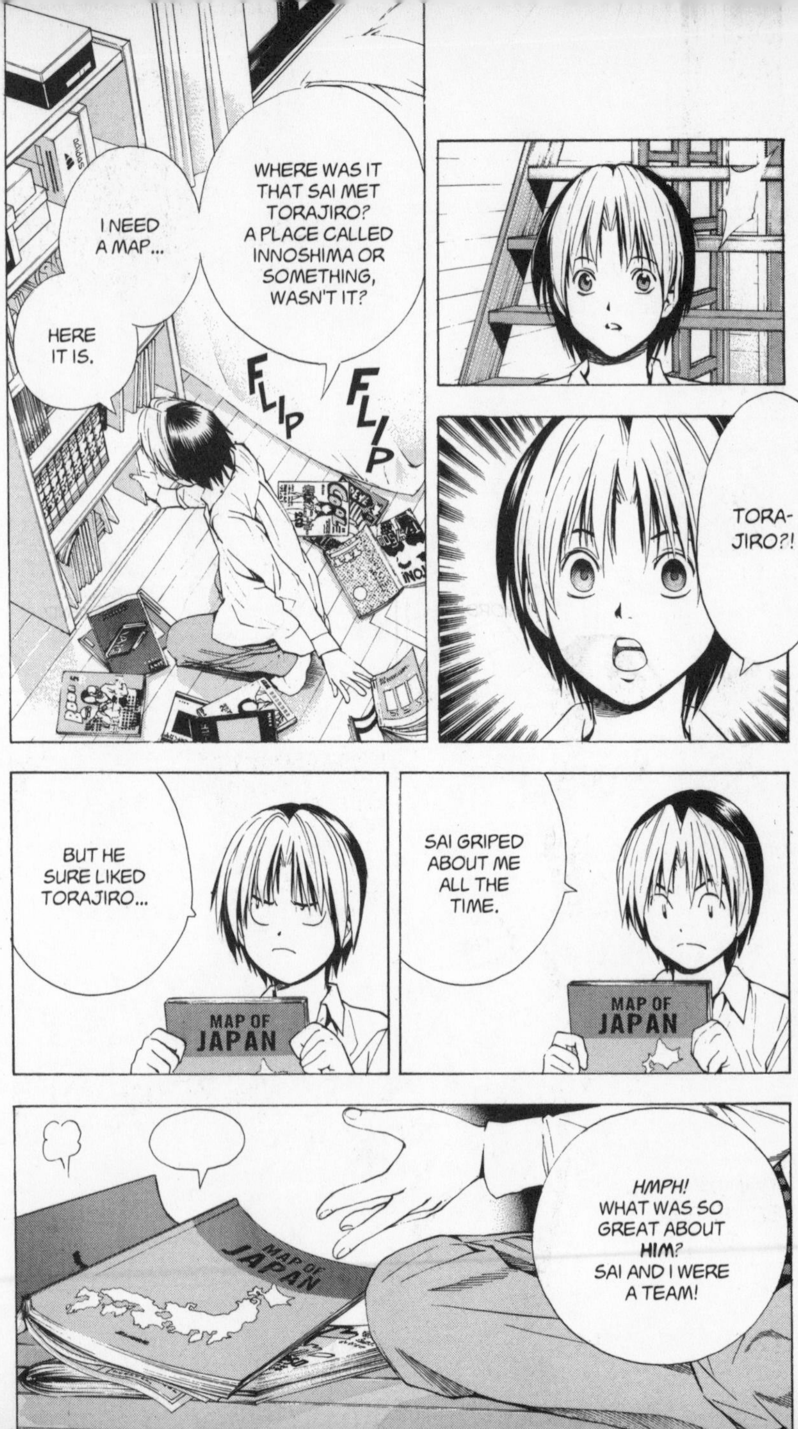
TORA-JIRO?!
WHERE WAS IT THAT SAI MET TORAJIRO? A PLACE CALLED INNOSHIMA OR SOMETHING, WASN'T IT?
FLIP
FLIP
I NEED A MAP...
HERE IT IS.
SAI GRIPED ABOUT ME ALL THE TIME.
MAP OF JAPAN
BUT HE SURE LIKED TORAJIRO...
MAP OF JAPAN
HMPH! WHAT WAS SO GREAT ABOUT HIM? SAI AND I WERE A TEAM!
MAP OF JAPAN

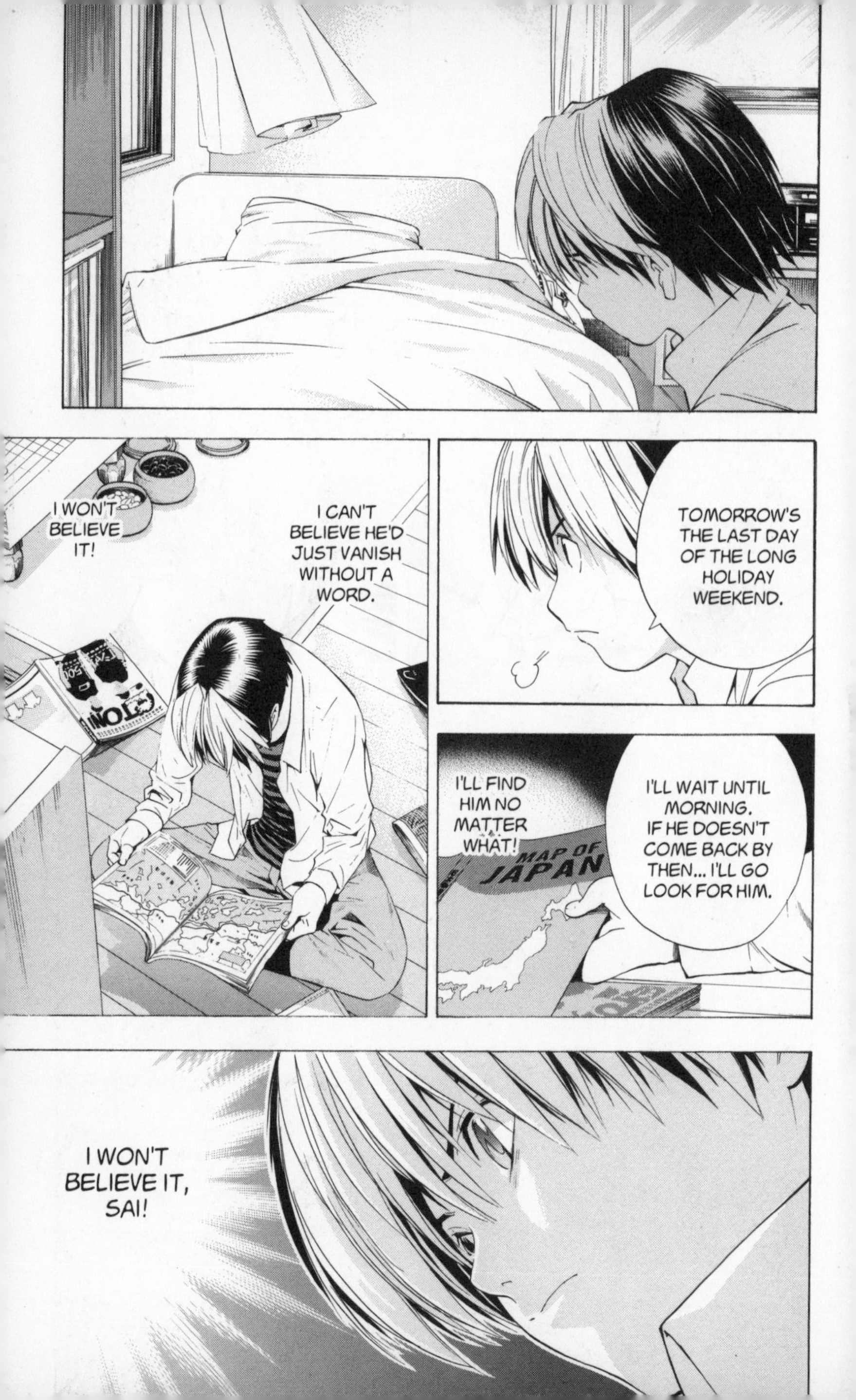
TOMORROW'S THE LAST DAY OF THE LONG HOLIDAY WEEKEND.
I'LL WAIT UNTIL MORNING. IF HE DOESN'T COME BACK BY THEN... I'LL GO LOOK FOR HIM.
I'LL FIND HIM NO MATTER WHAT!
MAP OF JAPAN
I CAN'T BELIEVE HE'D JUST VANISH WITHOUT A WORD.
I WON'T BELIEVE IT!
I WON'T BELIEVE IT, SAI!

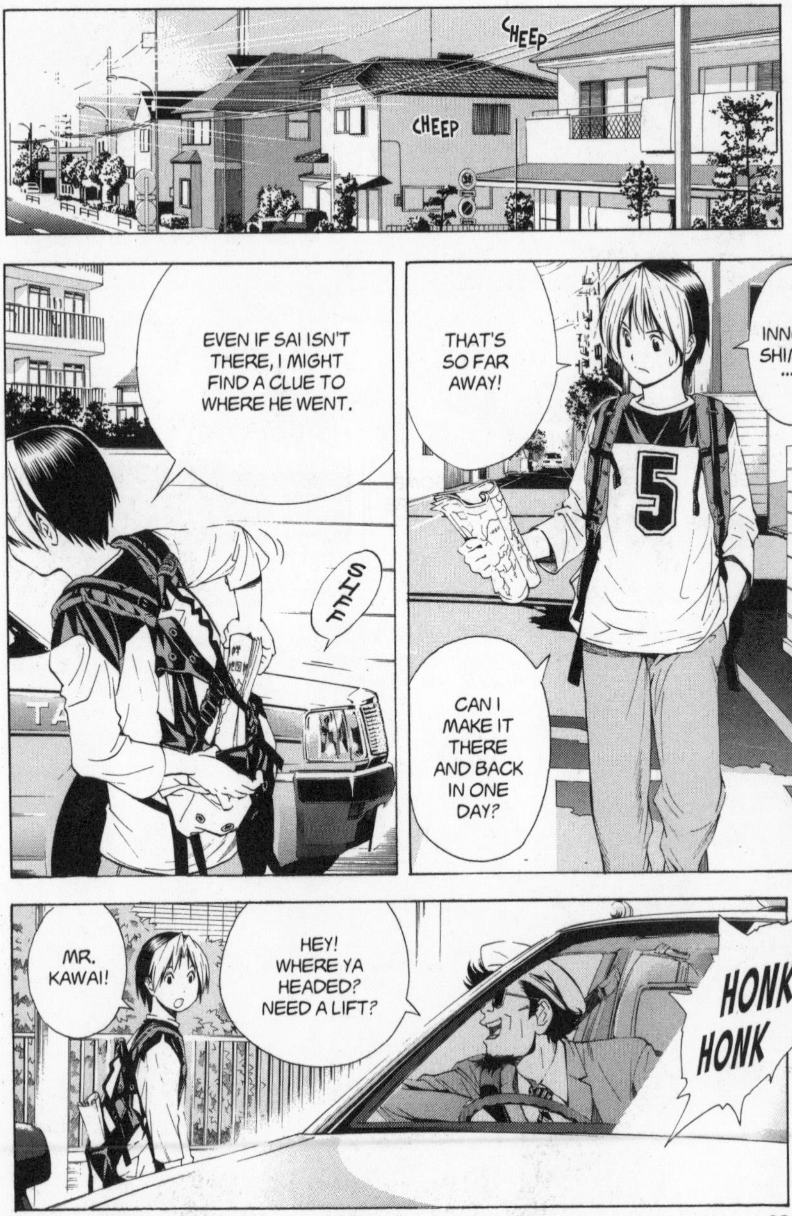
CHEEP
CHEEP
INNO-SHIMA ...
THAT'S SO FAR AWAY!
CAN I MAKE IT THERE AND BACK IN ONE DAY?
EVEN IF SAI ISN'T THERE, I MIGHT FIND A CLUE TO WHERE HE WENT.
SHFF
HONK HONK
HEY! WHERE YA HEADED? NEED A LIFT?
MR. KAWAI!

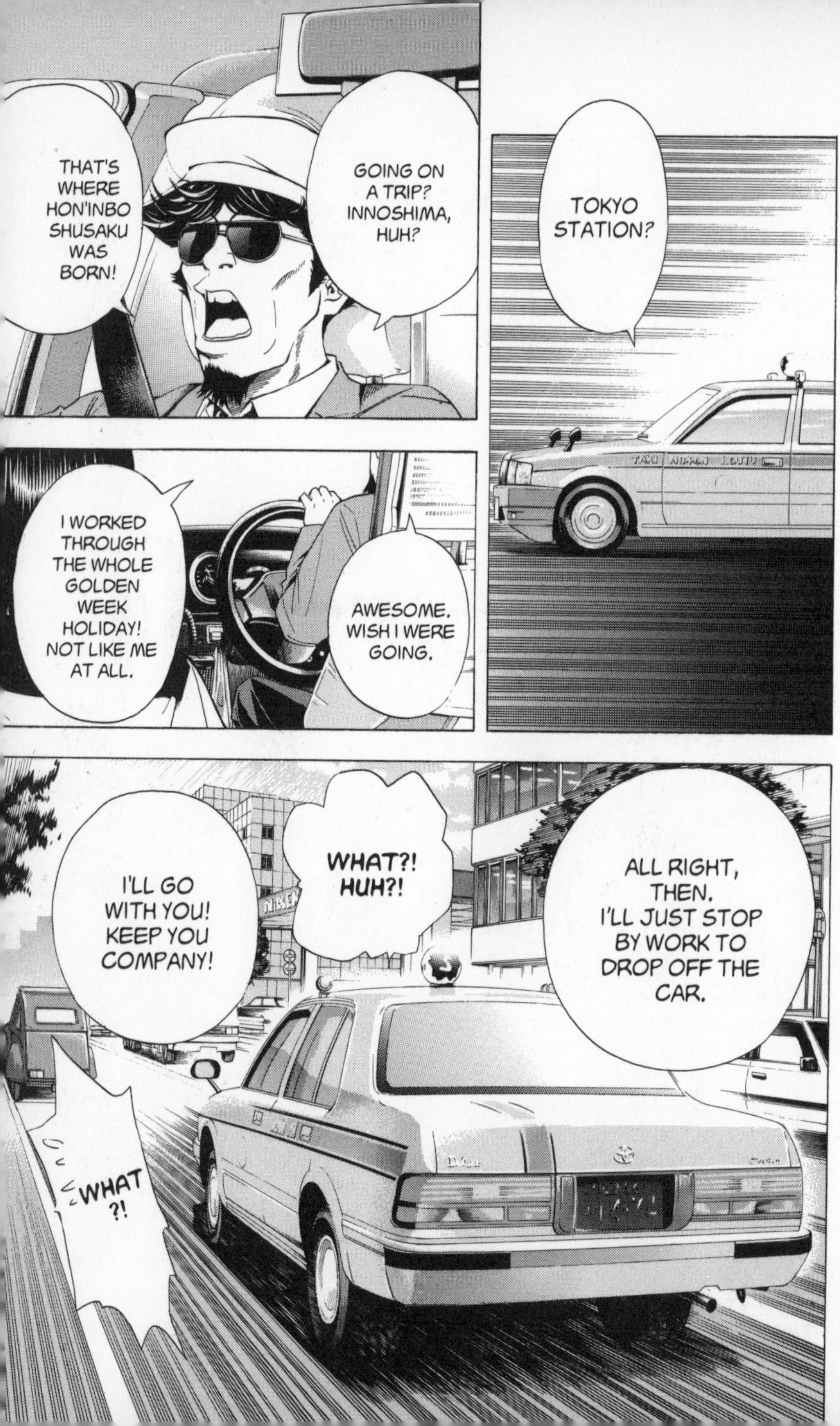
TOKYO STATION?
GOING ON A TRIP? INNOSHIMA, HUH?
THAT'S WHERE HON'INBO SHUSAKU WAS BORN!
AWESOME. WISH I WERE GOING.
I WORKED THROUGH THE WHOLE GOLDEN WEEK HOLIDAY! NOT LIKE ME AT ALL.
ALL RIGHT, THEN. I'LL JUST STOP BY WORK TO DROP OFF THE CAR.
WHAT?! HUH?!
I'LL GO WITH YOU! KEEP YOU COMPANY!
WHAT ?!

HIKARU NO GO

STORYBOARDS

40

YUMI HOTTA

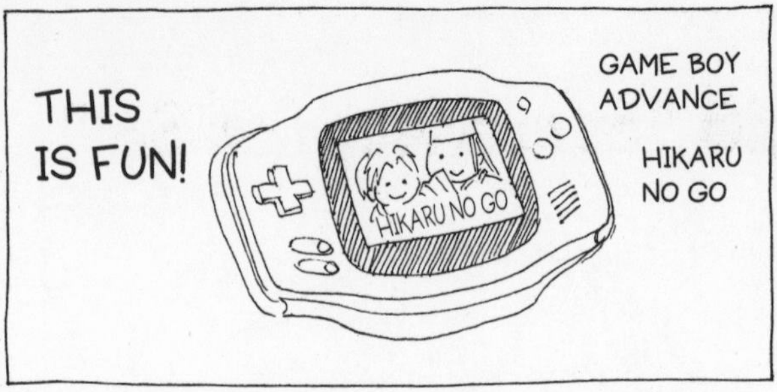
GAME BOY ADVANCE
HIKARU NO GO
HIKARU NO GO
THIS IS FUN!

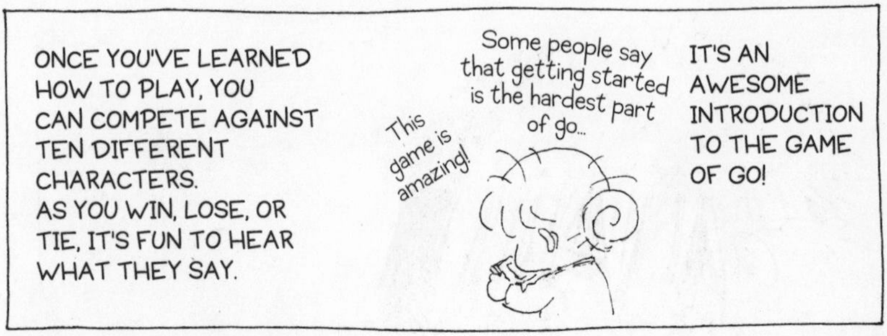
IT'S AN AWESOME INTRODUCTION TO THE GAME OF GO!
Some people say that getting started is the hardest part of go...
This game is amazing!
ONCE YOU'VE LEARNED HOW TO PLAY, YOU CAN COMPETE AGAINST TEN DIFFERENT CHARACTERS.
AS YOU WIN, LOSE, OR TIE, IT'S FUN TO HEAR WHAT THEY SAY.

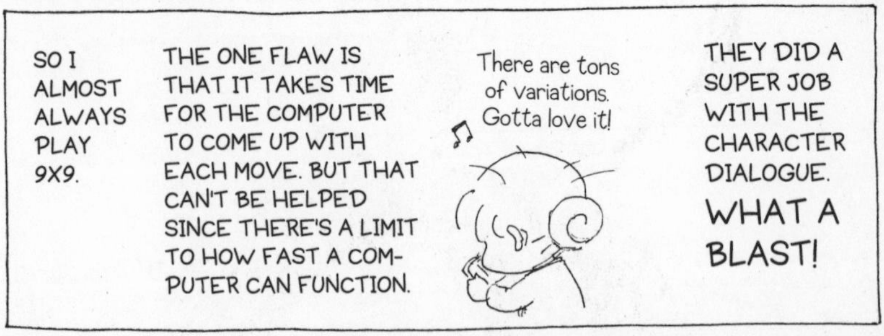
THEY DID A SUPER JOB WITH THE CHARACTER DIALOGUE.
WHAT A BLAST!
There are tons of variations. Gotta love it!
THE ONE FLAW IS THAT IT TAKES TIME FOR THE COMPUTER TO COME UP WITH EACH MOVE. BUT THAT CAN'T BE HELPED SINCE THERE'S A LIMIT TO HOW FAST A COMPUTER CAN FUNCTION.
SO I ALMOST ALWAYS PLAY 9X9.

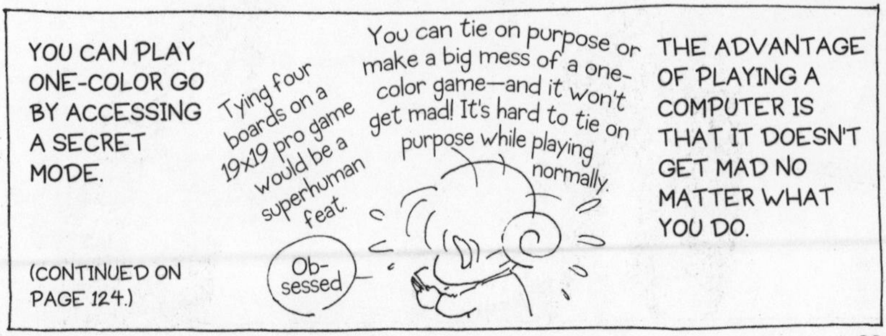
THE ADVANTAGE OF PLAYING A COMPUTER IS THAT IT DOESN'T GET MAD NO MATTER WHAT YOU DO.
You can tie on purpose or make a big mess of a one-color game—and it won't get mad! It's hard to tie on purpose while playing normally.
Tying four boards on a 19x19 pro game would be a superhuman feat.
Ob-sessed
YOU CAN PLAY ONE-COLOR GO BY ACCESSING A SECRET MODE.
(CONTINUED ON PAGE 124.)

Game 126 "Searching for Sai"

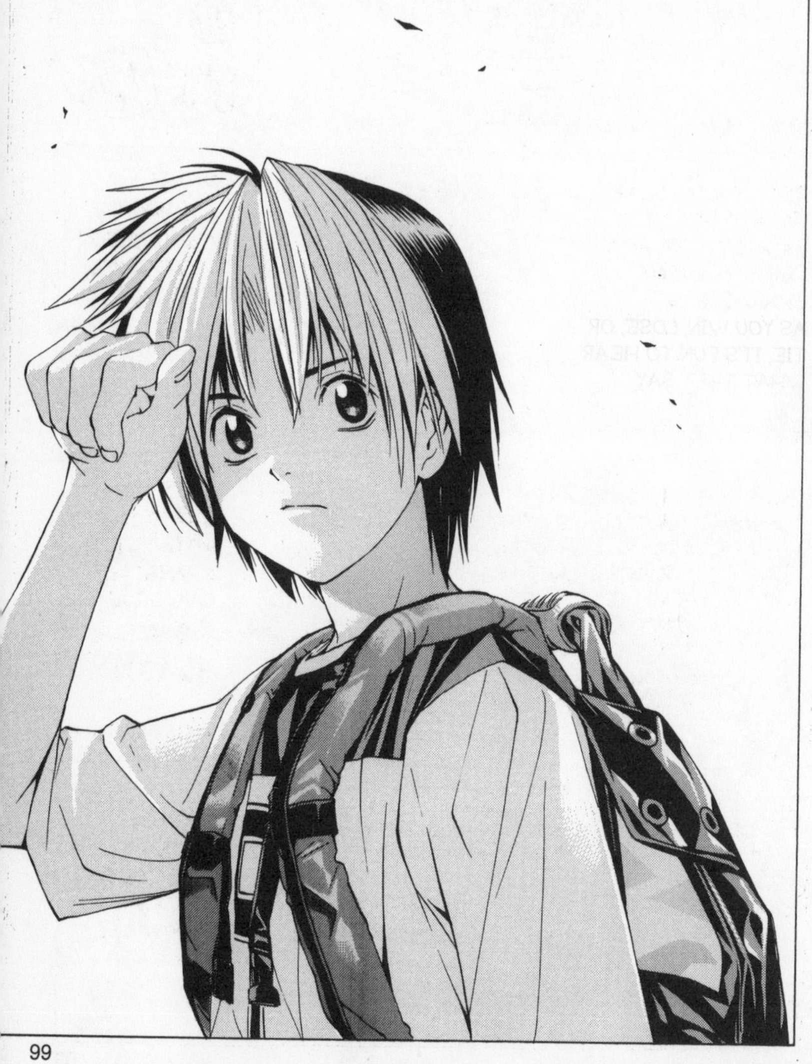

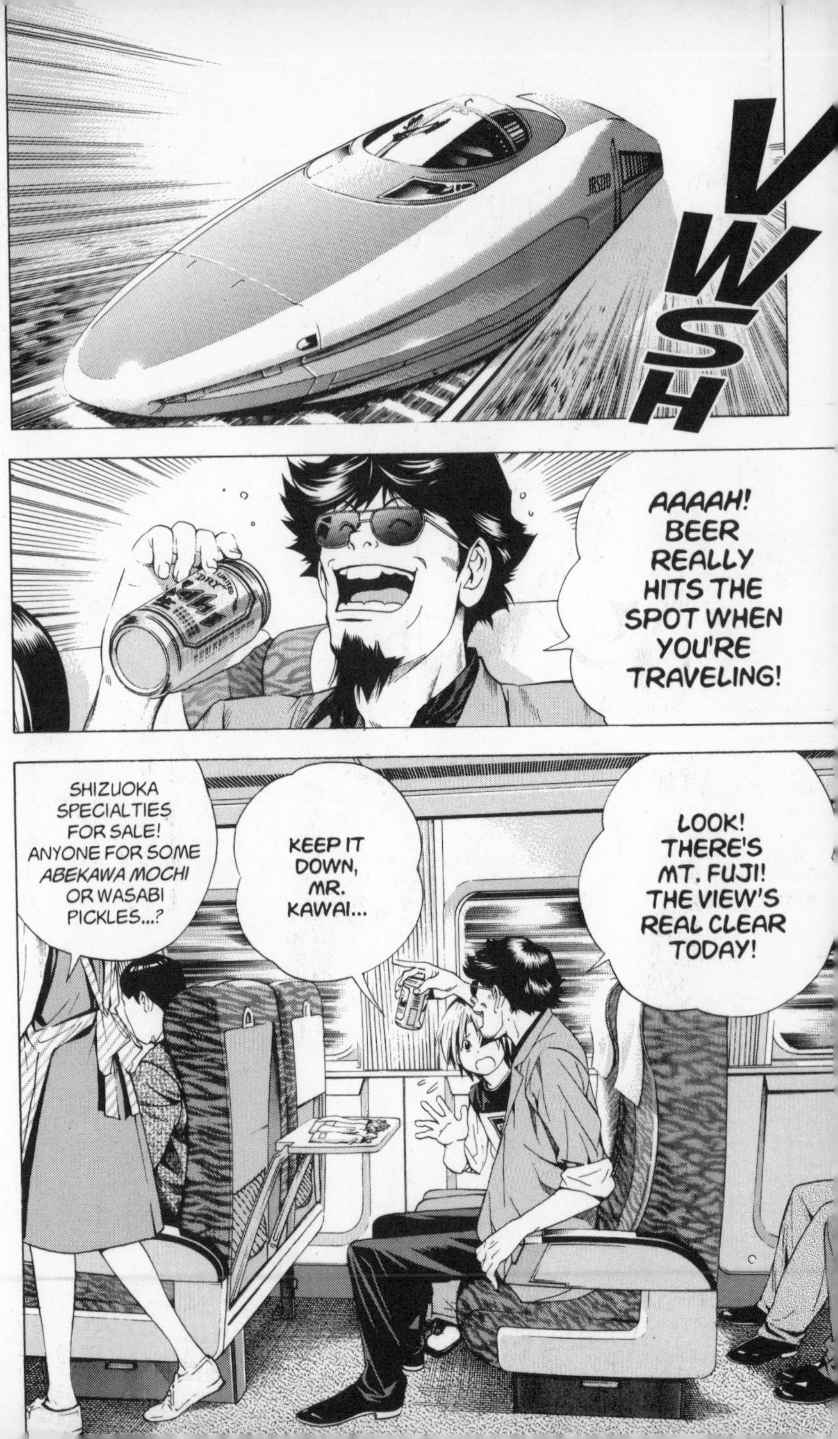
VWSH
AAAAH! BEER REALLY HITS THE SPOT WHEN YOU'RE TRAVELING!
LOOK! THERE'S MT. FUJI! THE VIEW'S REAL CLEAR TODAY!
KEEP IT DOWN, MR. KAWAI...
SHIZUOKA SPECIALTIES FOR SALE! ANYONE FOR SOME ABEKAWA MOCHI OR WASABI PICKLES...?

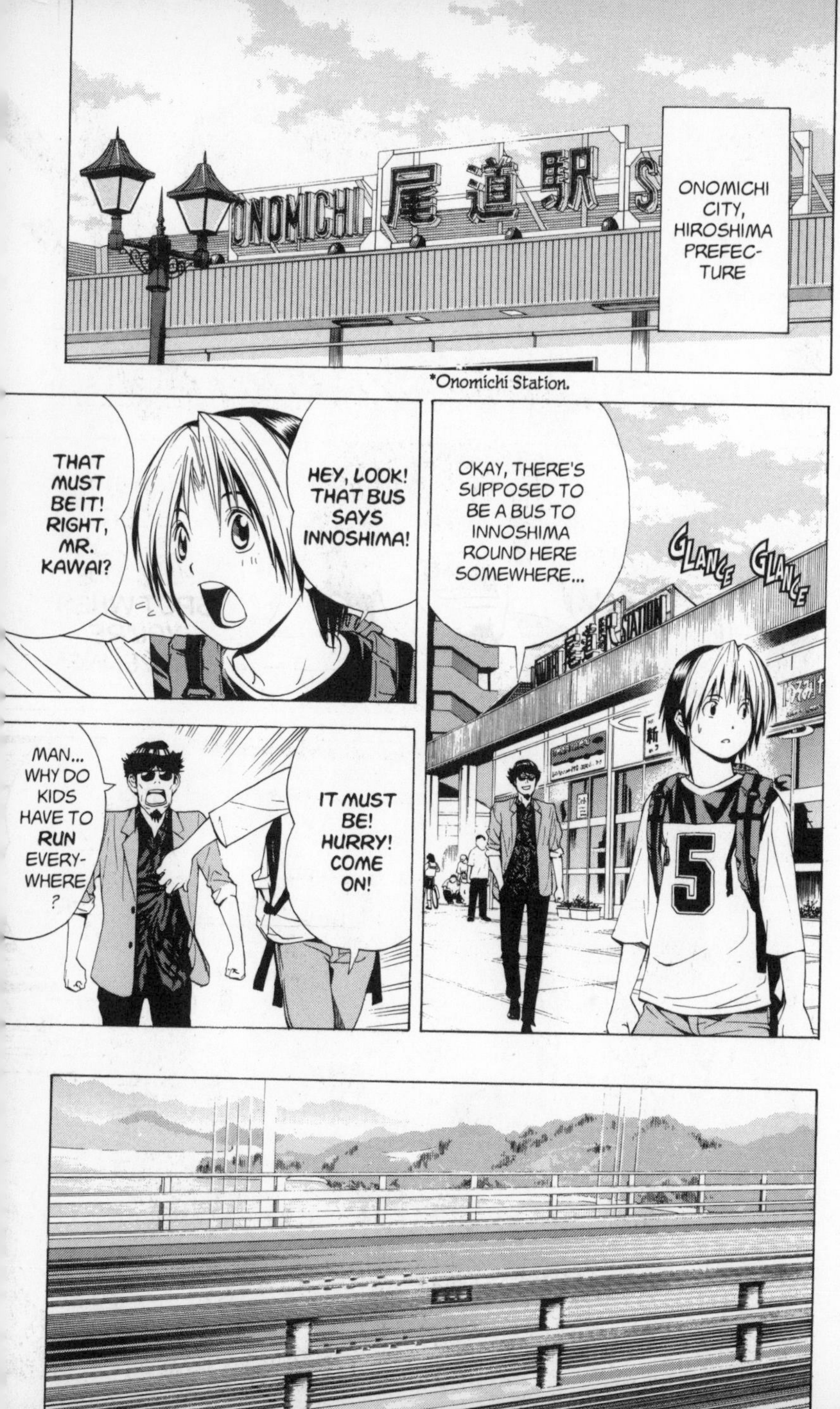
ONOMICHI 尾道駅 S
ONOMICHI CITY, HIROSHIMA PREFEC-TURE
*Onomichi Station.
OKAY, THERE'S SUPPOSED TO BE A BUS TO INNOSHIMA ROUND HERE SOMEWHERE...
GLANCE GLANCE
尾道駅 STATION
HEY, LOOK! THAT BUS SAYS INNOSHIMA!
THAT MUST BE IT! RIGHT, MR. KAWAI?
IT MUST BE! HURRY! COME ON!
MAN... WHY DO KIDS HAVE TO **RUN** EVERY-WHERE?

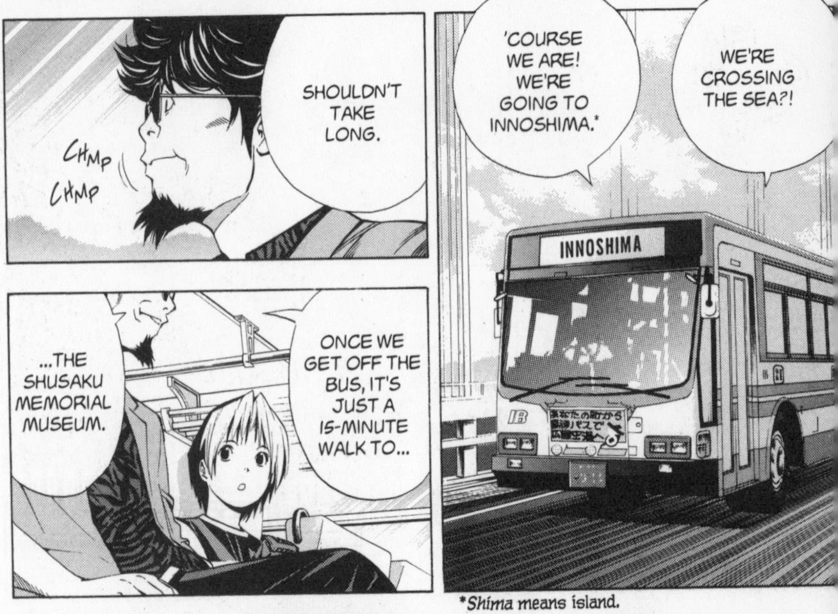
WE'RE CROSSING THE SEA?!
'COURSE WE ARE! WE'RE GOING TO INNOSHIMA.*
INNOSHIMA
SHOULDN'T TAKE LONG.
CHMP CHMP
ONCE WE GET OFF THE BUS, IT'S JUST A 15-MINUTE WALK TO...
...THE SHUSAKU MEMORIAL MUSEUM.

*Shima means island.

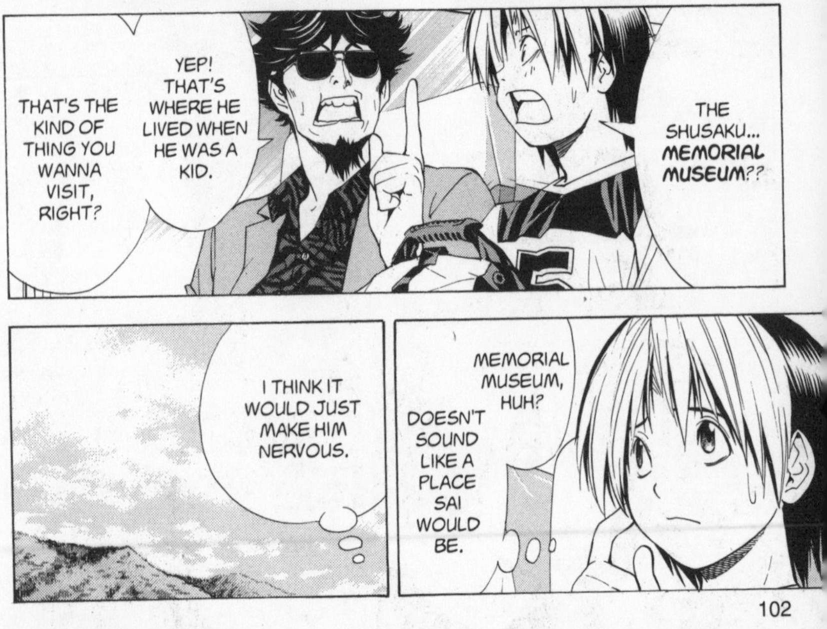
THE SHUSAKU... MEMORIAL MUSEUM??
YEP! THAT'S WHERE HE LIVED WHEN HE WAS A KID.
THAT'S THE KIND OF THING YOU WANNA VISIT, RIGHT?
MEMORIAL MUSEUM, HUH?
DOESN'T SOUND LIKE A PLACE SAI WOULD BE.
I THINK IT WOULD JUST MAKE HIM NERVOUS.

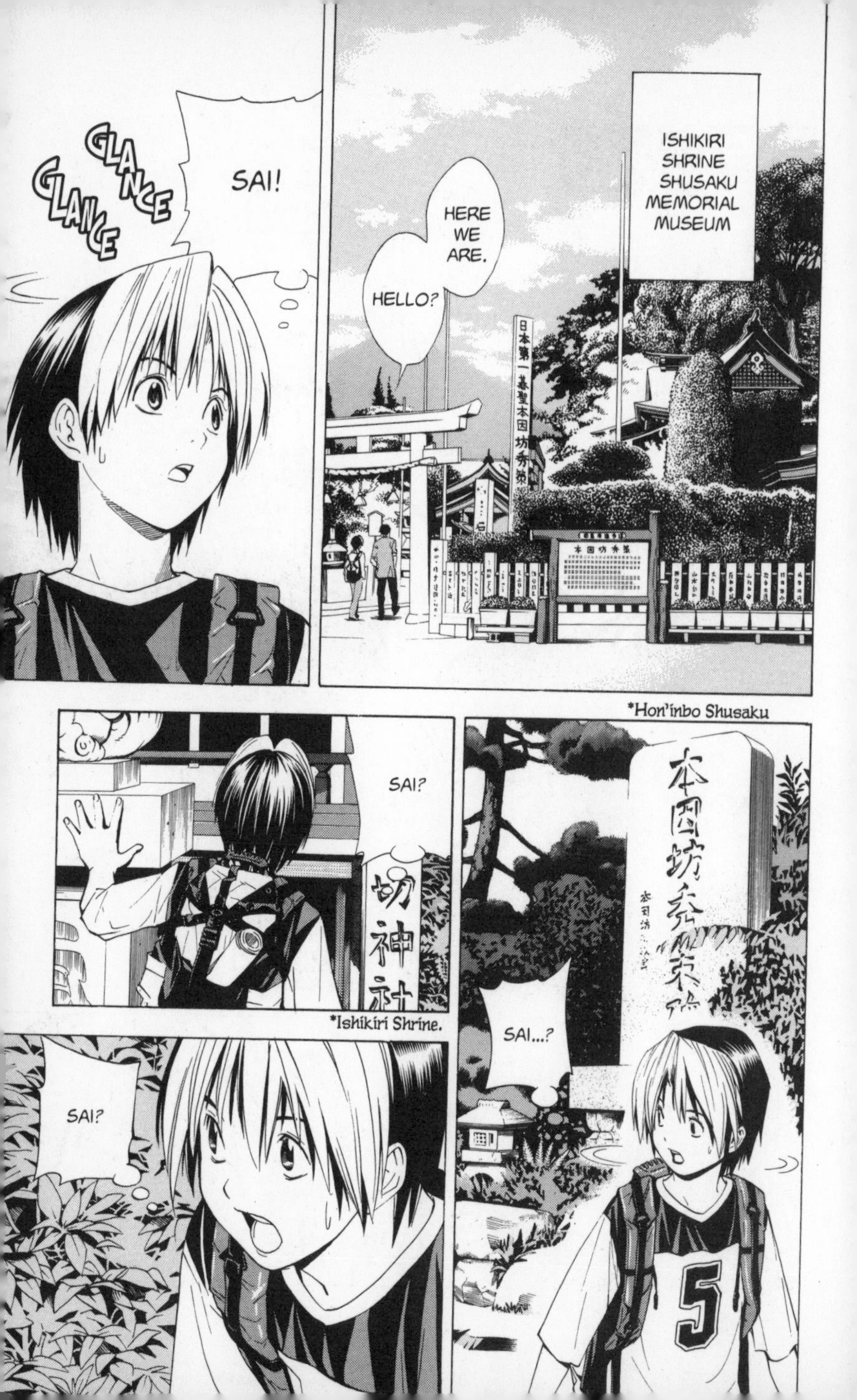
ISHIKIRI SHRINE SHUSAKU MEMORIAL MUSEUM
HERE WE ARE.
HELLO?
*Hon'inbo Shusaku
SAI!
GLANCE GLANCE
SAI...?
SAI?
*Ishikiri Shrine.
SAI?

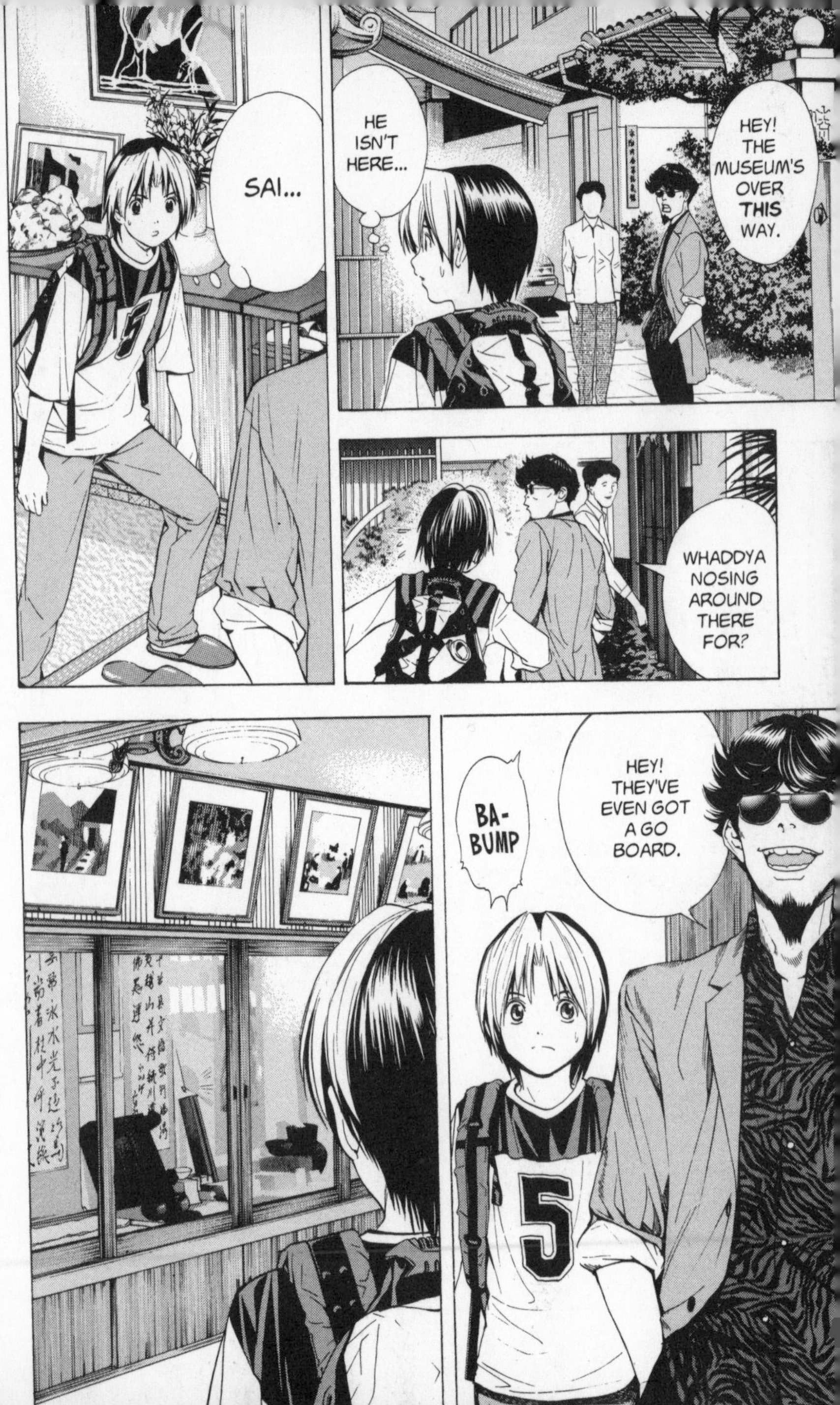
HEY! THE MUSEUM'S OVER THIS WAY.
HE ISN'T HERE...
WHADDYA NOSING AROUND THERE FOR?
SAI...
HEY! THEY'VE EVEN GOT A GO BOARD.
BA-BUMP

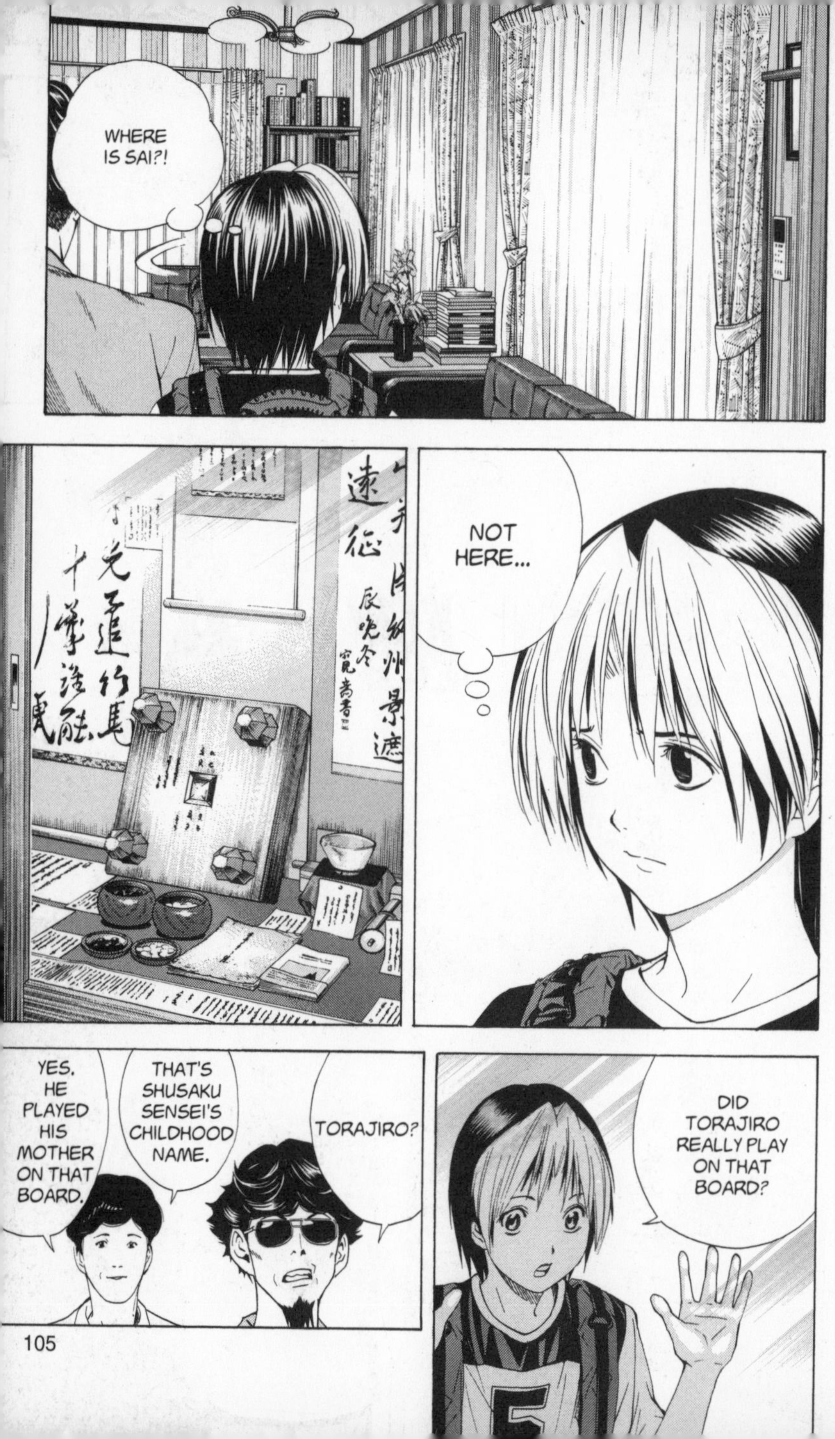
WHERE IS SAI?!
NOT HERE...
DID TORAJIRO REALLY PLAY ON THAT BOARD?
TORAJIRO?
THAT'S SHUSAKU SENSEI'S CHILDHOOD NAME.
YES. HE PLAYED HIS MOTHER ON THAT BOARD.

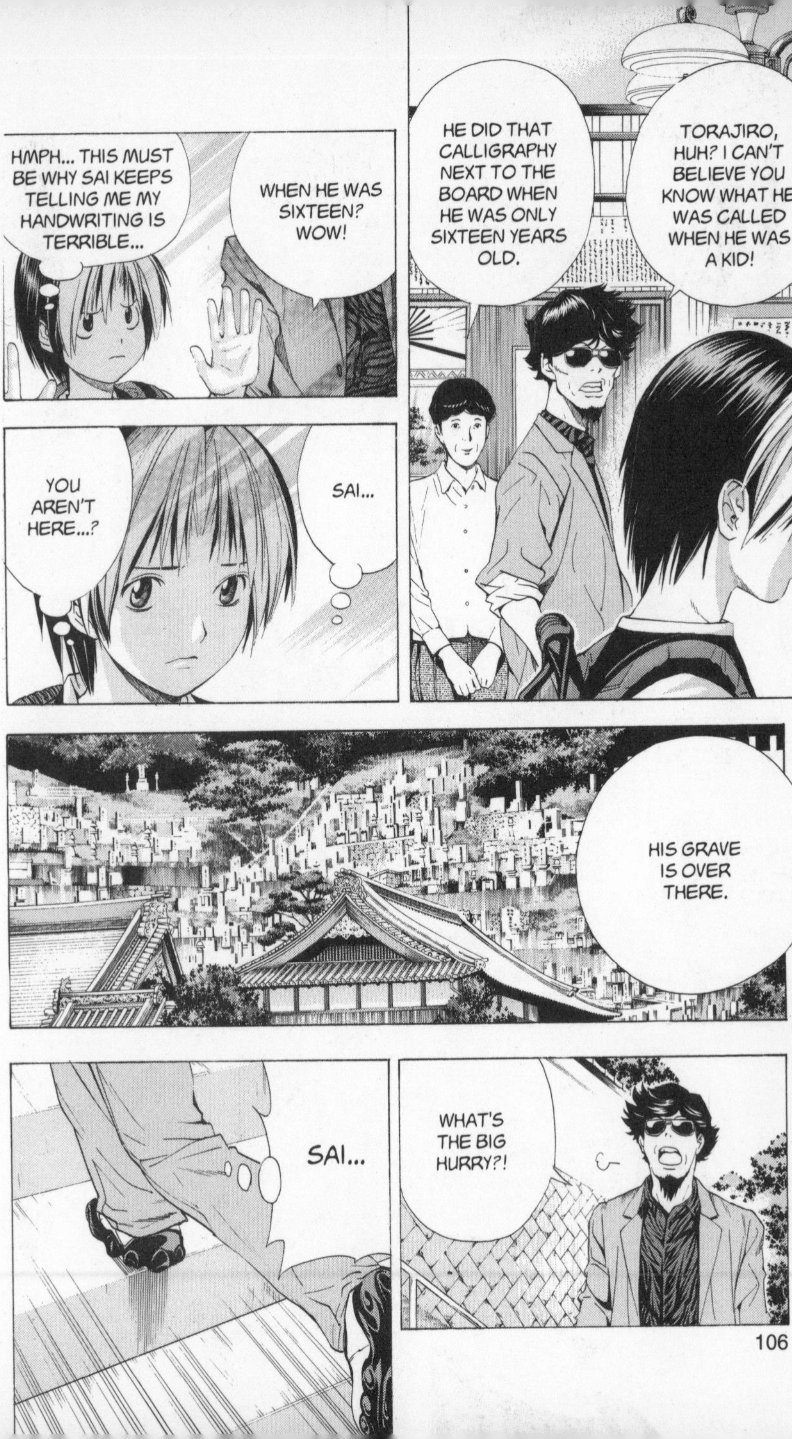
TORAJIRO, HUH? I CAN'T BELIEVE YOU KNOW WHAT HE WAS CALLED WHEN HE WAS A KID!
HE DID THAT CALLIGRAPHY NEXT TO THE BOARD WHEN HE WAS ONLY SIXTEEN YEARS OLD.
WHEN HE WAS SIXTEEN? WOW!
HMPH... THIS MUST BE WHY SAI KEEPS TELLING ME MY HANDWRITING IS TERRIBLE...
SAI...
YOU AREN'T HERE...?
HIS GRAVE IS OVER THERE.
WHAT'S THE BIG HURRY?!
SAI...

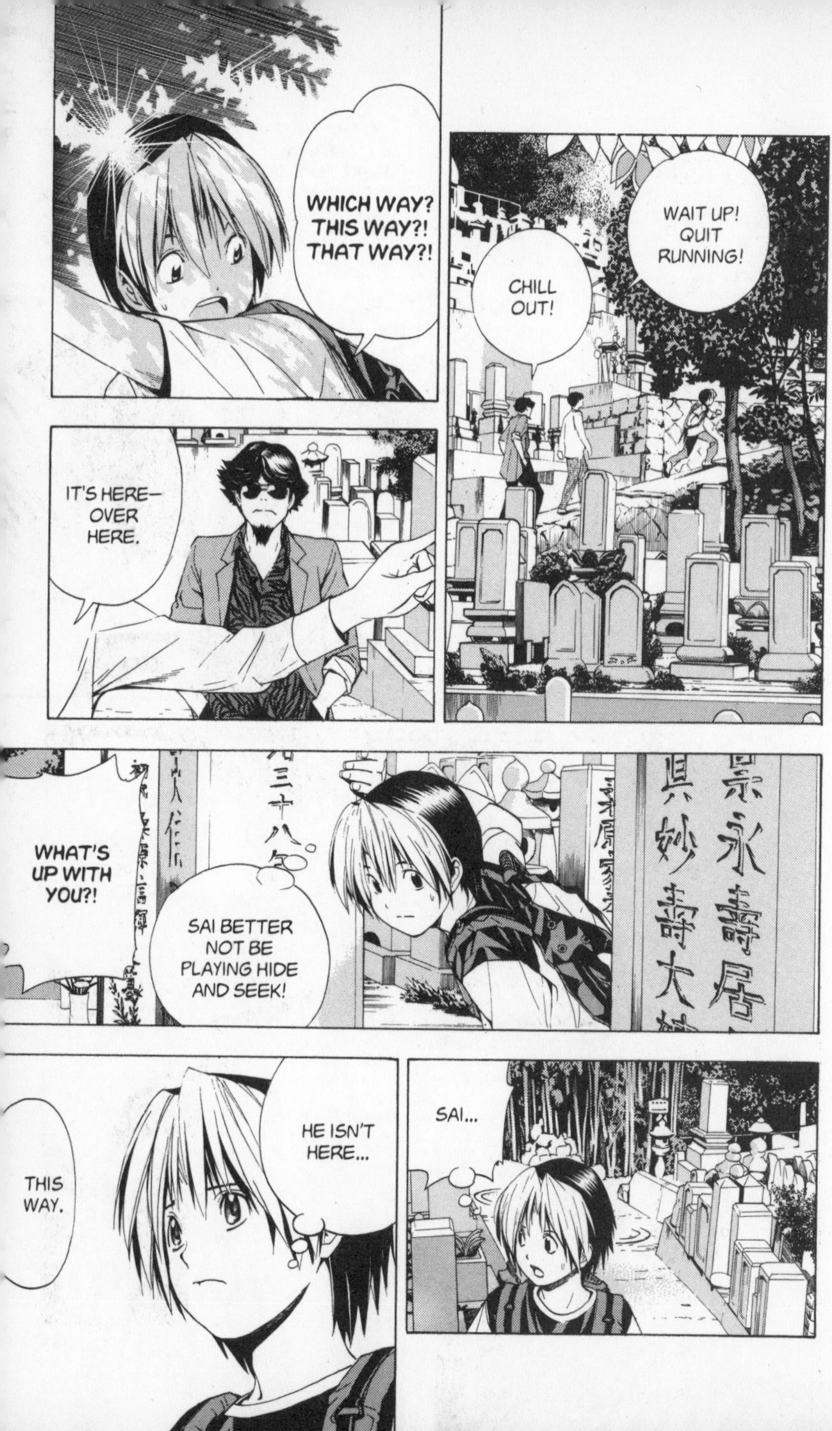
WAIT UP! QUIT RUNNING!
CHILL OUT!
WHICH WAY? THIS WAY?! THAT WAY?!
IT'S HERE—OVER HERE.
SAI BETTER NOT BE PLAYING HIDE AND SEEK!
WHAT'S UP WITH YOU?!
SAI...
HE ISN'T HERE...
THIS WAY.

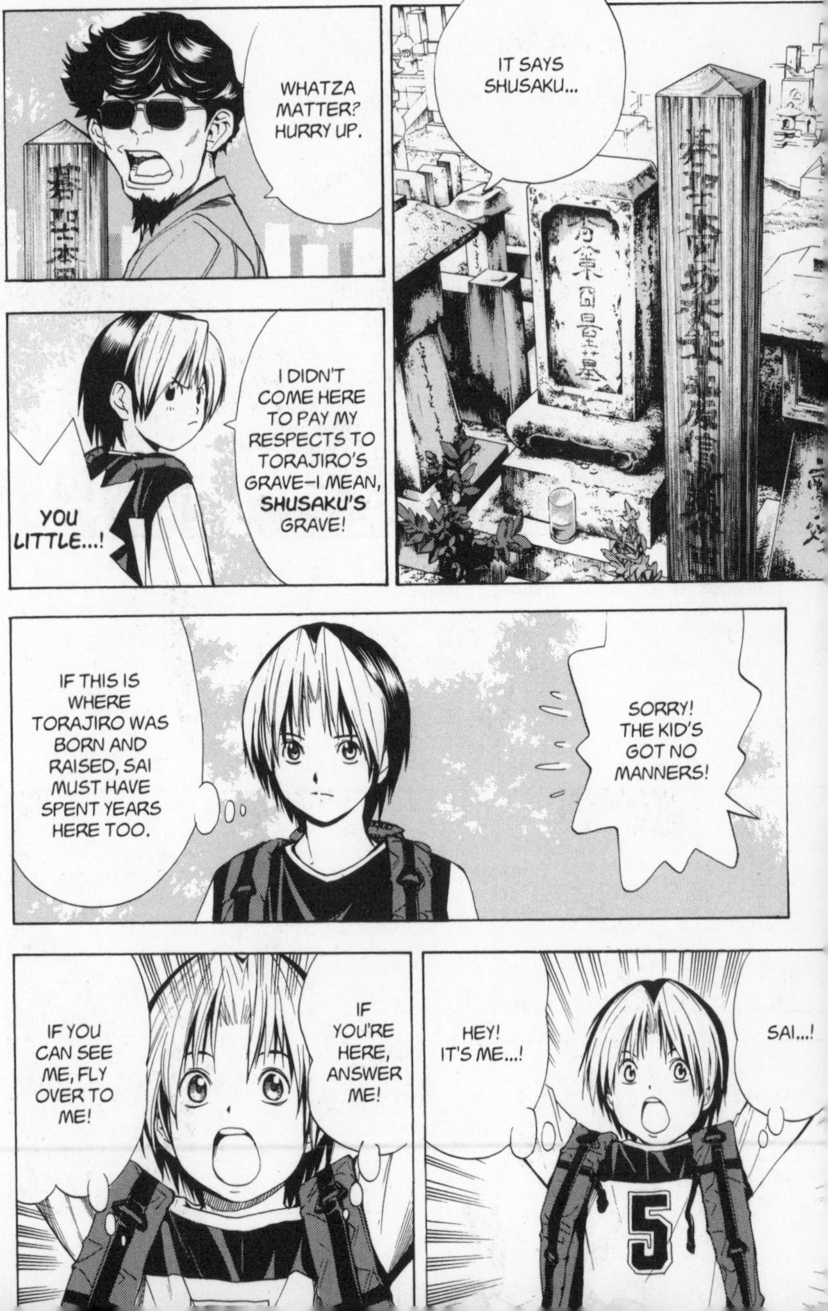
IT SAYS SHUSAKU...
WHATZA MATTER? HURRY UP.
I DIDN'T COME HERE TO PAY MY RESPECTS TO TORAJIRO'S GRAVE—I MEAN, SHUSAKU'S GRAVE!
YOU LITTLE...!
SORRY! THE KID'S GOT NO MANNERS!
IF THIS IS WHERE TORAJIRO WAS BORN AND RAISED, SAI MUST HAVE SPENT YEARS HERE TOO.
SAI...!
HEY! IT'S ME...!
IF YOU'RE HERE, ANSWER ME!
IF YOU CAN SEE ME, FLY OVER TO ME!

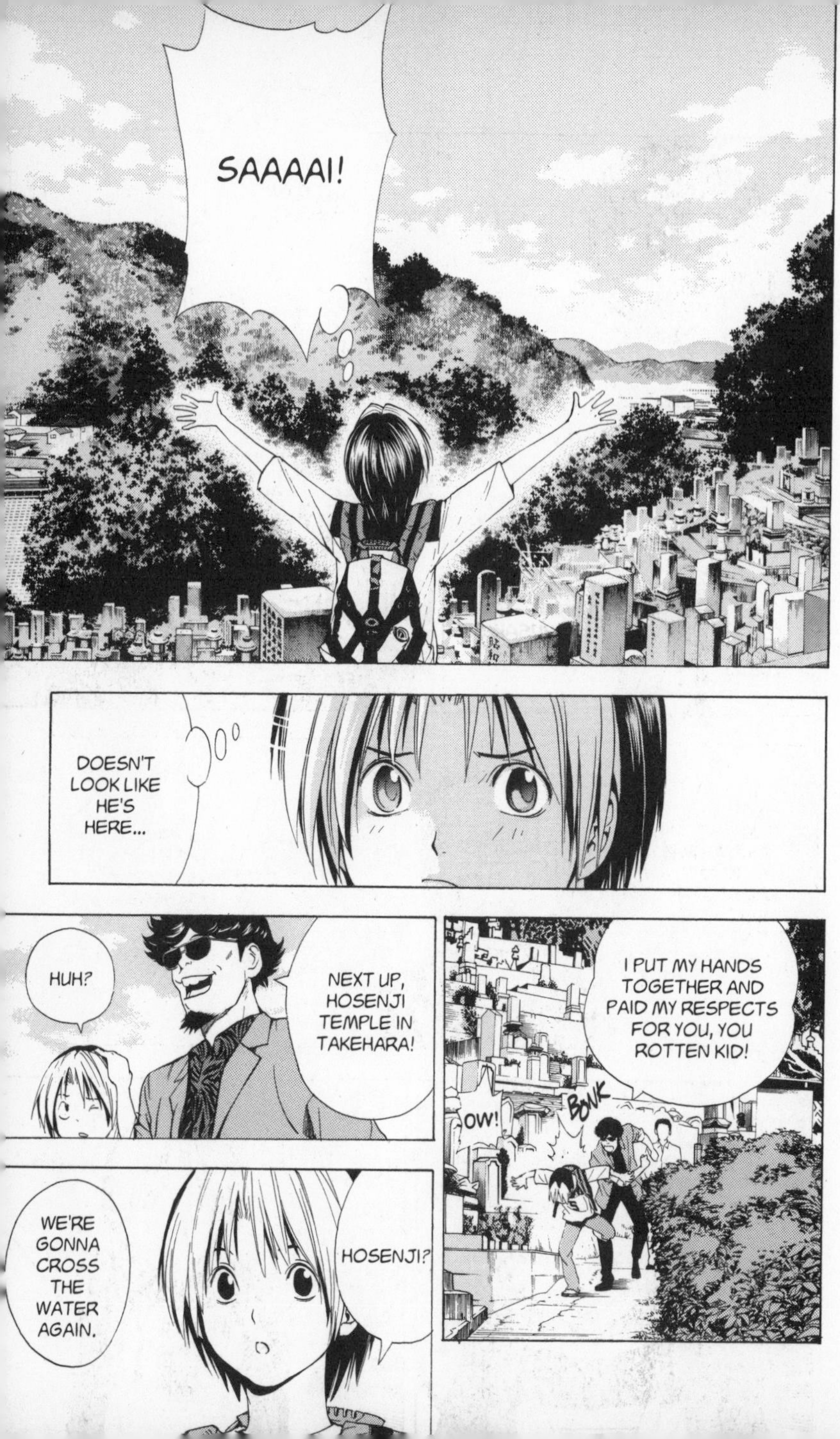
SAAAAI!
DOESN'T LOOK LIKE HE'S HERE...
I PUT MY HANDS TOGETHER AND PAID MY RESPECTS FOR YOU, YOU ROTTEN KID!
BONK
OW!
NEXT UP, HOSENJI TEMPLE IN TAKEHARA!
HUH?
HOSENJI?
WE'RE GONNA CROSS THE WATER AGAIN.

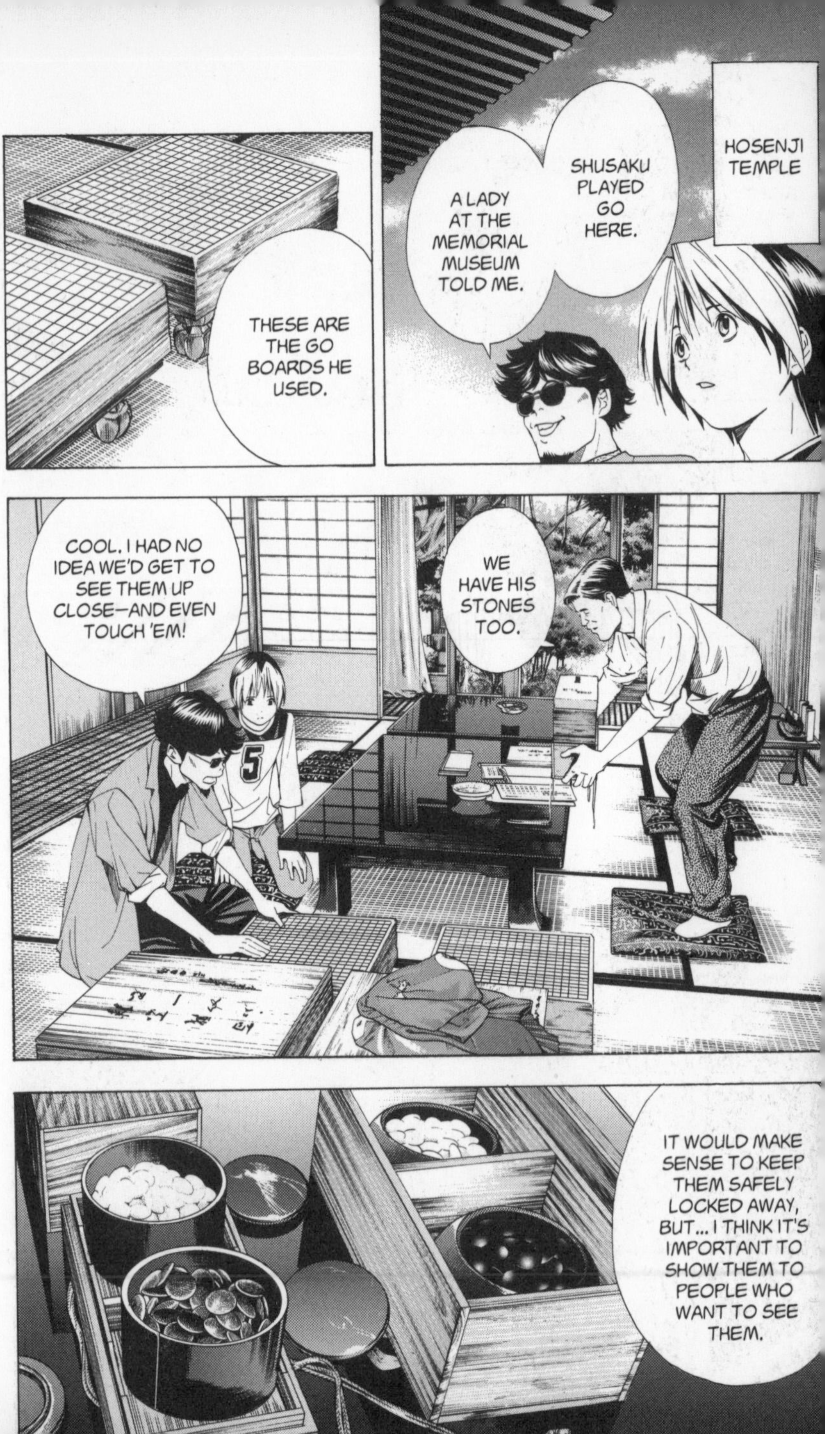
HOSENJI TEMPLE
SHUSAKU PLAYED GO HERE.
A LADY AT THE MEMORIAL MUSEUM TOLD ME.
THESE ARE THE GO BOARDS HE USED.
WE HAVE HIS STONES TOO.
COOL. I HAD NO IDEA WE'D GET TO SEE THEM UP CLOSE—AND EVEN TOUCH 'EM!
IT WOULD MAKE SENSE TO KEEP THEM SAFELY LOCKED AWAY, BUT... I THINK IT'S IMPORTANT TO SHOW THEM TO PEOPLE WHO WANT TO SEE THEM.

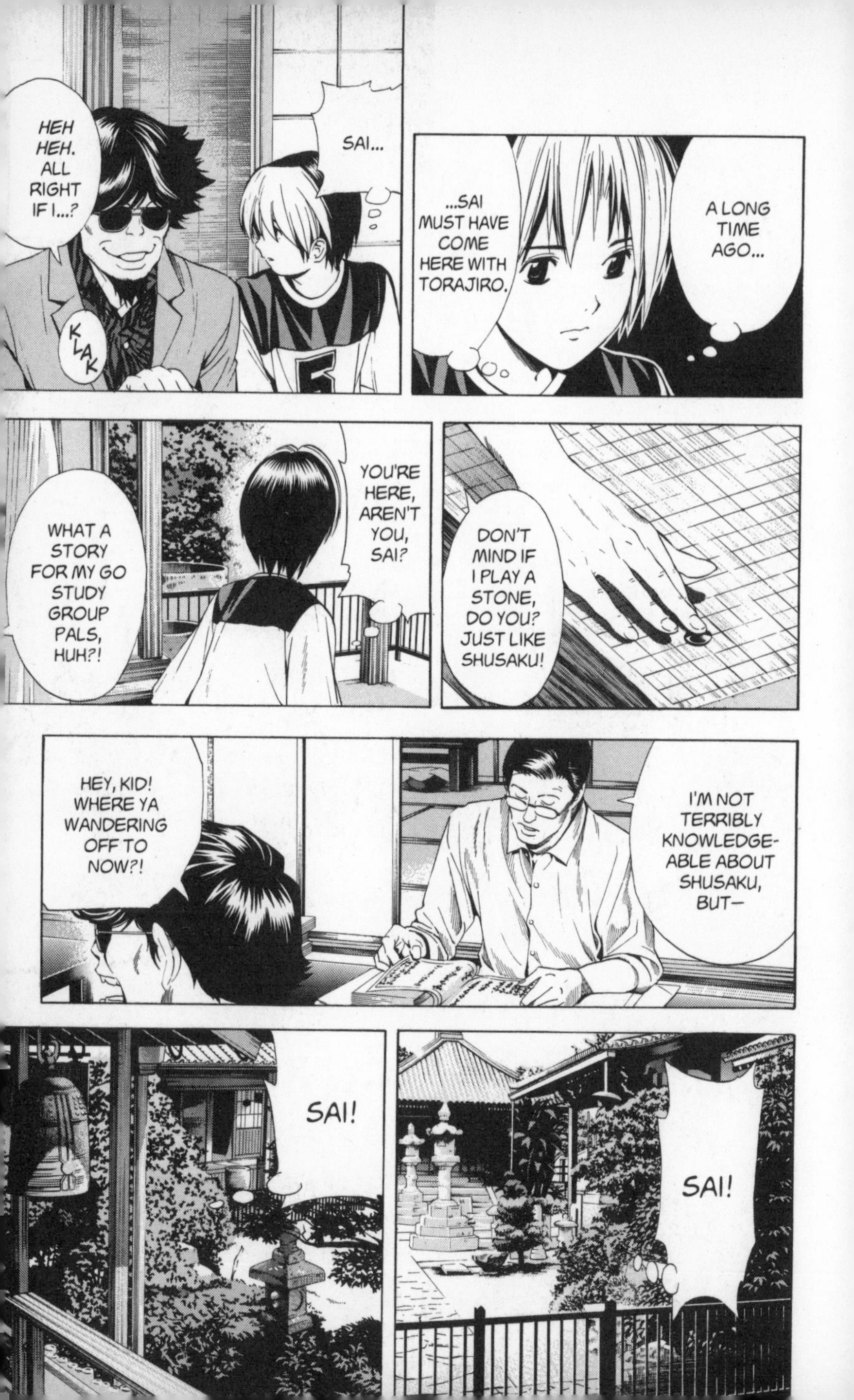
A LONG TIME AGO...
...SAI MUST HAVE COME HERE WITH TORAJIRO.
SAI...
HEH HEH. ALL RIGHT IF I...?
KLAK
DON'T MIND IF I PLAY A STONE, DO YOU? JUST LIKE SHUSAKU!
YOU'RE HERE, AREN'T YOU, SAI?
WHAT A STORY FOR MY GO STUDY GROUP PALS, HUH?!
I'M NOT TERRIBLY KNOWLEDGE-ABLE ABOUT SHUSAKU, BUT—
HEY, KID! WHERE YA WANDERING OFF TO NOW?!
SAI!
SAI!

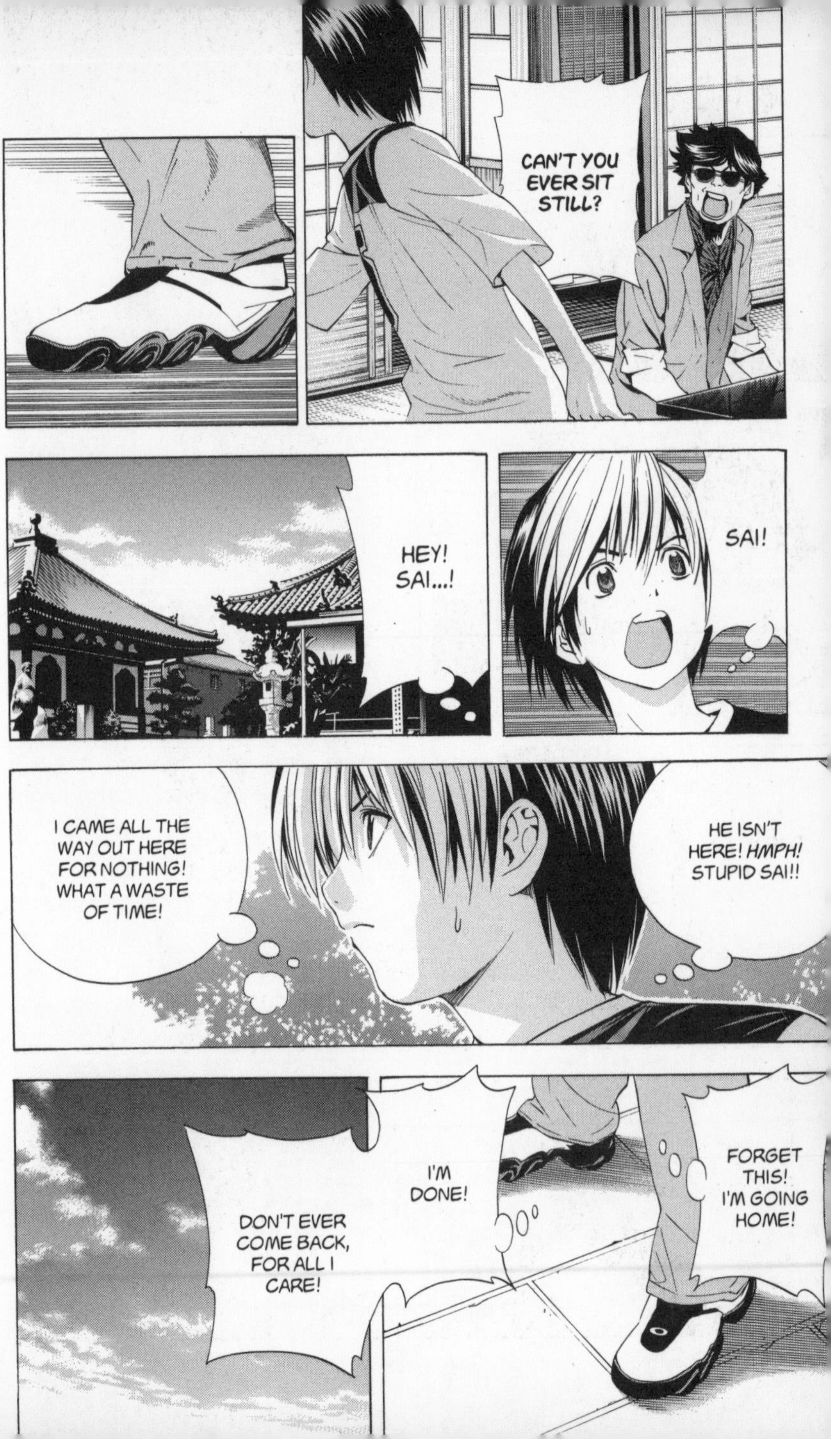
CAN'T YOU EVER SIT STILL?
SAI!
HEY! SAI...!
HE ISN'T HERE! *HMPH!* STUPID SAI!!
I CAME ALL THE WAY OUT HERE FOR NOTHING! WHAT A WASTE OF TIME!
FORGET THIS! I'M GOING HOME!
I'M DONE!
DON'T EVER COME BACK, FOR ALL I CARE!

READ THIS WAY

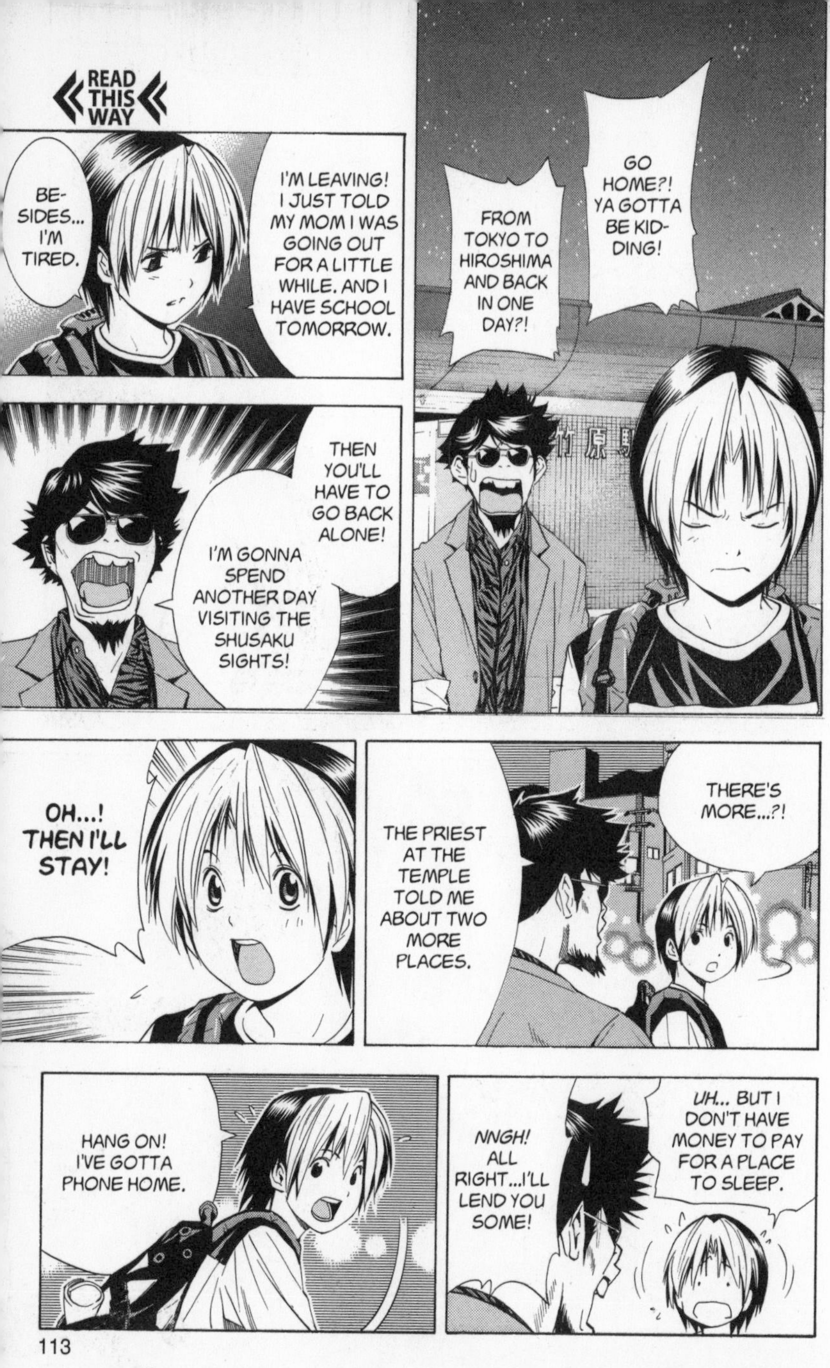
GO HOME?! YA GOTTA BE KID-DING!
FROM TOKYO TO HIROSHIMA AND BACK IN ONE DAY?!
I'M LEAVING! I JUST TOLD MY MOM I WAS GOING OUT FOR A LITTLE WHILE. AND I HAVE SCHOOL TOMORROW.
BE-SIDES... I'M TIRED.
THEN YOU'LL HAVE TO GO BACK ALONE!
I'M GONNA SPEND ANOTHER DAY VISITING THE SHUSAKU SIGHTS!
THERE'S MORE...?!
THE PRIEST AT THE TEMPLE TOLD ME ABOUT TWO MORE PLACES.
OH...! THEN I'LL STAY!
UH... BUT I DON'T HAVE MONEY TO PAY FOR A PLACE TO SLEEP.
NNGH! ALL RIGHT...I'LL LEND YOU SOME!
HANG ON! I'VE GOTTA PHONE HOME.

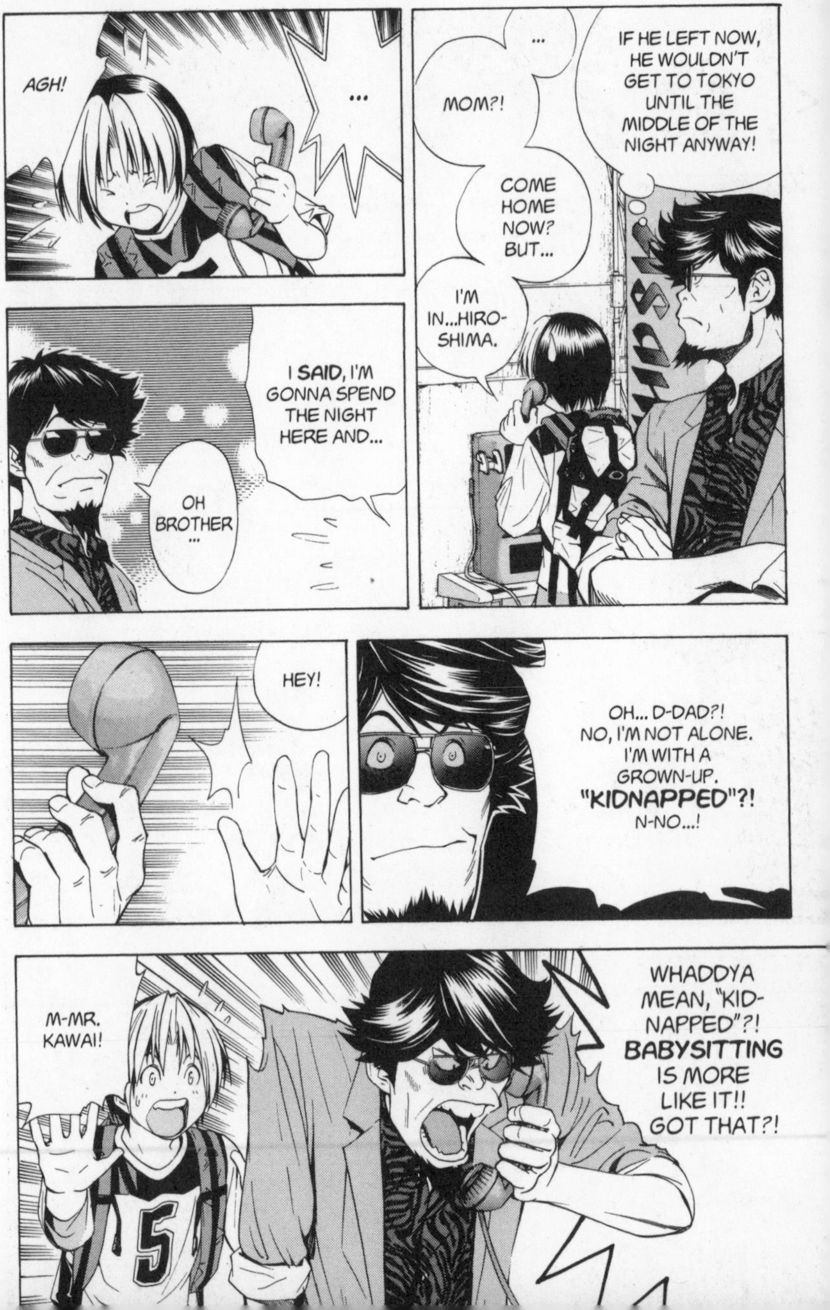
IF HE LEFT NOW, HE WOULDN'T GET TO TOKYO UNTIL THE MIDDLE OF THE NIGHT ANYWAY!
...
MOM?!
COME HOME NOW? BUT...
I'M IN...HIRO-SHIMA.
...
AGH!
I **SAID**, I'M GONNA SPEND THE NIGHT HERE AND...
OH BROTHER ...
OH... D-DAD?! NO, I'M NOT ALONE. I'M WITH A GROWN-UP. **"KIDNAPPED"**?! N-NO...!
HEY!
WHADDYA MEAN, "KID-NAPPED"?! **BABYSITTING** IS MORE LIKE IT!! GOT THAT?!
M-MR. KAWAI!

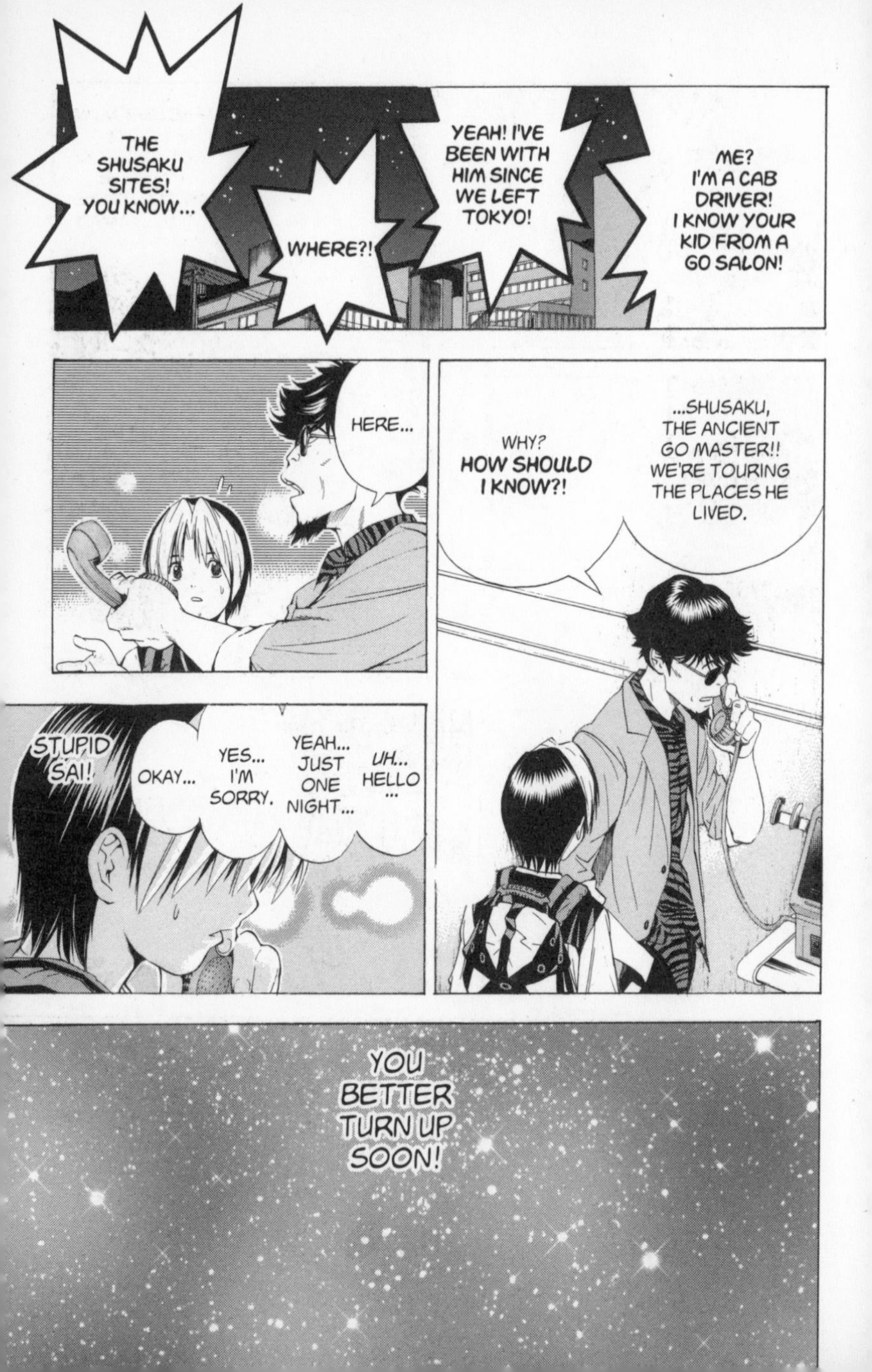
ME? I'M A CAB DRIVER! I KNOW YOUR KID FROM A GO SALON!
YEAH! I'VE BEEN WITH HIM SINCE WE LEFT TOKYO!
WHERE?!
THE SHUSAKU SITES! YOU KNOW...
...SHUSAKU, THE ANCIENT GO MASTER!! WE'RE TOURING THE PLACES HE LIVED.
WHY? **HOW SHOULD I KNOW?!**
HERE...
UH... HELLO ...
YEAH... JUST ONE NIGHT...
YES... I'M SORRY.
OKAY...
STUPID SAI!
YOU BETTER TURN UP SOON!

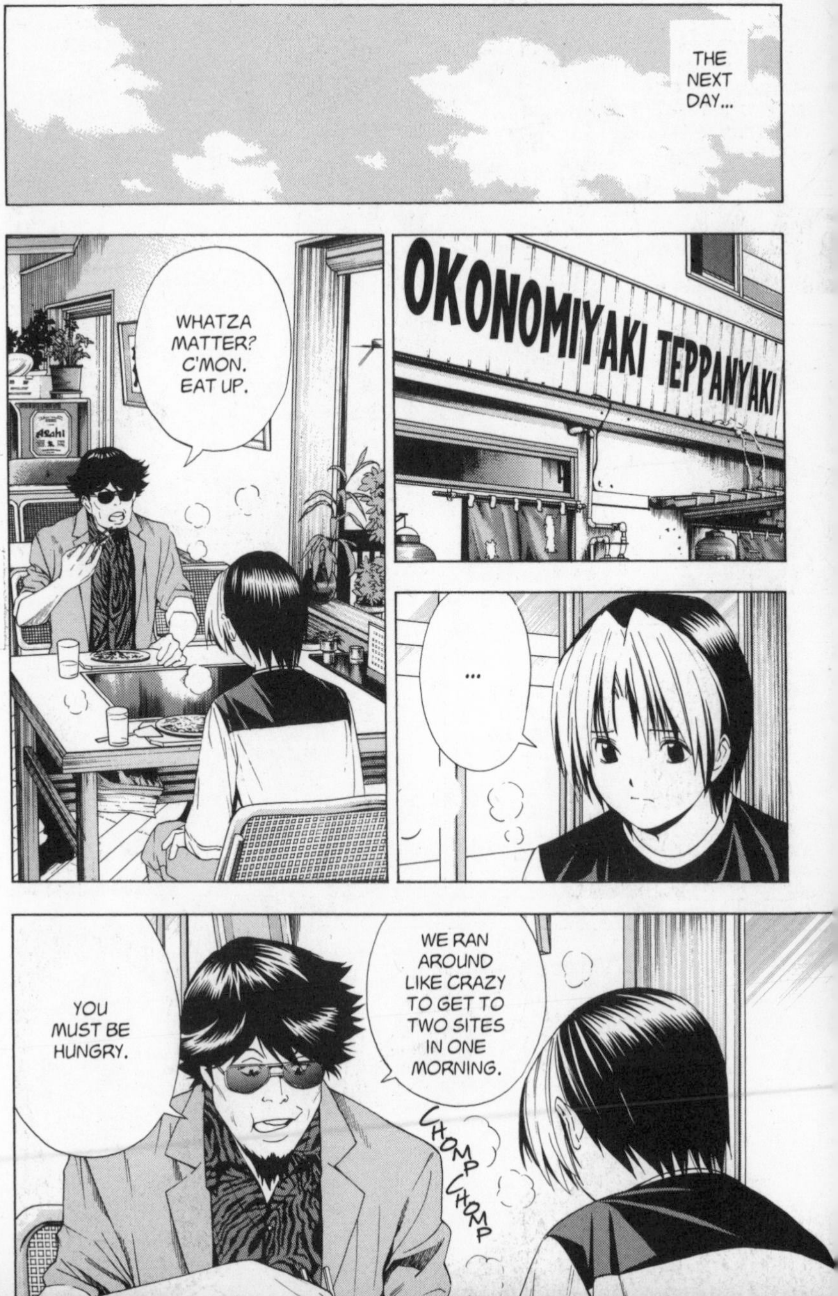
THE NEXT DAY...
OKONOMIYAKI TEPPANYAKI
...
WHATZA MATTER? C'MON. EAT UP.
WE RAN AROUND LIKE CRAZY TO GET TO TWO SITES IN ONE MORNING.
YOU MUST BE HUNGRY.
CHOMP CHOMP

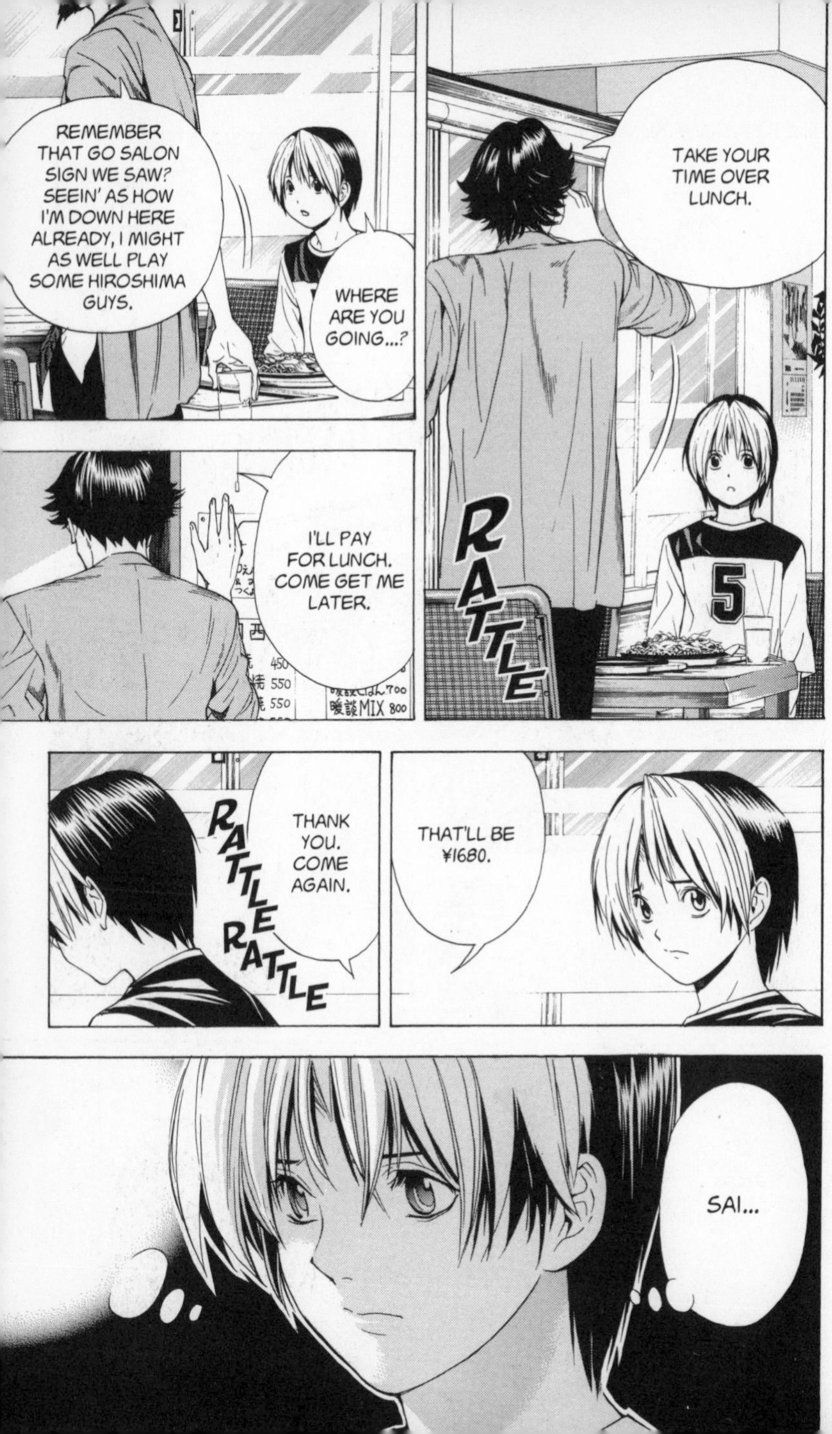
TAKE YOUR TIME OVER LUNCH.
RATTLE
WHERE ARE YOU GOING...?
REMEMBER THAT GO SALON SIGN WE SAW? SEEIN' AS HOW I'M DOWN HERE ALREADY, I MIGHT AS WELL PLAY SOME HIROSHIMA GUYS.
I'LL PAY FOR LUNCH. COME GET ME LATER.
THAT'LL BE ¥1680.
THANK YOU. COME AGAIN.
RATTLE RATTLE
SAI...

*Hon'inbo Shusaku Memorial

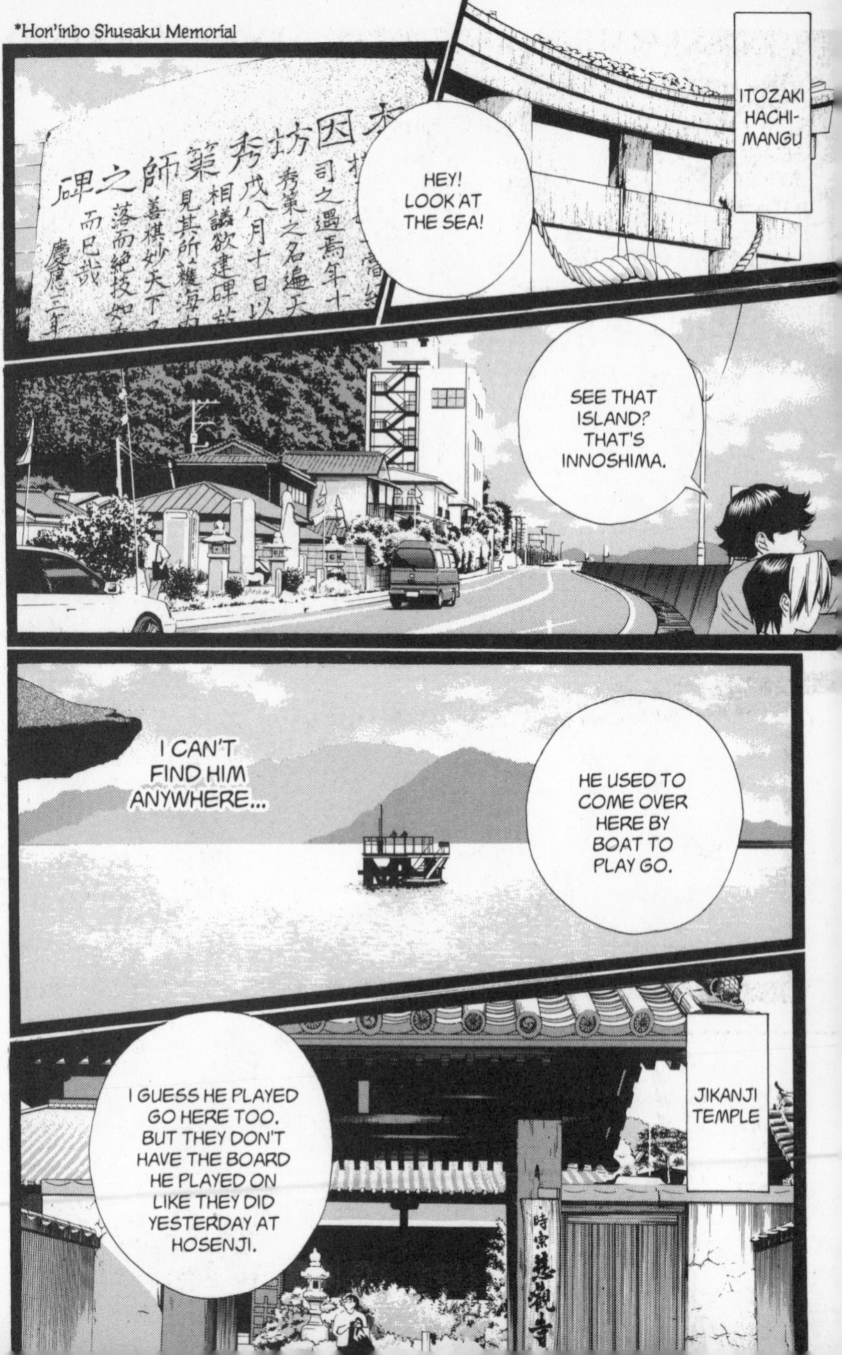
ITOZAKI HACHIMANGU
HEY! LOOK AT THE SEA!
本因坊秀策師之碑
SEE THAT ISLAND? THAT'S INNOSHIMA.
HE USED TO COME OVER HERE BY BOAT TO PLAY GO.
I CAN'T FIND HIM ANYWHERE...
JIKANJI TEMPLE
I GUESS HE PLAYED GO HERE TOO. BUT THEY DON'T HAVE THE BOARD HE PLAYED ON LIKE THEY DID YESTERDAY AT HOSENJI.
時宗 慈観寺

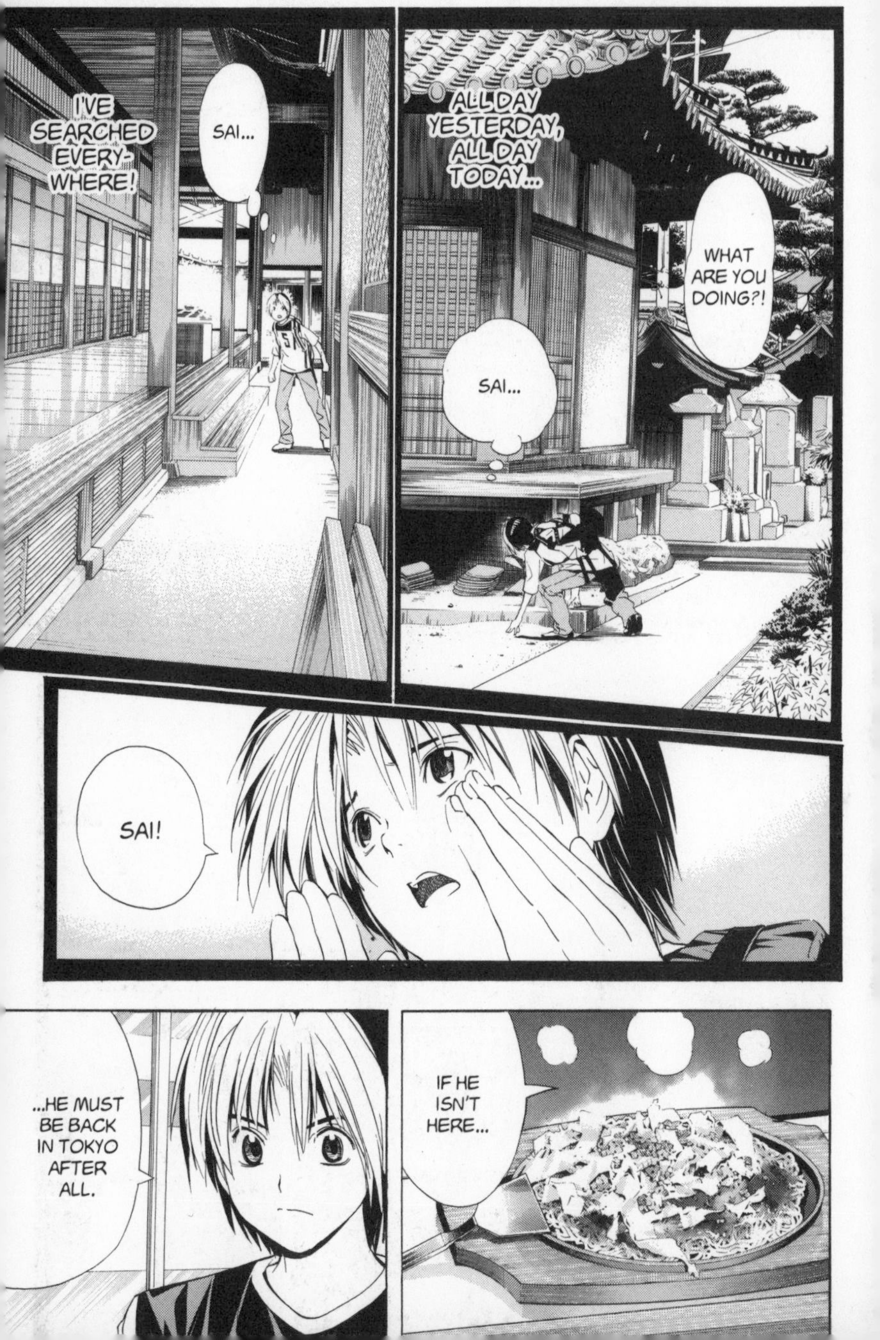
ALL DAY YESTERDAY, ALL DAY TODAY...
WHAT ARE YOU DOING?!
SAI...
SAI...
I'VE SEARCHED EVERY-WHERE!
SAI!
IF HE ISN'T HERE...
...HE MUST BE BACK IN TOKYO AFTER ALL.

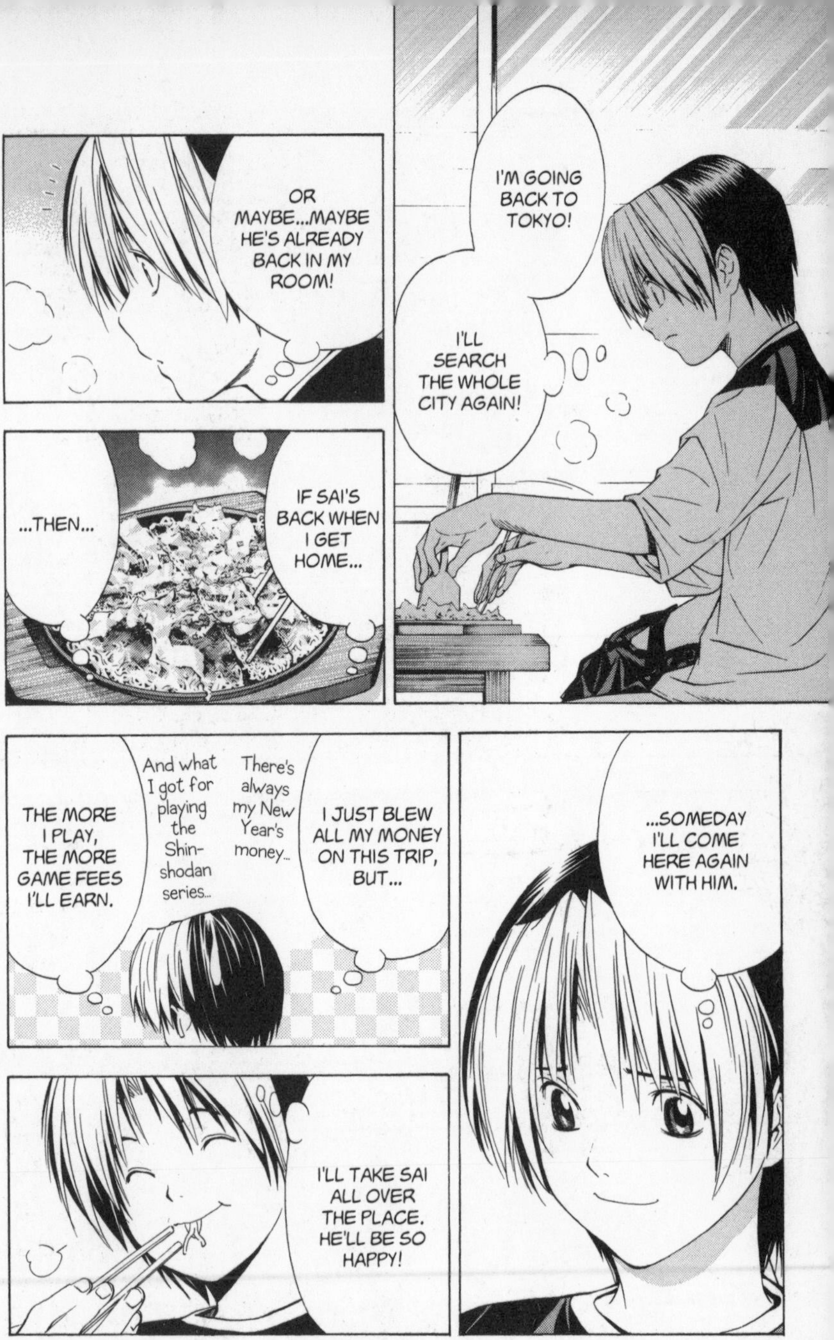

I'M GOING BACK TO TOKYO!
I'LL SEARCH THE WHOLE CITY AGAIN!
OR MAYBE...MAYBE HE'S ALREADY BACK IN MY ROOM!
IF SAI'S BACK WHEN I GET HOME...
...THEN...
...SOMEDAY I'LL COME HERE AGAIN WITH HIM.
I JUST BLEW ALL MY MONEY ON THIS TRIP, BUT...
There's always my New Year's money...
And what I got for playing the Shin-shodan series...
THE MORE I PLAY, THE MORE GAME FEES I'LL EARN.
I'LL TAKE SAI ALL OVER THE PLACE. HE'LL BE SO HAPPY!

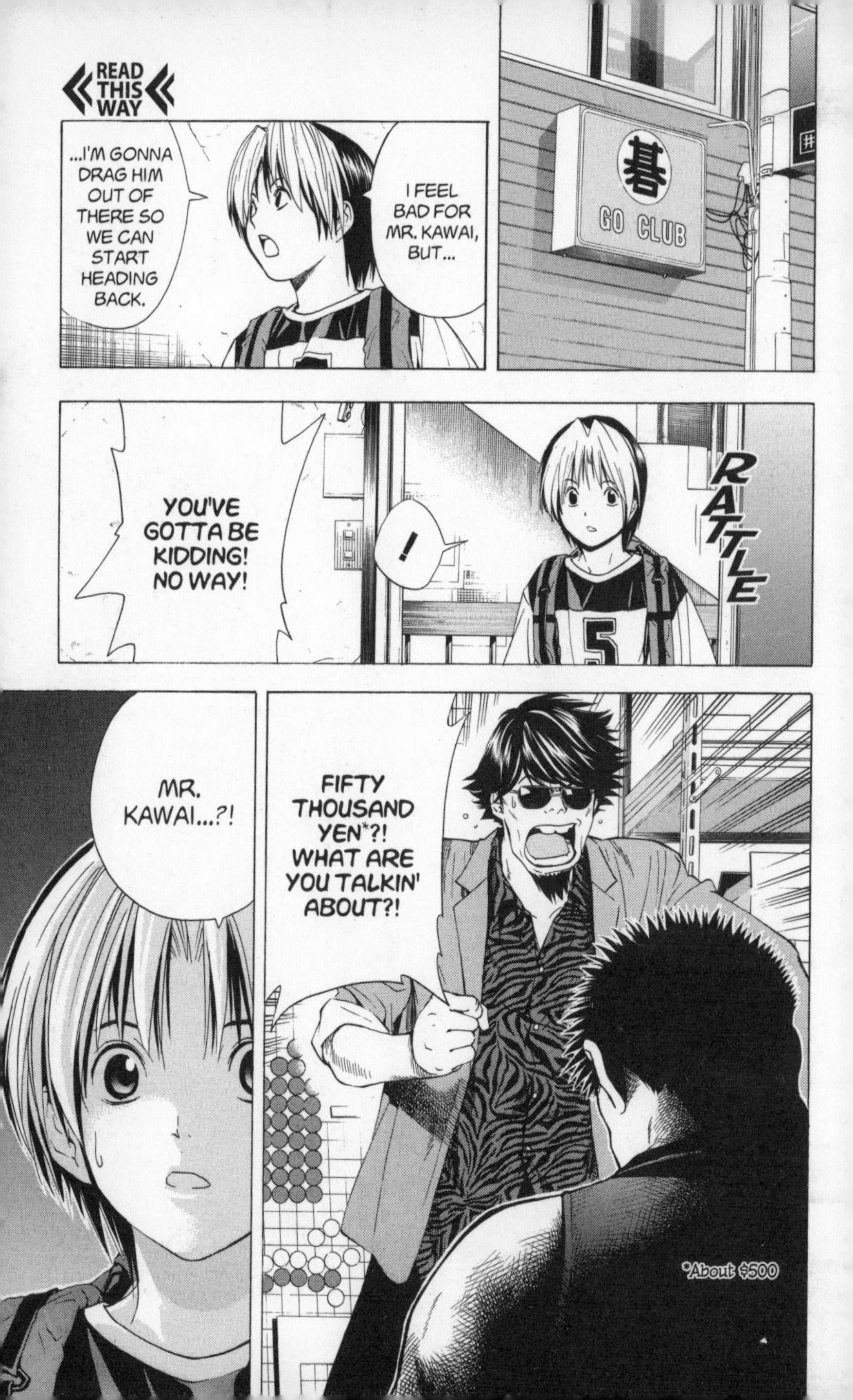
READ THIS WAY
碁
GO CLUB
I FEEL BAD FOR MR. KAWAI, BUT...
...I'M GONNA DRAG HIM OUT OF THERE SO WE CAN START HEADING BACK.
RATTLE
!
YOU'VE GOTTA BE KIDDING! NO WAY!
FIFTY THOUSAND YEN*?! WHAT ARE YOU TALKIN' ABOUT?!
*About $500
MR. KAWAI...?!

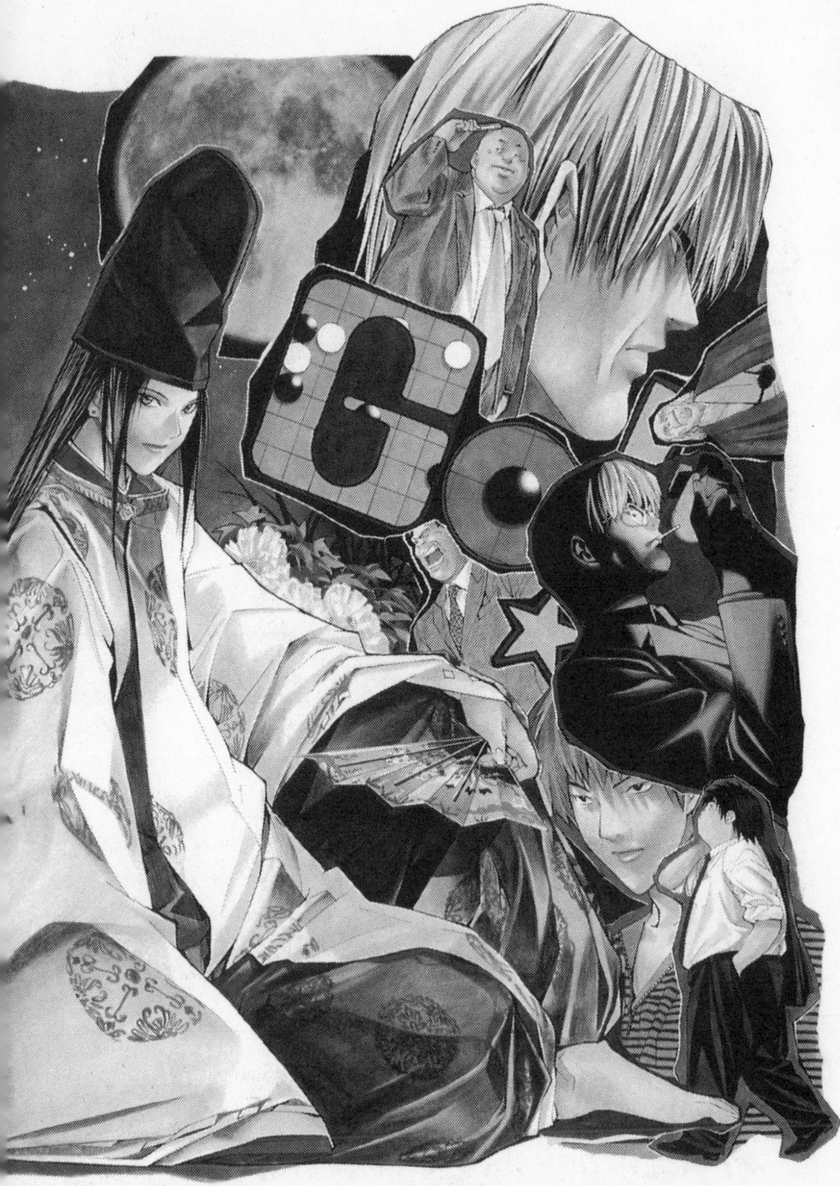

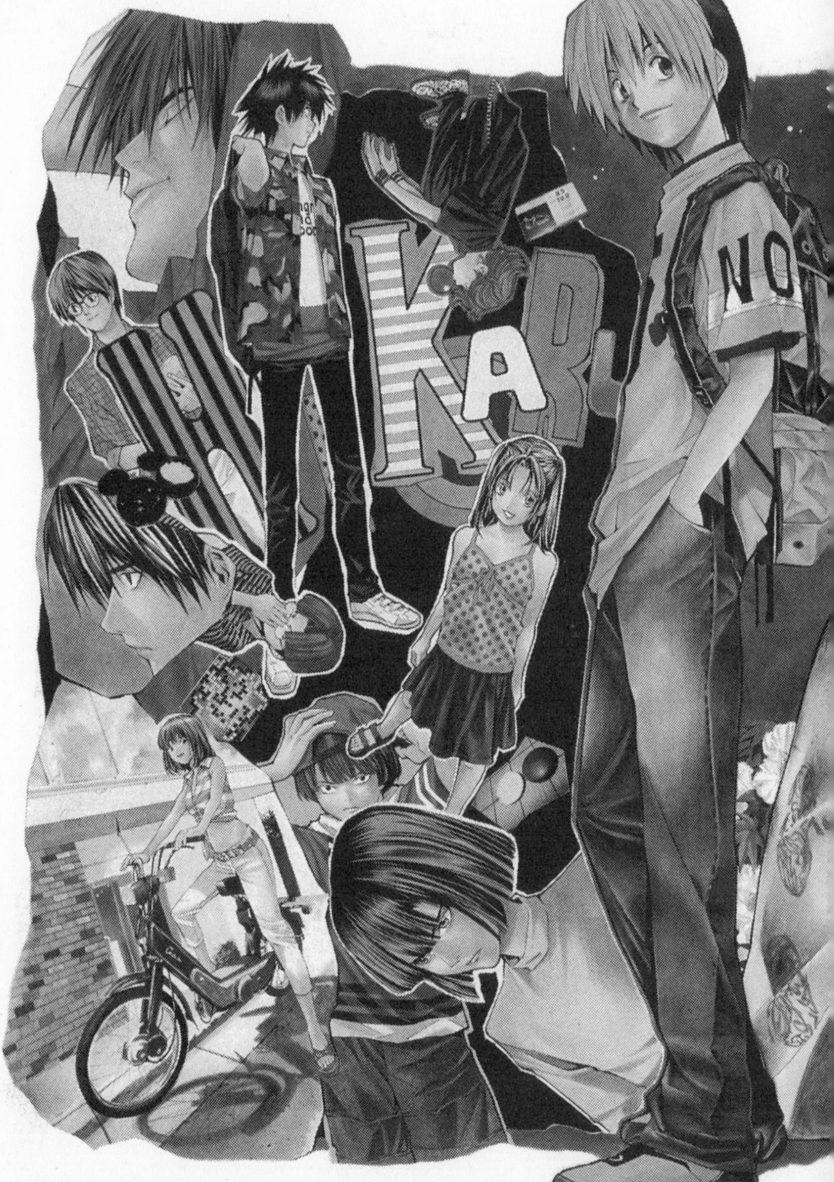
NO

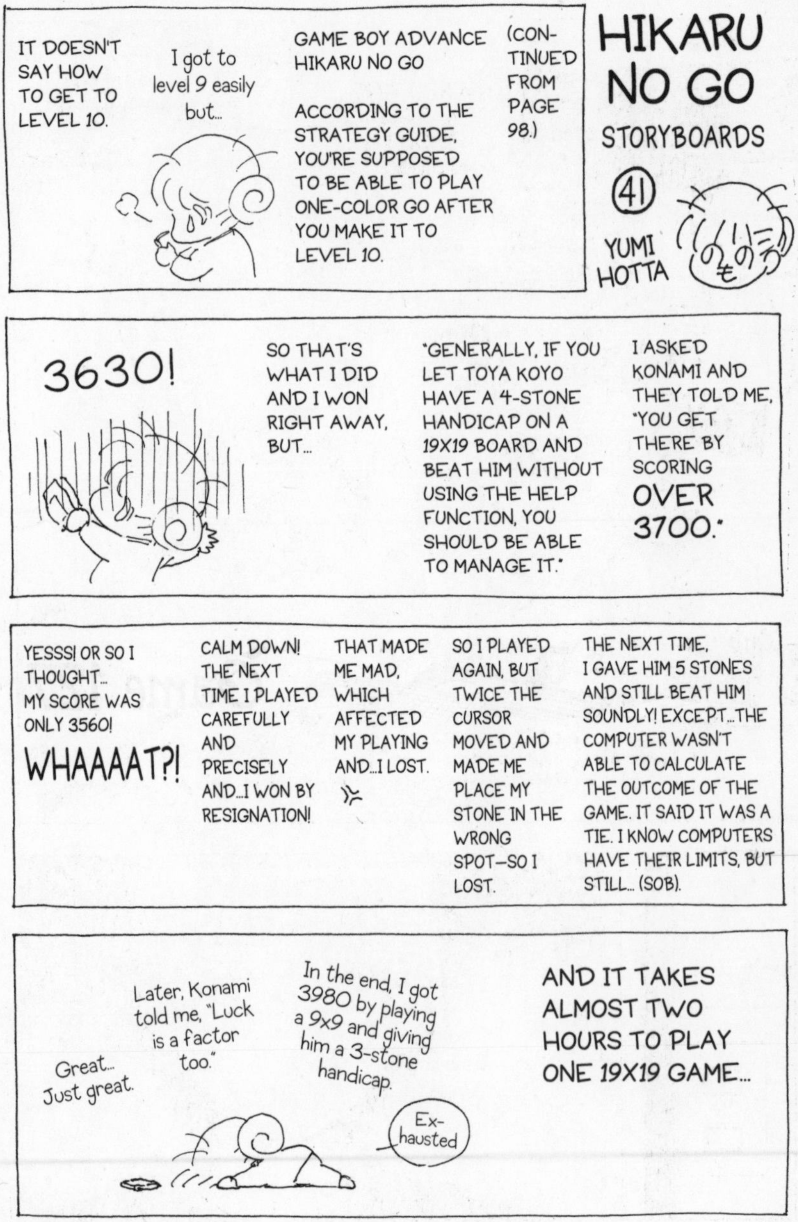
HIKARU NO GO
STORYBOARDS
41
YUMI HOTTA
(CONTINUED FROM PAGE 98.)
GAME BOY ADVANCE HIKARU NO GO
ACCORDING TO THE STRATEGY GUIDE, YOU'RE SUPPOSED TO BE ABLE TO PLAY ONE-COLOR GO AFTER YOU MAKE IT TO LEVEL 10.
I got to level 9 easily but...
IT DOESN'T SAY HOW TO GET TO LEVEL 10.
I ASKED KONAMI AND THEY TOLD ME, "YOU GET THERE BY SCORING OVER 3700."
"GENERALLY, IF YOU LET TOYA KOYO HAVE A 4-STONE HANDICAP ON A 19X19 BOARD AND BEAT HIM WITHOUT USING THE HELP FUNCTION, YOU SHOULD BE ABLE TO MANAGE IT."
SO THAT'S WHAT I DID AND I WON RIGHT AWAY, BUT...
3630!
THE NEXT TIME, I GAVE HIM 5 STONES AND STILL BEAT HIM SOUNDLY! EXCEPT...THE COMPUTER WASN'T ABLE TO CALCULATE THE OUTCOME OF THE GAME. IT SAID IT WAS A TIE. I KNOW COMPUTERS HAVE THEIR LIMITS, BUT STILL... (SOB).
SO I PLAYED AGAIN, BUT TWICE THE CURSOR MOVED AND MADE ME PLACE MY STONE IN THE WRONG SPOT—SO I LOST.
THAT MADE ME MAD, WHICH AFFECTED MY PLAYING AND...I LOST.
CALM DOWN! THE NEXT TIME I PLAYED CAREFULLY AND PRECISELY AND...I WON BY RESIGNATION!
YESSS! OR SO I THOUGHT... MY SCORE WAS ONLY 3560!
WHAAAAT?!
AND IT TAKES ALMOST TWO HOURS TO PLAY ONE 19X19 GAME...
In the end, I got 3980 by playing a 9x9 and giving him a 3-stone handicap.
Exhausted
Later, Konami told me, "Luck is a factor too."
Great... Just great.

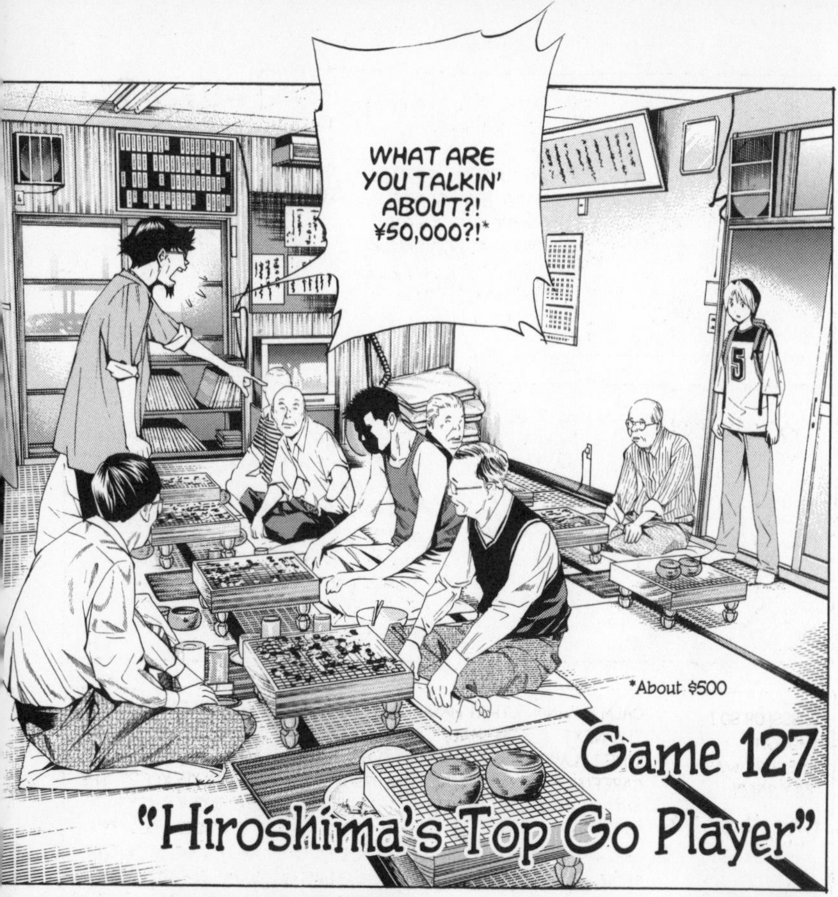
WHAT ARE YOU TALKIN' ABOUT?! ¥50,000?!*
*About $500
Game 127
"Hiroshima's Top Go Player"
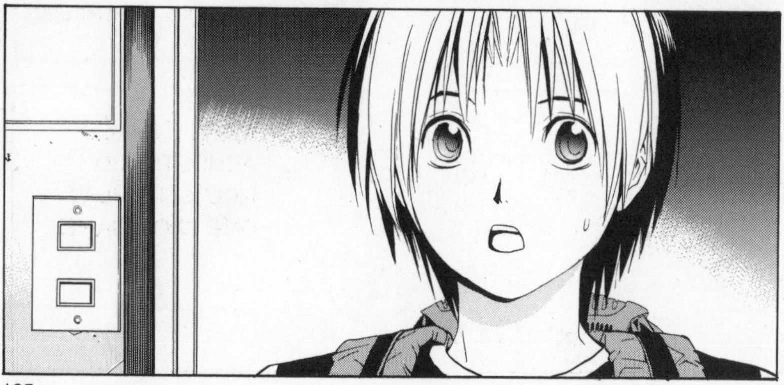

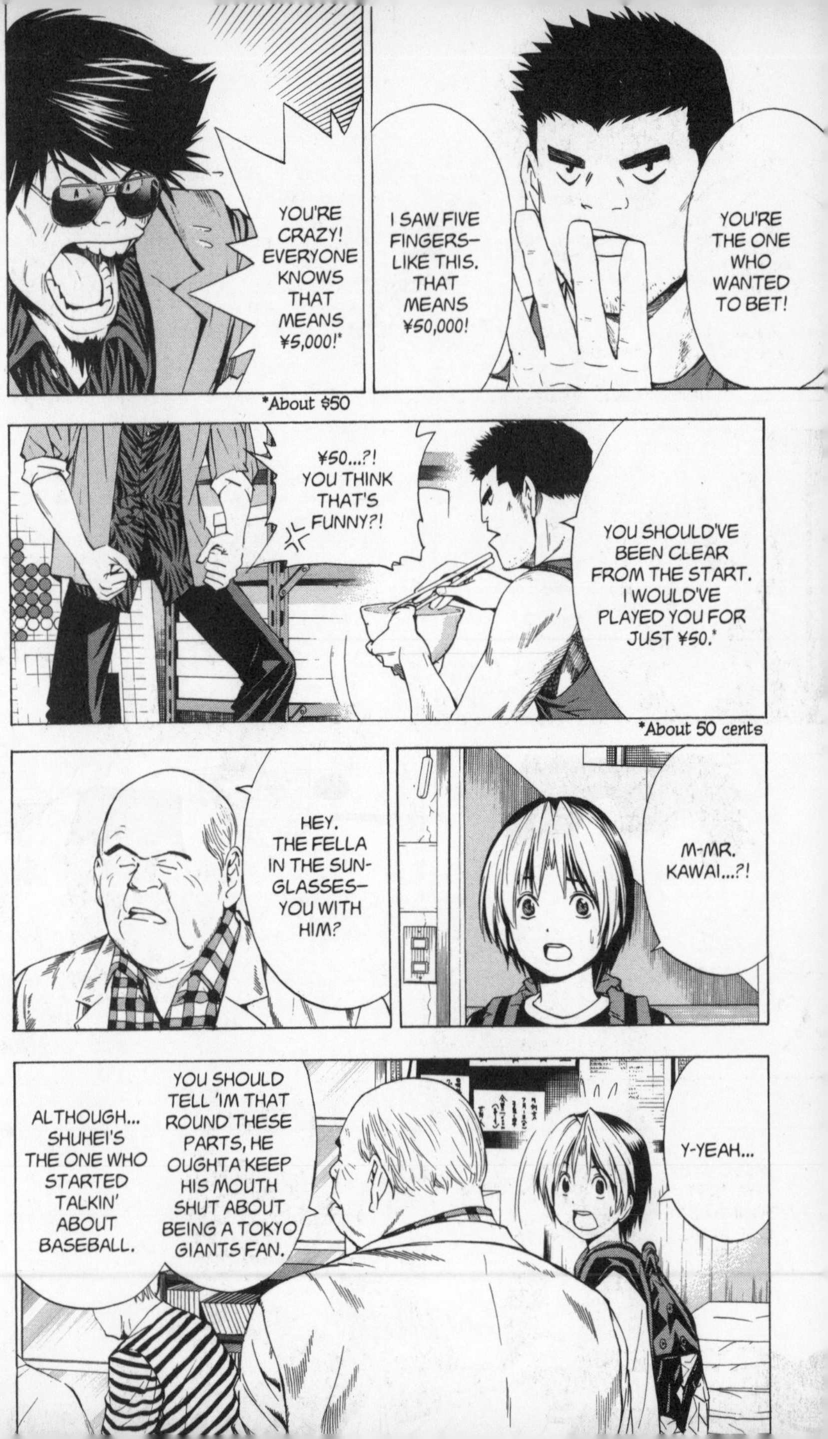
YOU'RE THE ONE WHO WANTED TO BET!
I SAW FIVE FINGERS— LIKE THIS. THAT MEANS ¥50,000!
YOU'RE CRAZY! EVERYONE KNOWS THAT MEANS ¥5,000!*
*About $50
YOU SHOULD'VE BEEN CLEAR FROM THE START. I WOULD'VE PLAYED YOU FOR JUST ¥50.*
¥50...?! YOU THINK THAT'S FUNNY?!
*About 50 cents
M-MR. KAWAI...?!
HEY. THE FELLA IN THE SUN-GLASSES— YOU WITH HIM?
Y-YEAH...
YOU SHOULD TELL 'IM THAT ROUND THESE PARTS, HE OUGHTA KEEP HIS MOUTH SHUT ABOUT BEING A TOKYO GIANTS FAN.
ALTHOUGH... SHUHEI'S THE ONE WHO STARTED TALKIN' ABOUT BASEBALL.

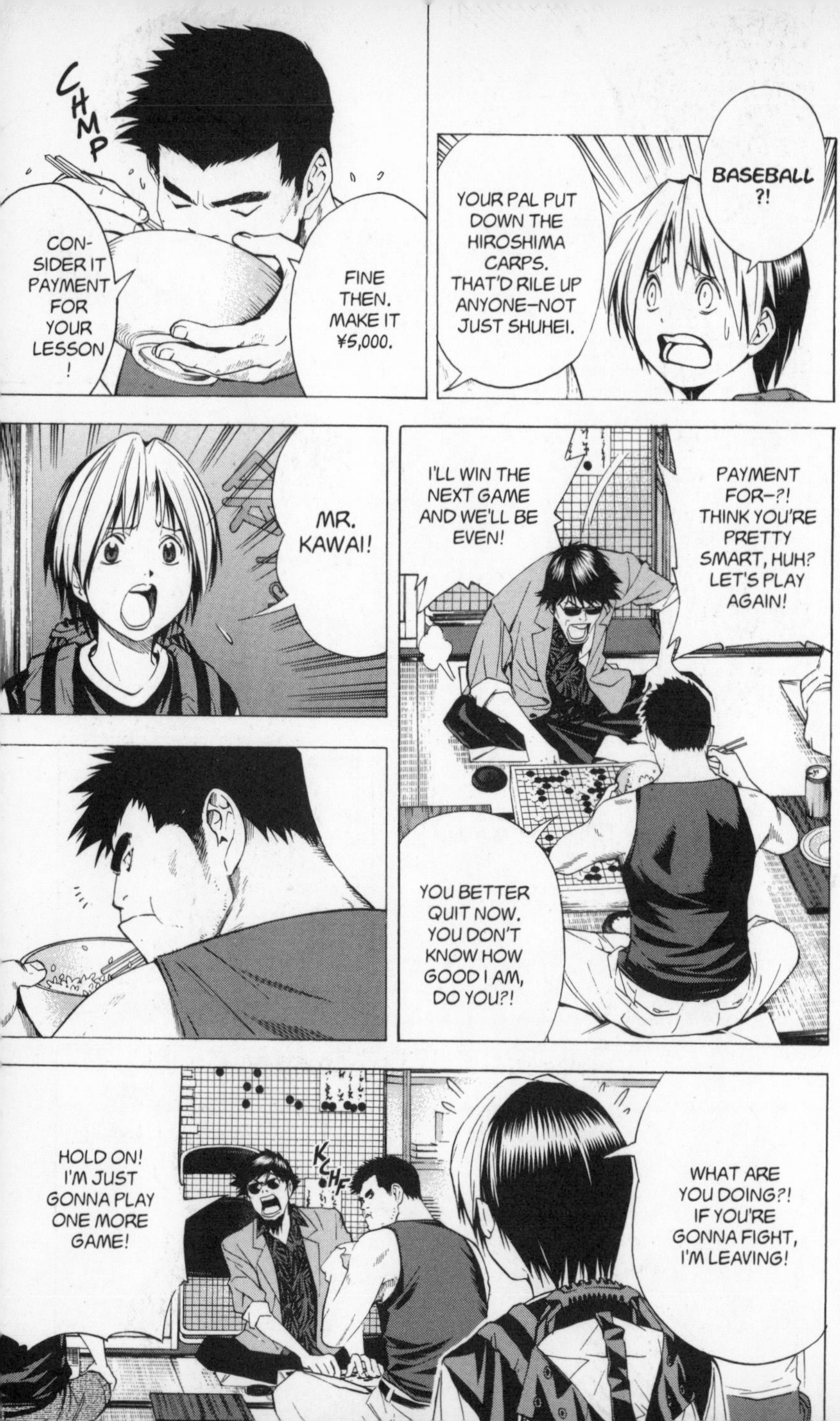
BASEBALL ?!
YOUR PAL PUT DOWN THE HIROSHIMA CARPS. THAT'D RILE UP ANYONE—NOT JUST SHUHEI.
FINE THEN. MAKE IT ¥5,000.
CHMP
CON-SIDER IT PAYMENT FOR YOUR LESSON !
PAYMENT FOR—?! THINK YOU'RE PRETTY SMART, HUH? LET'S PLAY AGAIN!
I'LL WIN THE NEXT GAME AND WE'LL BE EVEN!
YOU BETTER QUIT NOW. YOU DON'T KNOW HOW GOOD I AM, DO YOU?!
MR. KAWAI!
WHAT ARE YOU DOING?! IF YOU'RE GONNA FIGHT, I'M LEAVING!
KCHF
HOLD ON! I'M JUST GONNA PLAY ONE MORE GAME!

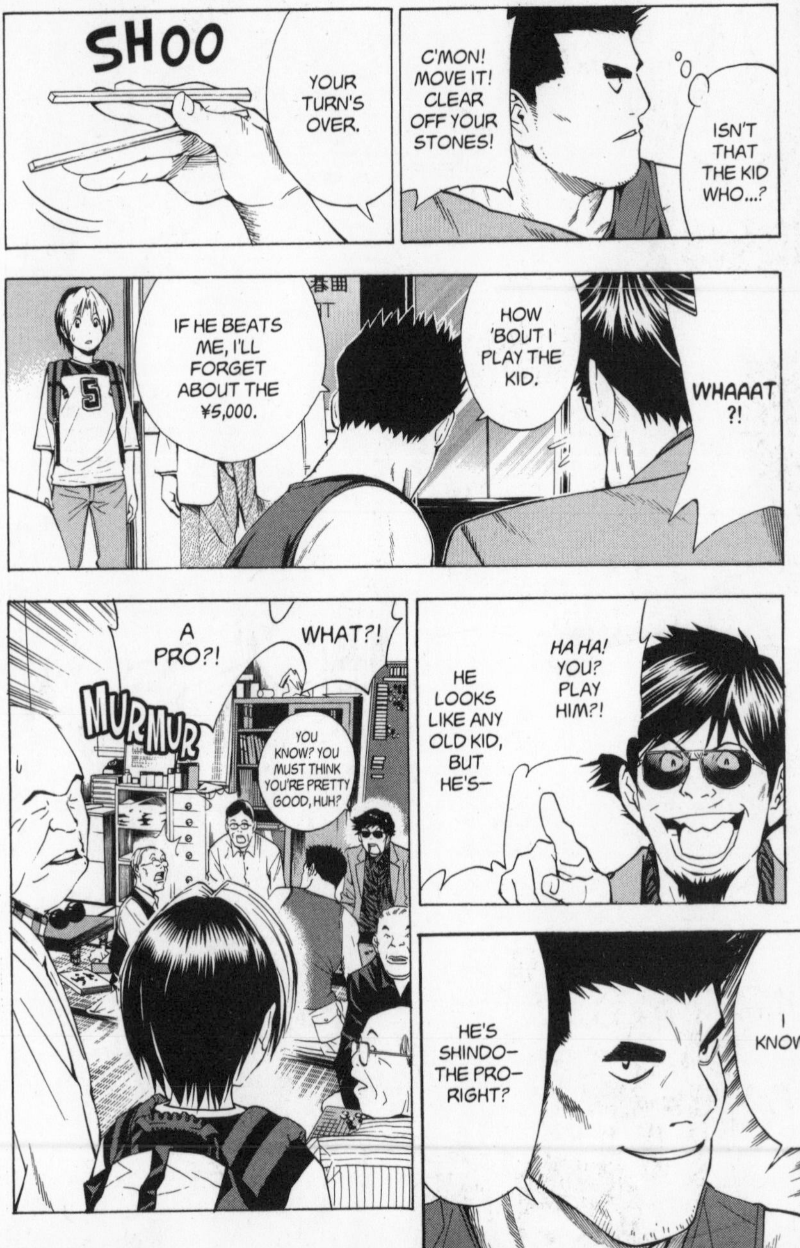
ISN'T THAT THE KID WHO...?
C'MON! MOVE IT! CLEAR OFF YOUR STONES!
YOUR TURN'S OVER.
SHOO
WHAAAT?!
HOW 'BOUT I PLAY THE KID.
IF HE BEATS ME, I'LL FORGET ABOUT THE ¥5,000.
HA HA! YOU? PLAY HIM?!
HE LOOKS LIKE ANY OLD KID, BUT HE'S—
I KNOW.
HE'S SHINDO—THE PRO—RIGHT?
WHAT?!
A PRO?!
MURMUR
YOU KNOW? YOU MUST THINK YOU'RE PRETTY GOOD, HUH?

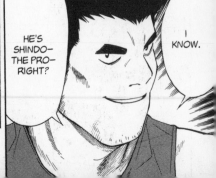

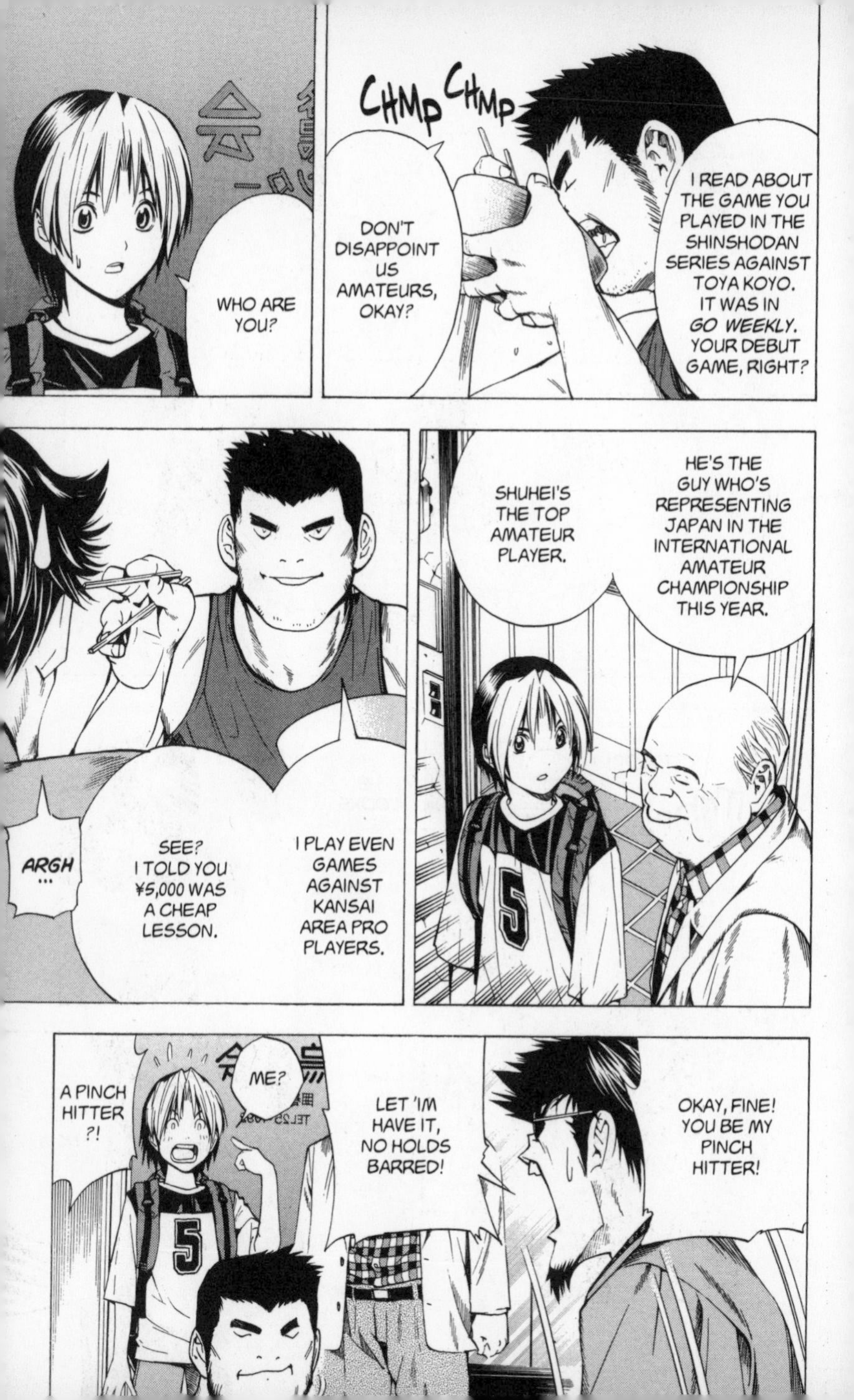
CHMP CHMP
I READ ABOUT THE GAME YOU PLAYED IN THE SHINSHODAN SERIES AGAINST TOYA KOYO. IT WAS IN *GO WEEKLY*. YOUR DEBUT GAME, RIGHT?
DON'T DISAPPOINT US AMATEURS, OKAY?
WHO ARE YOU?
SHUHEI'S THE TOP AMATEUR PLAYER.
HE'S THE GUY WHO'S REPRESENTING JAPAN IN THE INTERNATIONAL AMATEUR CHAMPIONSHIP THIS YEAR.
I PLAY EVEN GAMES AGAINST KANSAI AREA PRO PLAYERS.
SEE? I TOLD YOU ¥5,000 WAS A CHEAP LESSON.
ARGH...
OKAY, FINE! YOU BE MY PINCH HITTER!
LET 'IM HAVE IT, NO HOLDS BARRED!
ME?
A PINCH HITTER ?!

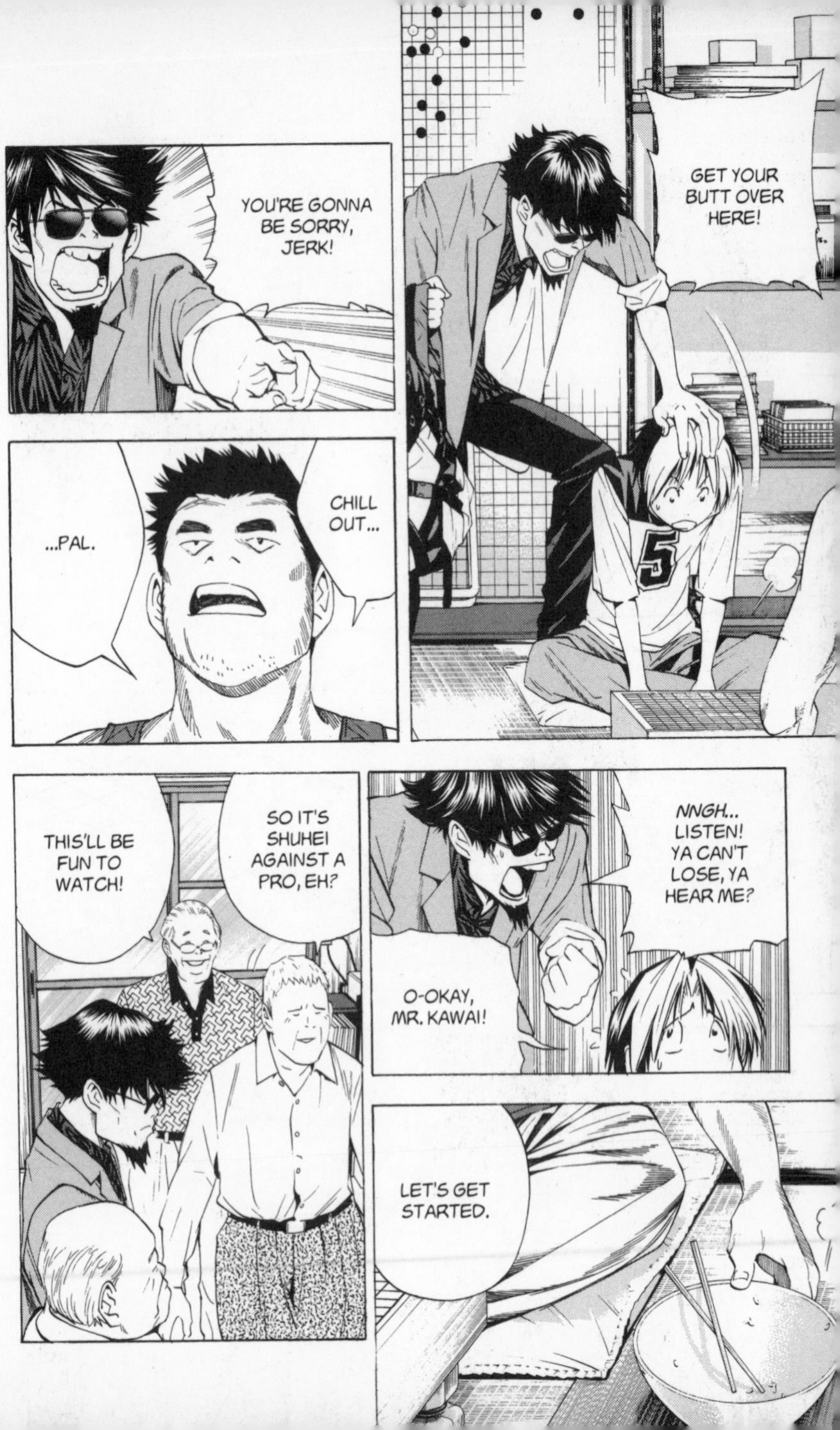
GET YOUR BUTT OVER HERE!
YOU'RE GONNA BE SORRY, JERK!
CHILL OUT...
...PAL.
NNGH... LISTEN! YA CAN'T LOSE, YA HEAR ME?
O-OKAY, MR. KAWAI!
LET'S GET STARTED.
SO IT'S SHUHEI AGAINST A PRO, EH?
THIS'LL BE FUN TO WATCH!

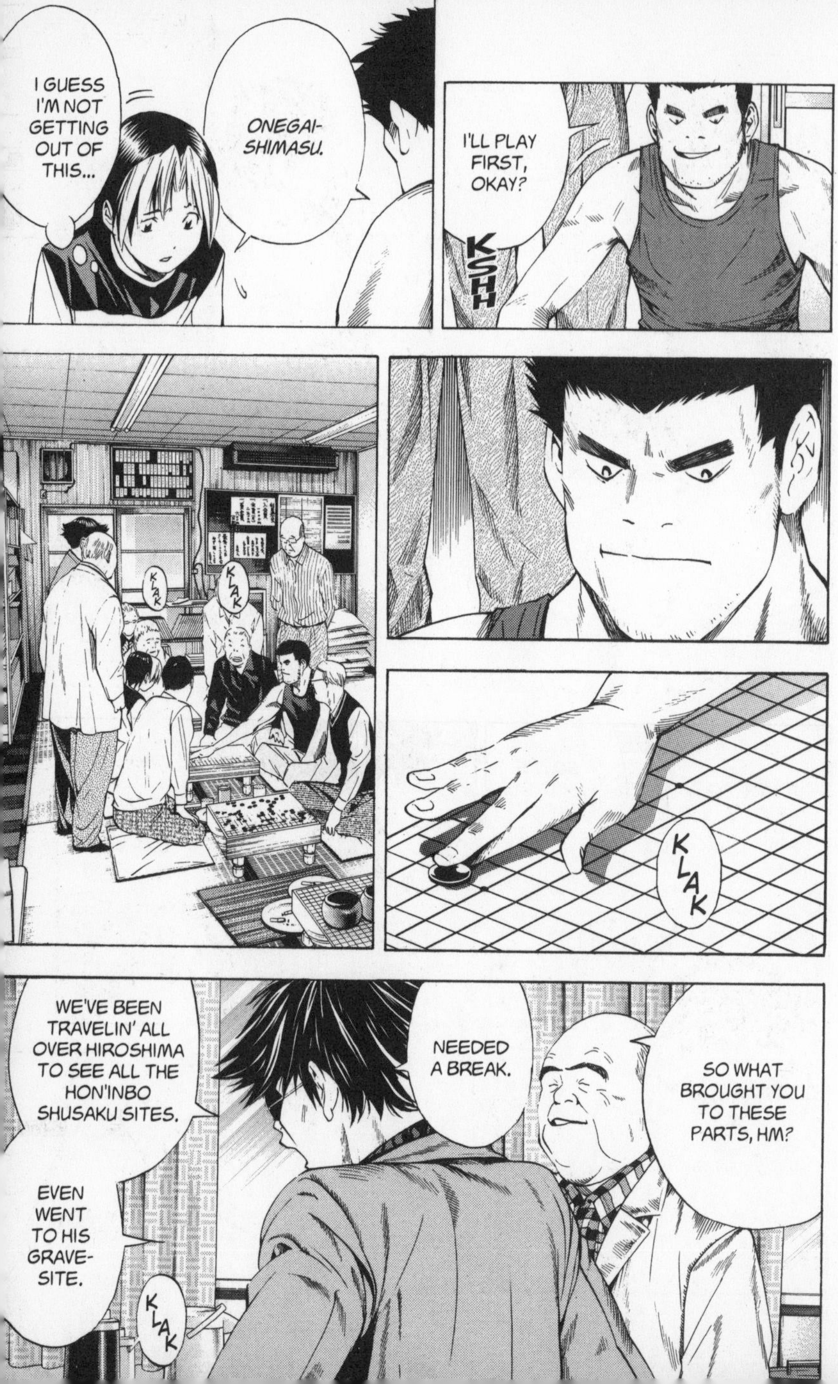
I'LL PLAY FIRST, OKAY?
KSHH
ONEGAI-SHIMASU.
I GUESS I'M NOT GETTING OUT OF THIS...
KLAK
KLAK
KLAK
SO WHAT BROUGHT YOU TO THESE PARTS, HM?
NEEDED A BREAK.
WE'VE BEEN TRAVELIN' ALL OVER HIROSHIMA TO SEE ALL THE HON'INBO SHUSAKU SITES.
EVEN WENT TO HIS GRAVE-SITE.
KLAK

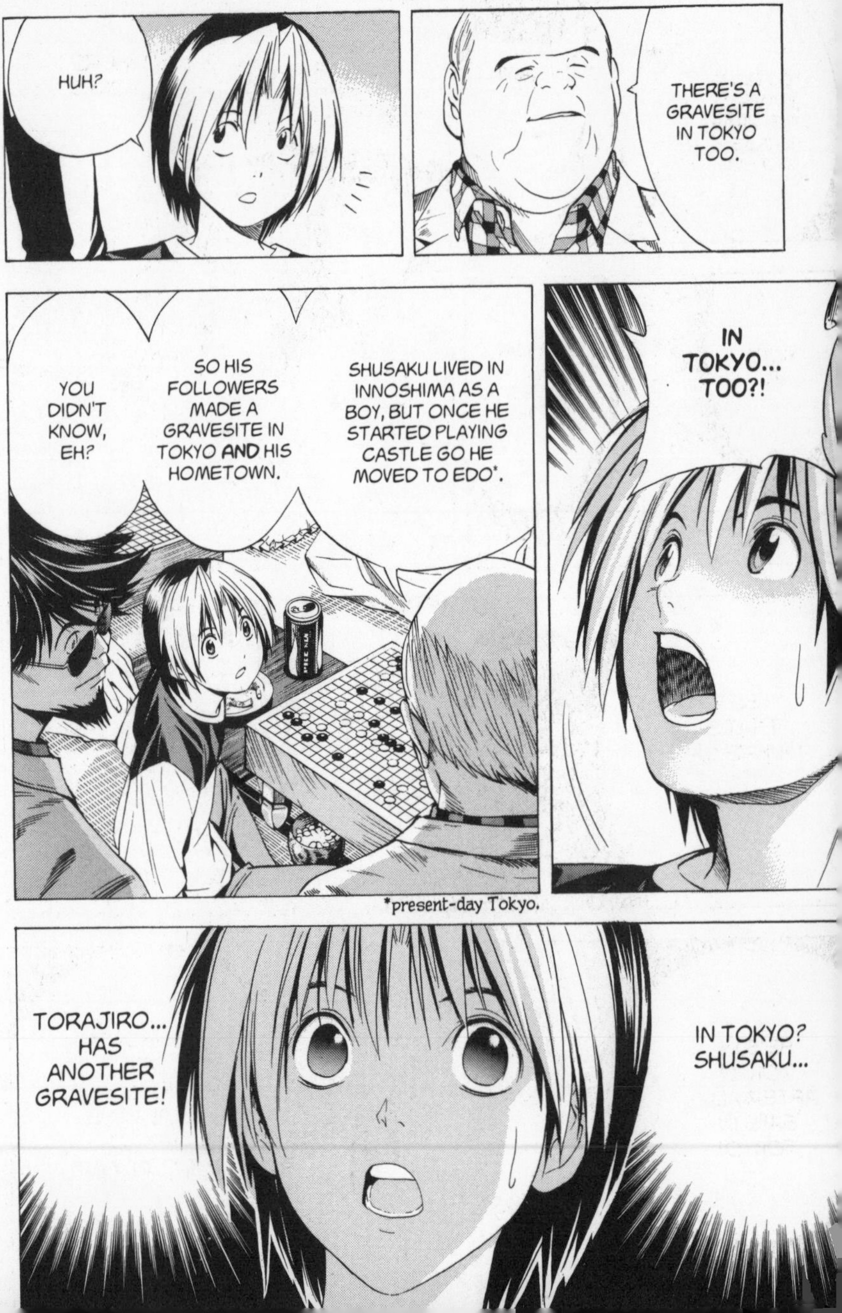
THERE'S A GRAVESITE IN TOKYO TOO.
HUH?
IN TOKYO... TOO?!
SHUSAKU LIVED IN INNOSHIMA AS A BOY, BUT ONCE HE STARTED PLAYING CASTLE GO HE MOVED TO EDO*.
SO HIS FOLLOWERS MADE A GRAVESITE IN TOKYO **AND** HIS HOMETOWN.
YOU DIDN'T KNOW, EH?
IN TOKYO? SHUSAKU...
TORAJIRO... HAS ANOTHER GRAVESITE!

*present-day Tokyo.

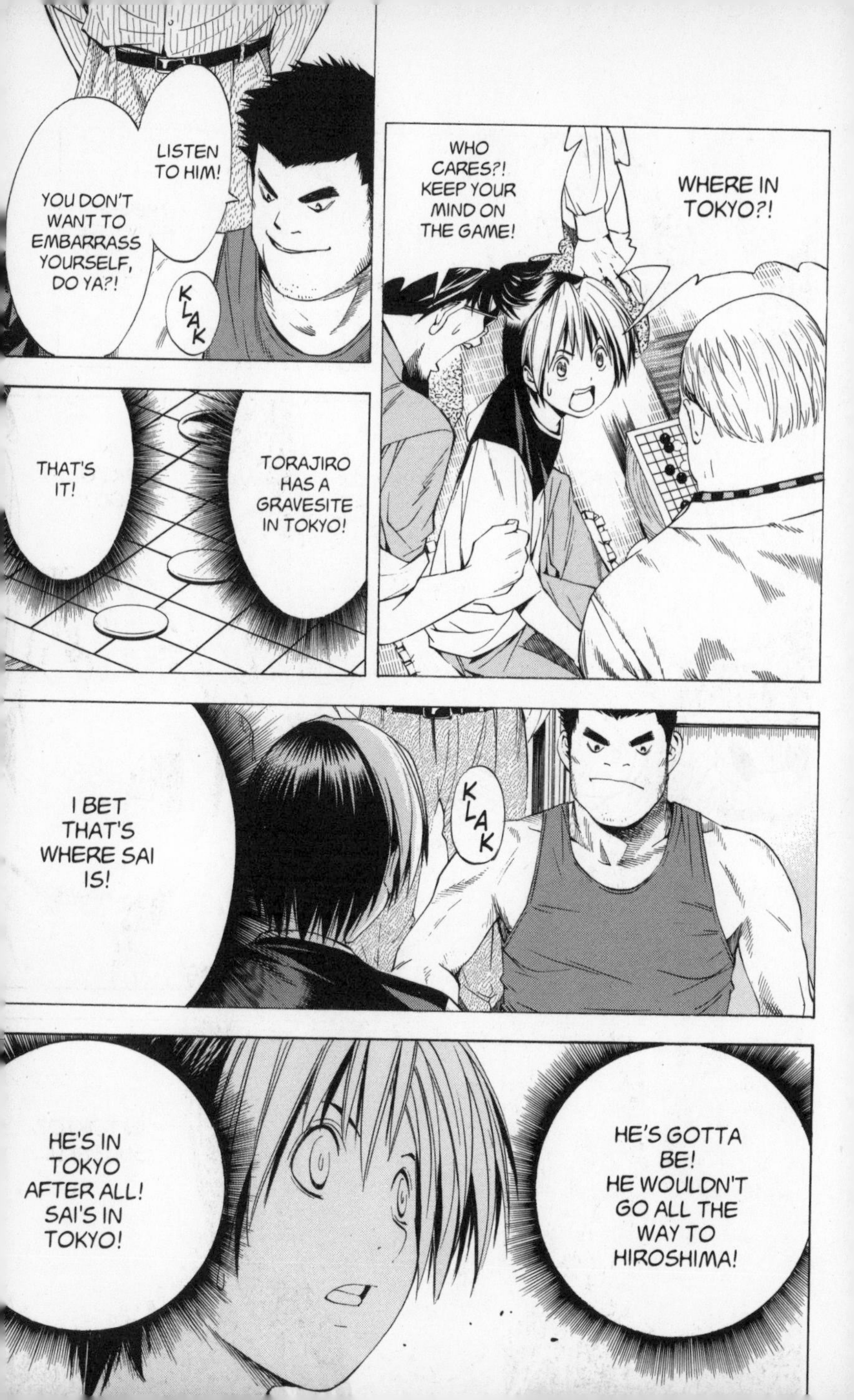
WHERE IN TOKYO?!
WHO CARES?! KEEP YOUR MIND ON THE GAME!
LISTEN TO HIM!
YOU DON'T WANT TO EMBARRASS YOURSELF, DO YA?!
KLAK
TORAJIRO HAS A GRAVESITE IN TOKYO!
THAT'S IT!
KLAK
I BET THAT'S WHERE SAI IS!
HE'S GOTTA BE! HE WOULDN'T GO ALL THE WAY TO HIROSHIMA!
HE'S IN TOKYO AFTER ALL! SAI'S IN TOKYO!

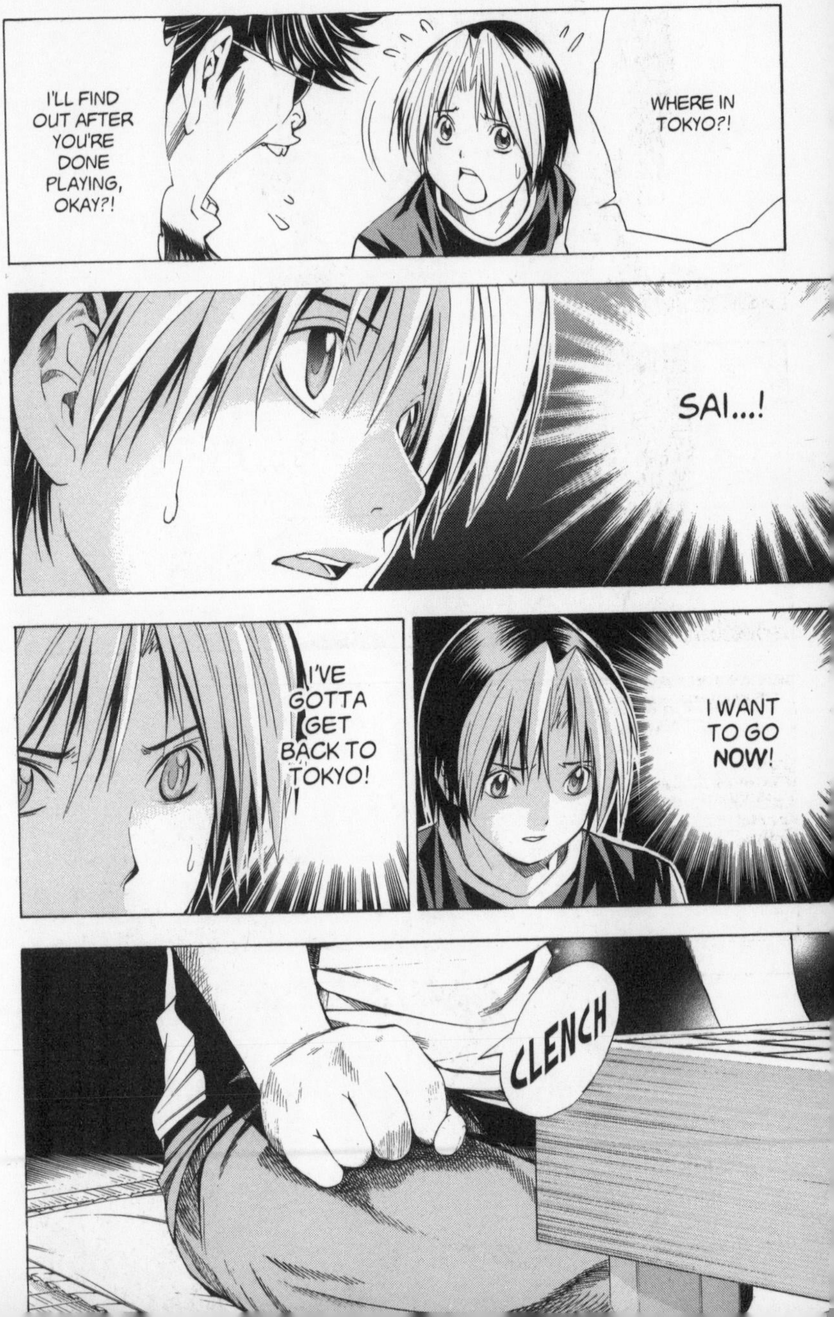
WHERE IN TOKYO?!
I'LL FIND OUT AFTER YOU'RE DONE PLAYING, OKAY?!
SAI...!
I WANT TO GO NOW!
I'VE GOTTA GET BACK TO TOKYO!
CLENCH

READ THIS WAY

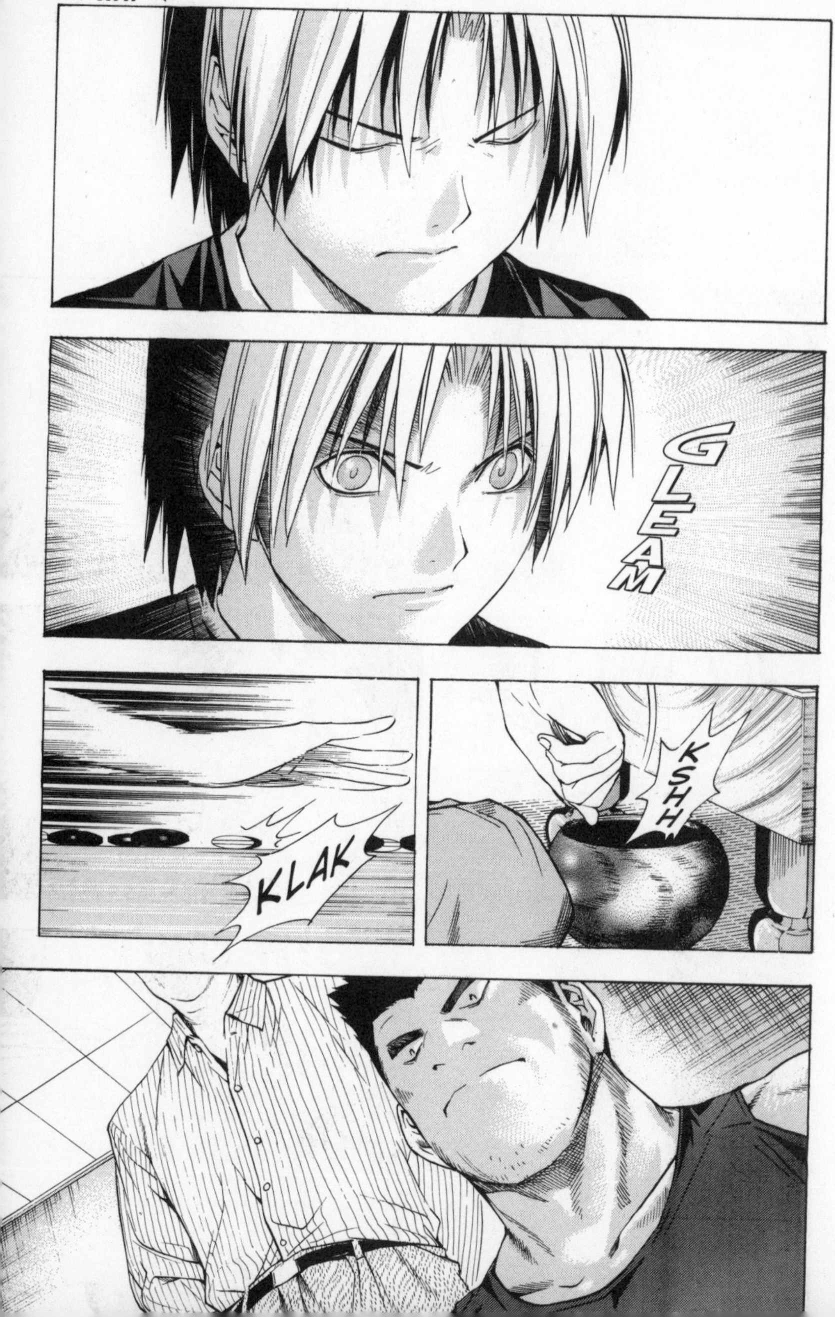
GLEAM
KSHH
KLAK

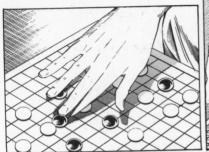

KLIK

KLAK

WHOA!

KLAK

...

OH! PLAYING SPEED GO?

KLIK

SHOULDN'T YOU PLAN YOUR MOVES MORE CAREFULLY...?

KLAK

READ THIS WAY

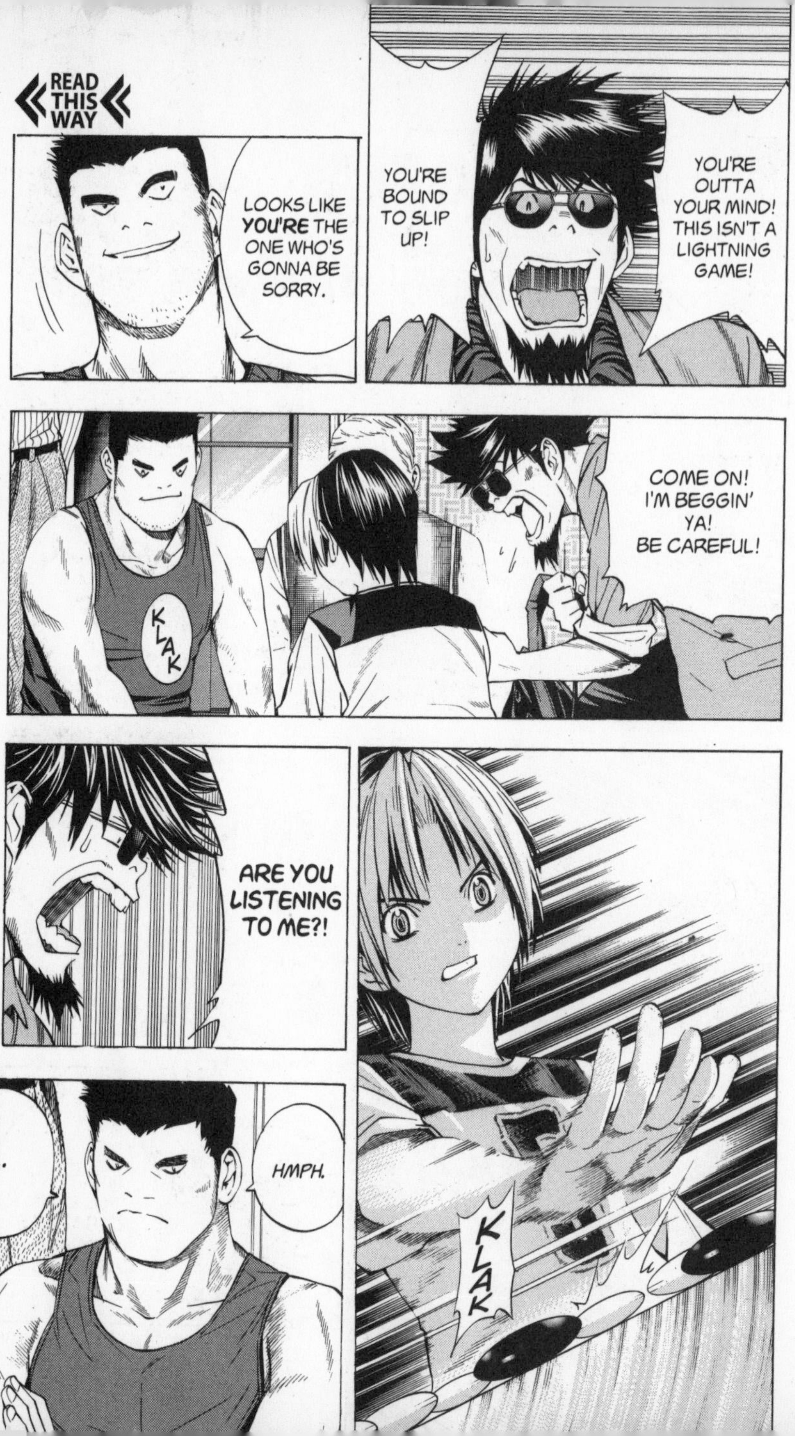
YOU'RE OUTTA YOUR MIND! THIS ISN'T A LIGHTNING GAME!
YOU'RE BOUND TO SLIP UP!
LOOKS LIKE YOU'RE THE ONE WHO'S GONNA BE SORRY.
COME ON! I'M BEGGIN' YA! BE CAREFUL!
KLAK
KLAK
ARE YOU LISTENING TO ME?!
HMPH.
...

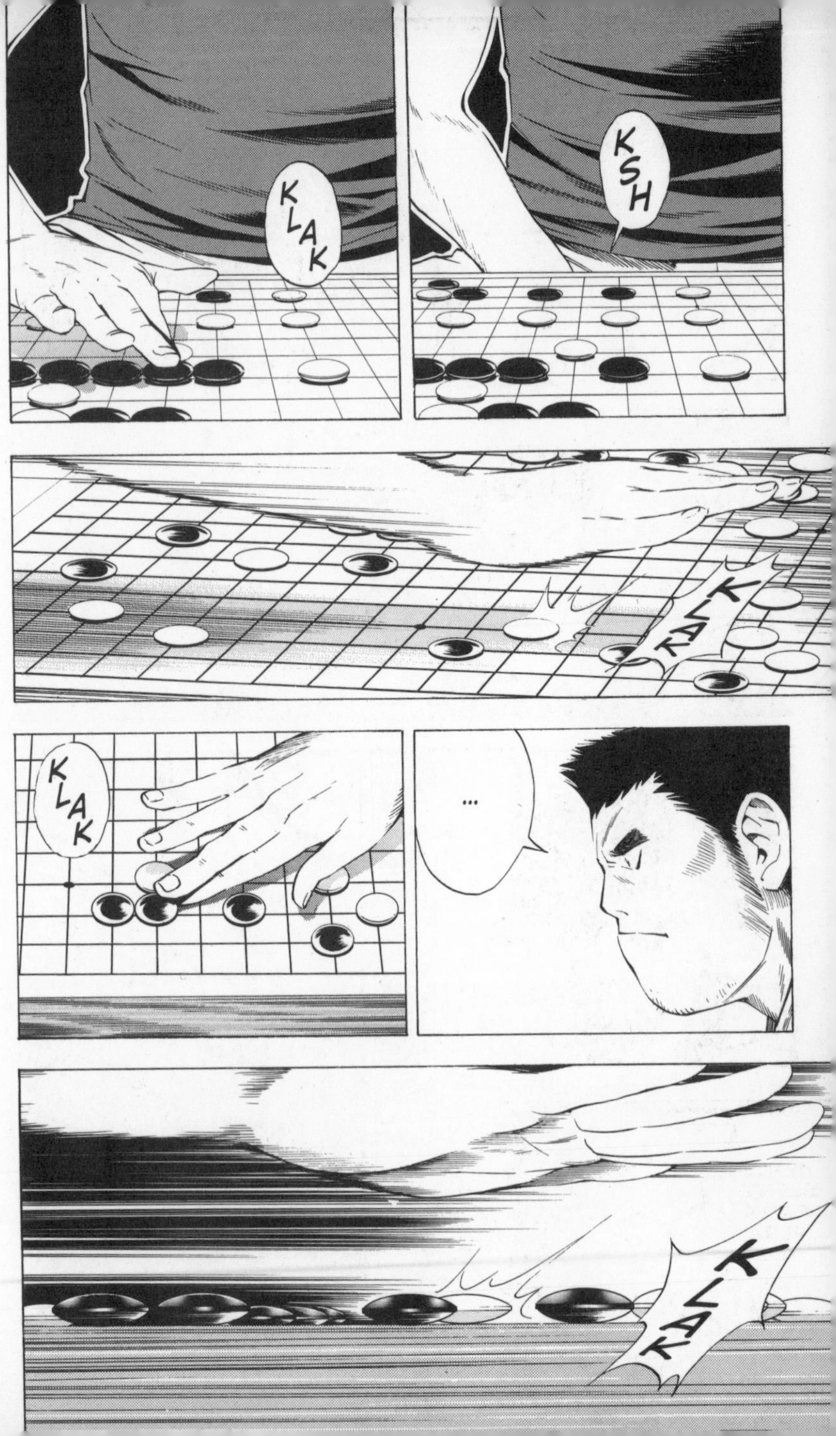
KSH
KLAK
KLAK
...
KLAK
KLAK

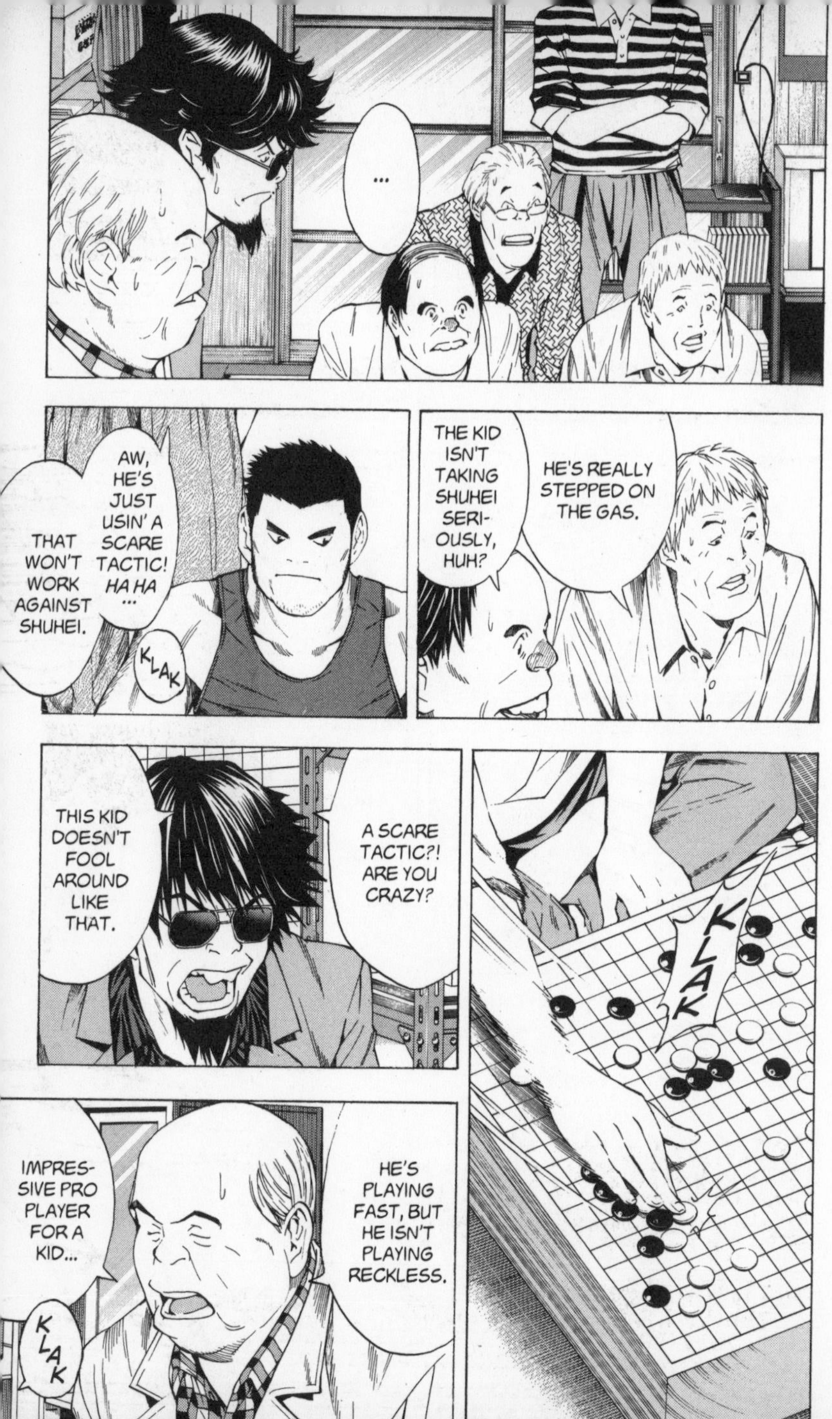
...
HE'S REALLY STEPPED ON THE GAS.
THE KID ISN'T TAKING SHUHEI SERIOUSLY, HUH?
AW, HE'S JUST USIN' A SCARE TACTIC! HA HA ...
THAT WON'T WORK AGAINST SHUHEI.
KLAK
KLAK
A SCARE TACTIC?! ARE YOU CRAZY?
THIS KID DOESN'T FOOL AROUND LIKE THAT.
HE'S PLAYING FAST, BUT HE ISN'T PLAYING RECKLESS.
IMPRESSIVE PRO PLAYER FOR A KID...
KLAK

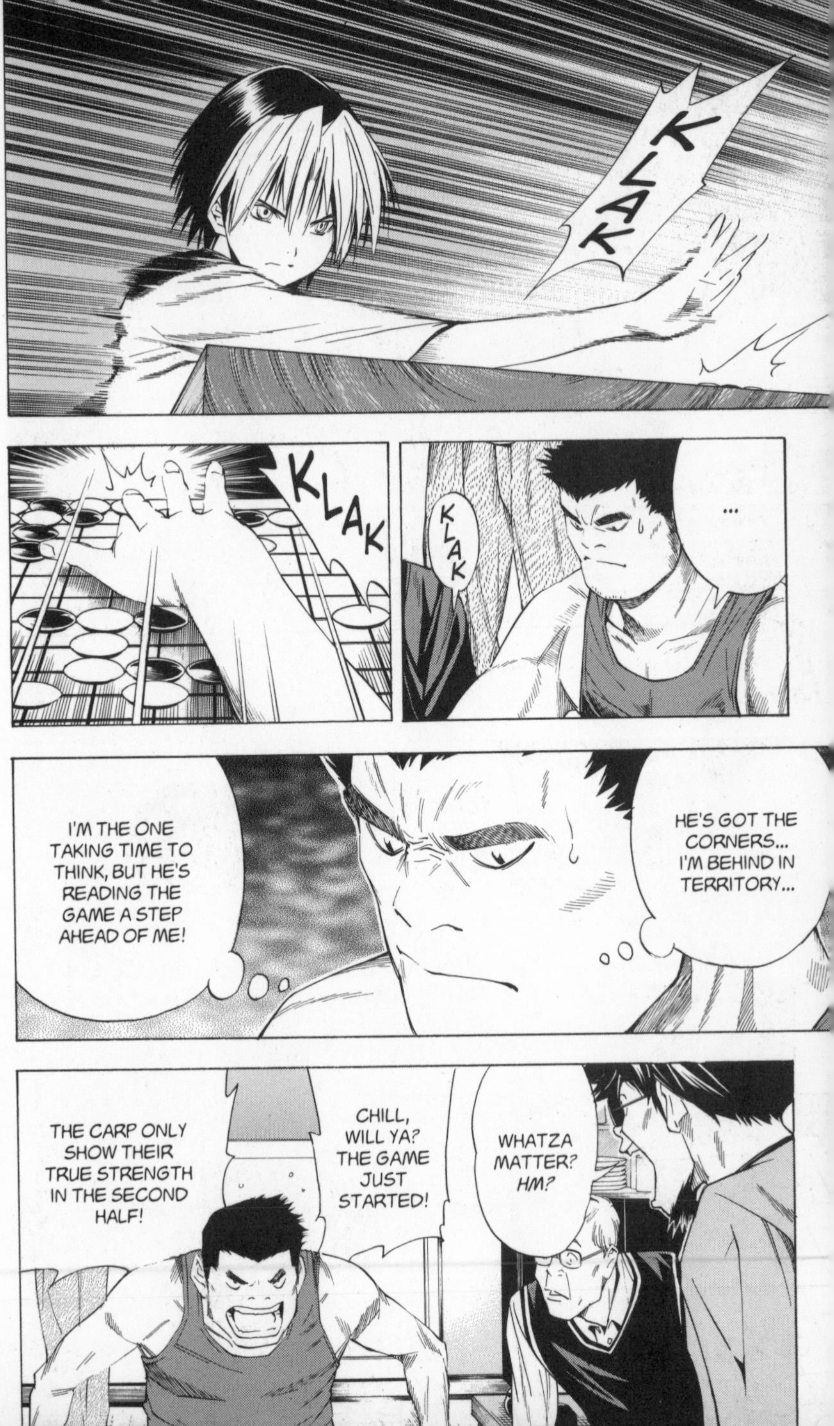
KLAK
...
KLAK
KLAK
HE'S GOT THE CORNERS... I'M BEHIND IN TERRITORY...
I'M THE ONE TAKING TIME TO THINK, BUT HE'S READING THE GAME A STEP AHEAD OF ME!
WHATZA MATTER? HM?
CHILL, WILL YA? THE GAME JUST STARTED!
THE CARP ONLY SHOW THEIR TRUE STRENGTH IN THE SECOND HALF!

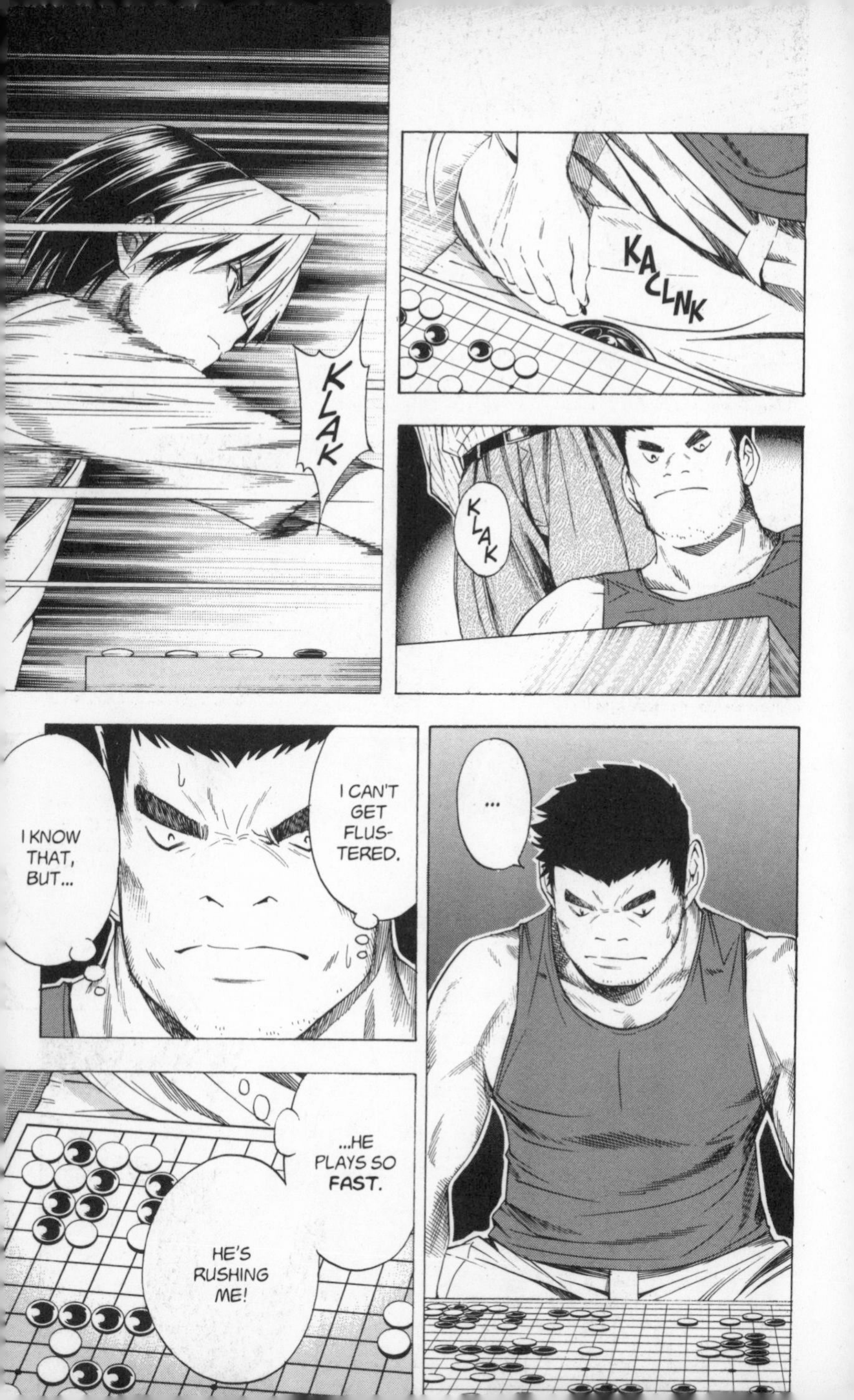
KACLNK
KLAK
KLAK
...
I CAN'T GET FLUSTERED.
I KNOW THAT, BUT...
...HE PLAYS SO **FAST.**
HE'S RUSHING ME!

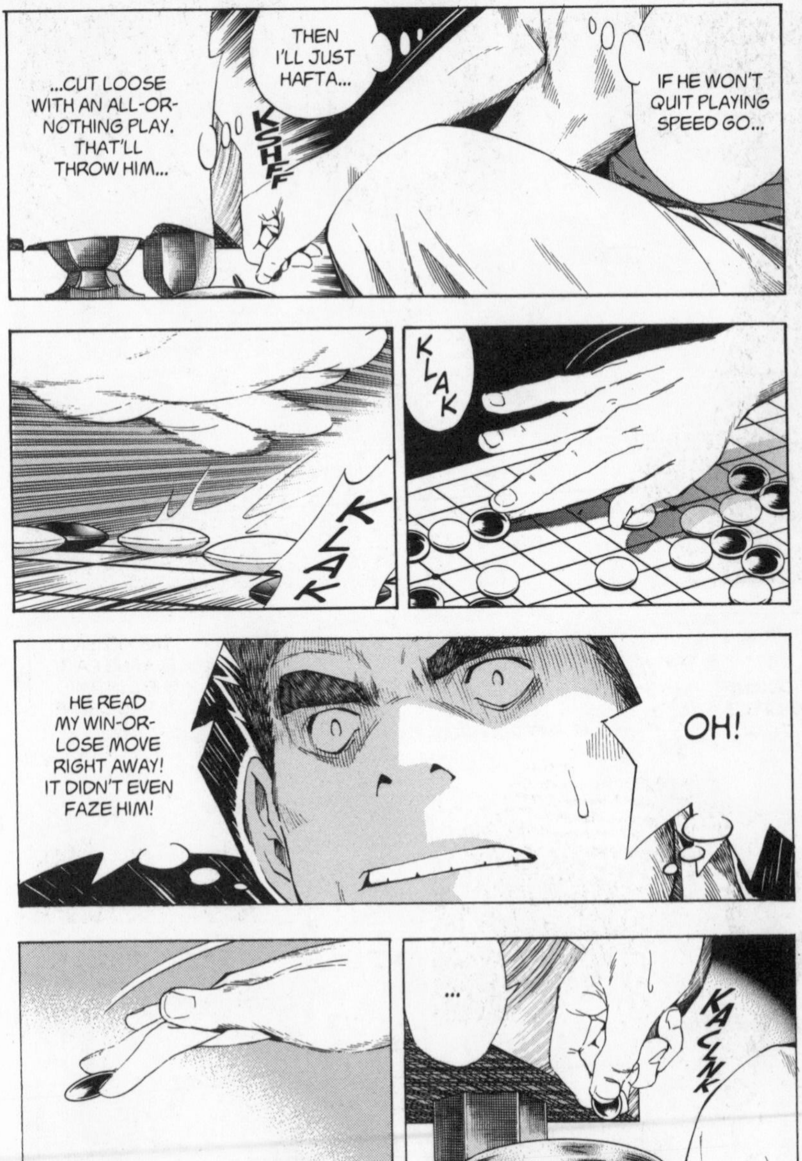
IF HE WON'T QUIT PLAYING SPEED GO...
THEN I'LL JUST HAFTA...
KSHFF
...CUT LOOSE WITH AN ALL-OR-NOTHING PLAY. THAT'LL THROW HIM...
KLAK
KLAK
OH!
HE READ MY WIN-OR-LOSE MOVE RIGHT AWAY! IT DIDN'T EVEN FAZE HIM!
...
KACLNK

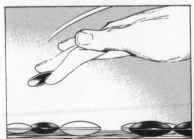

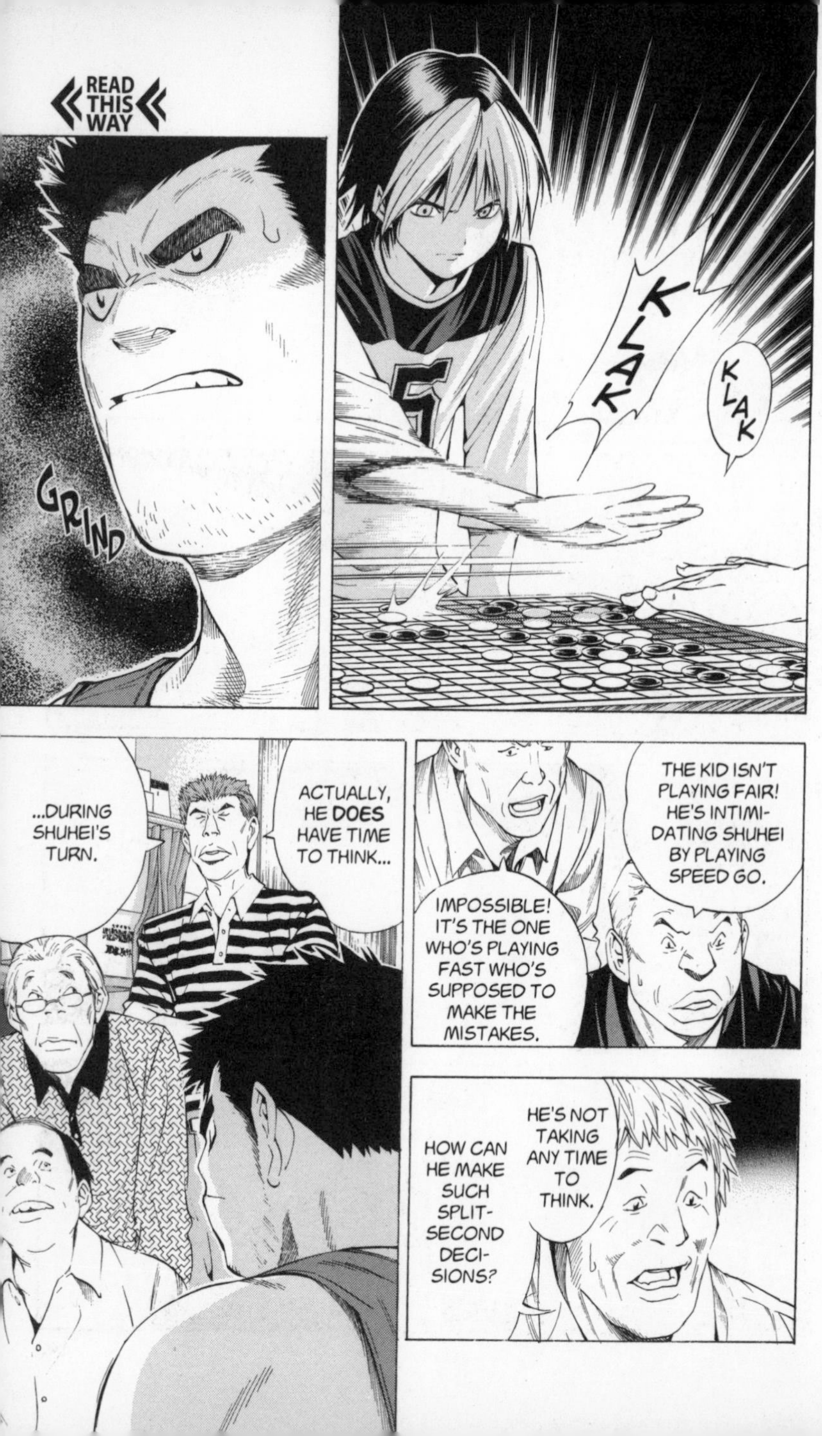
READ THIS WAY
KLAK
KLAK
GRIND
THE KID ISN'T PLAYING FAIR! HE'S INTIMI-DATING SHUHEI BY PLAYING SPEED GO.
IMPOSSIBLE! IT'S THE ONE WHO'S PLAYING FAST WHO'S SUPPOSED TO MAKE THE MISTAKES.
HE'S NOT TAKING ANY TIME TO THINK.
HOW CAN HE MAKE SUCH SPLIT-SECOND DECI-SIONS?
ACTUALLY, HE **DOES** HAVE TIME TO THINK...
...DURING SHUHEI'S TURN.

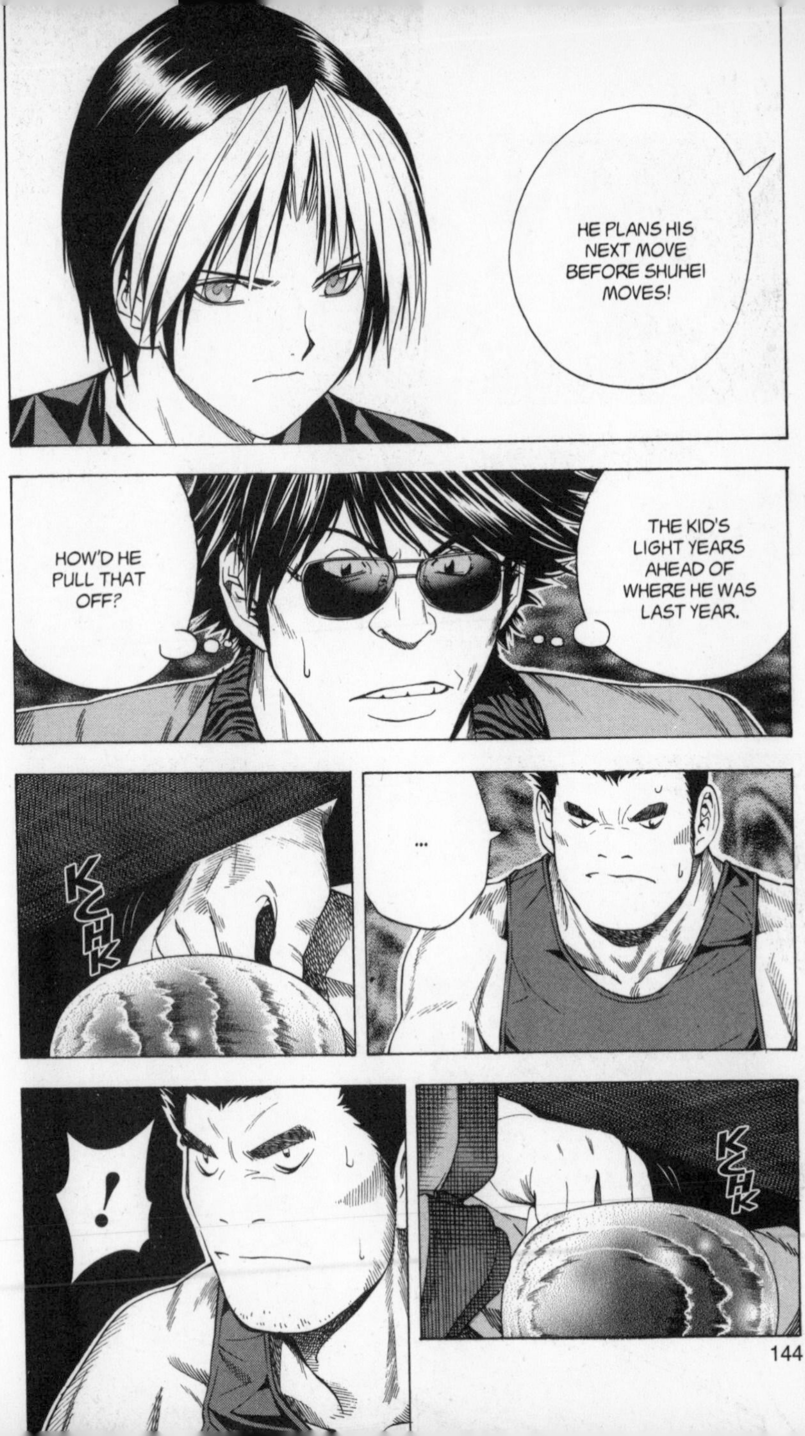
HE PLANS HIS NEXT MOVE BEFORE SHUHEI MOVES!
THE KID'S LIGHT YEARS AHEAD OF WHERE HE WAS LAST YEAR.
HOW'D HE PULL THAT OFF?
...
KCHK
KCHK
!

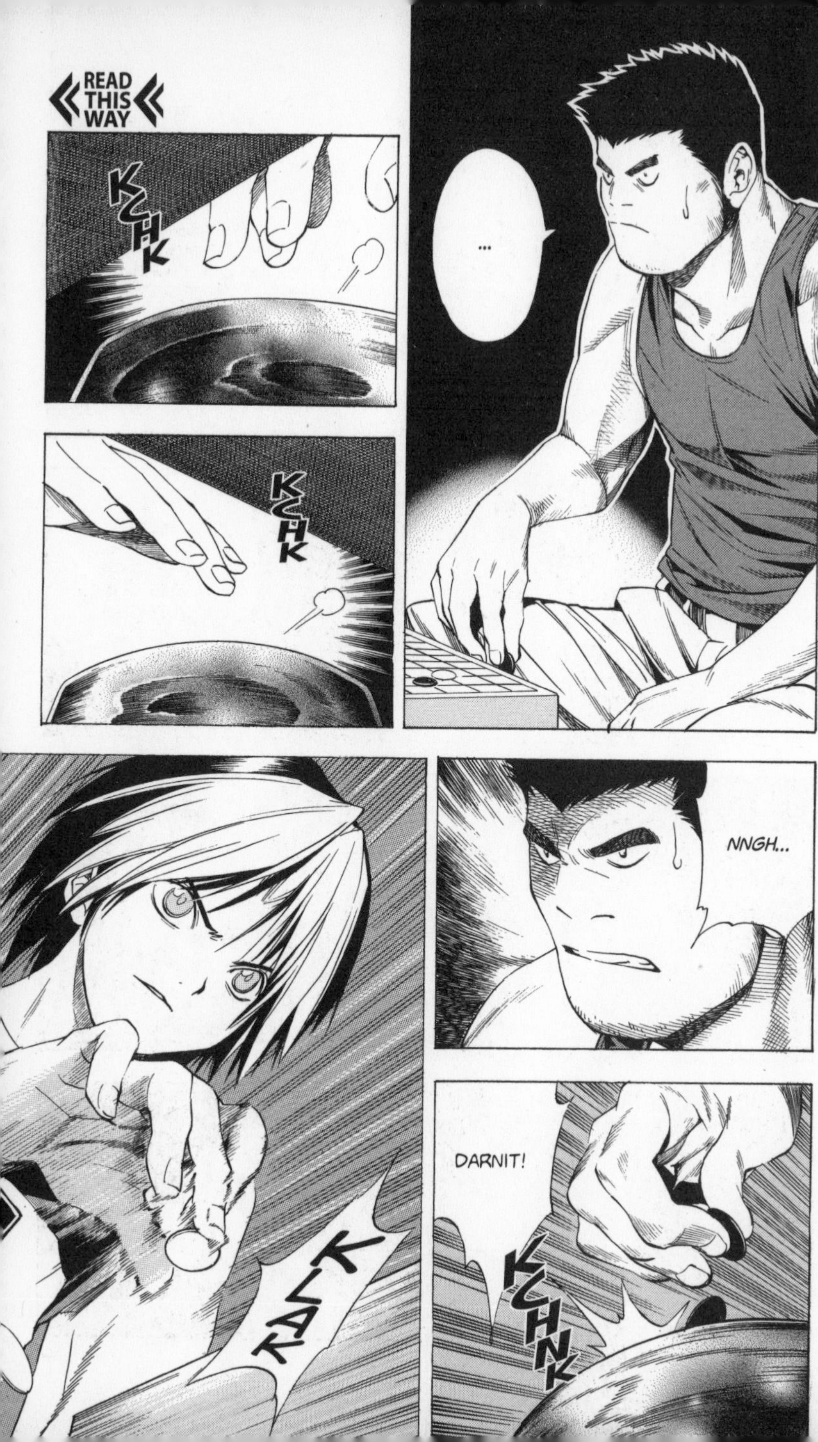
READ THIS WAY
...
KCHK
KCHK
NNGH...
DARNIT!
KCHNK
KLAK

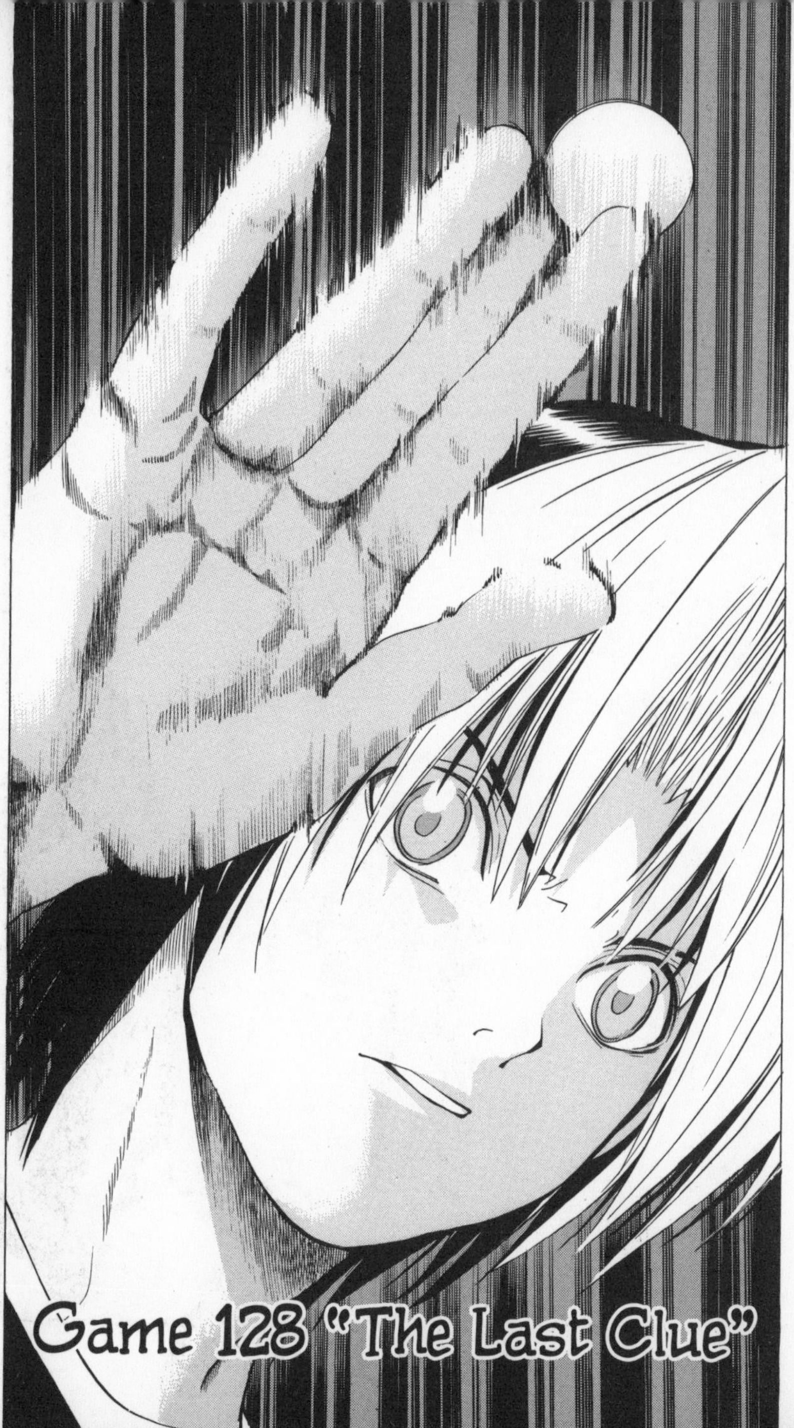
Game 128 "The Last Clue"

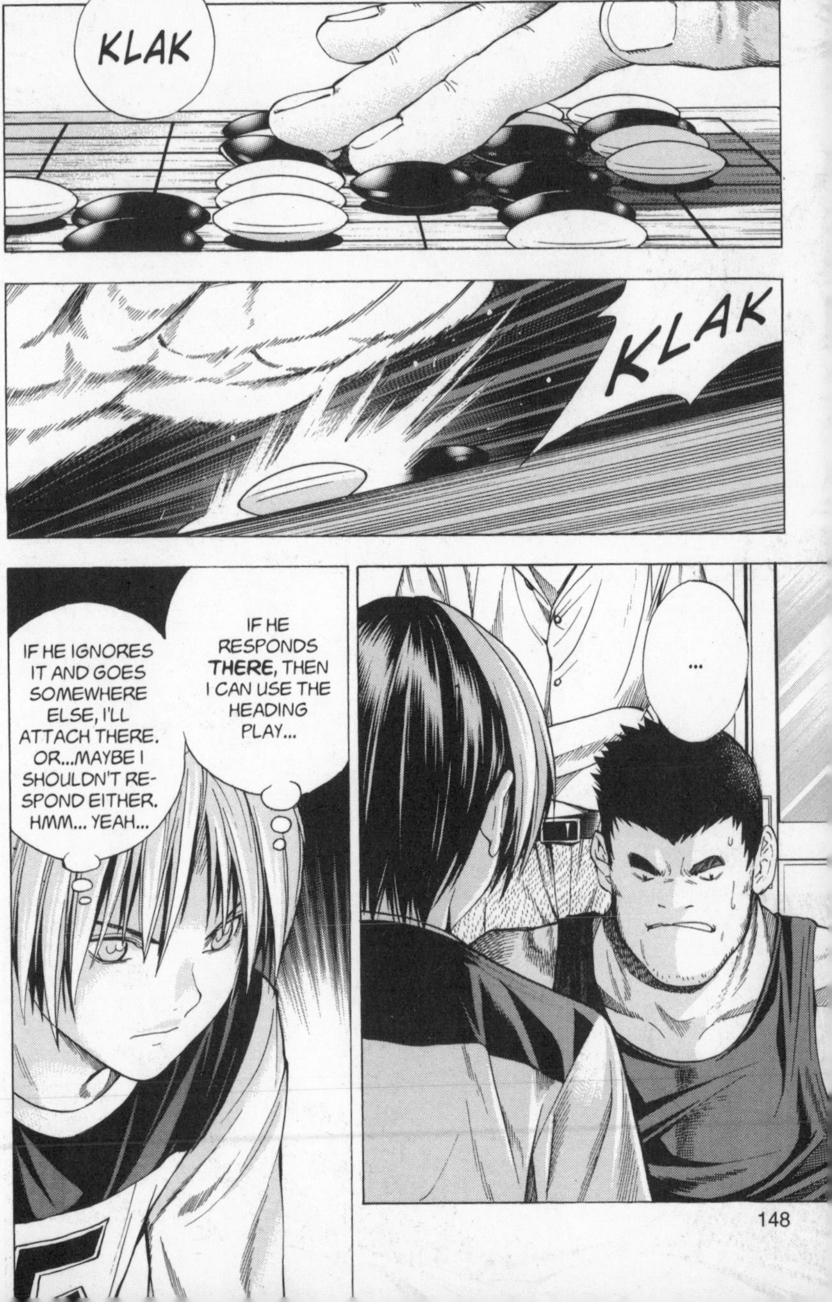
KLAK
KLAK
...
IF HE RESPONDS THERE, THEN I CAN USE THE HEADING PLAY...
IF HE IGNORES IT AND GOES SOMEWHERE ELSE, I'LL ATTACH THERE. OR...MAYBE I SHOULDN'T RE-SPOND EITHER. HMM... YEAH...

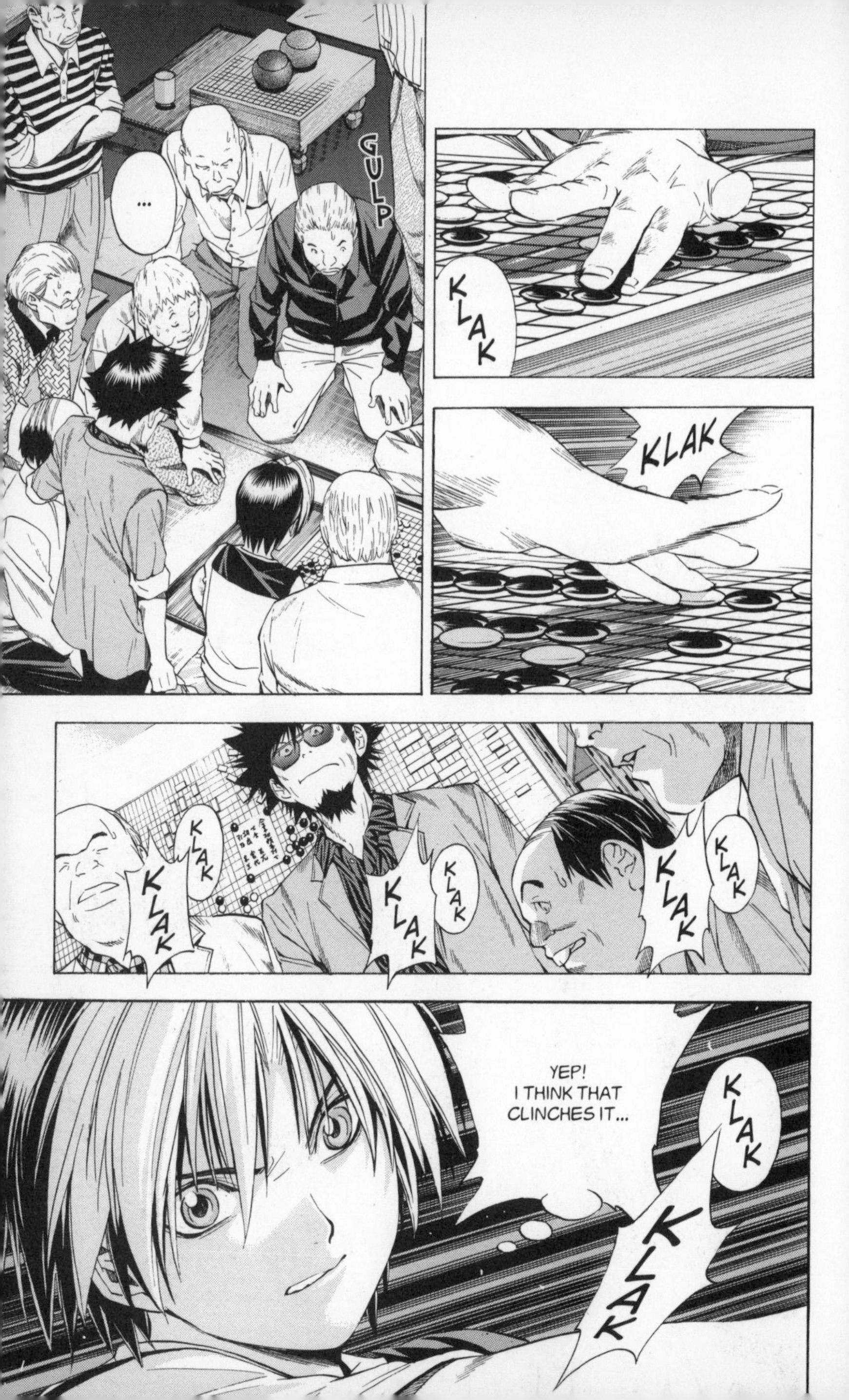
KLAK
KLAK
GULP
...
KLAK
KLAK
KLAK
KLAK
KLAK
KLAK
YEP! I THINK THAT CLINCHES IT...
KLAK
KLAK

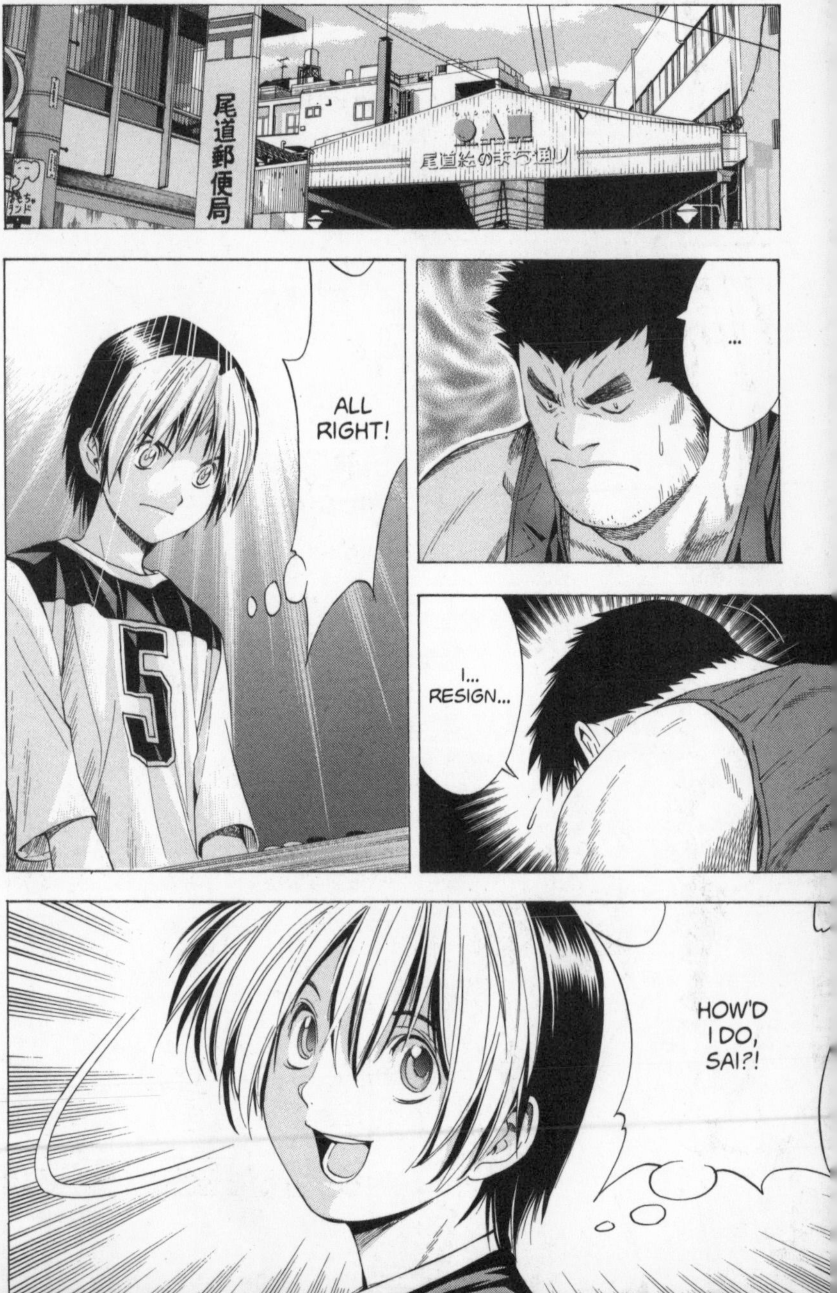
尾道郵便局
尾道絵のまち通り
...
I... RESIGN...
ALL RIGHT!
HOW'D I DO, SAI?!

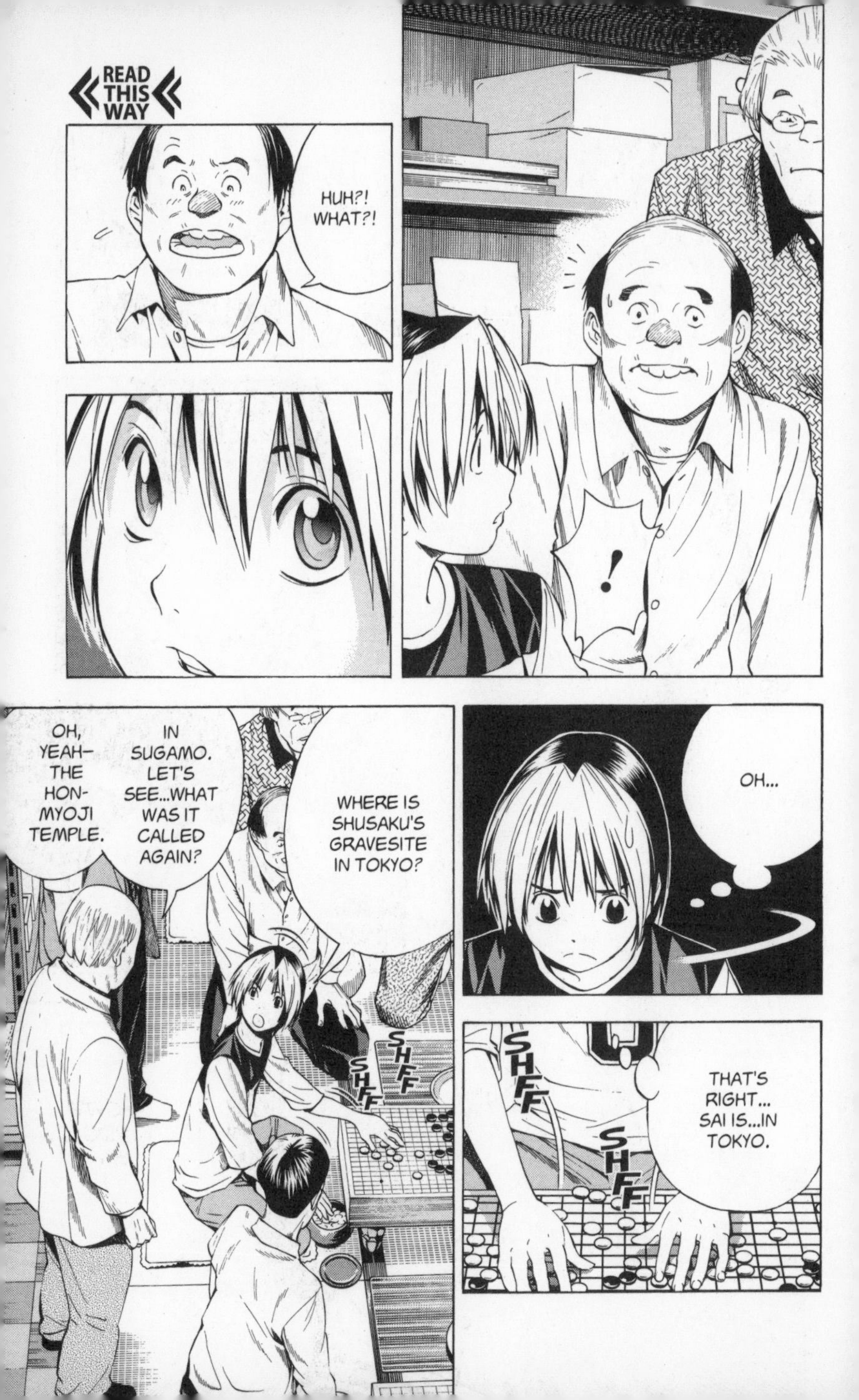
READ THIS WAY
!
HUH?! WHAT?!
OH...
SHFF
SHFF
THAT'S RIGHT... SAI IS...IN TOKYO.
WHERE IS SHUSAKU'S GRAVESITE IN TOKYO?
IN SUGAMO. LET'S SEE...WHAT WAS IT CALLED AGAIN?
OH, YEAH— THE HON-MYOJI TEMPLE.
SHFF
SHFF

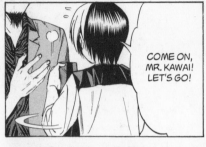

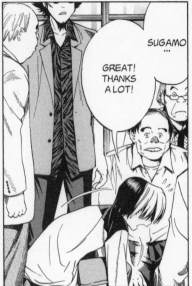

SUGAMO ...
GREAT! THANKS A LOT!
COME ON, MR. KAWAI! LET'S GO!
WAIT!
!
UH-OH! WAS I TOO AGGRESSIVE? ARE WE IN TROUBLE?
I'LL GIVE YOU A RIDE TO THE STATION.
COME ON!

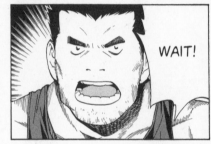

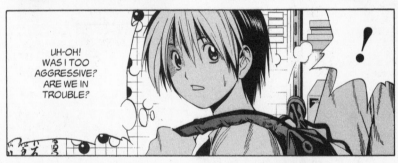

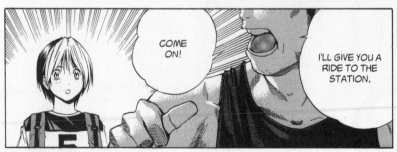

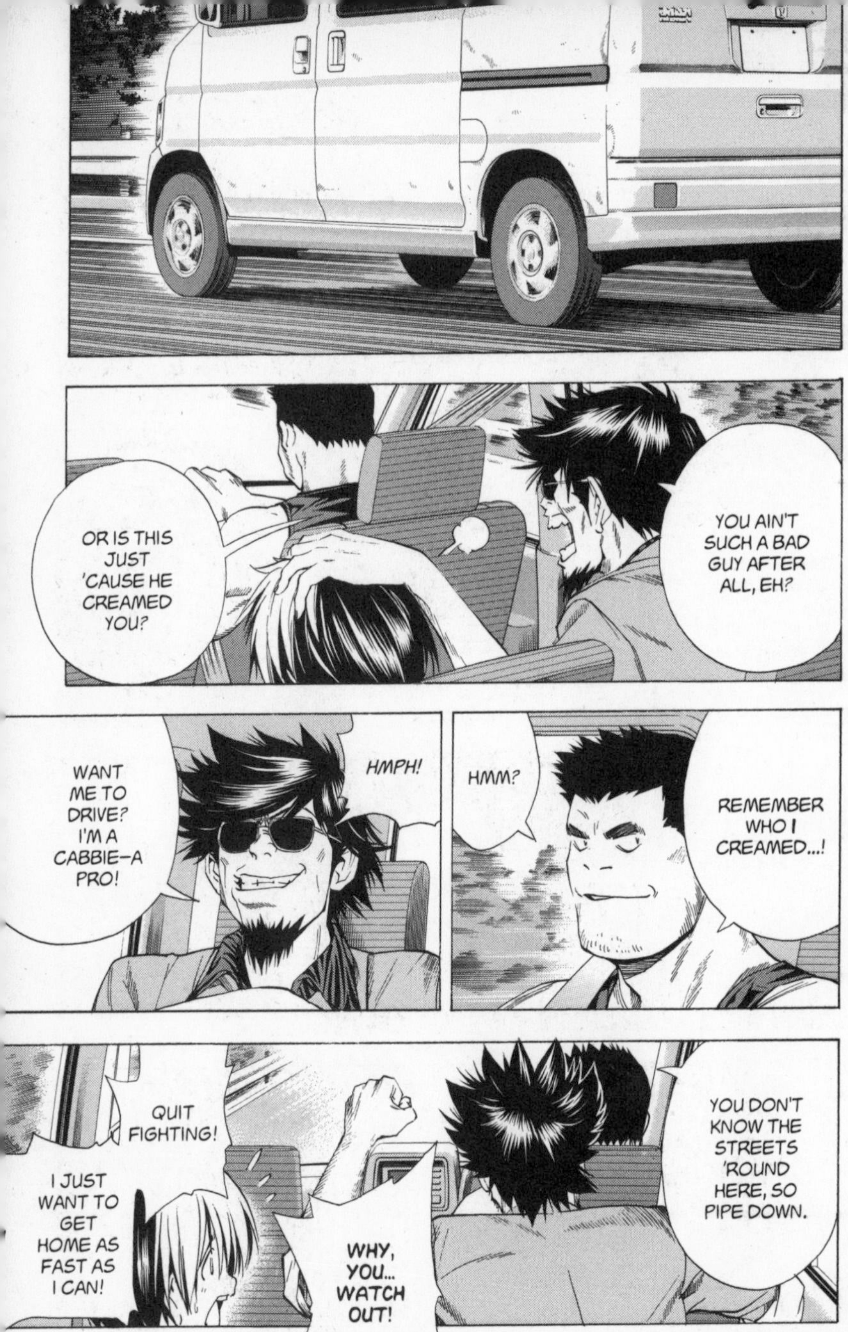
YOU AIN'T SUCH A BAD GUY AFTER ALL, EH?
OR IS THIS JUST 'CAUSE HE CREAMED YOU?
REMEMBER WHO I CREAMED...!
HMM?
HMPH!
WANT ME TO DRIVE? I'M A CABBIE—A PRO!
YOU DON'T KNOW THE STREETS 'ROUND HERE, SO PIPE DOWN.
WHY, YOU... WATCH OUT!
QUIT FIGHTING!
I JUST WANT TO GET HOME AS FAST AS I CAN!

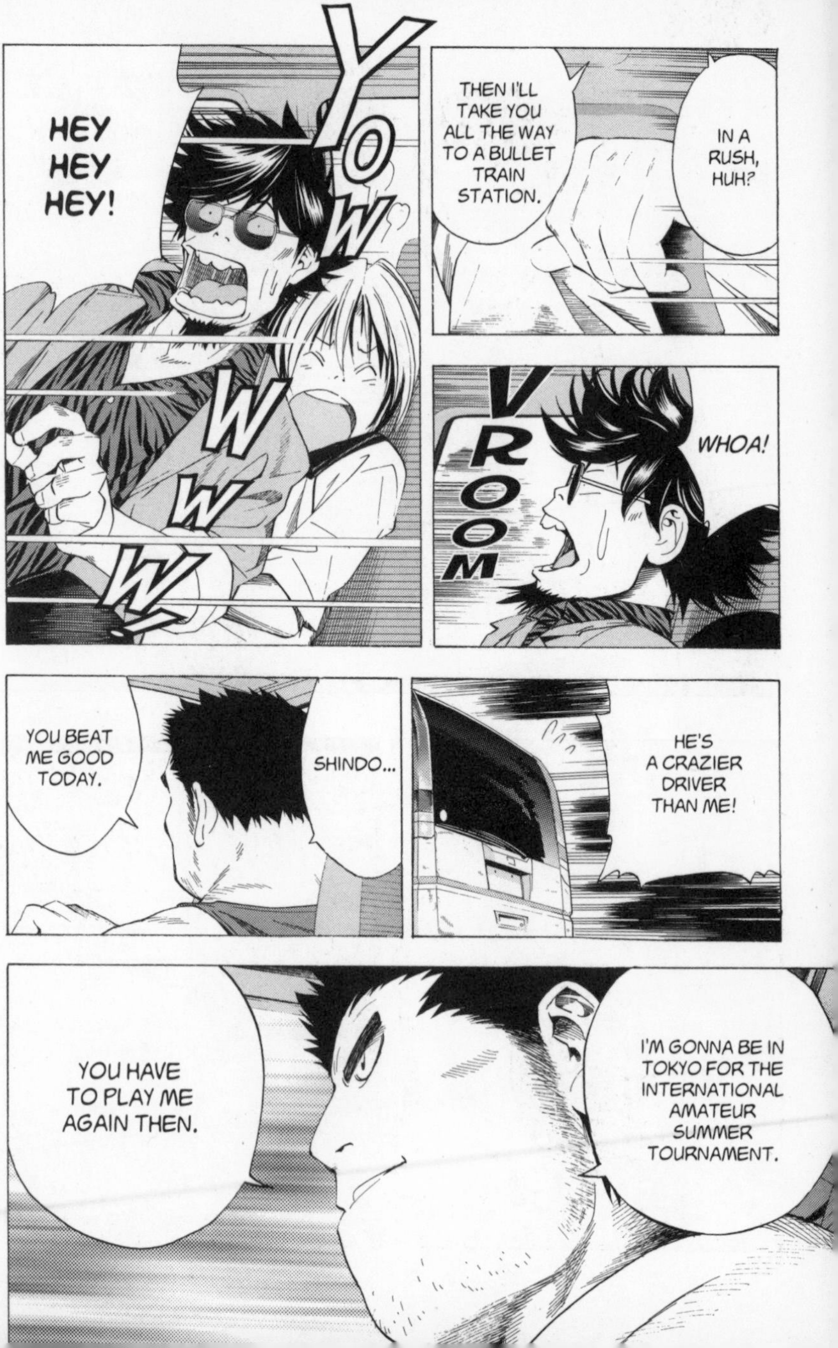
IN A RUSH, HUH?
THEN I'LL TAKE YOU ALL THE WAY TO A BULLET TRAIN STATION.
VROOM
WHOA!
YOWWWW!
HEY HEY HEY!
HE'S A CRAZIER DRIVER THAN ME!
SHINDO...
YOU BEAT ME GOOD TODAY.
I'M GONNA BE IN TOKYO FOR THE INTERNATIONAL AMATEUR SUMMER TOURNAMENT.
YOU HAVE TO PLAY ME AGAIN THEN.

READ THIS WAY

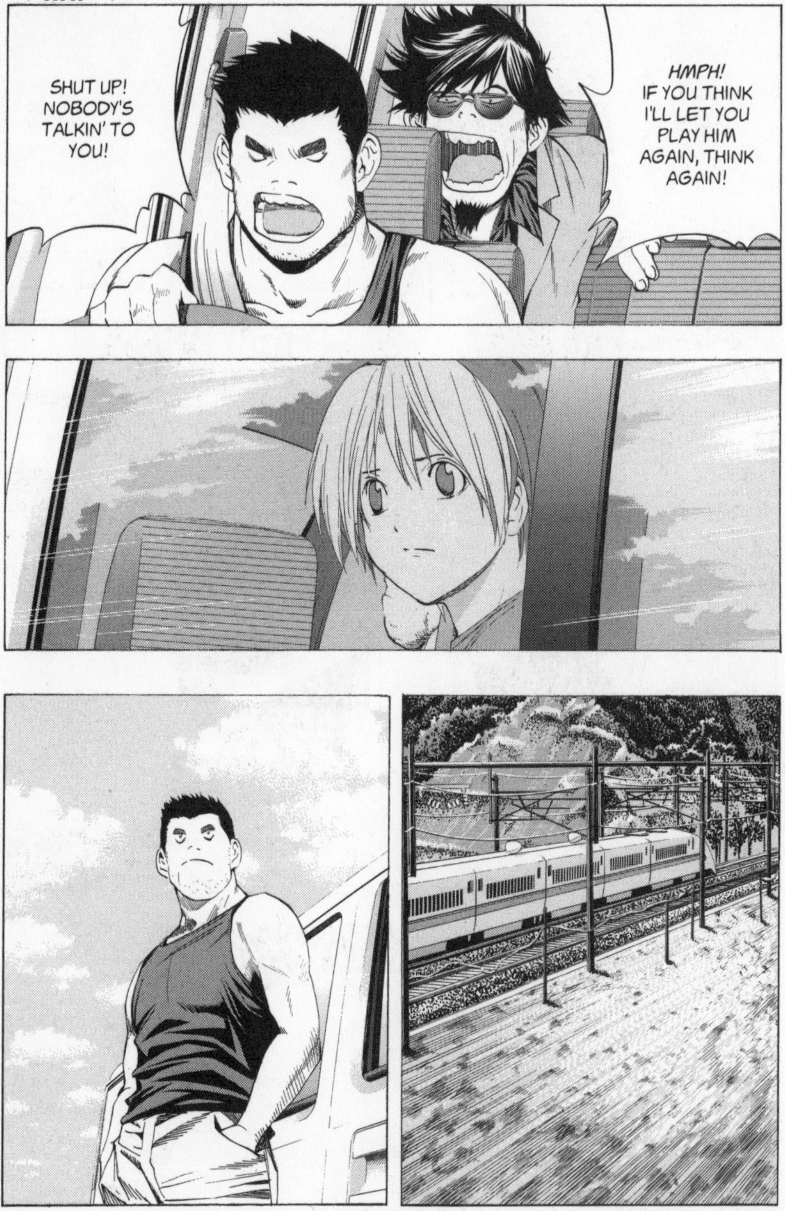
HMPH! IF YOU THINK I'LL LET YOU PLAY HIM AGAIN, THINK AGAIN!
SHUT UP! NOBODY'S TALKIN' TO YOU!

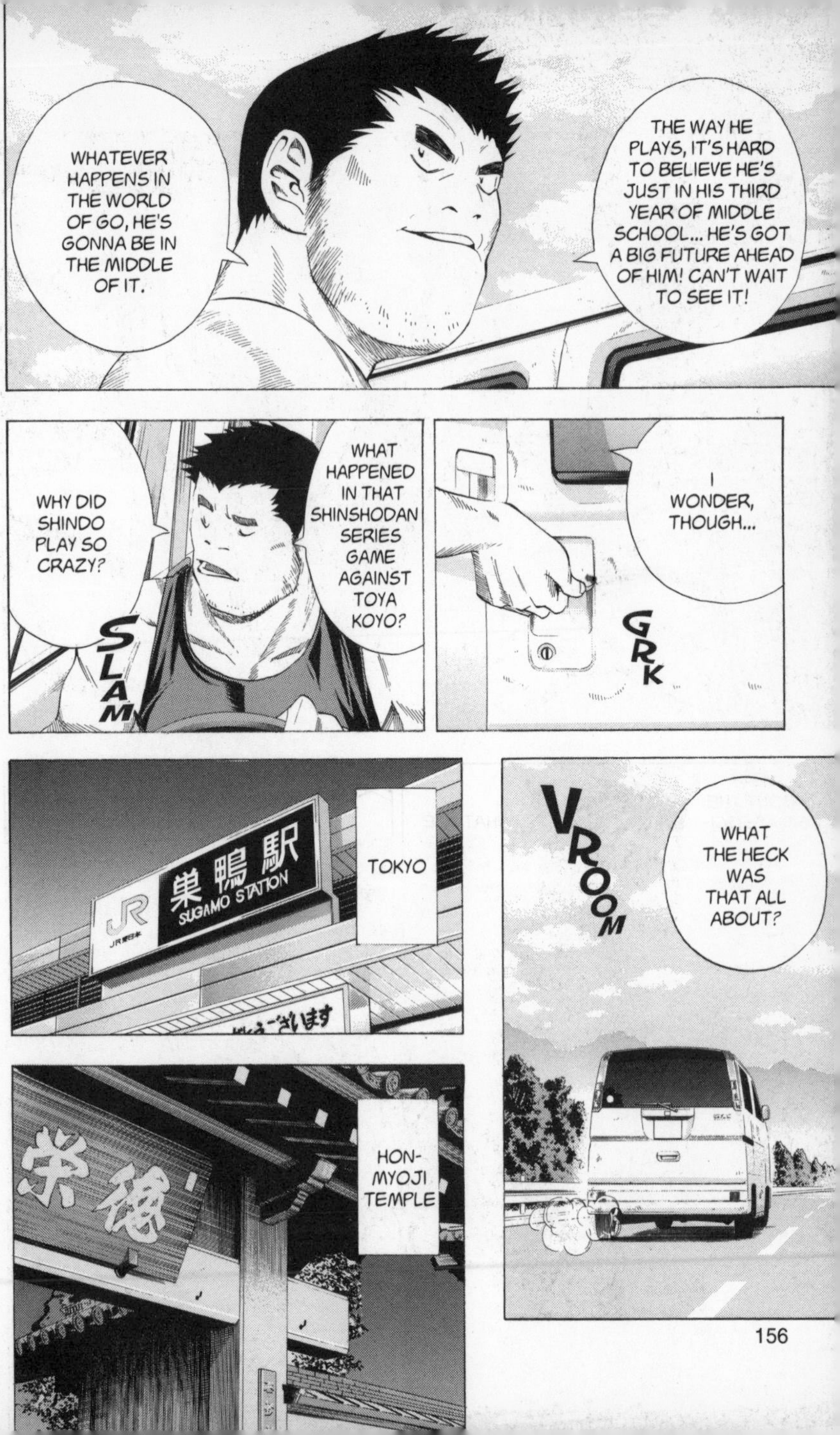
THE WAY HE PLAYS, IT'S HARD TO BELIEVE HE'S JUST IN HIS THIRD YEAR OF MIDDLE SCHOOL... HE'S GOT A BIG FUTURE AHEAD OF HIM! CAN'T WAIT TO SEE IT!
WHATEVER HAPPENS IN THE WORLD OF GO, HE'S GONNA BE IN THE MIDDLE OF IT.
I WONDER, THOUGH...
GRK
WHAT HAPPENED IN THAT SHINSHODAN SERIES GAME AGAINST TOYA KOYO?
WHY DID SHINDO PLAY SO CRAZY?
SLAM
VROOM
WHAT THE HECK WAS THAT ALL ABOUT?
TOKYO
JR
巣鴨駅
SUGAMO STATION
HON-MYOJI TEMPLE

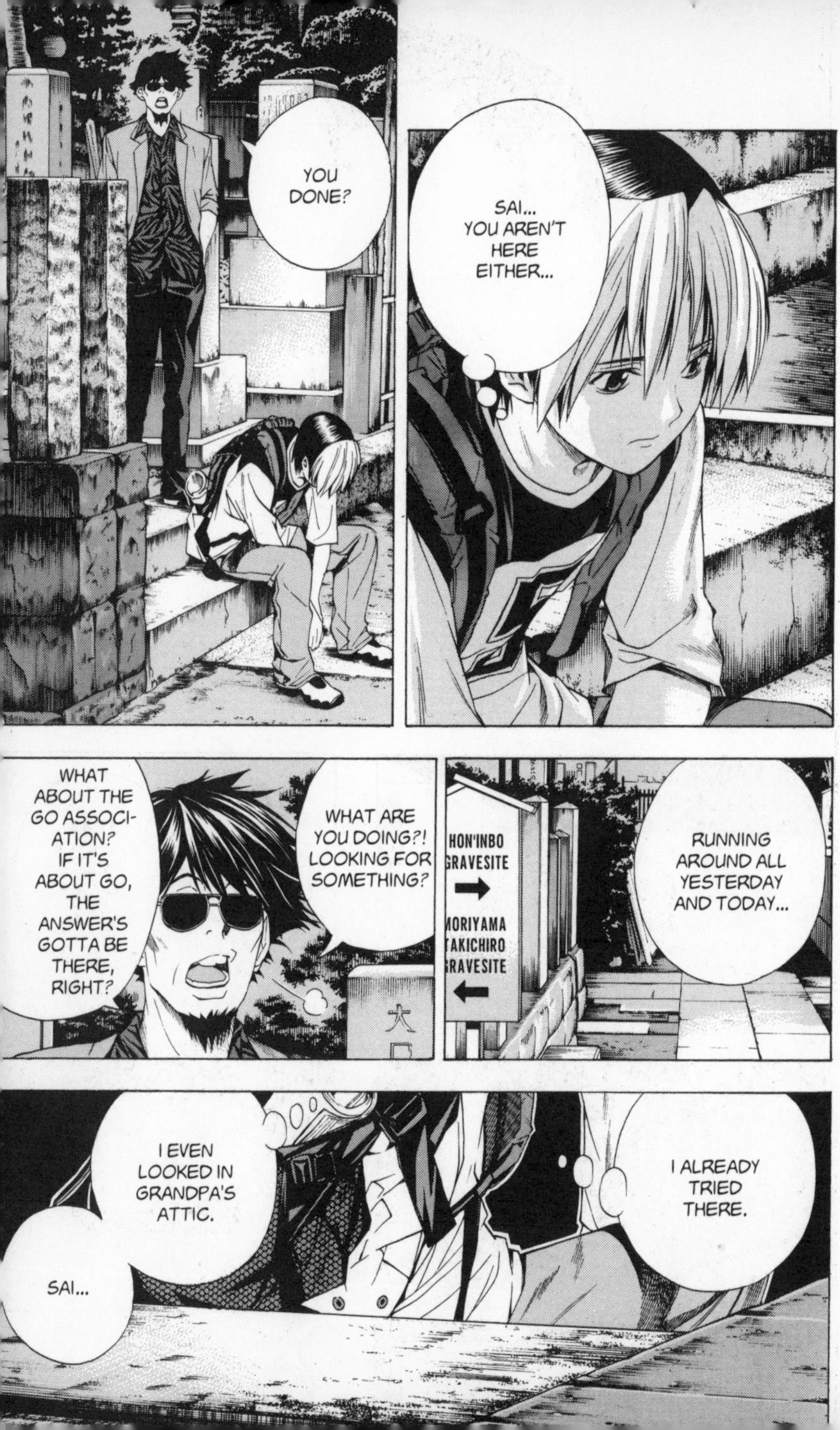
SAI... YOU AREN'T HERE EITHER...
YOU DONE?
RUNNING AROUND ALL YESTERDAY AND TODAY...
HON'INBO GRAVESITE
MORIYAMA TAKICHIRO GRAVESITE
WHAT ARE YOU DOING?! LOOKING FOR SOMETHING?
WHAT ABOUT THE GO ASSOCI-ATION? IF IT'S ABOUT GO, THE ANSWER'S GOTTA BE THERE, RIGHT?
I ALREADY TRIED THERE.
I EVEN LOOKED IN GRANDPA'S ATTIC.
SAI...

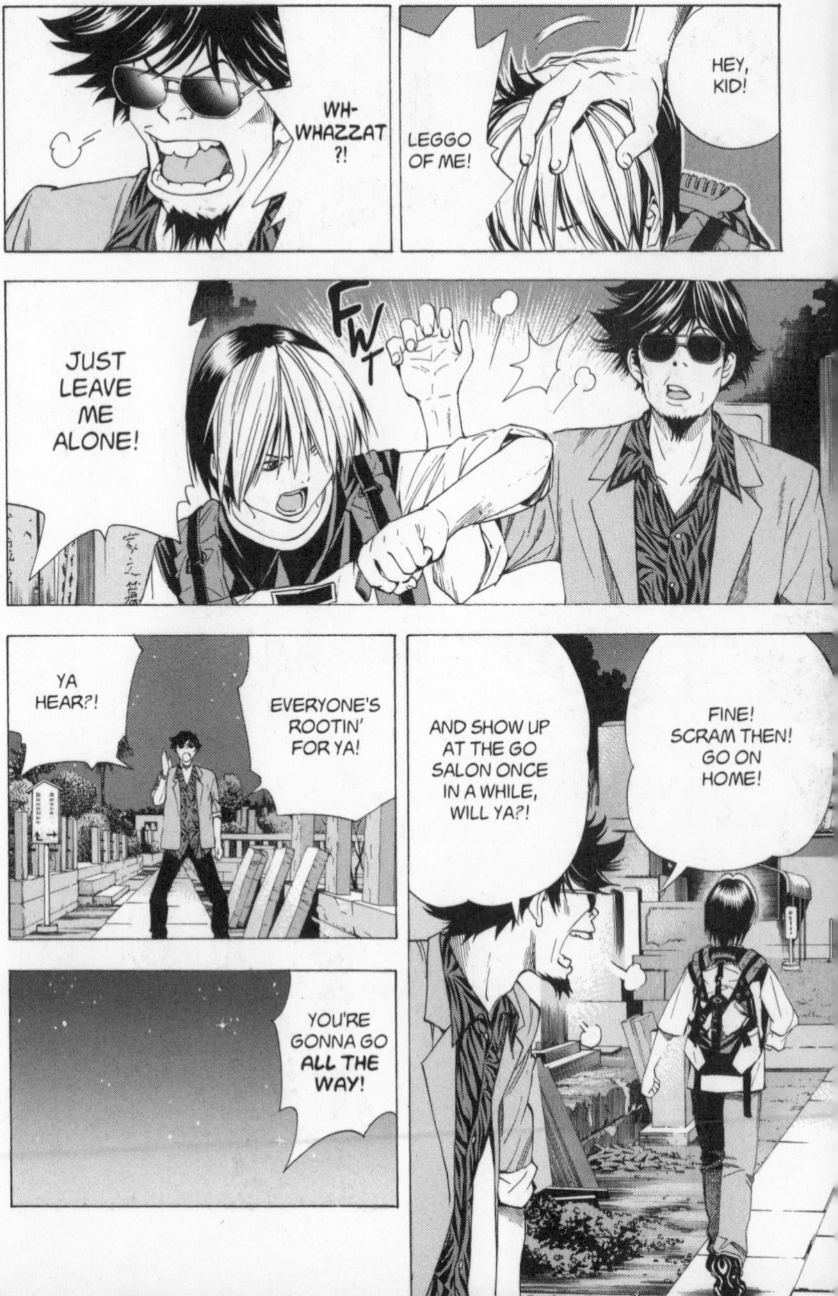
HEY, KID!
LEGGO OF ME!
WH-WHAZZAT?!
FWT
JUST LEAVE ME ALONE!
FINE! SCRAM THEN! GO ON HOME!
AND SHOW UP AT THE GO SALON ONCE IN A WHILE, WILL YA?!
EVERYONE'S ROOTIN' FOR YA!
YA HEAR?!
YOU'RE GONNA GO ALL THE WAY!

READ THIS WAY

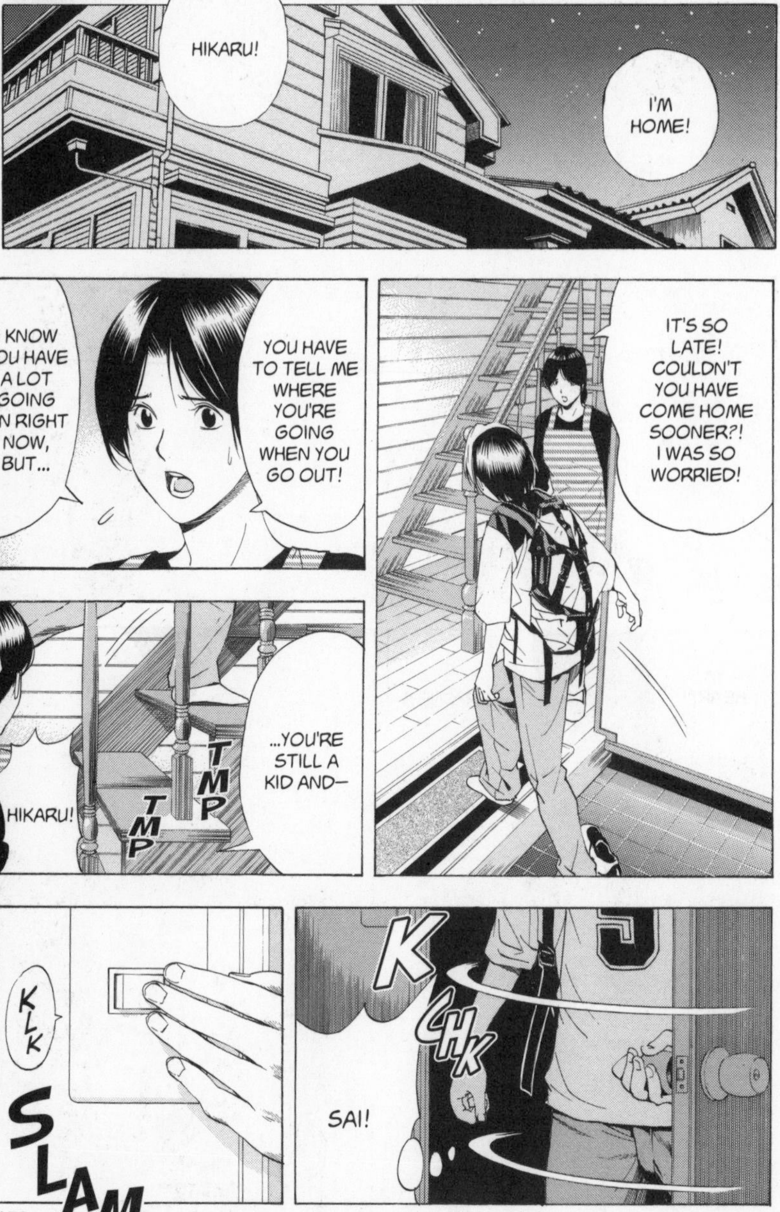

I'M HOME!
HIKARU!
IT'S SO LATE! COULDN'T YOU HAVE COME HOME SOONER?! I WAS SO WORRIED!
YOU HAVE TO TELL ME WHERE YOU'RE GOING WHEN YOU GO OUT!
I KNOW YOU HAVE A LOT GOING ON RIGHT NOW, BUT...
...YOU'RE STILL A KID AND—
TMP
TMP
HIKARU!
KCHK
SAI!
KLK
SLAM

...

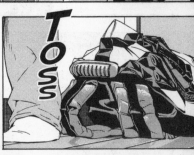

TOSS

I'M WIPED OUT FROM THAT GAME WITH THAT SHUHEI GUY.

FWMP

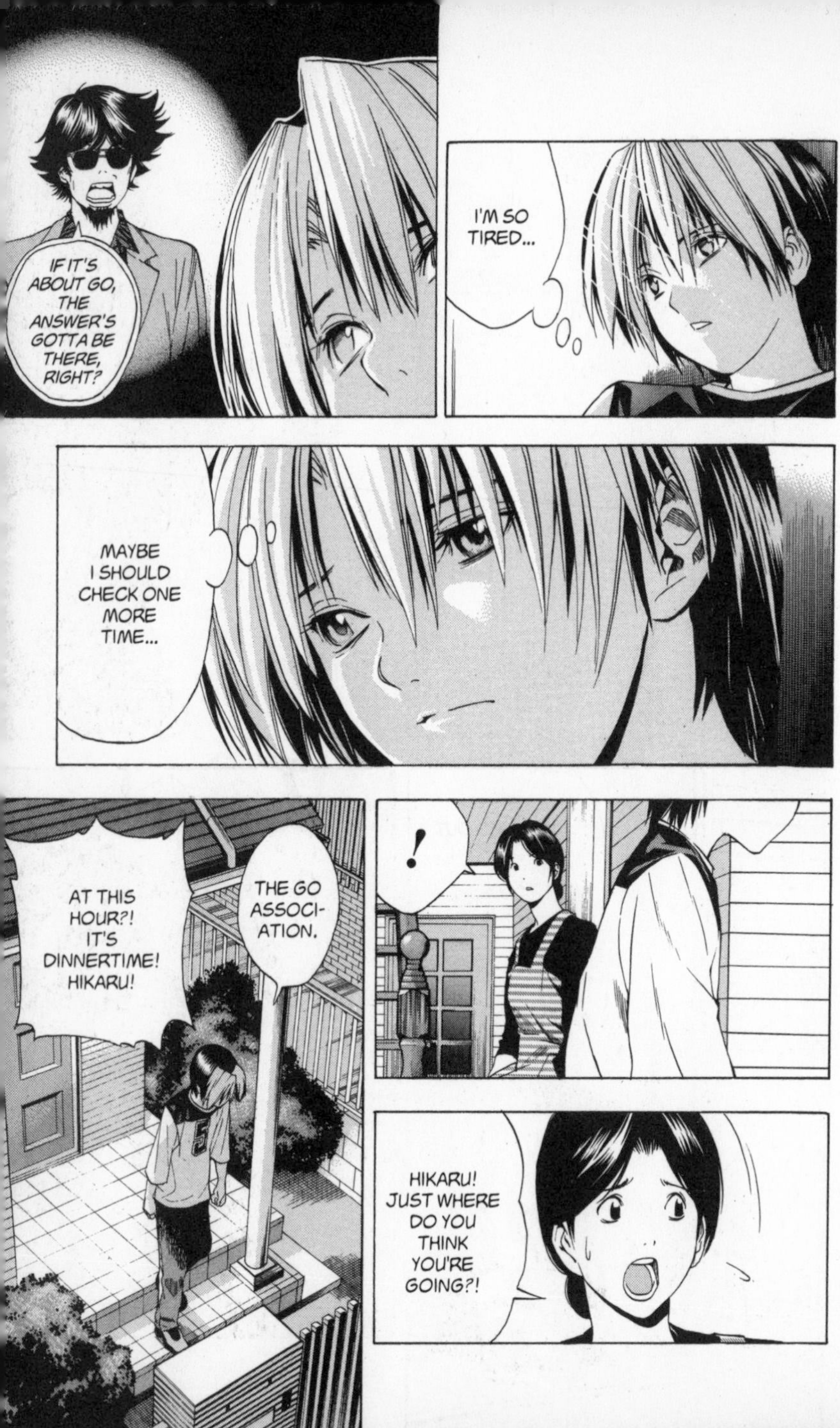
I'M SO TIRED...
IF IT'S ABOUT GO, THE ANSWER'S GOTTA BE THERE, RIGHT?
MAYBE I SHOULD CHECK ONE MORE TIME...
!
HIKARU! JUST WHERE DO YOU THINK YOU'RE GOING?!
THE GO ASSOCIATION.
AT THIS HOUR?! IT'S DINNERTIME! HIKARU!

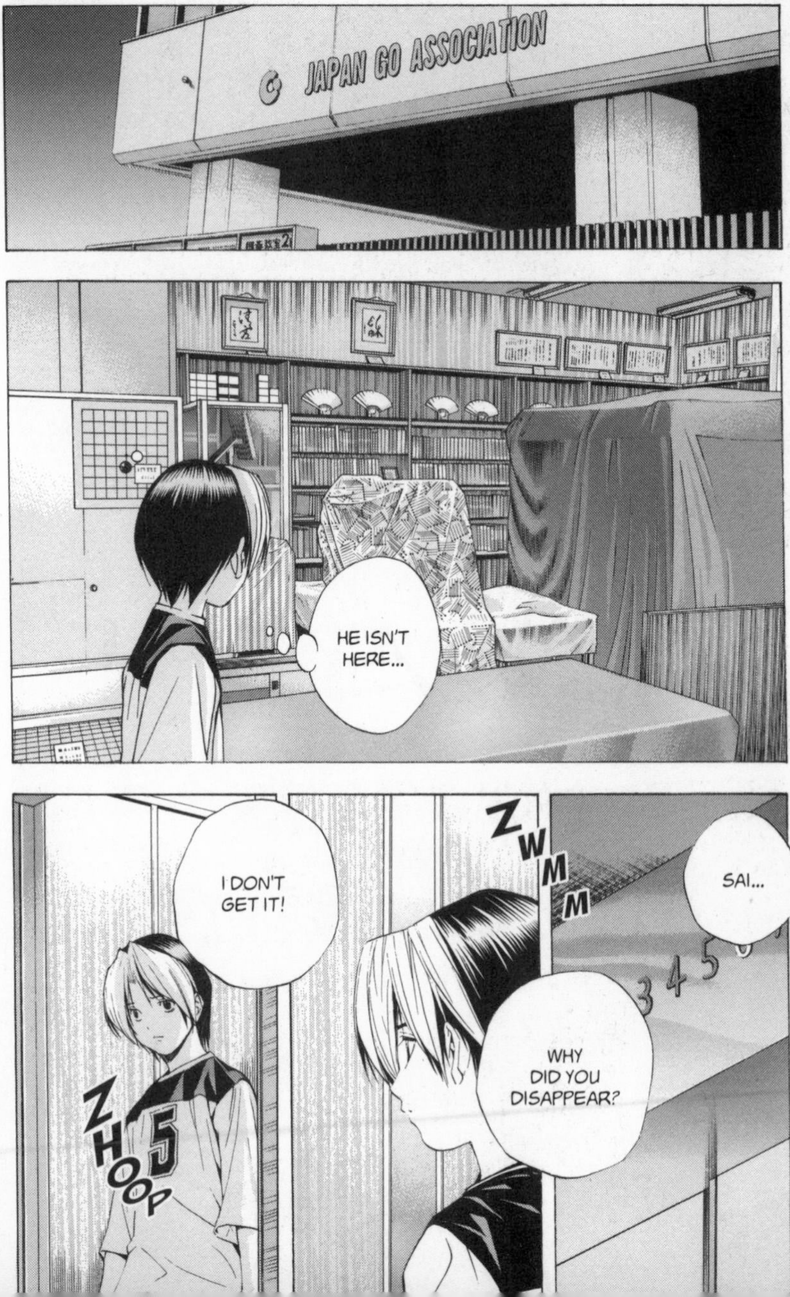
JAPAN GO ASSOCIATION
HE ISN'T HERE...
SAI...
ZWMM
WHY DID YOU DISAPPEAR?
I DON'T GET IT!
ZHOOP

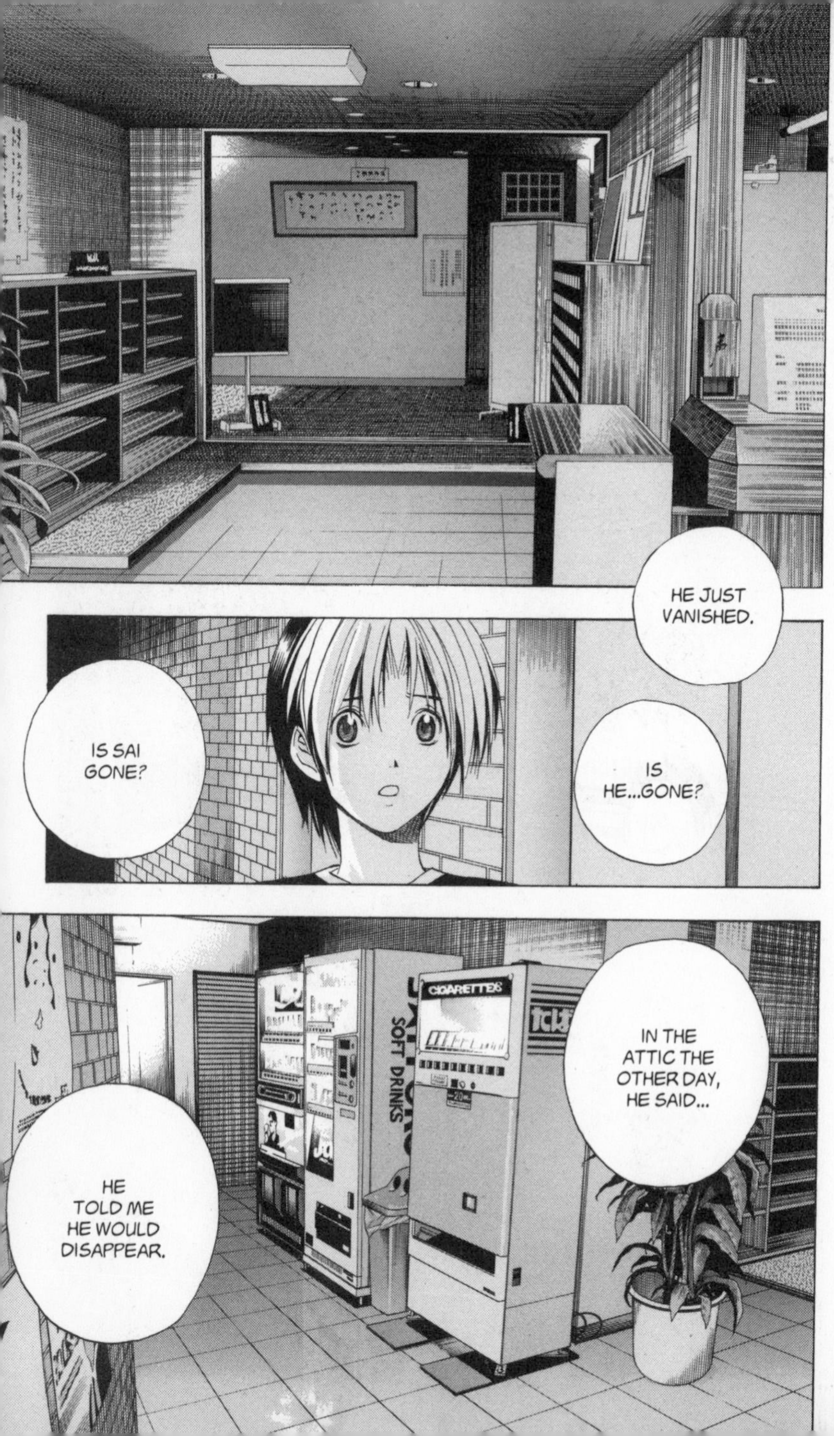
HE JUST VANISHED.
IS HE...GONE?
IS SAI GONE?
IN THE ATTIC THE OTHER DAY, HE SAID...
CIGARETTES
SOFT DRINKS
HE TOLD ME HE WOULD DISAPPEAR.

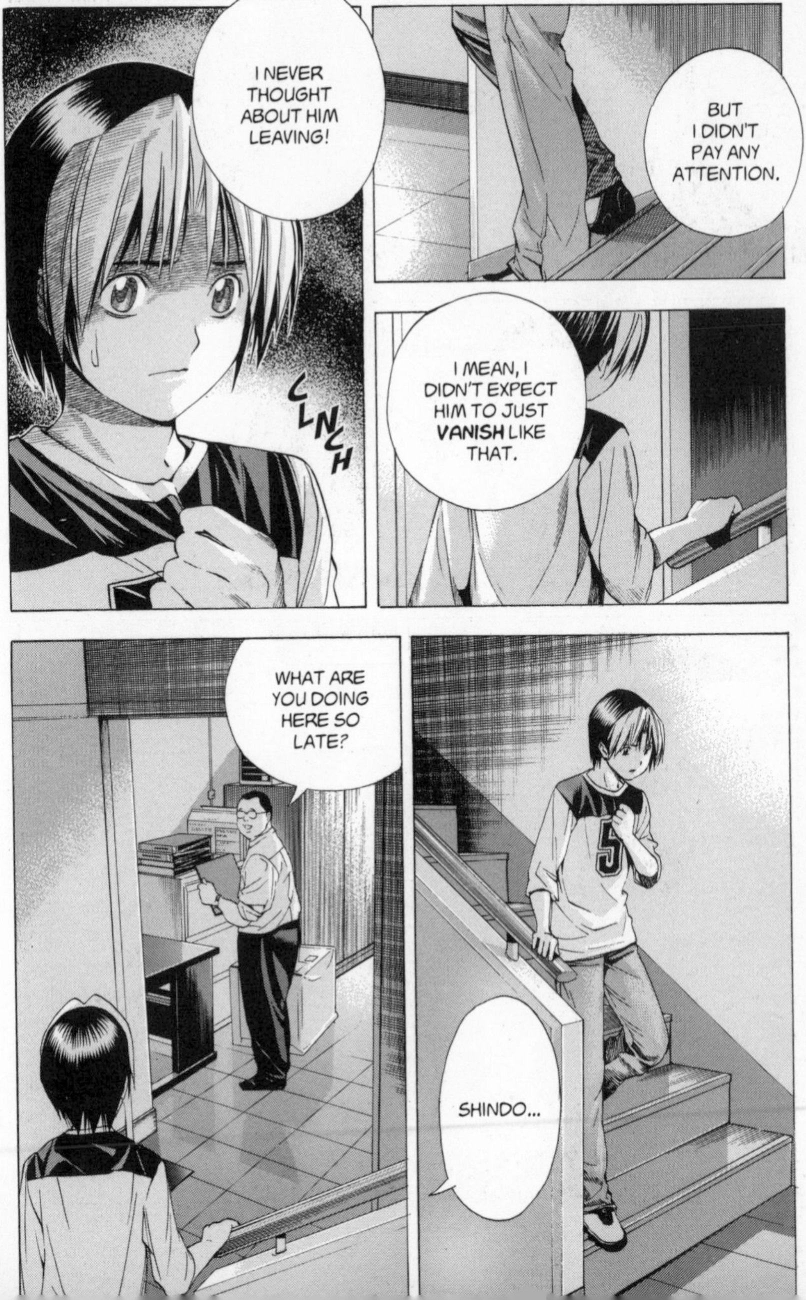
BUT I DIDN'T PAY ANY ATTENTION.
I MEAN, I DIDN'T EXPECT HIM TO JUST **VANISH** LIKE THAT.
I NEVER THOUGHT ABOUT HIM LEAVING!
CLNCH
SHINDO...
WHAT ARE YOU DOING HERE SO LATE?

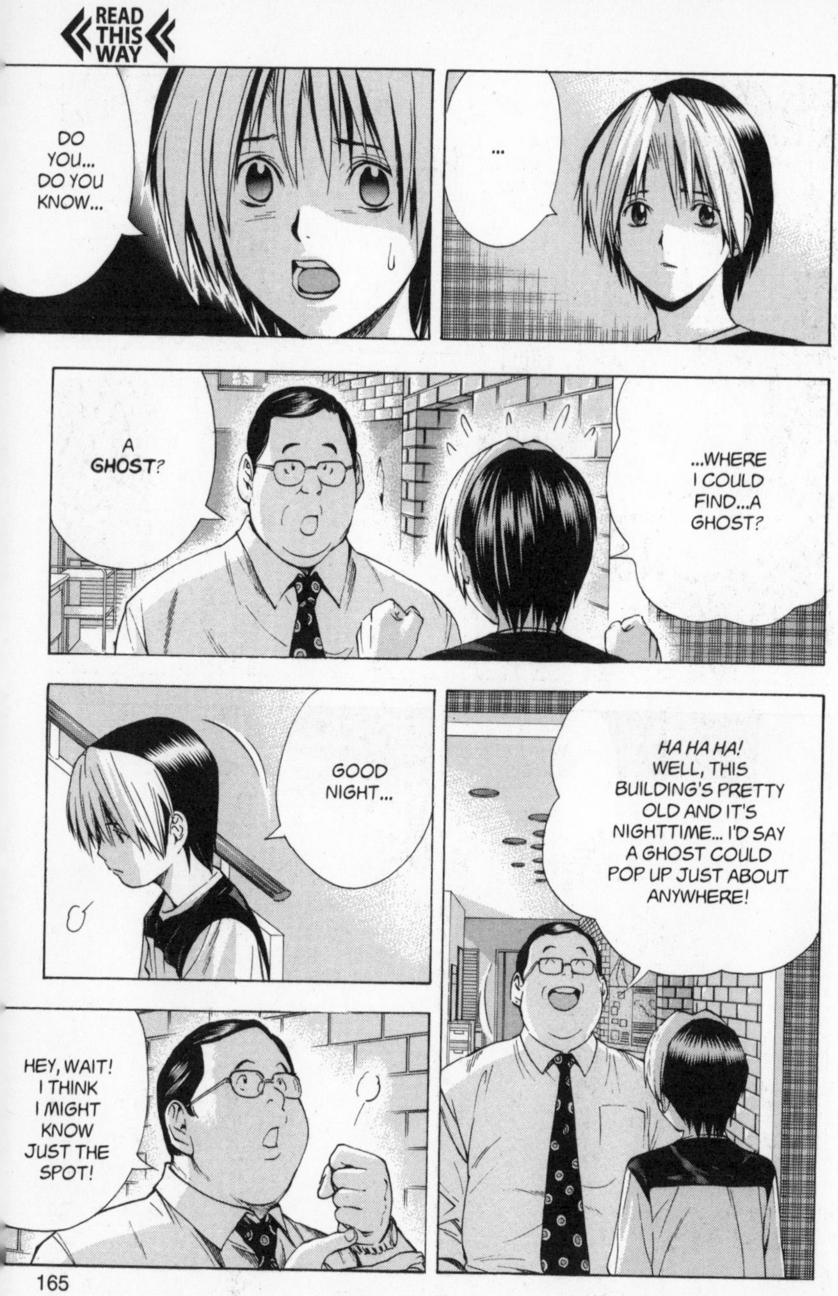
READ THIS WAY
...
DO YOU... DO YOU KNOW...
...WHERE I COULD FIND...A GHOST?
A GHOST?
HA HA HA! WELL, THIS BUILDING'S PRETTY OLD AND IT'S NIGHTTIME... I'D SAY A GHOST COULD POP UP JUST ABOUT ANYWHERE!
GOOD NIGHT...
HEY, WAIT! I THINK I MIGHT KNOW JUST THE SPOT!

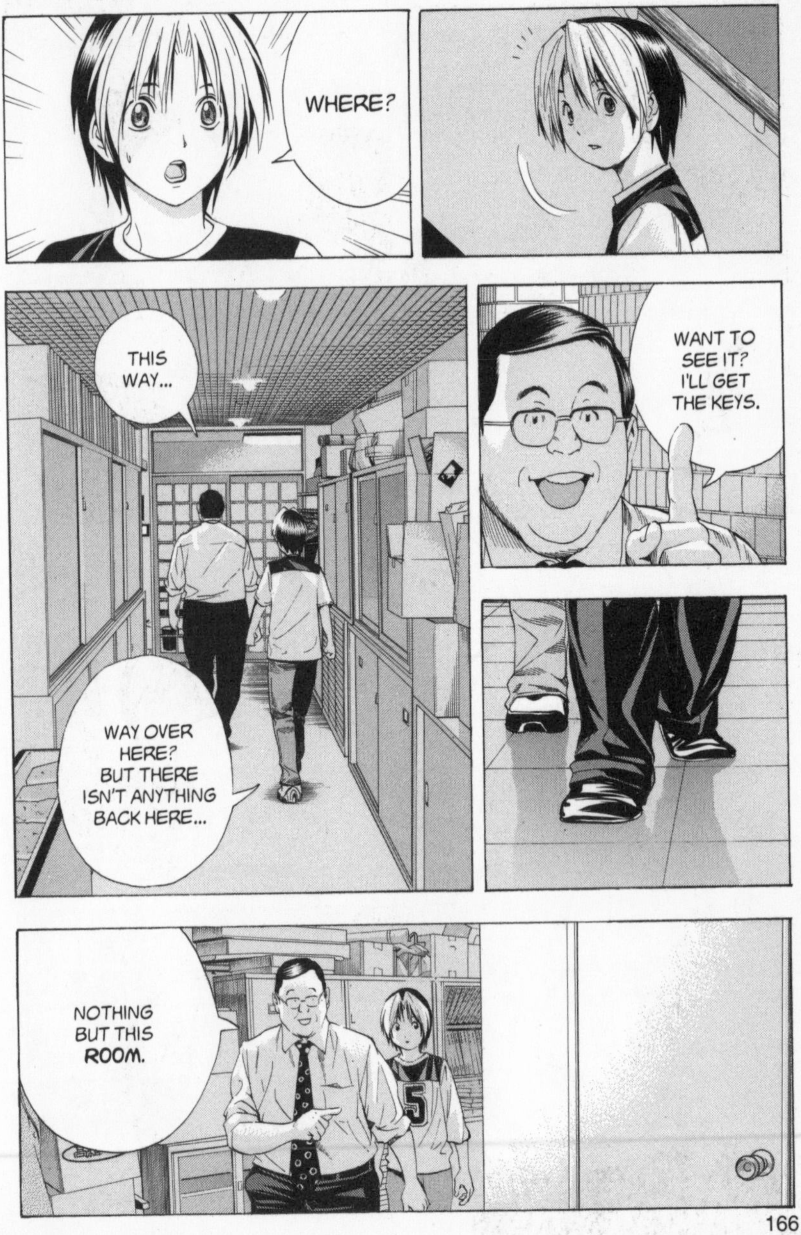
WHERE?
WANT TO SEE IT? I'LL GET THE KEYS.
THIS WAY...
WAY OVER HERE? BUT THERE ISN'T ANYTHING BACK HERE...
NOTHING BUT THIS **ROOM.**

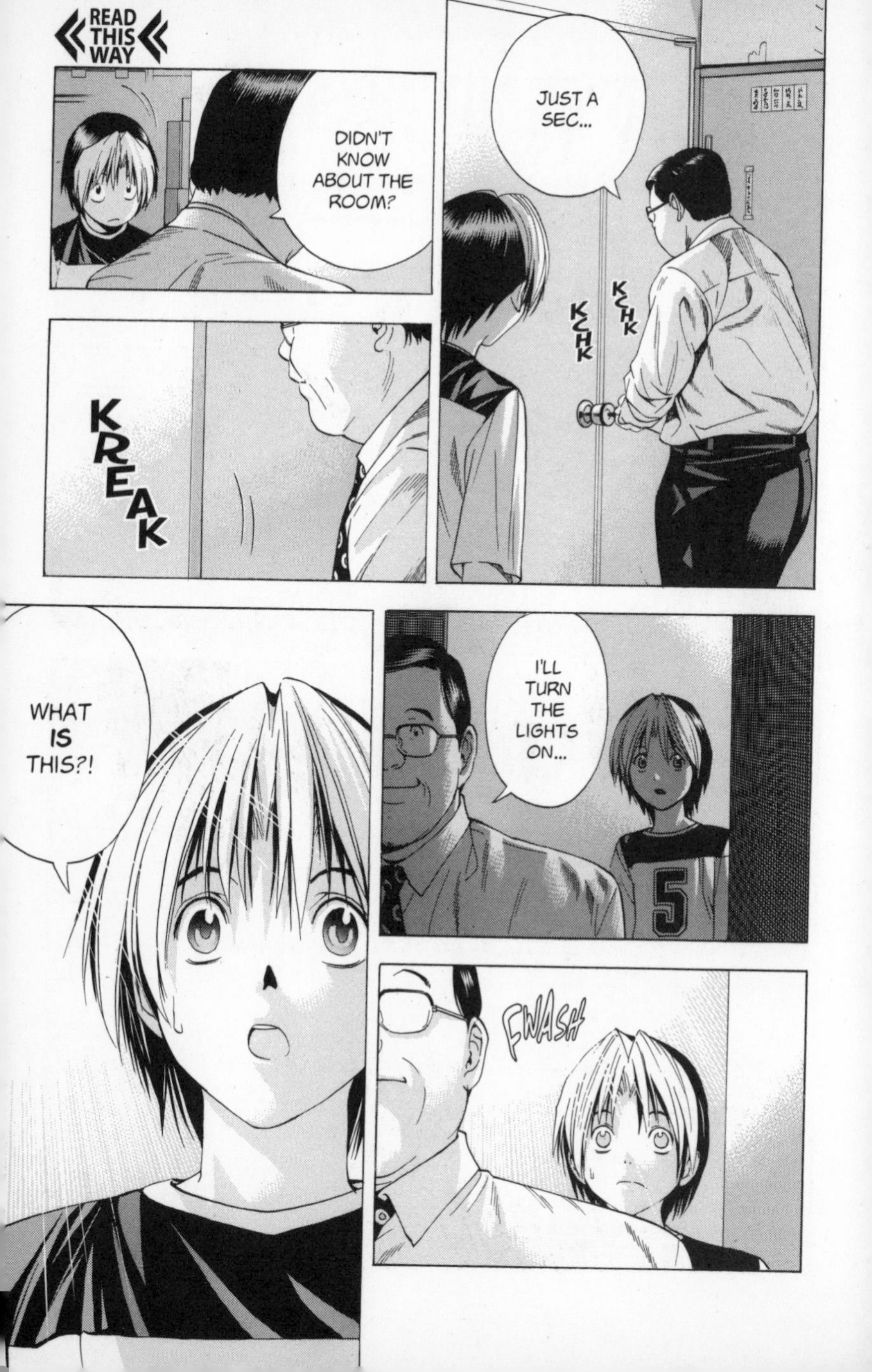
READ THIS WAY
JUST A SEC...
KCHK
KCHK
DIDN'T KNOW ABOUT THE ROOM?
KREAK
I'LL TURN THE LIGHTS ON...
FWASH
WHAT IS THIS?!

A WORD ABOUT HIKARU NO GO

A STUDY OF THE HIROSHIMA DIALECT

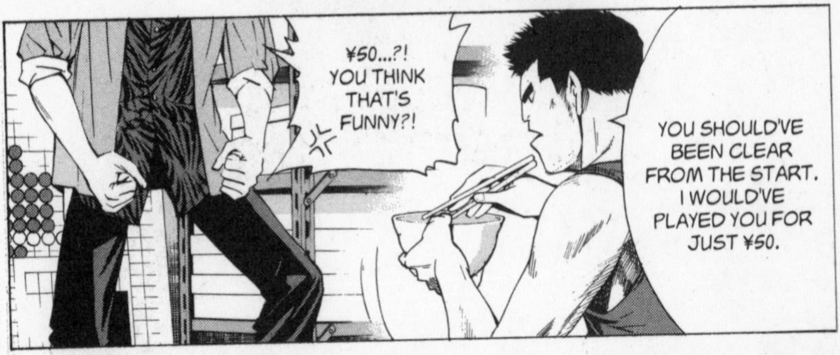
YOU SHOULD'VE BEEN CLEAR FROM THE START. I WOULD'VE PLAYED YOU FOR JUST ¥50.
¥50...?! YOU THINK THAT'S FUNNY?!

I HAD SOMEONE FROM HIROSHIMA GO OVER THE HIROSHIMA DIALECT THAT APPEARS IN GAMES 127 THROUGH 129.
FOR THE PANEL ABOVE, THE LINE I ORIGINALLY HAD IN THE STORYBOARD WAS, "*NARA HAJIME KARA HAKKIRI IE YA! 50 EN DEN UTTEYATTAKEE.*" DIALECTS SURE ARE DIFFICULT. (LAUGH)
BY THE WAY, IN THE DIALECT OF NAGOYA, THAT LINE WOULD BE "*NARA HAJIMEKKARA CHANTO IYAA! 50 EN DEMO UTTATANI.*"*

*ALTHOUGH THE EFFECT IS LOST IN TRANSLATION, IN THE ORIGINAL JAPANESE THE HIROSHIMA CHARACTERS USE A HIROSHIMA DIALECT. THERE ARE MANY REGIONAL DIALECTS IN JAPAN. SOMETIMES THE DIFFERENCES ARE SUBTLE, AS IN THE EXAMPLE ABOVE.

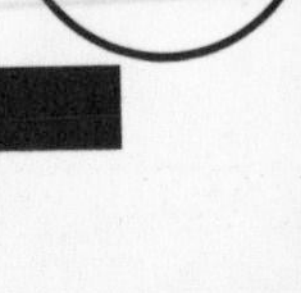

Game 129 "Come Back!"

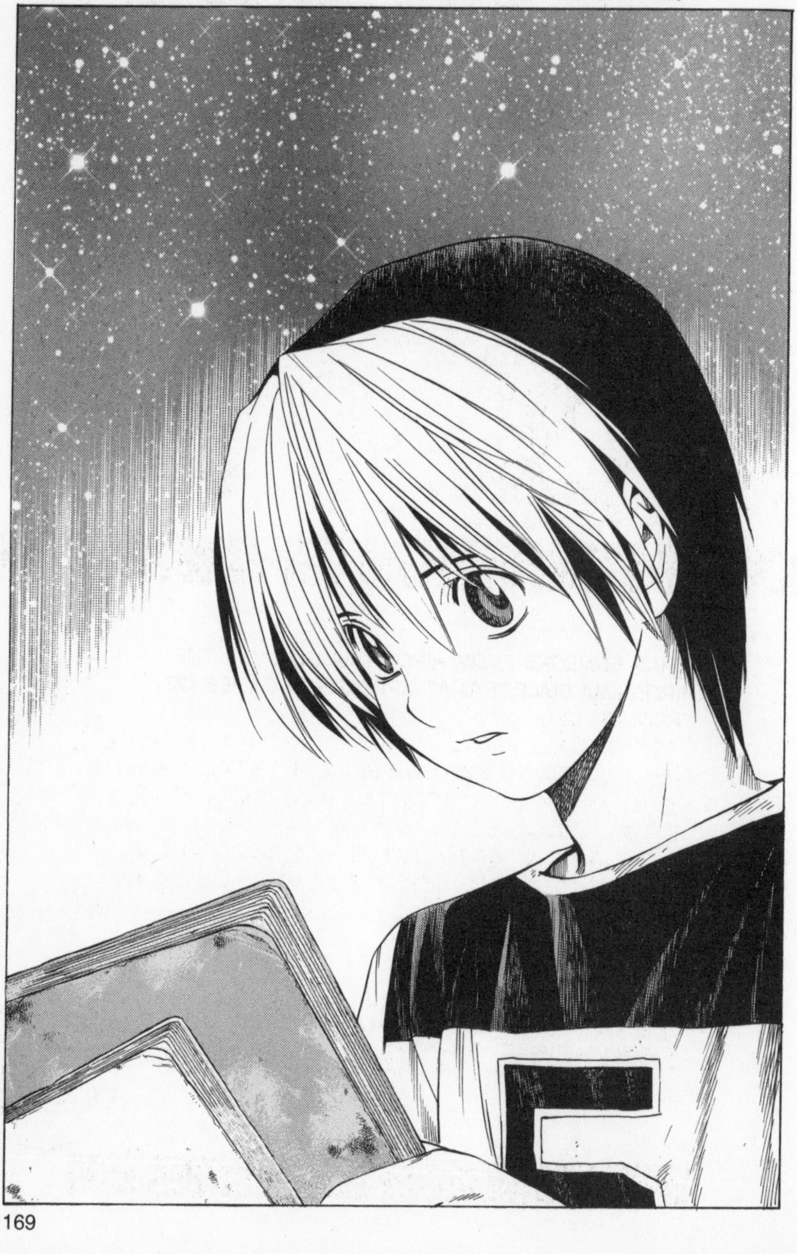

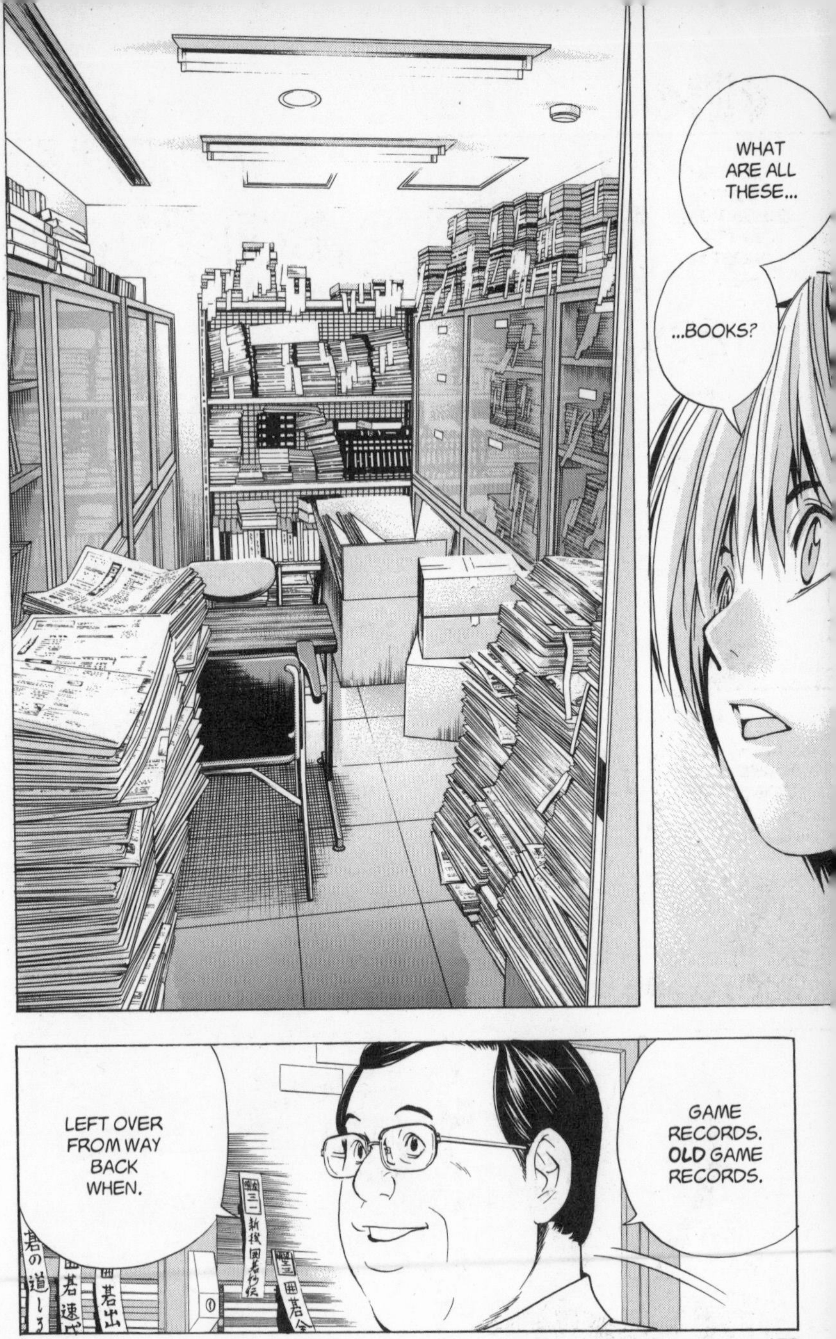
WHAT ARE ALL THESE...
...BOOKS?
GAME RECORDS. OLD GAME RECORDS.
LEFT OVER FROM WAY BACK WHEN.

READ THIS WAY

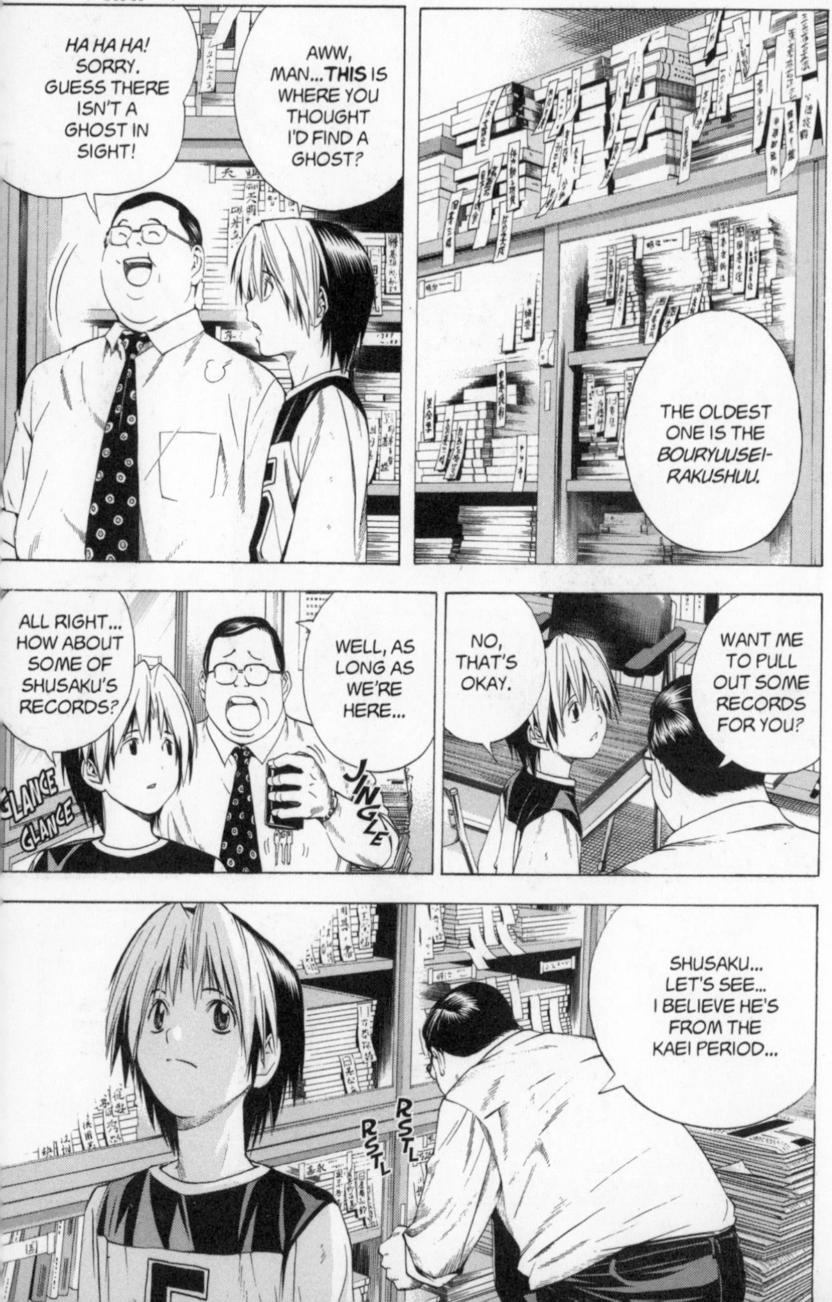
THE OLDEST ONE IS THE BOURYUUSEI-RAKUSHUU.
AWW, MAN... THIS IS WHERE YOU THOUGHT I'D FIND A GHOST?
HA HA HA! SORRY. GUESS THERE ISN'T A GHOST IN SIGHT!
WANT ME TO PULL OUT SOME RECORDS FOR YOU?
NO, THAT'S OKAY.
WELL, AS LONG AS WE'RE HERE...
JINGLE
ALL RIGHT... HOW ABOUT SOME OF SHUSAKU'S RECORDS?
GLANCE GLANCE
SHUSAKU... LET'S SEE... I BELIEVE HE'S FROM THE KAEI PERIOD...
RSTL RSTL

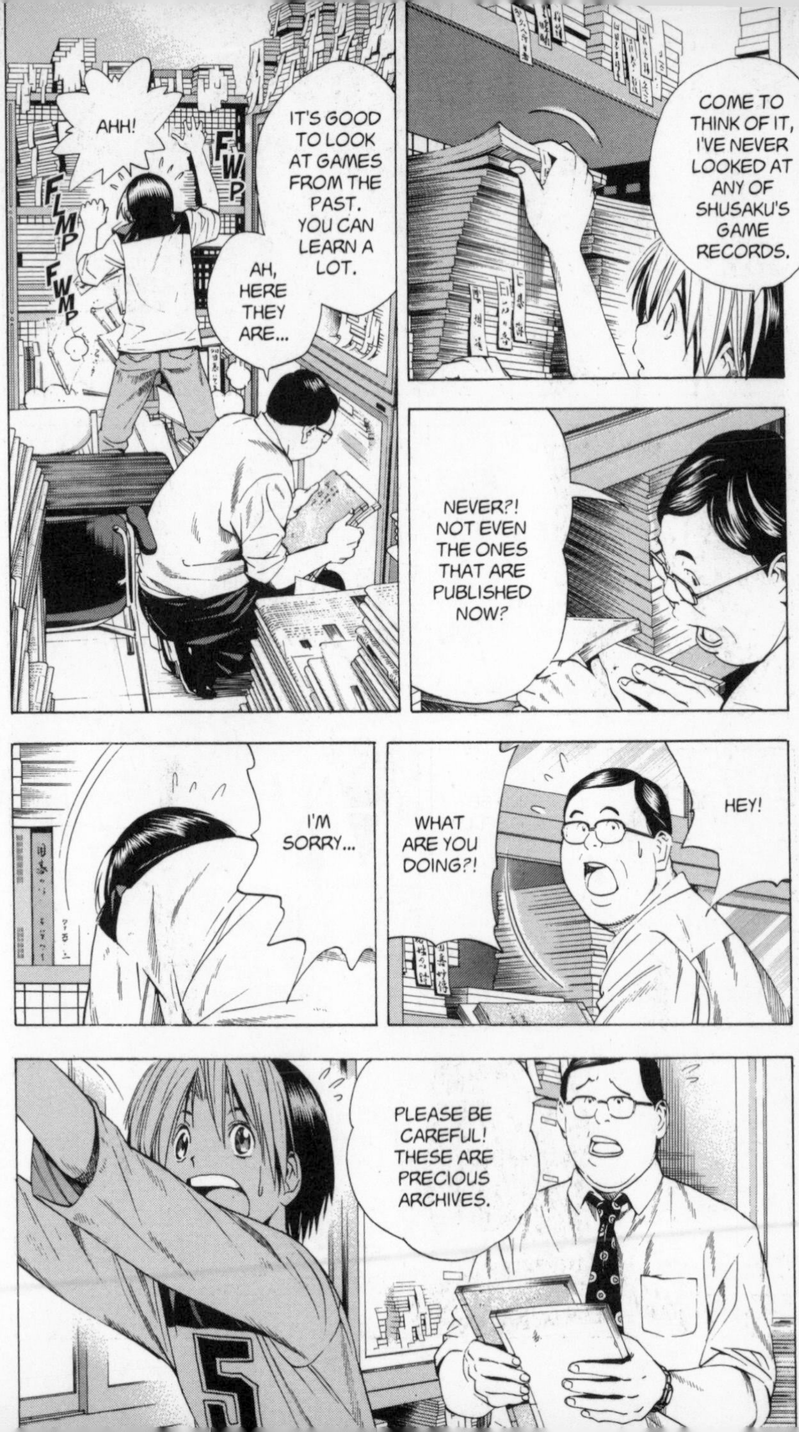
COME TO THINK OF IT, I'VE NEVER LOOKED AT ANY OF SHUSAKU'S GAME RECORDS.
NEVER?! NOT EVEN THE ONES THAT ARE PUBLISHED NOW?
IT'S GOOD TO LOOK AT GAMES FROM THE PAST. YOU CAN LEARN A LOT.
FWP
AHH!
AH, HERE THEY ARE...
FLMP
FWMP
HEY!
WHAT ARE YOU DOING?!
I'M SORRY...
PLEASE BE CAREFUL! THESE ARE PRECIOUS ARCHIVES.

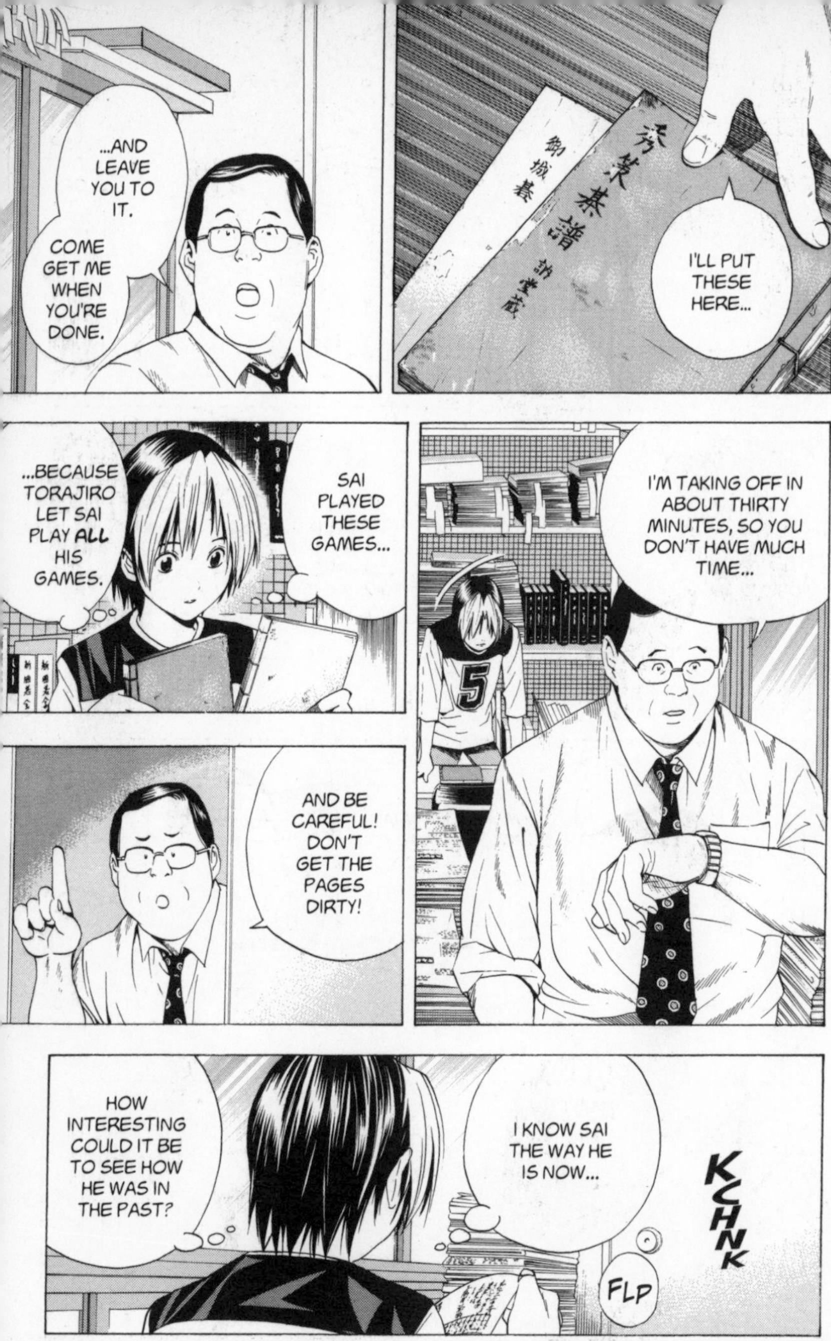
I'LL PUT THESE HERE...
...AND LEAVE YOU TO IT.
COME GET ME WHEN YOU'RE DONE.
I'M TAKING OFF IN ABOUT THIRTY MINUTES, SO YOU DON'T HAVE MUCH TIME...
SAI PLAYED THESE GAMES...
...BECAUSE TORAJIRO LET SAI PLAY ALL HIS GAMES.
AND BE CAREFUL! DON'T GET THE PAGES DIRTY!
KCHNK
FLP
I KNOW SAI THE WAY HE IS NOW...
HOW INTERESTING COULD IT BE TO SEE HOW HE WAS IN THE PAST?

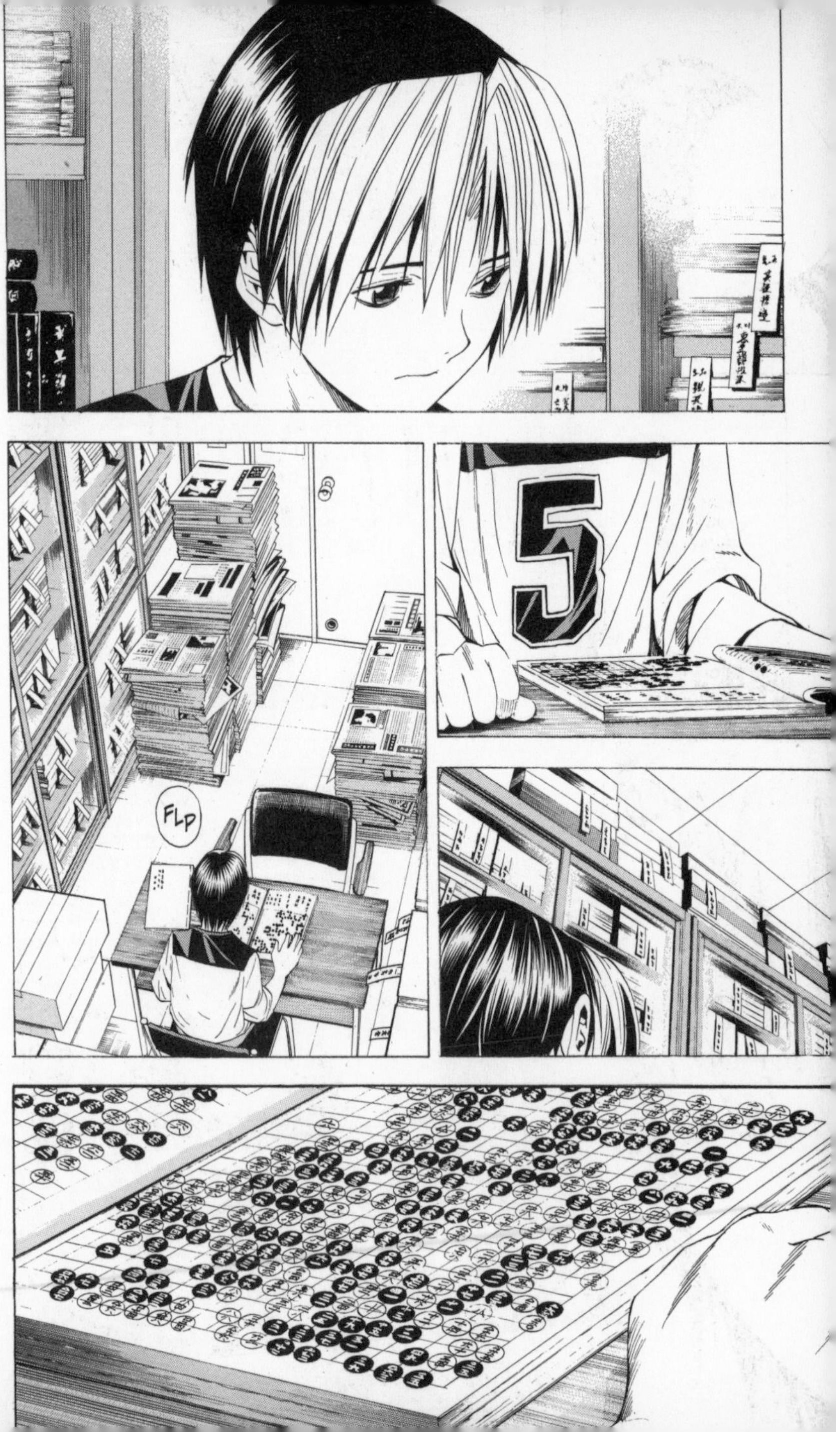
FLP

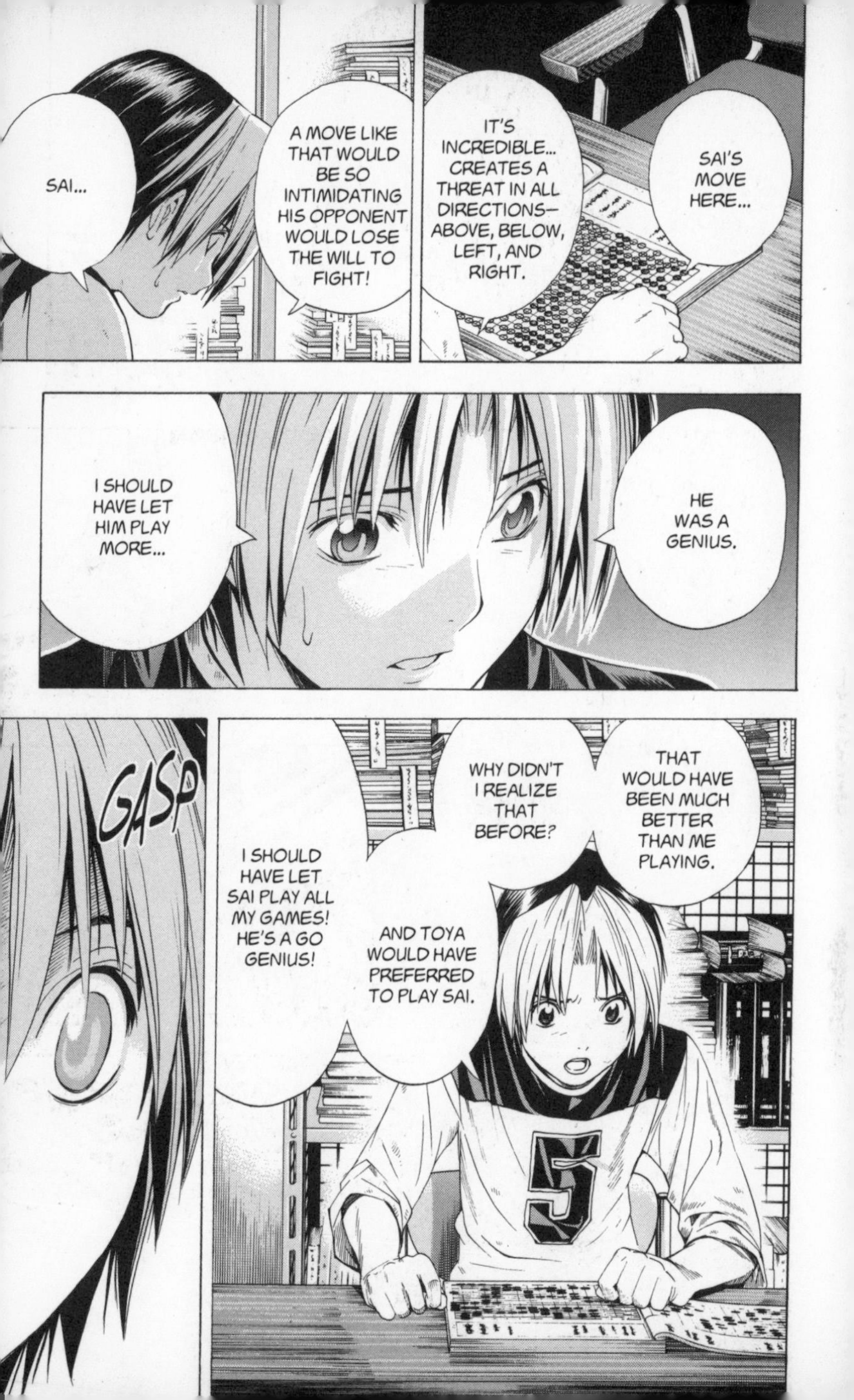
SAI'S MOVE HERE...
IT'S INCREDIBLE... CREATES A THREAT IN ALL DIRECTIONS—ABOVE, BELOW, LEFT, AND RIGHT.
A MOVE LIKE THAT WOULD BE SO INTIMIDATING HIS OPPONENT WOULD LOSE THE WILL TO FIGHT!
SAI...
HE WAS A GENIUS.
I SHOULD HAVE LET HIM PLAY MORE...
THAT WOULD HAVE BEEN MUCH BETTER THAN ME PLAYING.
WHY DIDN'T I REALIZE THAT BEFORE?
AND TOYA WOULD HAVE PREFERRED TO PLAY SAI.
I SHOULD HAVE LET SAI PLAY ALL MY GAMES! HE'S A GO GENIUS!
GASP

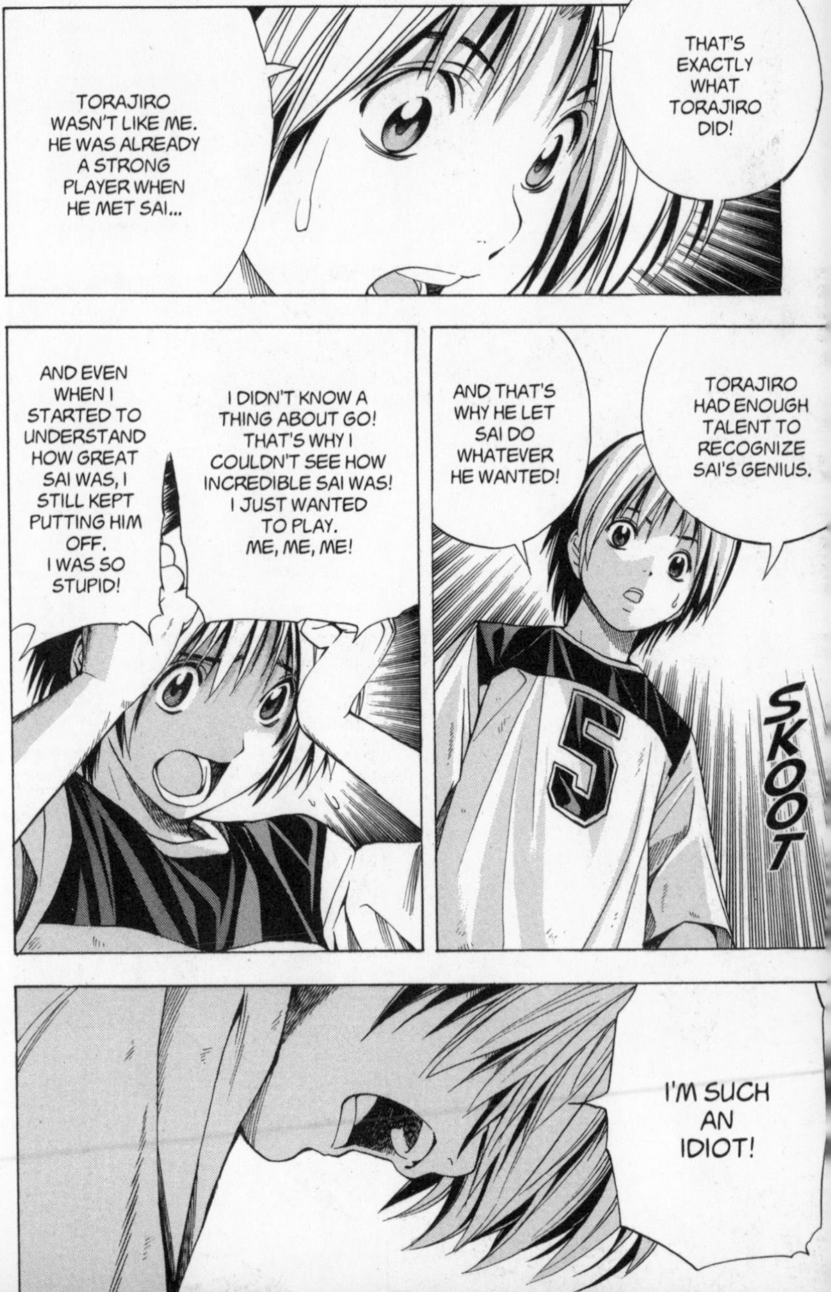
THAT'S EXACTLY WHAT TORAJIRO DID!
TORAJIRO WASN'T LIKE ME. HE WAS ALREADY A STRONG PLAYER WHEN HE MET SAI...
TORAJIRO HAD ENOUGH TALENT TO RECOGNIZE SAI'S GENIUS.
AND THAT'S WHY HE LET SAI DO WHATEVER HE WANTED!
SKOOT
I DIDN'T KNOW A THING ABOUT GO! THAT'S WHY I COULDN'T SEE HOW INCREDIBLE SAI WAS! I JUST WANTED TO PLAY. ME, ME, ME!
AND EVEN WHEN I STARTED TO UNDERSTAND HOW GREAT SAI WAS, I STILL KEPT PUTTING HIM OFF. I WAS SO STUPID!
I'M SUCH AN IDIOT!

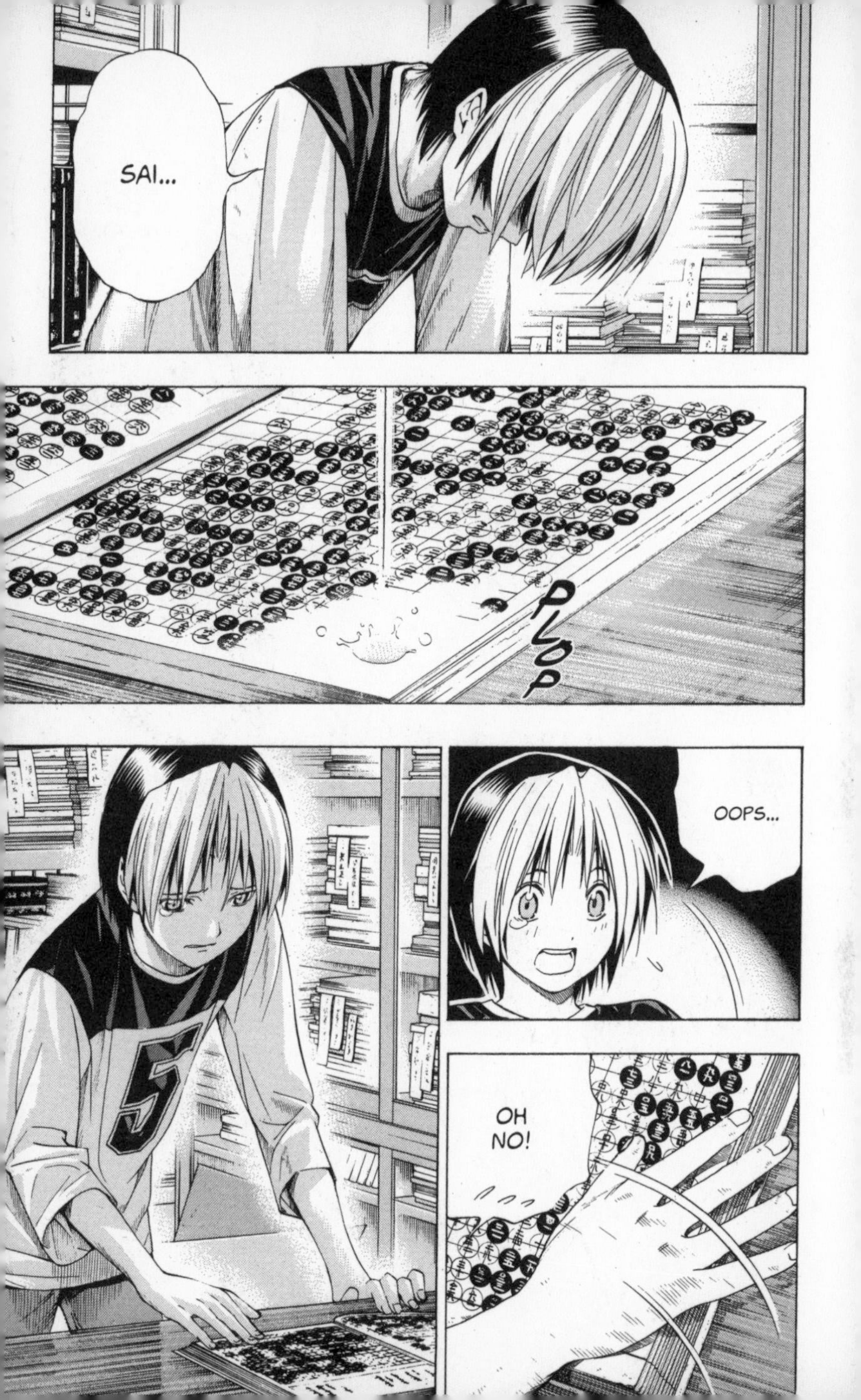
SAI...
PLOP
OOPS...
OH NO!

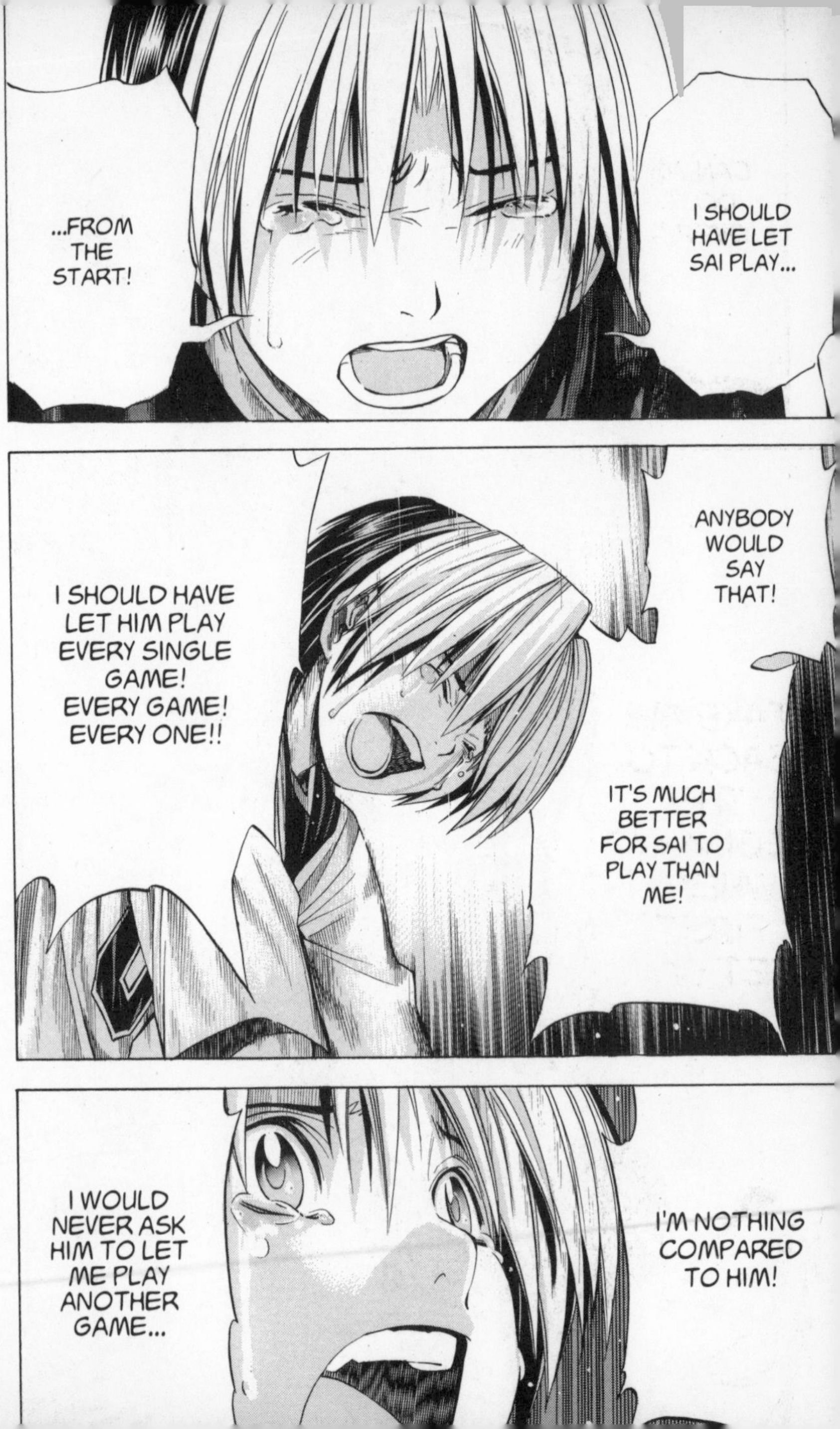
I SHOULD HAVE LET SAI PLAY...
...FROM THE START!
ANYBODY WOULD SAY THAT!
I SHOULD HAVE LET HIM PLAY EVERY SINGLE GAME! EVERY GAME! EVERY ONE!!
IT'S MUCH BETTER FOR SAI TO PLAY THAN ME!
I'M NOTHING COMPARED TO HIM!
I WOULD NEVER ASK HIM TO LET ME PLAY ANOTHER GAME...

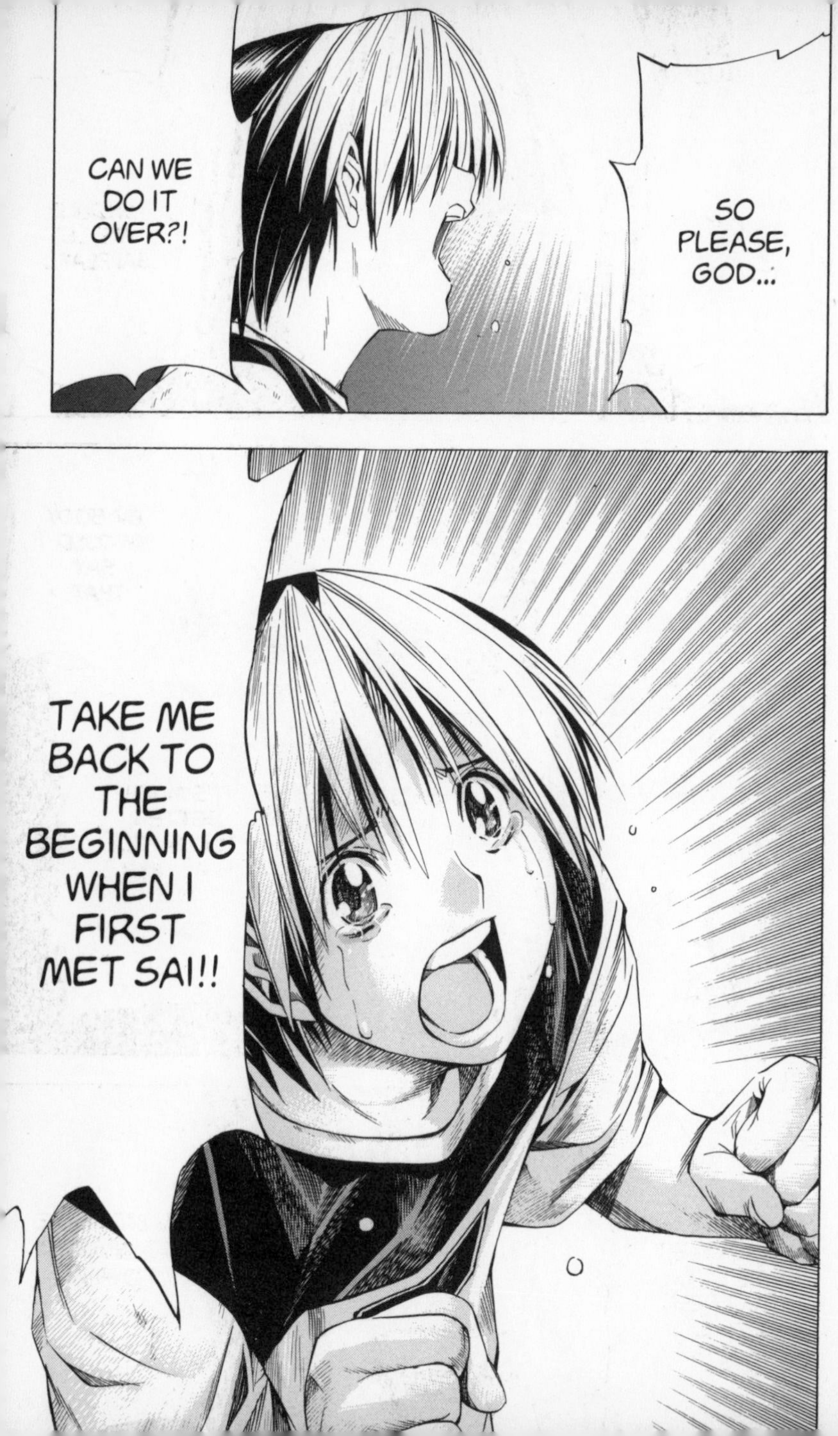
SO PLEASE, GOD...
CAN WE DO IT OVER?!
TAKE ME BACK TO THE BEGINNING WHEN I FIRST MET SAI!!

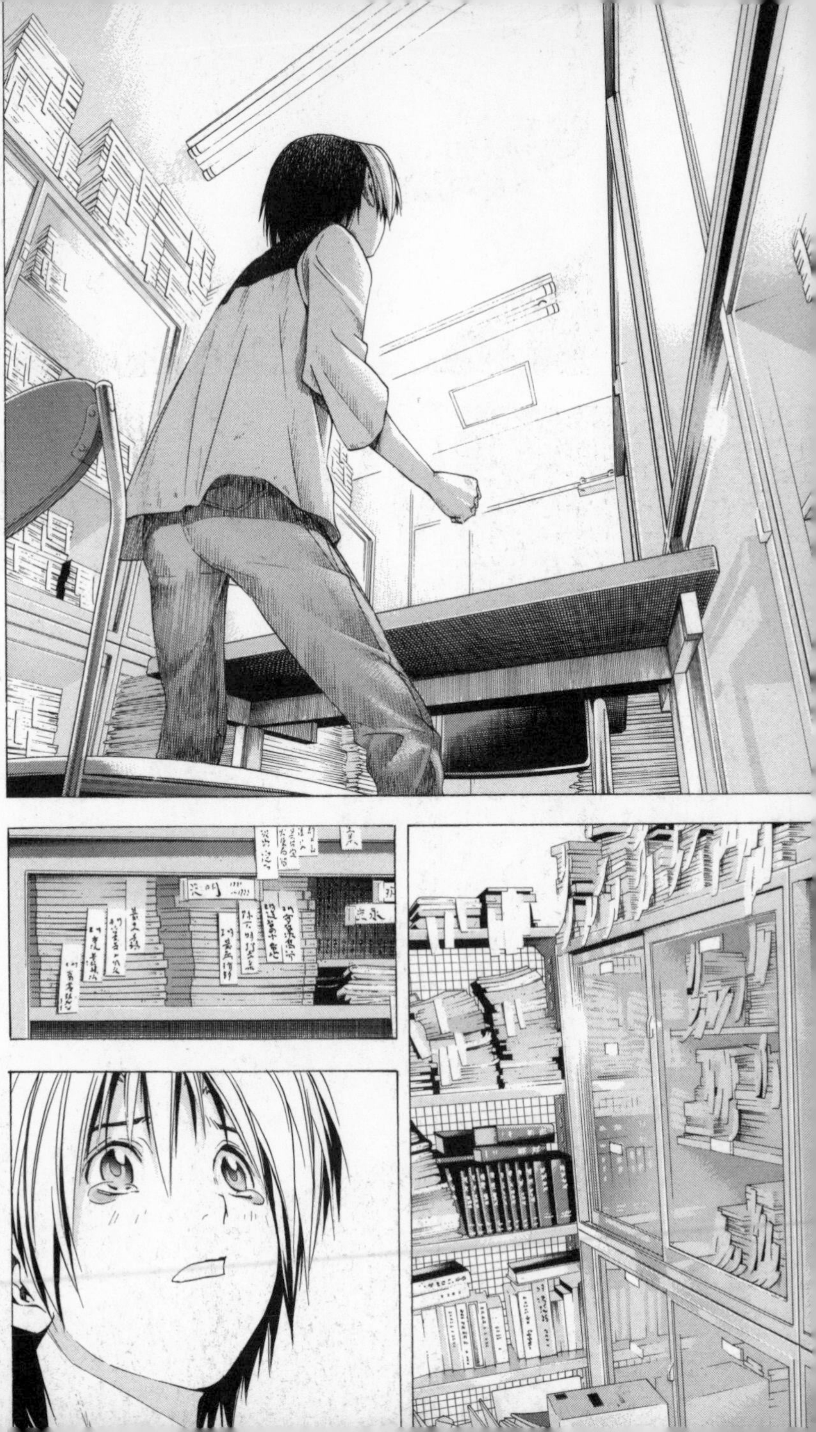

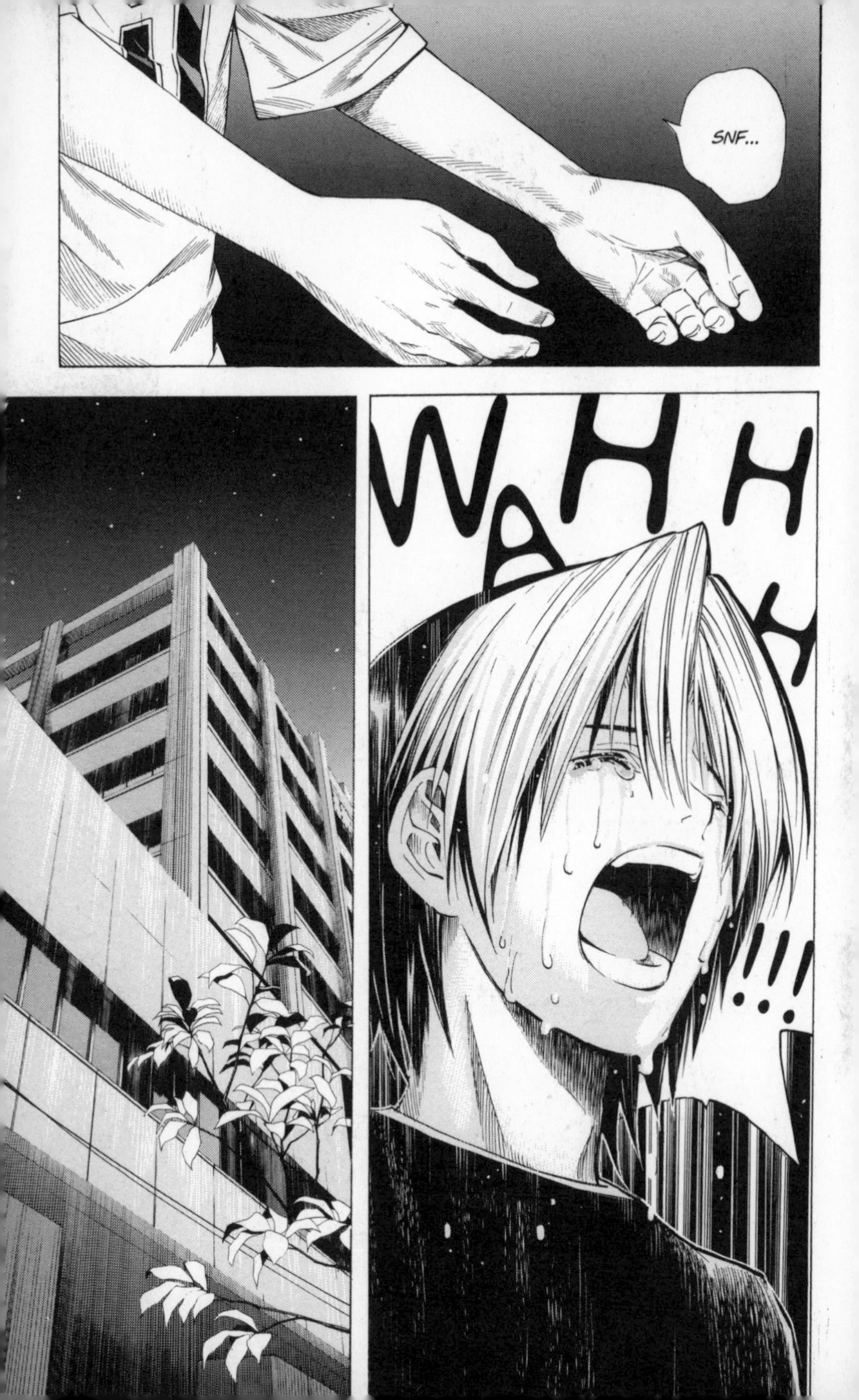
SNF...
WAHHH!!!...

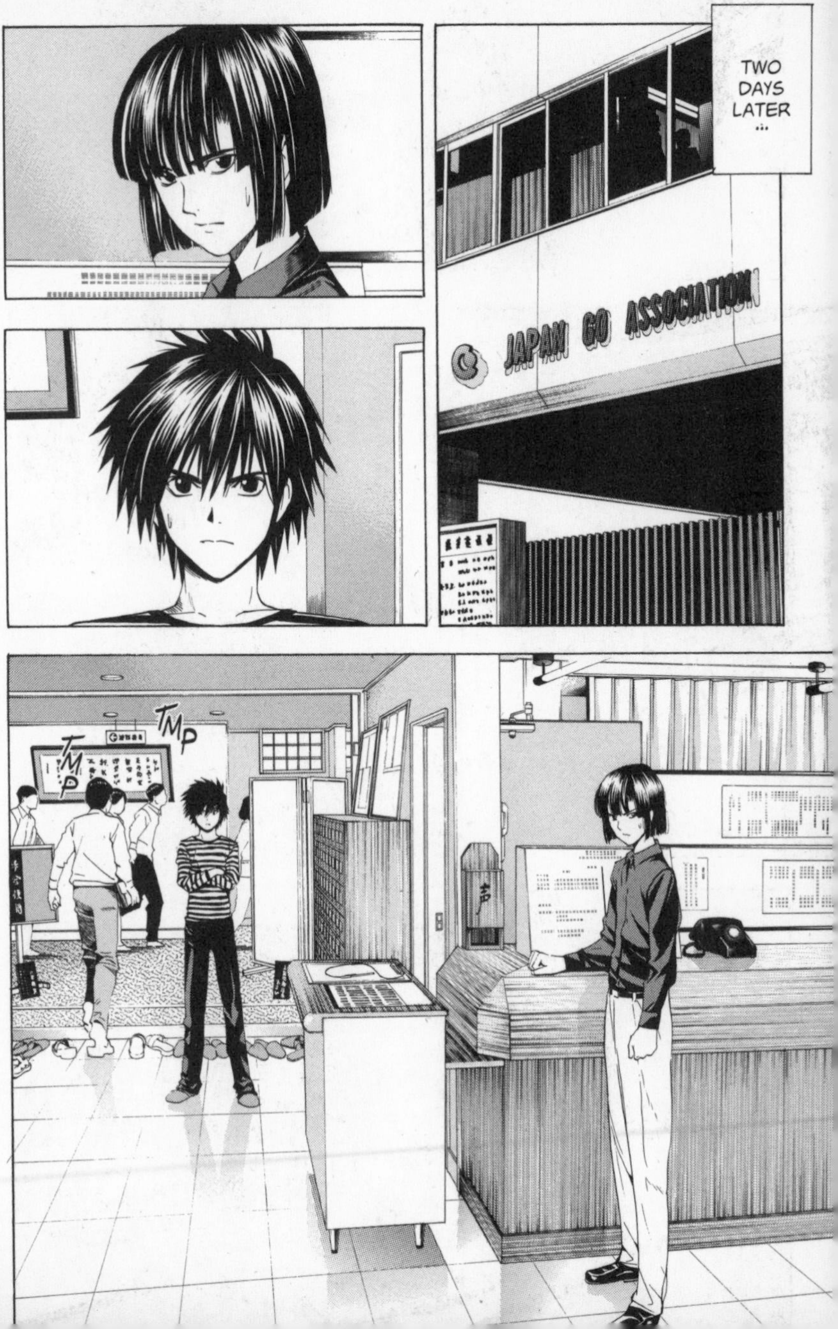
TWO DAYS LATER ...
JAPAN GO ASSOCIATION
TMP
TMP

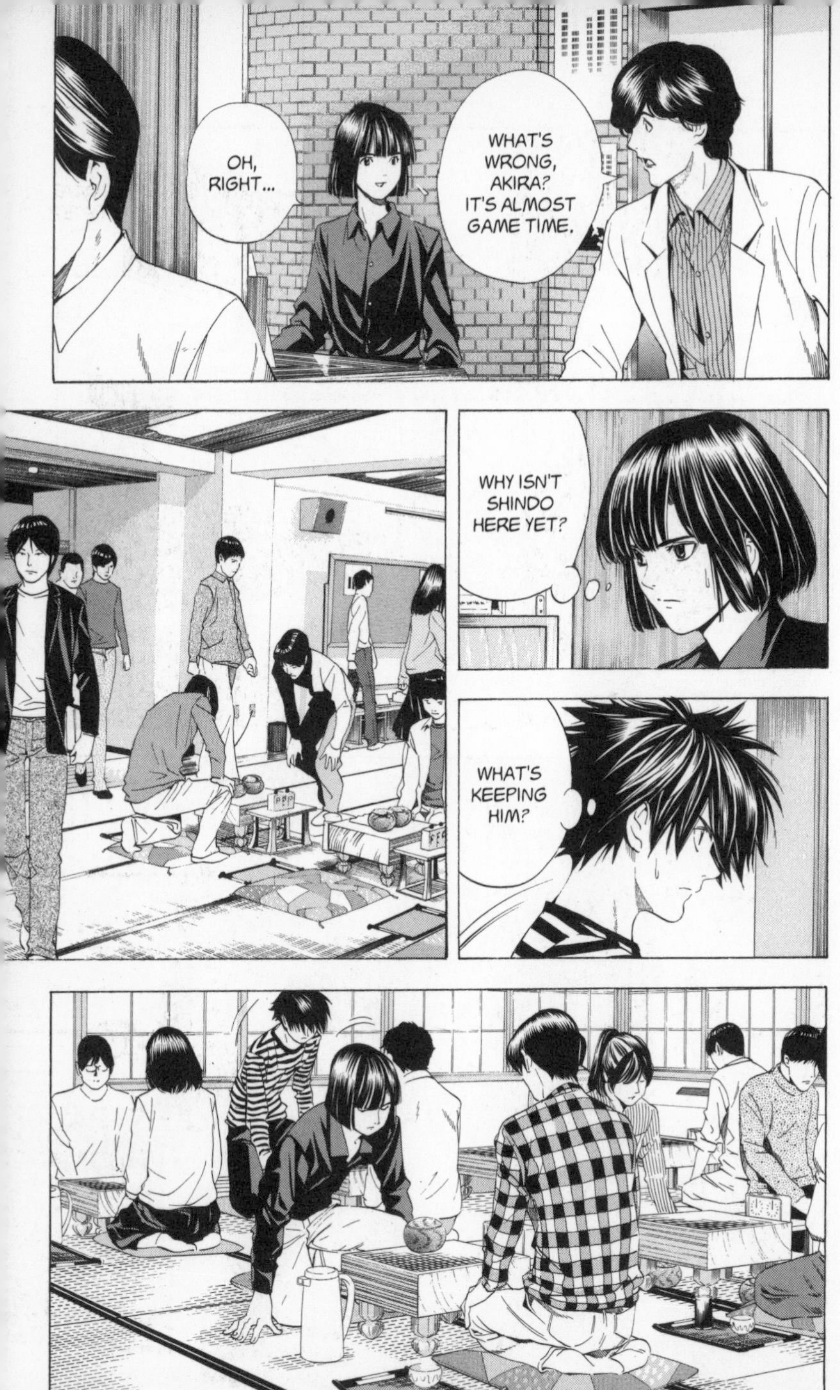
WHAT'S WRONG, AKIRA? IT'S ALMOST GAME TIME.
OH, RIGHT...
WHY ISN'T SHINDO HERE YET?
WHAT'S KEEPING HIM?

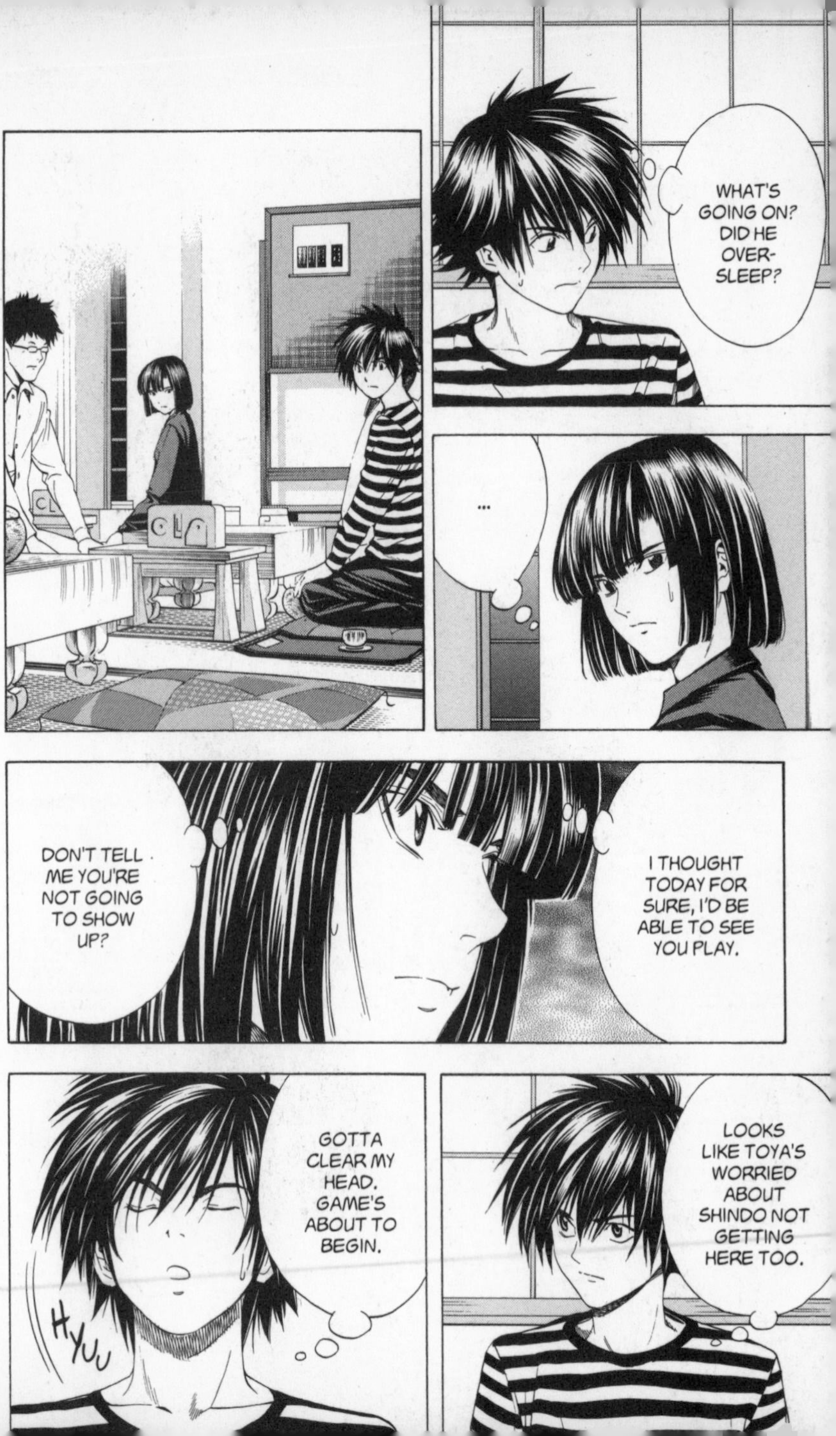
WHAT'S GOING ON? DID HE OVER-SLEEP?
...
I THOUGHT TODAY FOR SURE, I'D BE ABLE TO SEE YOU PLAY.
DON'T TELL ME YOU'RE NOT GOING TO SHOW UP?
LOOKS LIKE TOYA'S WORRIED ABOUT SHINDO NOT GETTING HERE TOO.
GOTTA CLEAR MY HEAD. GAME'S ABOUT TO BEGIN.
HYUU

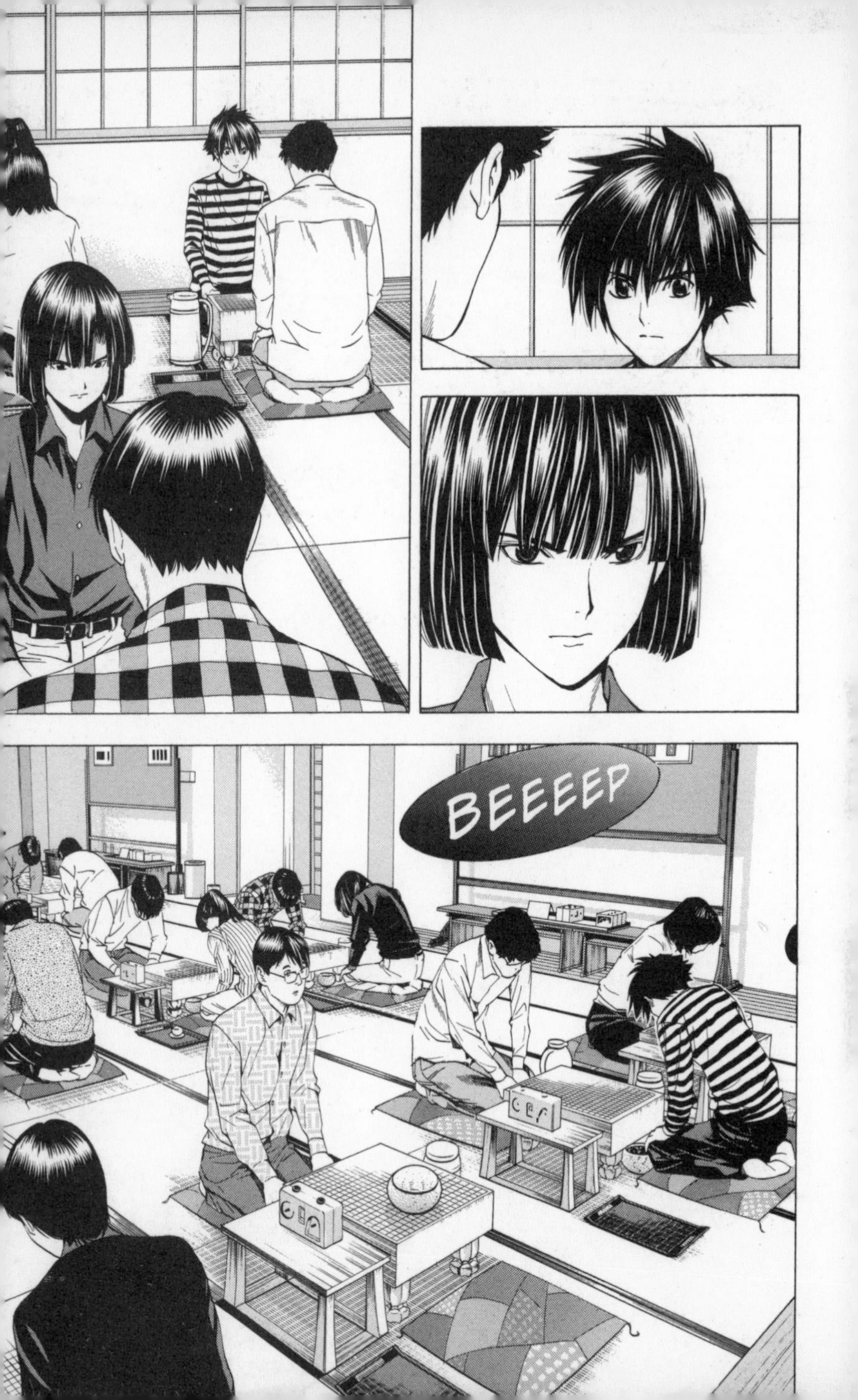
BEEEEP

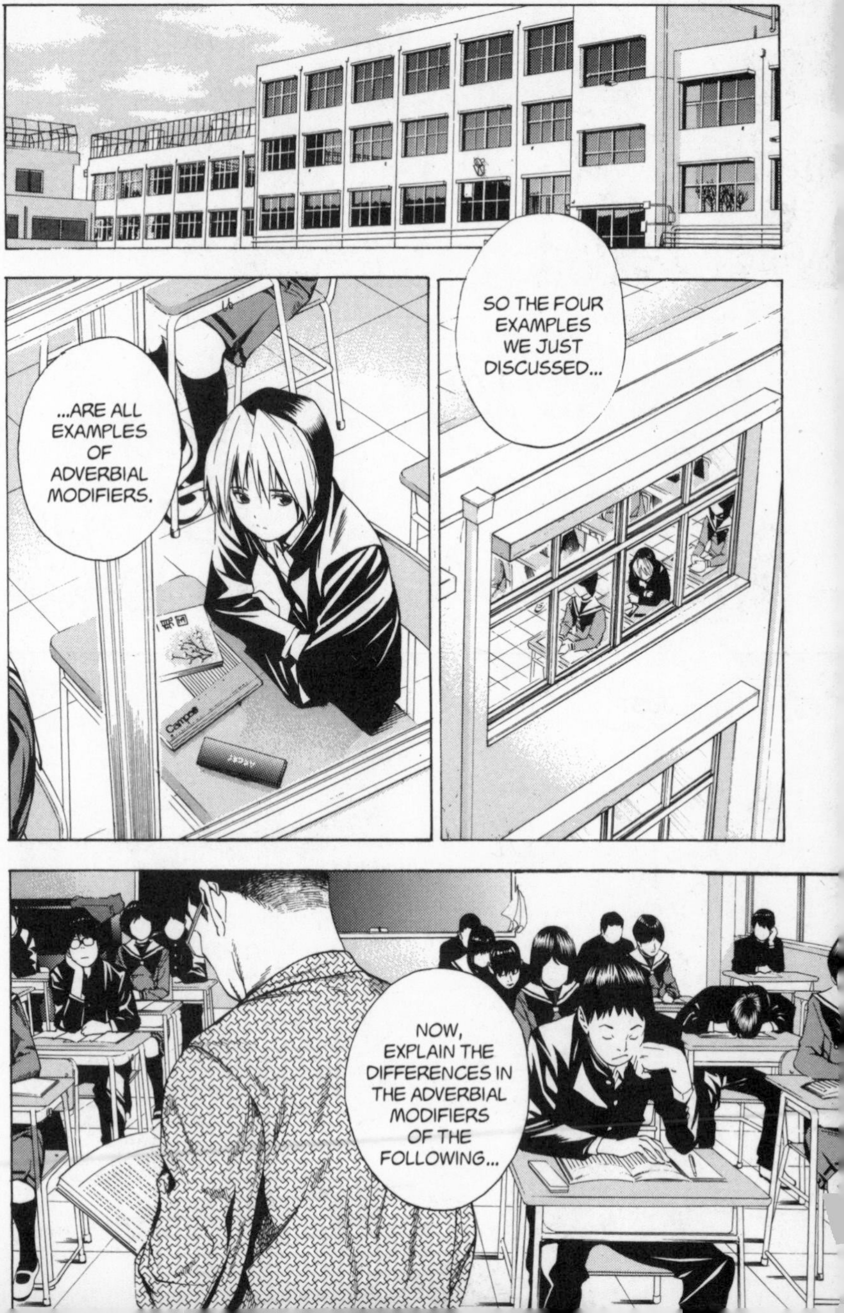
SO THE FOUR EXAMPLES WE JUST DISCUSSED...
...ARE ALL EXAMPLES OF ADVERBIAL MODIFIERS.
NOW, EXPLAIN THE DIFFERENCES IN THE ADVERBIAL MODIFIERS OF THE FOLLOWING...

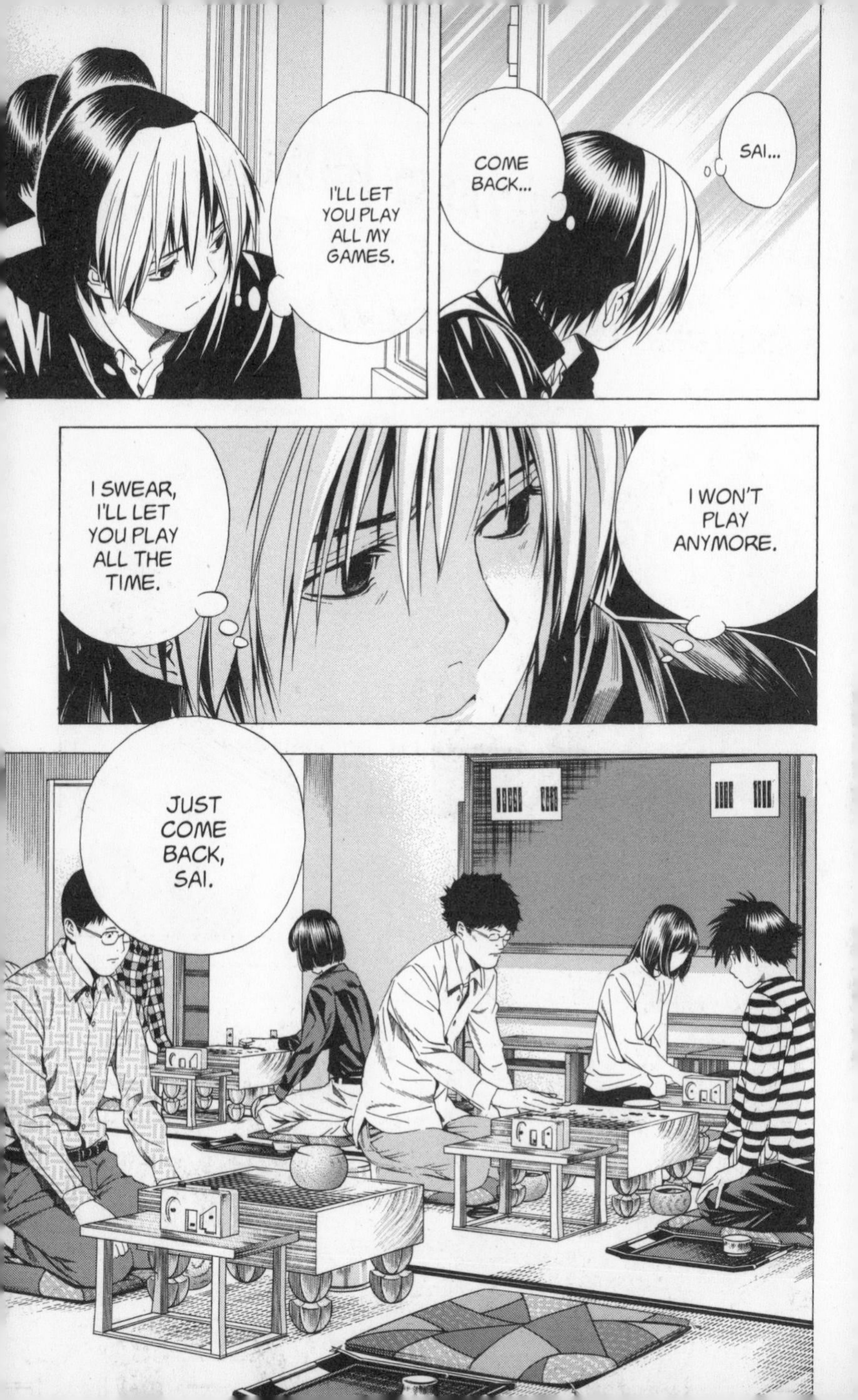
SAI...
COME BACK...
I'LL LET YOU PLAY ALL MY GAMES.
I WON'T PLAY ANYMORE.
I SWEAR, I'LL LET YOU PLAY ALL THE TIME.
JUST COME BACK, SAI.

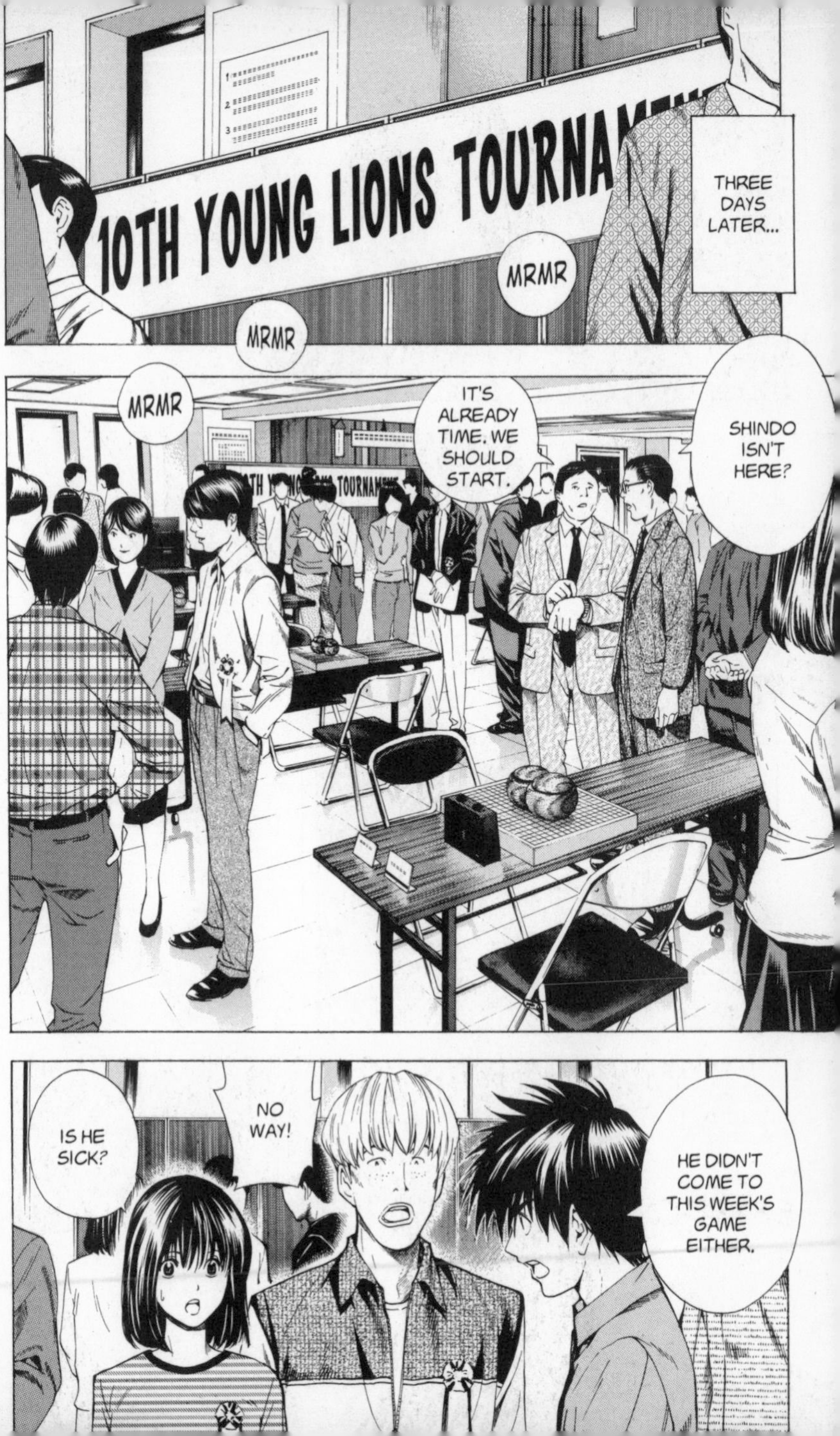
THREE DAYS LATER...
10TH YOUNG LIONS TOURNAM
MRMR
MRMR
SHINDO ISN'T HERE?
IT'S ALREADY TIME. WE SHOULD START.
MRMR
HE DIDN'T COME TO THIS WEEK'S GAME EITHER.
NO WAY!
IS HE SICK?

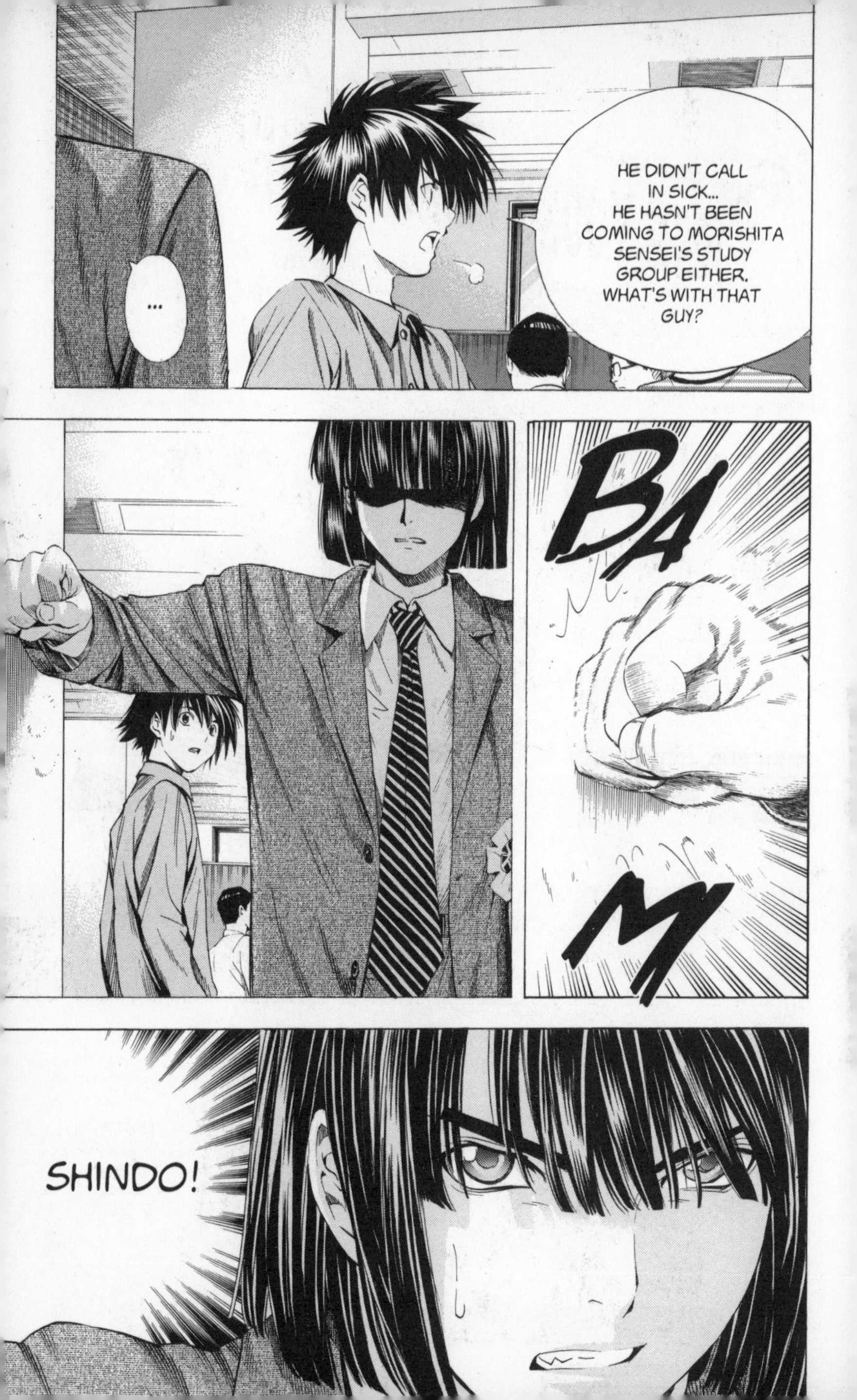
HE DIDN'T CALL IN SICK... HE HASN'T BEEN COMING TO MORISHITA SENSEI'S STUDY GROUP EITHER. WHAT'S WITH THAT GUY?
...
BAM
SHINDO!

A WORD ABOUT HIKARU NO GO

THE REFERENCE ROOM

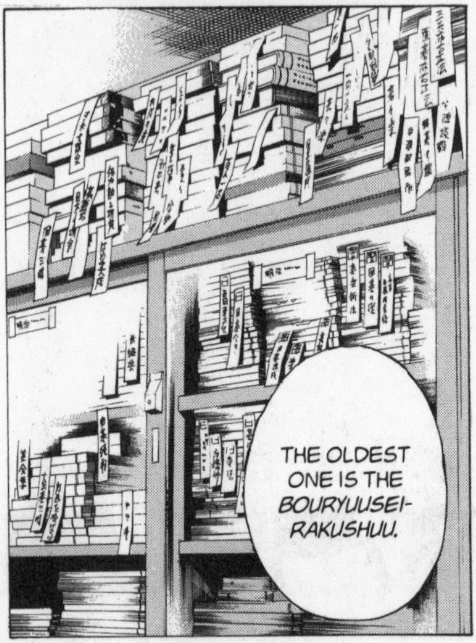
THE OLDEST ONE IS THE *BOURYUUSEI-RAKUSHUU*.

A REAL PROFESSIONAL GO PLAYER TOLD ME HE HADN'T HEARD OF THIS ROOM UNTIL HE READ ABOUT IT IN *HIKARU NO GO*.
SO EVEN INSIDERS DON'T KNOW OF IT.
NO WONDER HIKARU DIDN'T KNOW ABOUT IT.

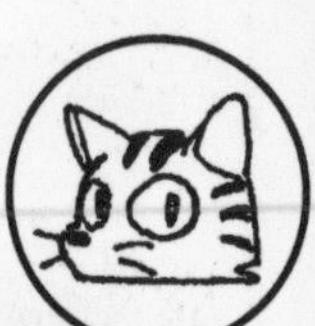

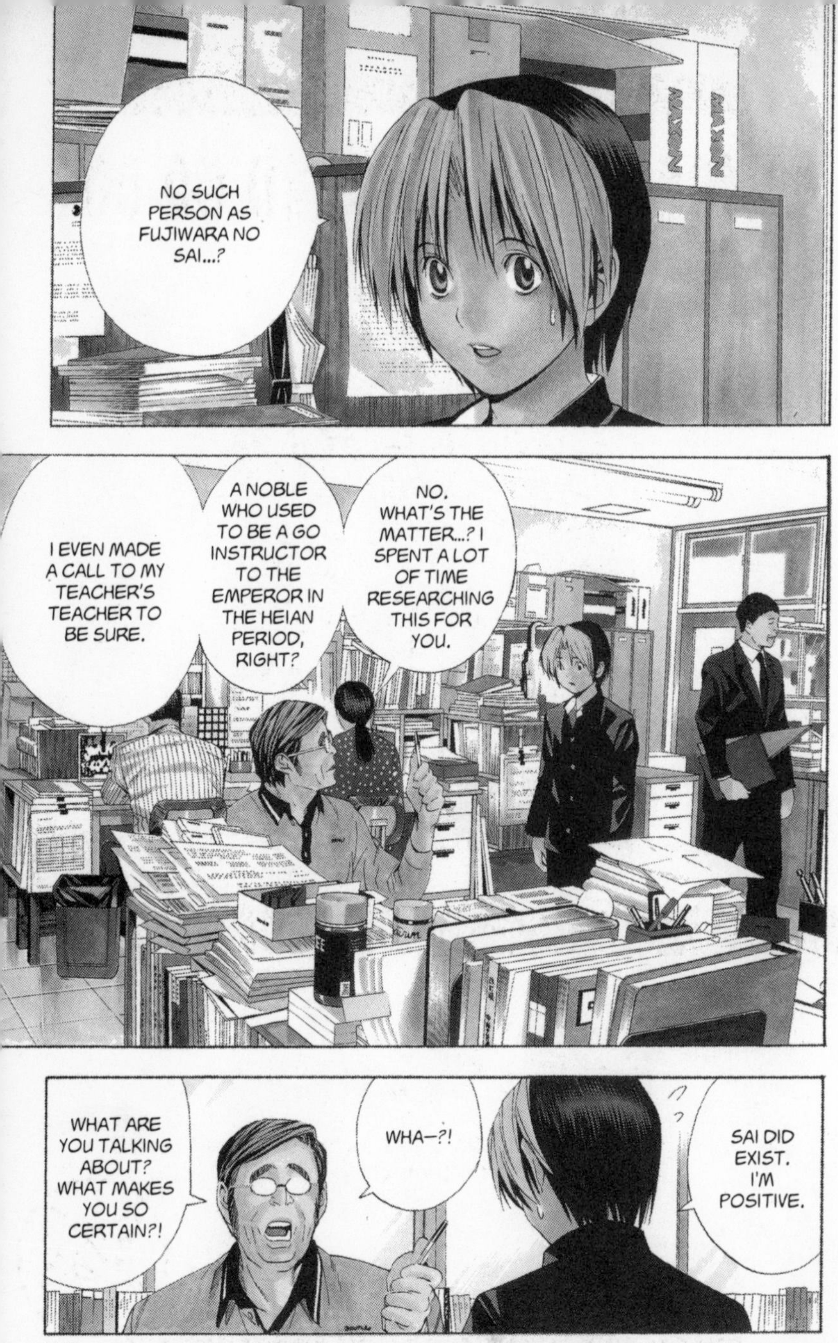
NO SUCH PERSON AS FUJIWARA NO SAI...?
NO. WHAT'S THE MATTER...? I SPENT A LOT OF TIME RESEARCHING THIS FOR YOU.
A NOBLE WHO USED TO BE A GO INSTRUCTOR TO THE EMPEROR IN THE HEIAN PERIOD, RIGHT?
I EVEN MADE A CALL TO MY TEACHER'S TEACHER TO BE SURE.
SAI DID EXIST. I'M POSITIVE.
WHA–?!
WHAT ARE YOU TALKING ABOUT? WHAT MAKES YOU SO CERTAIN?!

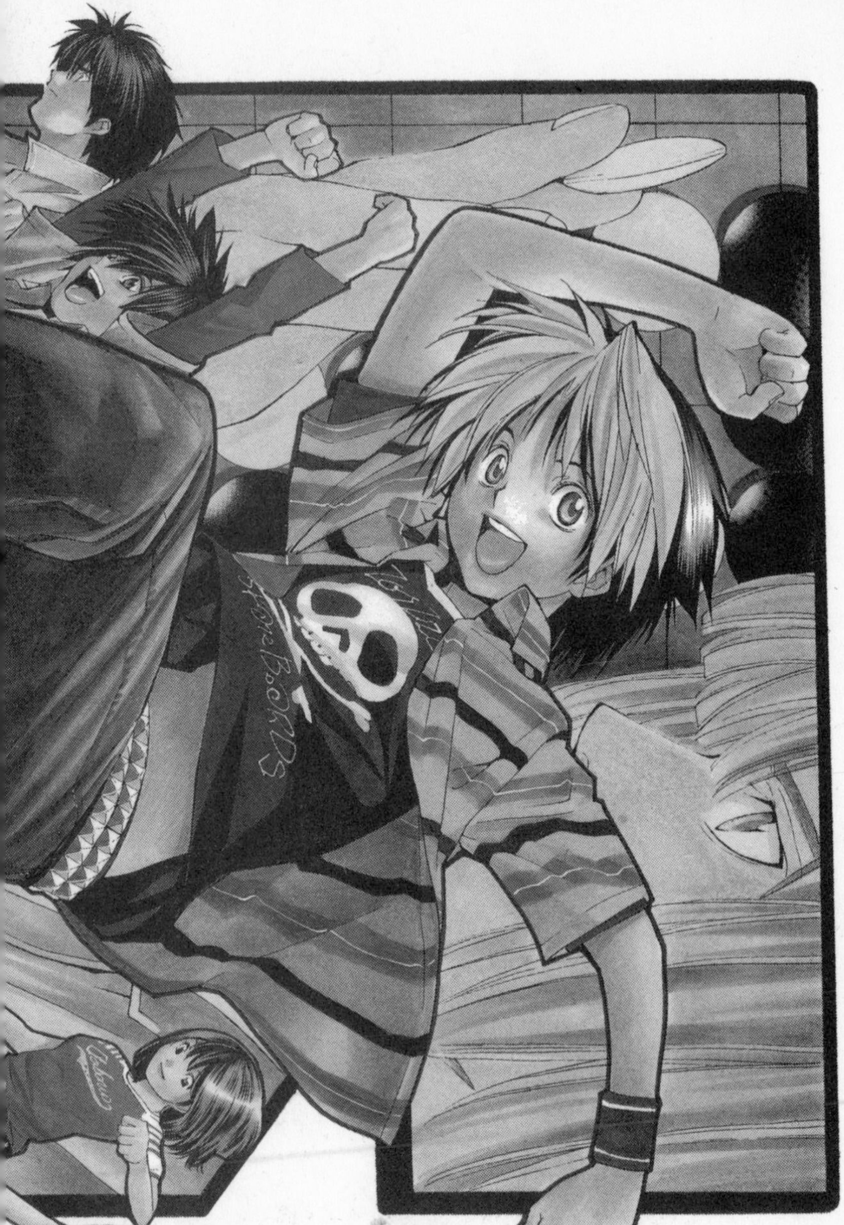

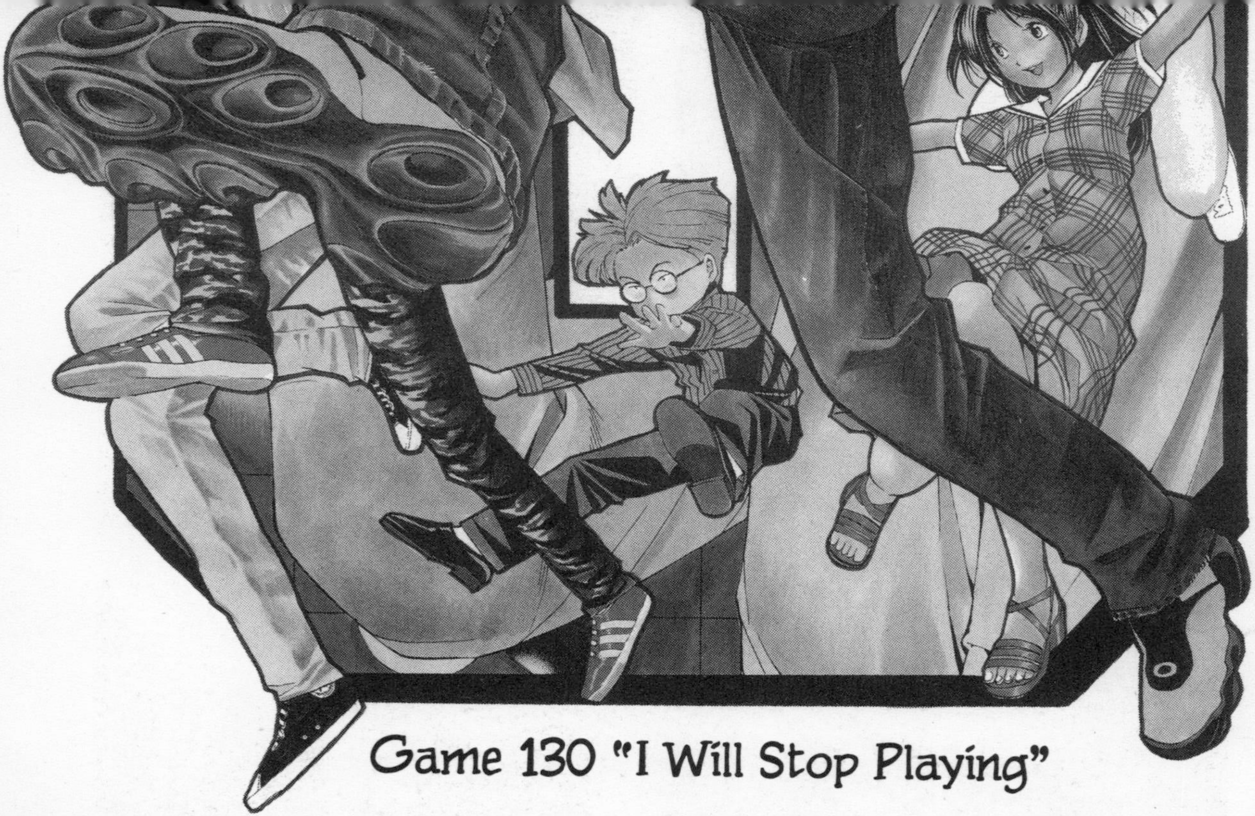

Game 130 "I Will Stop Playing"

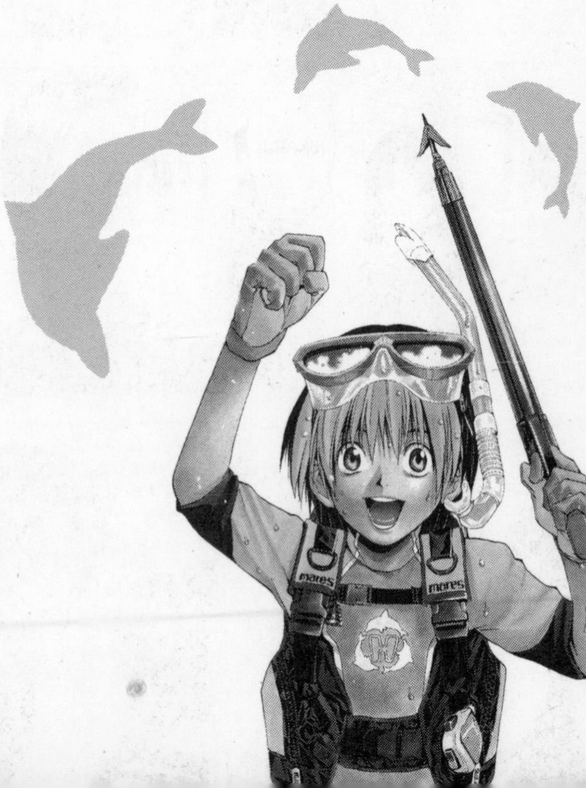
mares
mares

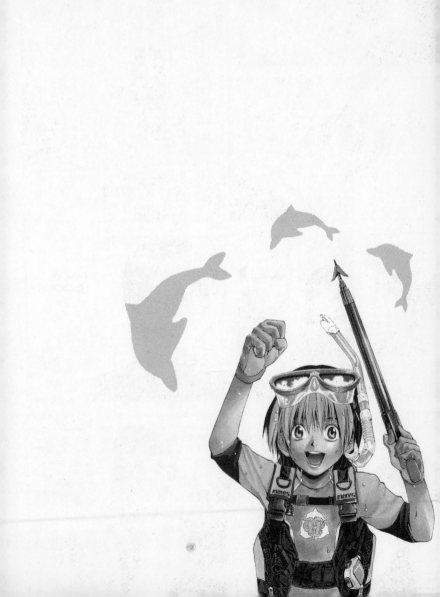

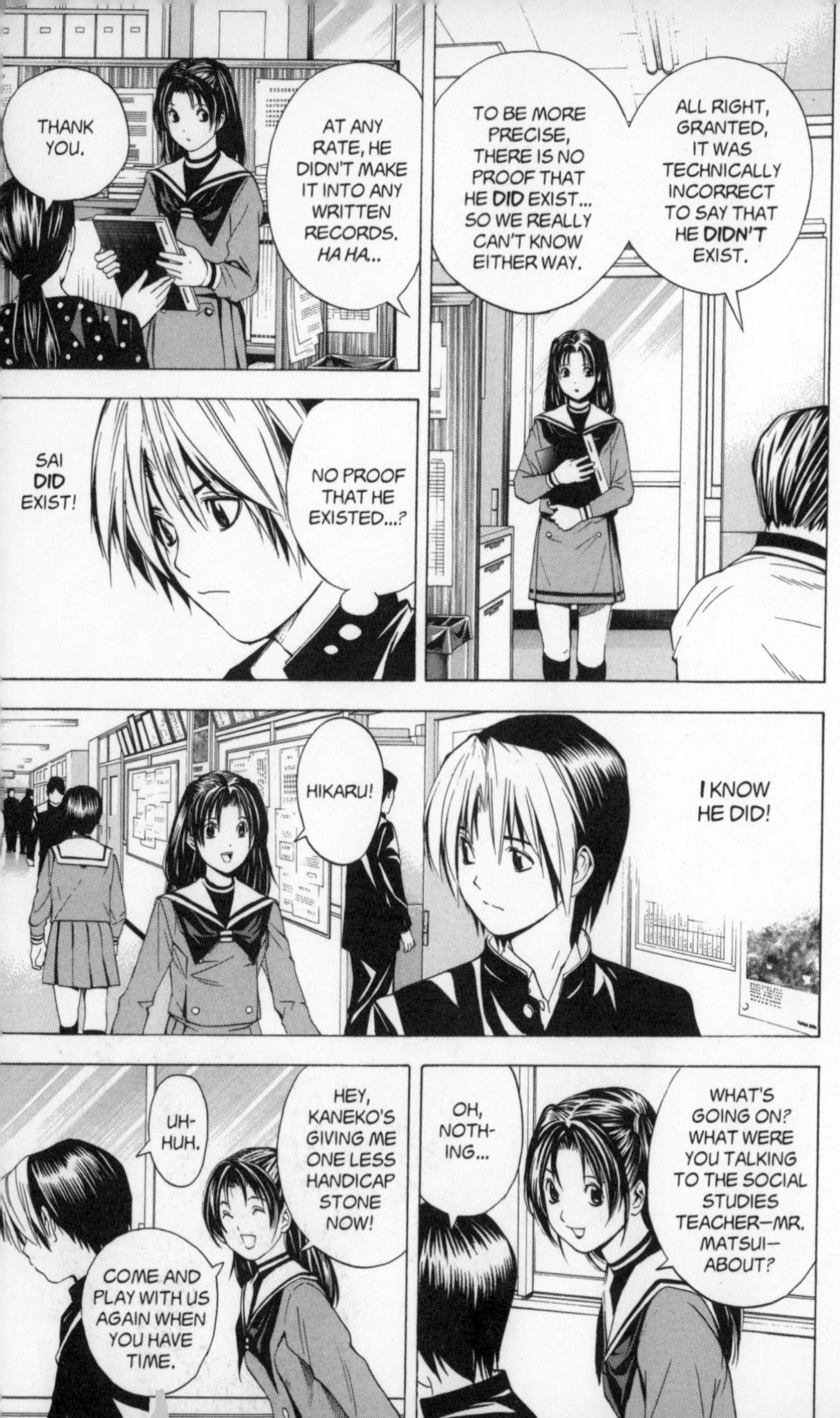
ALL RIGHT, GRANTED, IT WAS TECHNICALLY INCORRECT TO SAY THAT HE **DIDN'T** EXIST.
TO BE MORE PRECISE, THERE IS NO PROOF THAT HE **DID** EXIST... SO WE REALLY CAN'T KNOW EITHER WAY.
AT ANY RATE, HE DIDN'T MAKE IT INTO ANY WRITTEN RECORDS. *HA HA...*
THANK YOU.
NO PROOF THAT HE EXISTED...?
SAI **DID** EXIST!
I KNOW HE DID!
HIKARU!
WHAT'S GOING ON? WHAT WERE YOU TALKING TO THE SOCIAL STUDIES TEACHER—MR. MATSUI—ABOUT?
OH, NOTHING...
HEY, KANEKO'S GIVING ME ONE LESS HANDICAP STONE NOW!
UH-HUH.
COME AND PLAY WITH US AGAIN WHEN YOU HAVE TIME.

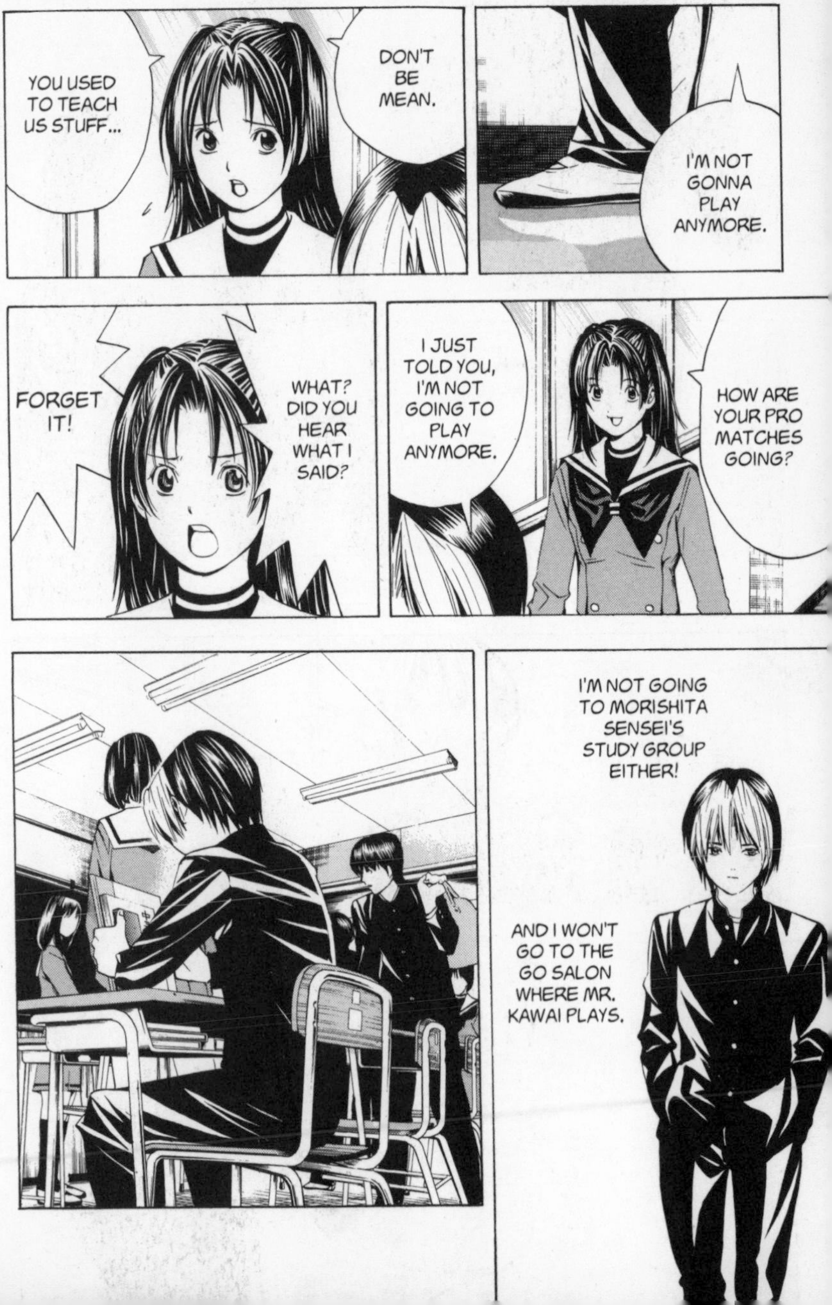
I'M NOT GONNA PLAY ANYMORE.
DON'T BE MEAN.
YOU USED TO TEACH US STUFF...
HOW ARE YOUR PRO MATCHES GOING?
I JUST TOLD YOU, I'M NOT GOING TO PLAY ANYMORE.
WHAT? DID YOU HEAR WHAT I SAID?
FORGET IT!
I'M NOT GOING TO MORISHITA SENSEI'S STUDY GROUP EITHER!
AND I WON'T GO TO THE GO SALON WHERE MR. KAWAI PLAYS.

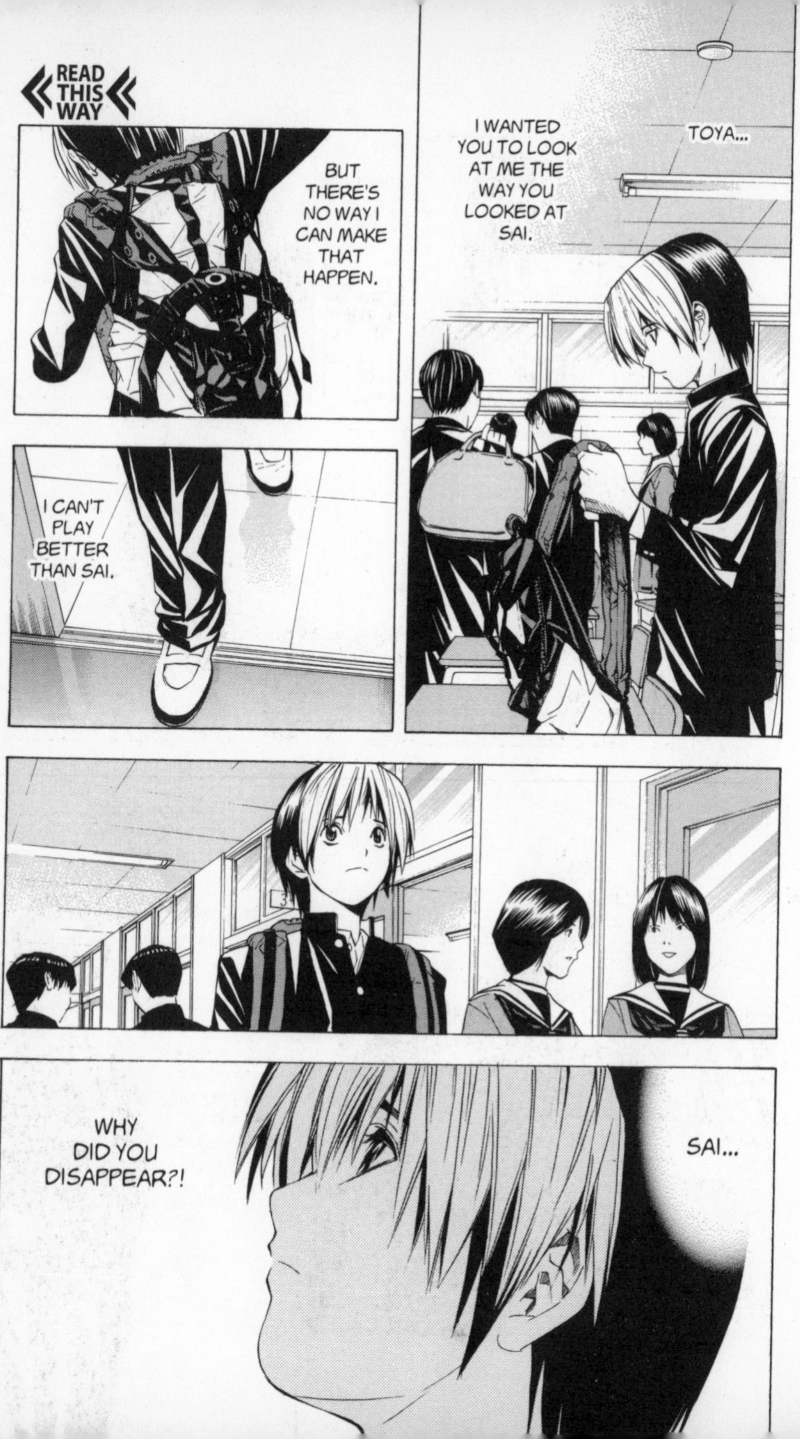
READ THIS WAY
TOYA...
I WANTED YOU TO LOOK AT ME THE WAY YOU LOOKED AT SAI.
BUT THERE'S NO WAY I CAN MAKE THAT HAPPEN.
I CAN'T PLAY BETTER THAN SAI.
SAI...
WHY DID YOU DISAPPEAR?!

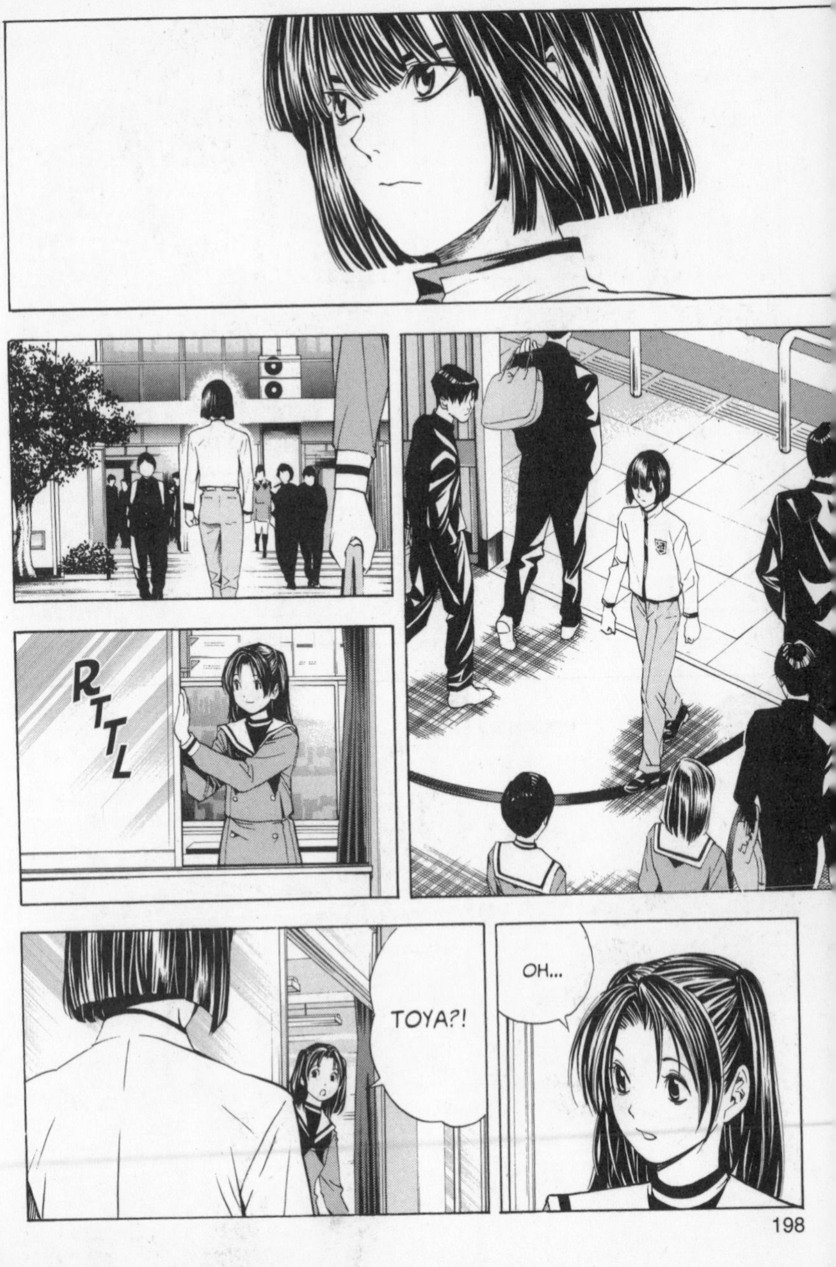
RTTL
OH...
TOYA?!

READ THIS WAY

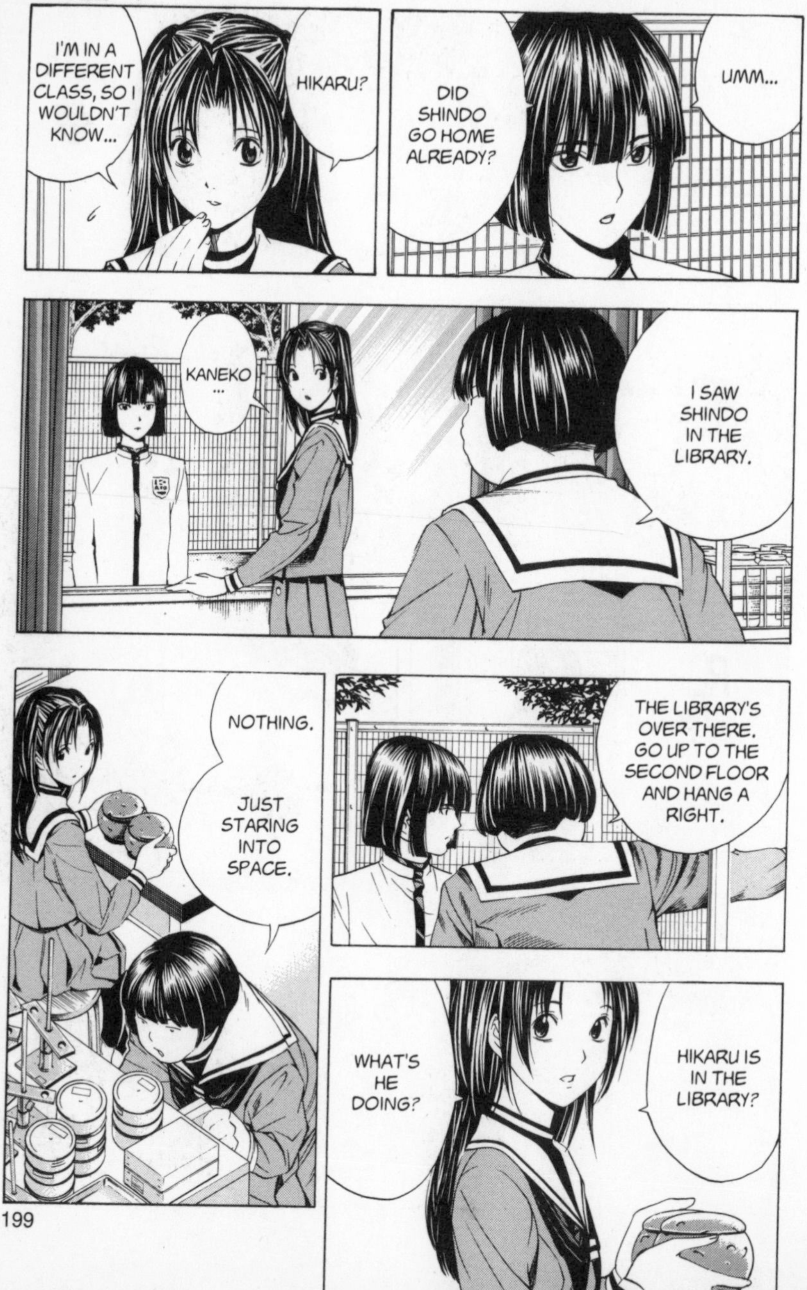
UMM...
DID SHINDO GO HOME ALREADY?
HIKARU?
I'M IN A DIFFERENT CLASS, SO I WOULDN'T KNOW...
I SAW SHINDO IN THE LIBRARY.
KANEKO...
THE LIBRARY'S OVER THERE. GO UP TO THE SECOND FLOOR AND HANG A RIGHT.
HIKARU IS IN THE LIBRARY?
WHAT'S HE DOING?
NOTHING.
JUST STARING INTO SPACE.

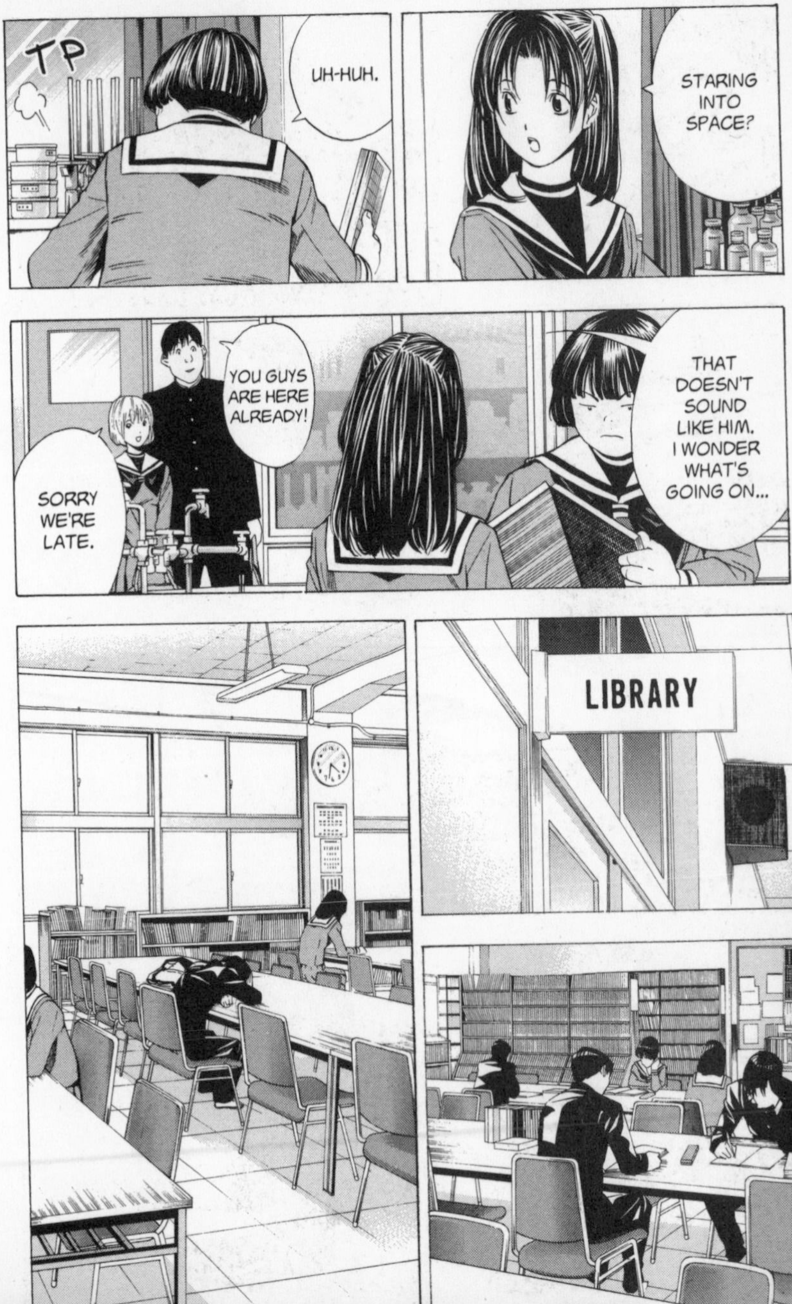
STARING INTO SPACE?
UH-HUH.
TP
THAT DOESN'T SOUND LIKE HIM. I WONDER WHAT'S GOING ON...
YOU GUYS ARE HERE ALREADY!
SORRY WE'RE LATE.
LIBRARY

READ THIS WAY

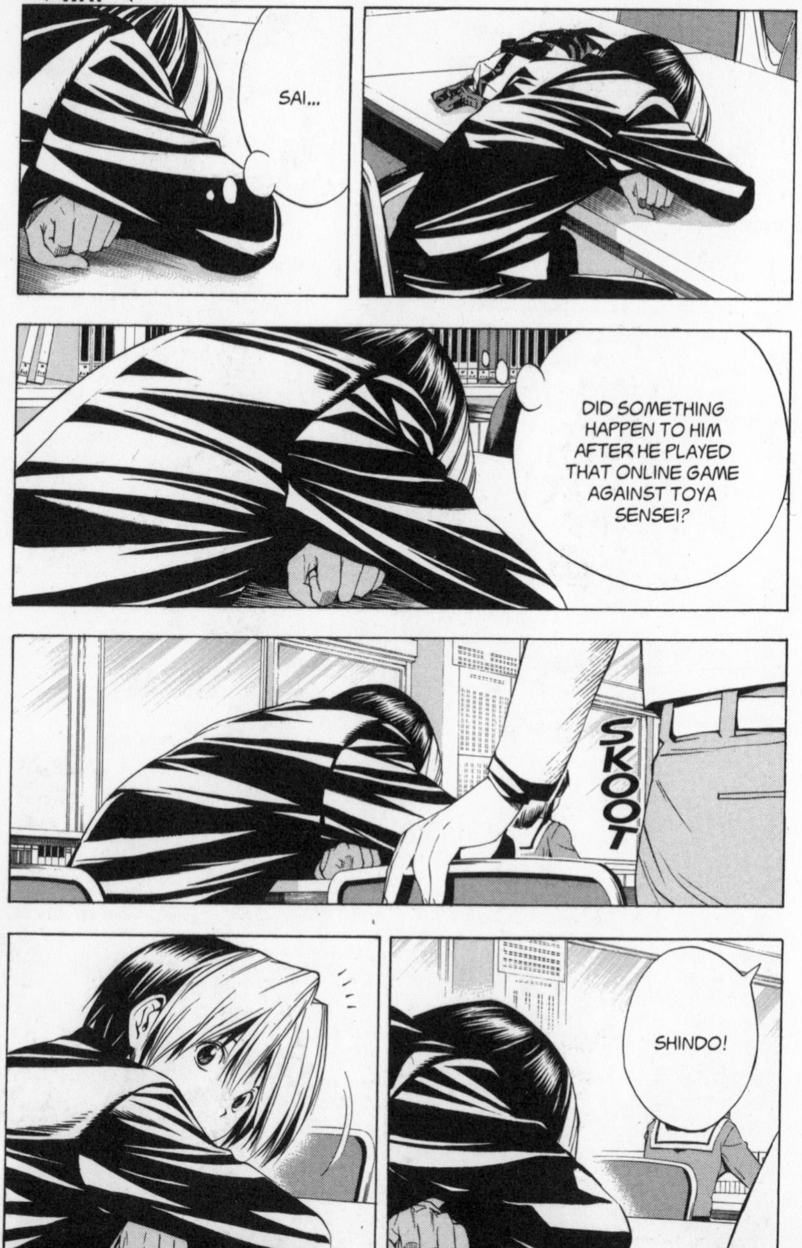
SAI...
DID SOMETHING HAPPEN TO HIM AFTER HE PLAYED THAT ONLINE GAME AGAINST TOYA SENSEI?
SKOOT
SHINDO!

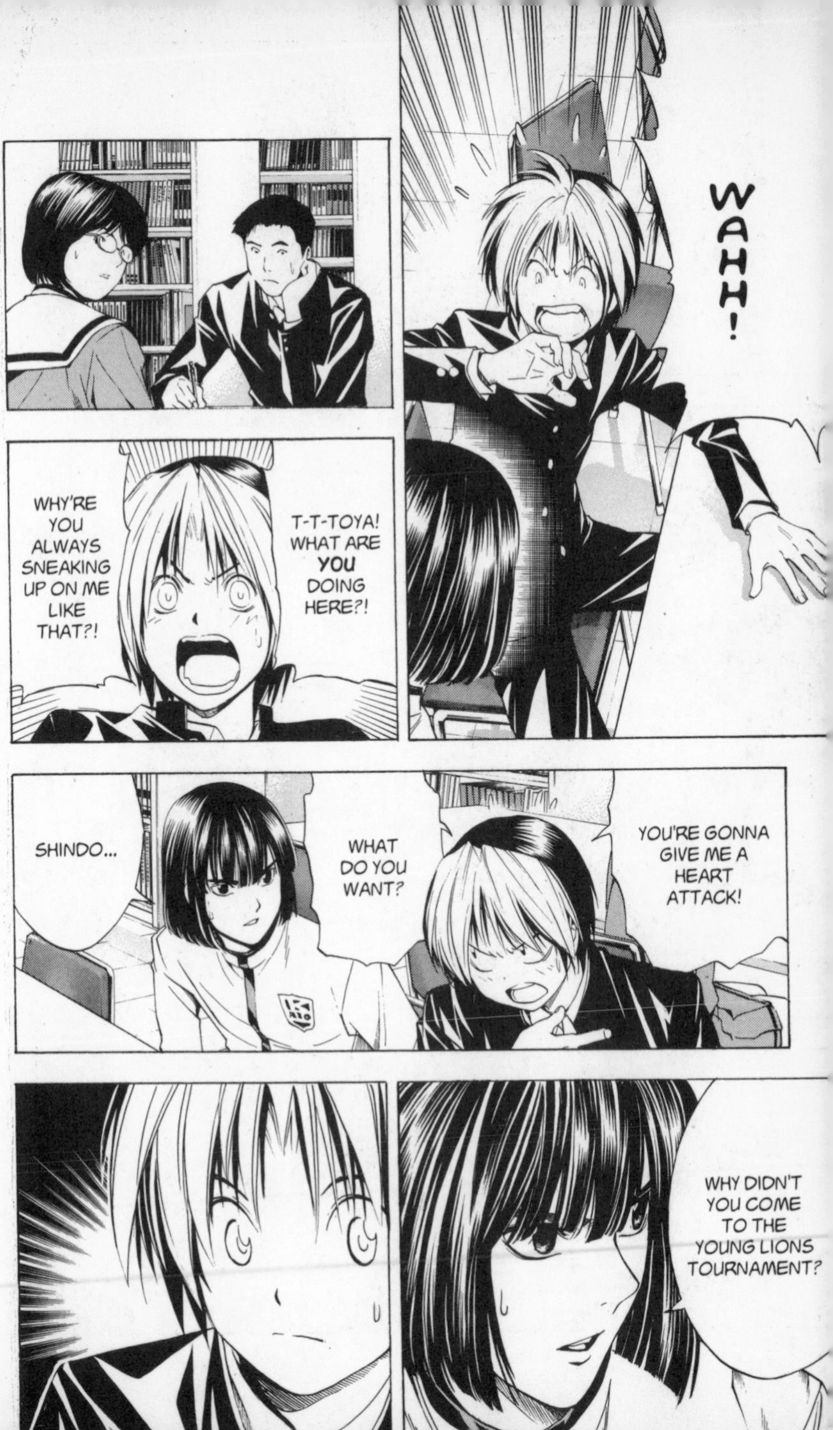
WAHH!
T-T-TOYA! WHAT ARE **YOU** DOING HERE?!
WHY'RE YOU ALWAYS SNEAKING UP ON ME LIKE THAT?!
YOU'RE GONNA GIVE ME A HEART ATTACK!
WHAT DO YOU WANT?
SHINDO...
WHY DIDN'T YOU COME TO THE YOUNG LIONS TOURNAMENT?

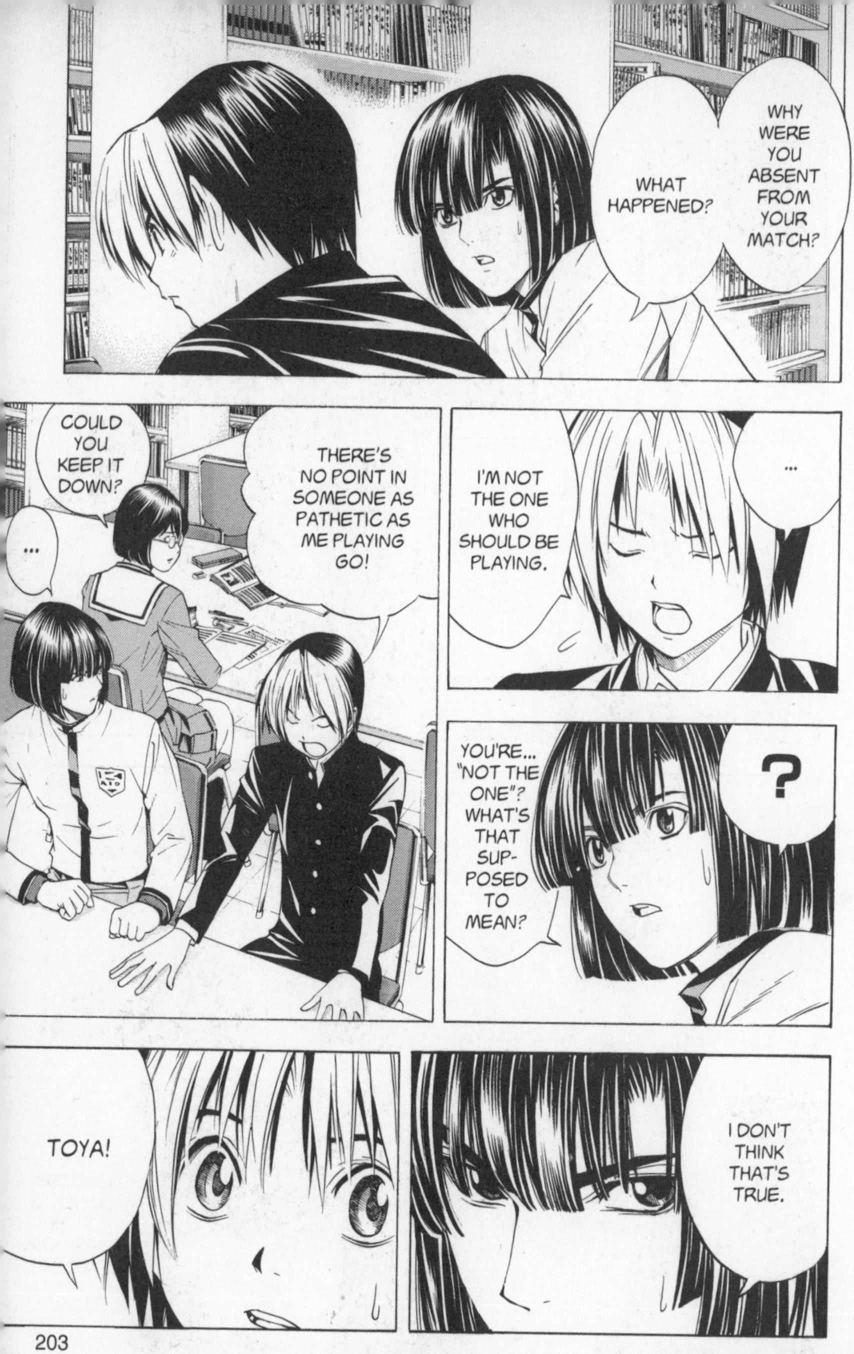
WHY WERE YOU ABSENT FROM YOUR MATCH?
WHAT HAPPENED?
...
I'M NOT THE ONE WHO SHOULD BE PLAYING.
?
YOU'RE... "NOT THE ONE"? WHAT'S THAT SUP-POSED TO MEAN?
THERE'S NO POINT IN SOMEONE AS PATHETIC AS ME PLAYING GO!
COULD YOU KEEP IT DOWN?
...
I DON'T THINK THAT'S TRUE.
TOYA!

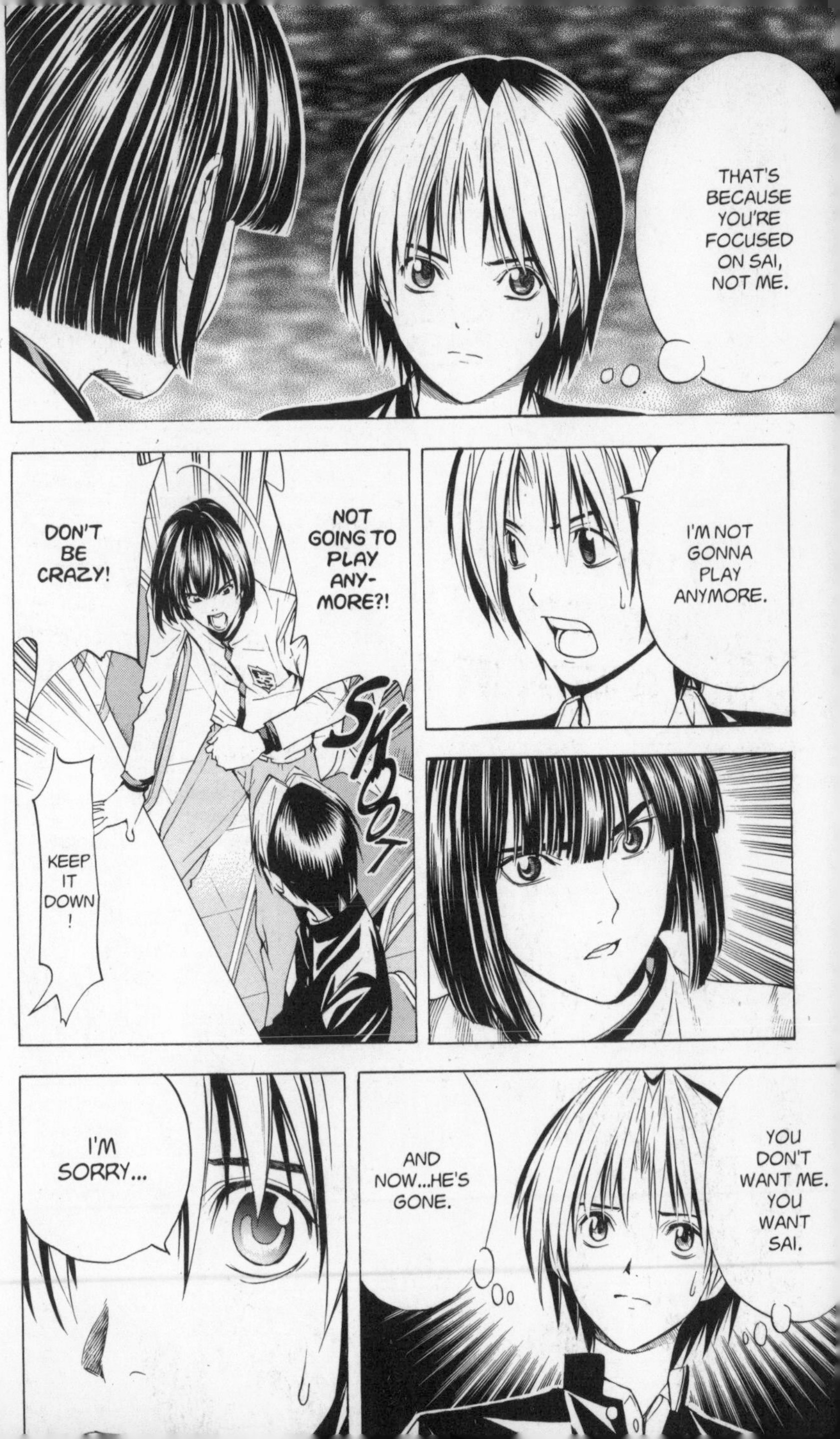
THAT'S BECAUSE YOU'RE FOCUSED ON SAI, NOT ME.
I'M NOT GONNA PLAY ANYMORE.
NOT GOING TO PLAY ANYMORE?!
DON'T BE CRAZY!
SHOOT
KEEP IT DOWN!
YOU DON'T WANT ME. YOU WANT SAI.
AND NOW...HE'S GONE.
I'M SORRY...

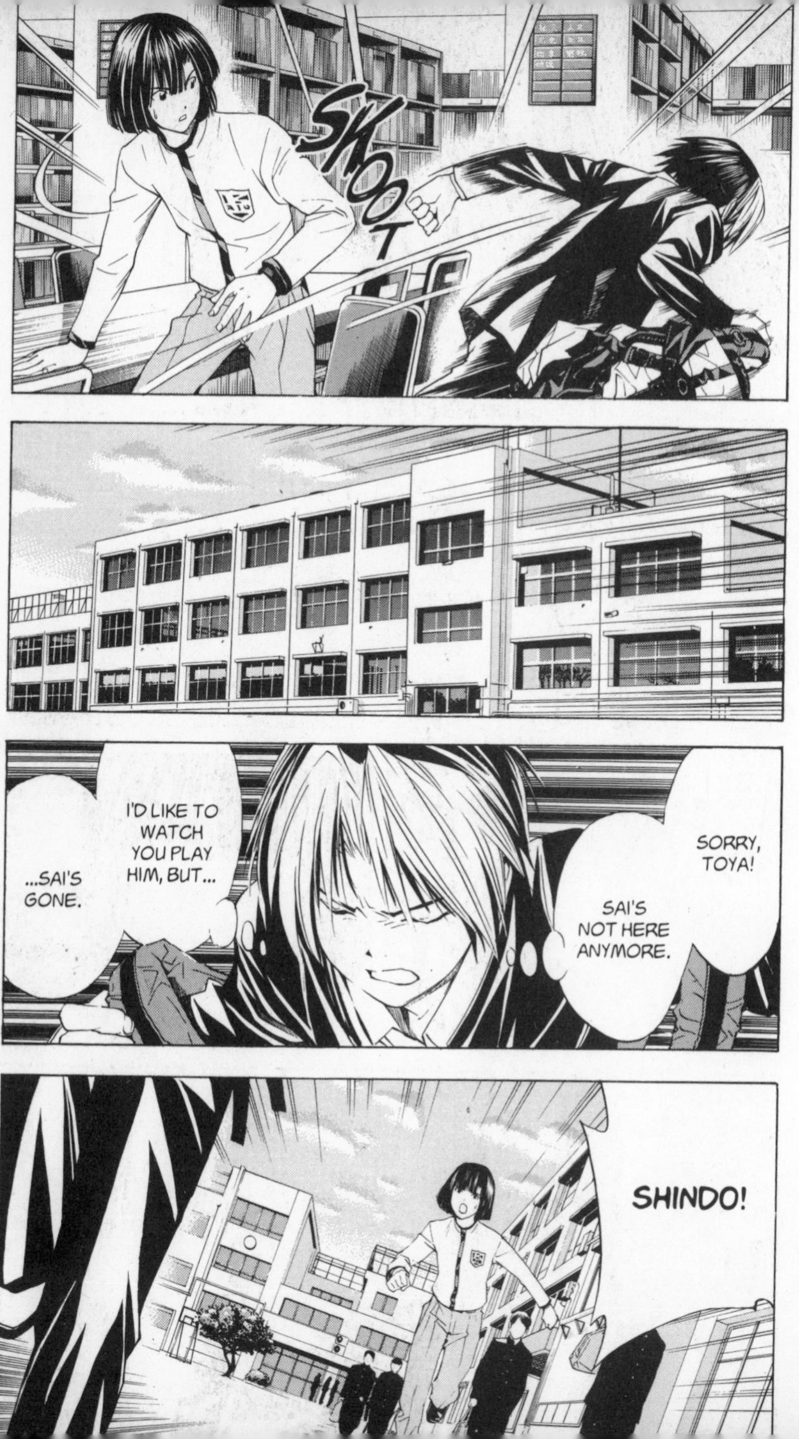
SHOOT
SORRY, TOYA!
SAI'S NOT HERE ANYMORE.
I'D LIKE TO WATCH YOU PLAY HIM, BUT...
...SAI'S GONE.
SHINDO!

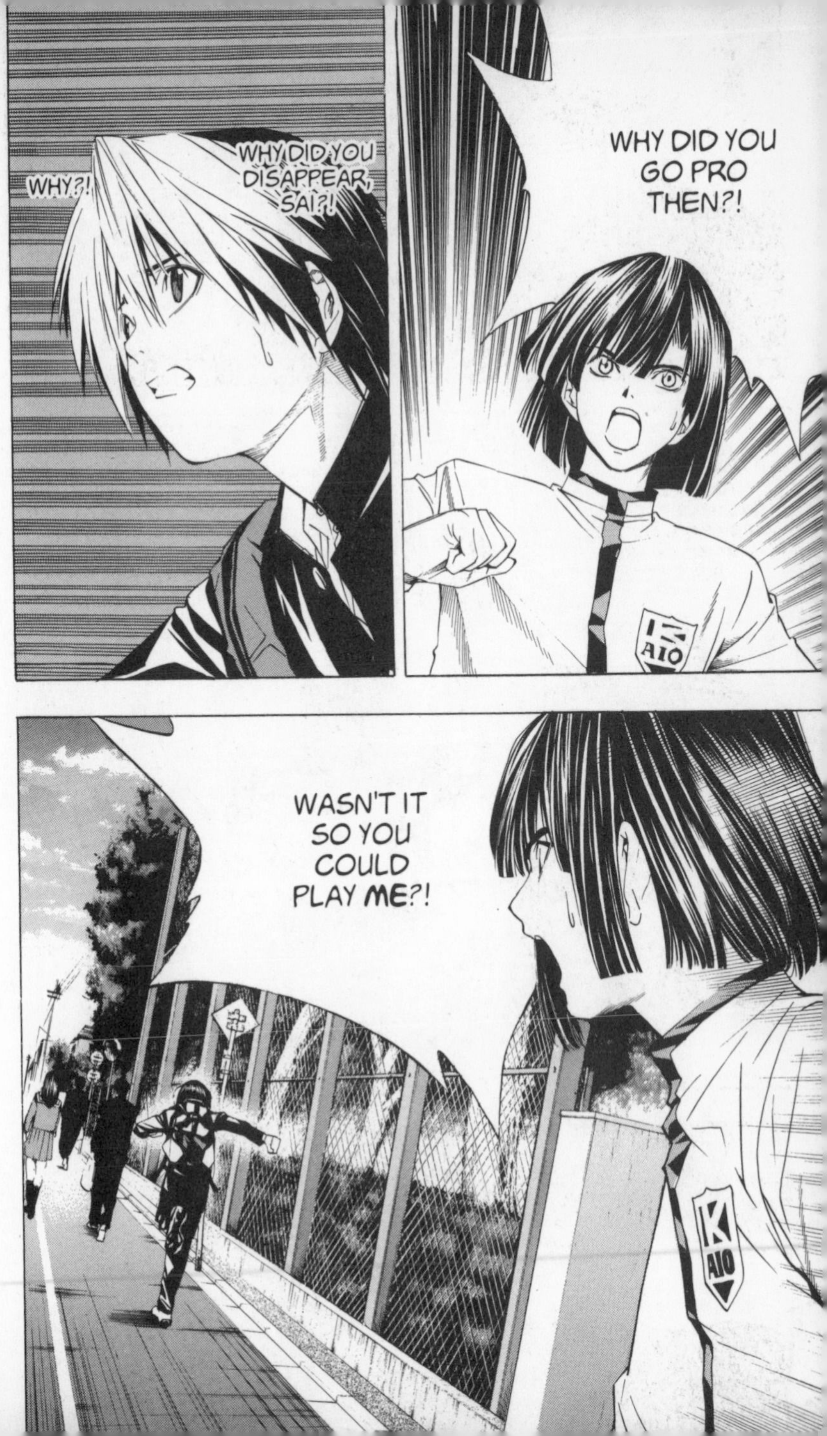
WHY DID YOU GO PRO THEN?!
WHY DID YOU DISAPPEAR, SAI?!
WHY?!
WASN'T IT SO YOU COULD PLAY ME?!

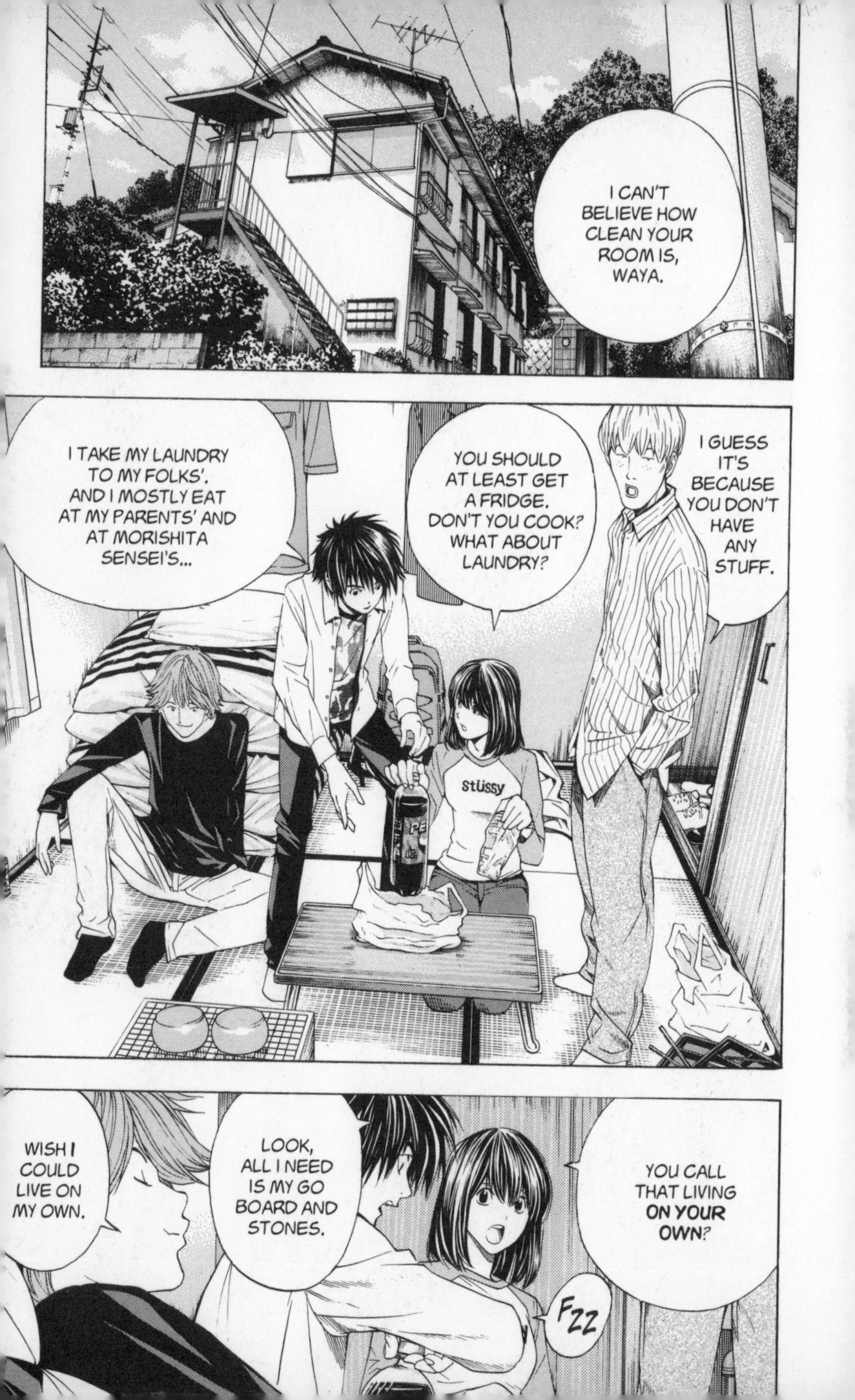
I CAN'T BELIEVE HOW CLEAN YOUR ROOM IS, WAYA.
I GUESS IT'S BECAUSE YOU DON'T HAVE ANY STUFF.
YOU SHOULD AT LEAST GET A FRIDGE. DON'T YOU COOK? WHAT ABOUT LAUNDRY?
I TAKE MY LAUNDRY TO MY FOLKS'. AND I MOSTLY EAT AT MY PARENTS' AND AT MORISHITA SENSEI'S...
Stüssy
YOU CALL THAT LIVING **ON YOUR OWN**?
FZZ
LOOK, ALL I NEED IS MY GO BOARD AND STONES.
WISH I COULD LIVE ON MY OWN.

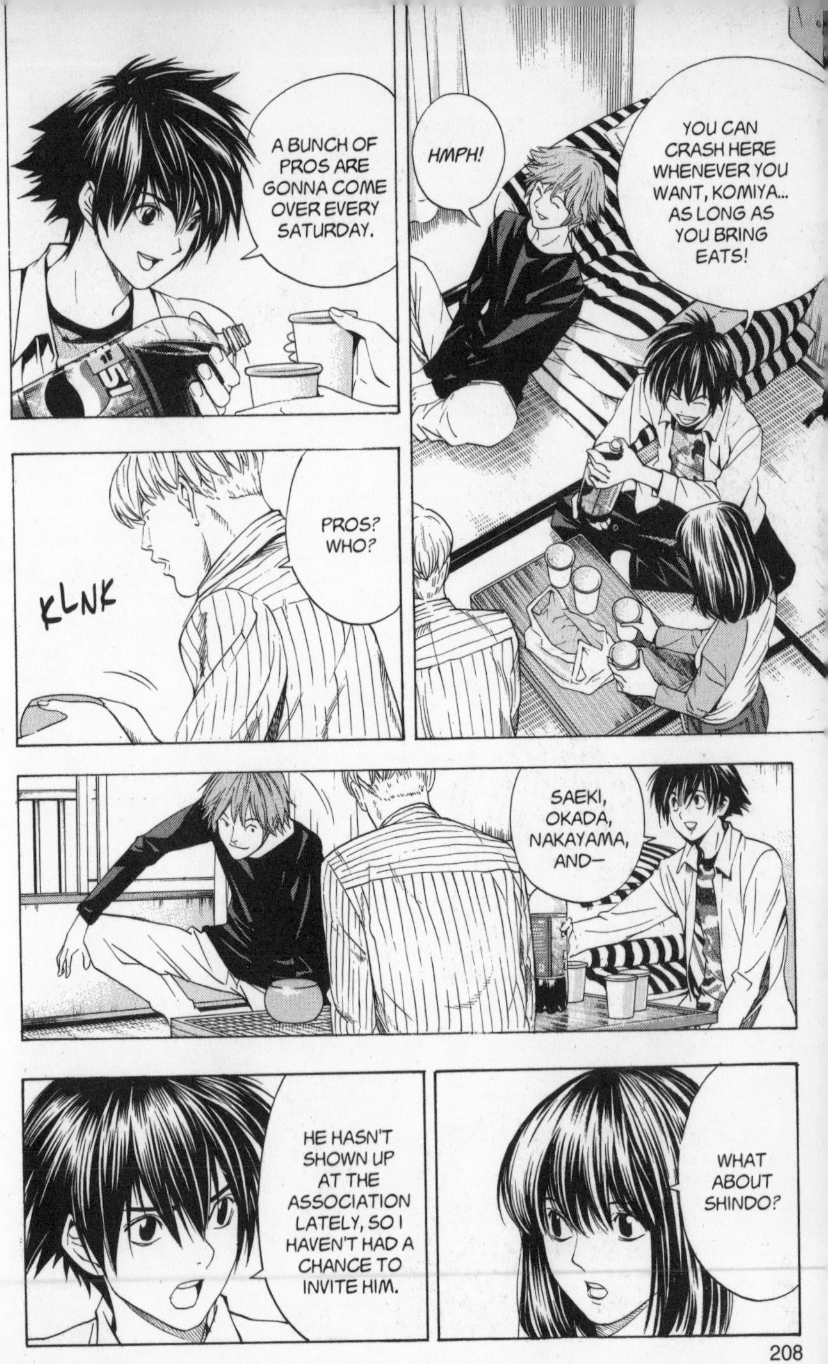
YOU CAN CRASH HERE WHENEVER YOU WANT, KOMIYA... AS LONG AS YOU BRING EATS!
HMPH!
A BUNCH OF PROS ARE GONNA COME OVER EVERY SATURDAY.
PROS? WHO?
KLNK
SAEKI, OKADA, NAKAYAMA, AND—
WHAT ABOUT SHINDO?
HE HASN'T SHOWN UP AT THE ASSOCIATION LATELY, SO I HAVEN'T HAD A CHANCE TO INVITE HIM.

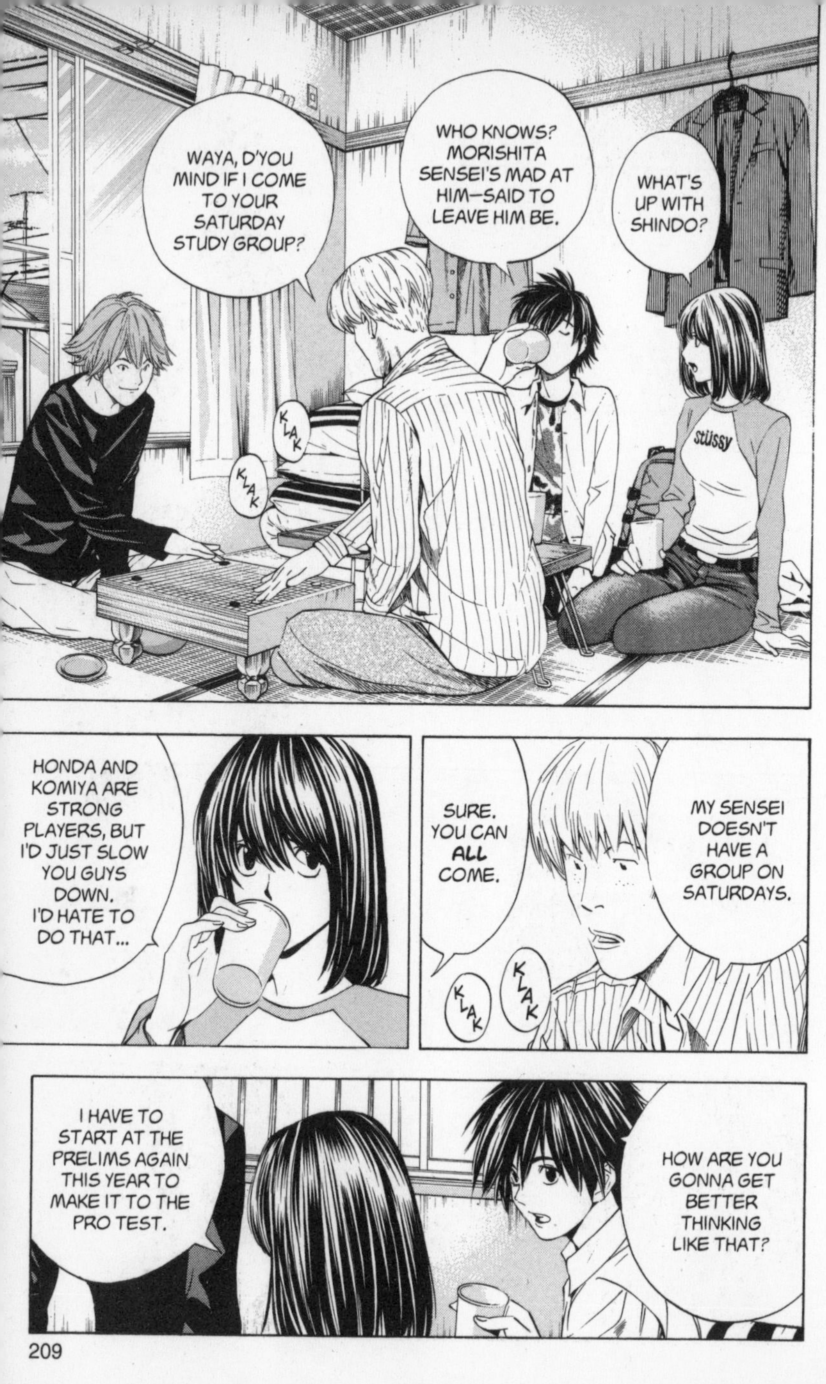
WHAT'S UP WITH SHINDO?
WHO KNOWS? MORISHITA SENSEI'S MAD AT HIM—SAID TO LEAVE HIM BE.
WAYA, D'YOU MIND IF I COME TO YOUR SATURDAY STUDY GROUP?
stüssy
KLAK
KLAK
MY SENSEI DOESN'T HAVE A GROUP ON SATURDAYS.
SURE. YOU CAN **ALL** COME.
KLAK
KLAK
HONDA AND KOMIYA ARE STRONG PLAYERS, BUT I'D JUST SLOW YOU GUYS DOWN. I'D HATE TO DO THAT...
HOW ARE YOU GONNA GET BETTER THINKING LIKE THAT?
I HAVE TO START AT THE PRELIMS AGAIN THIS YEAR TO MAKE IT TO THE PRO TEST.

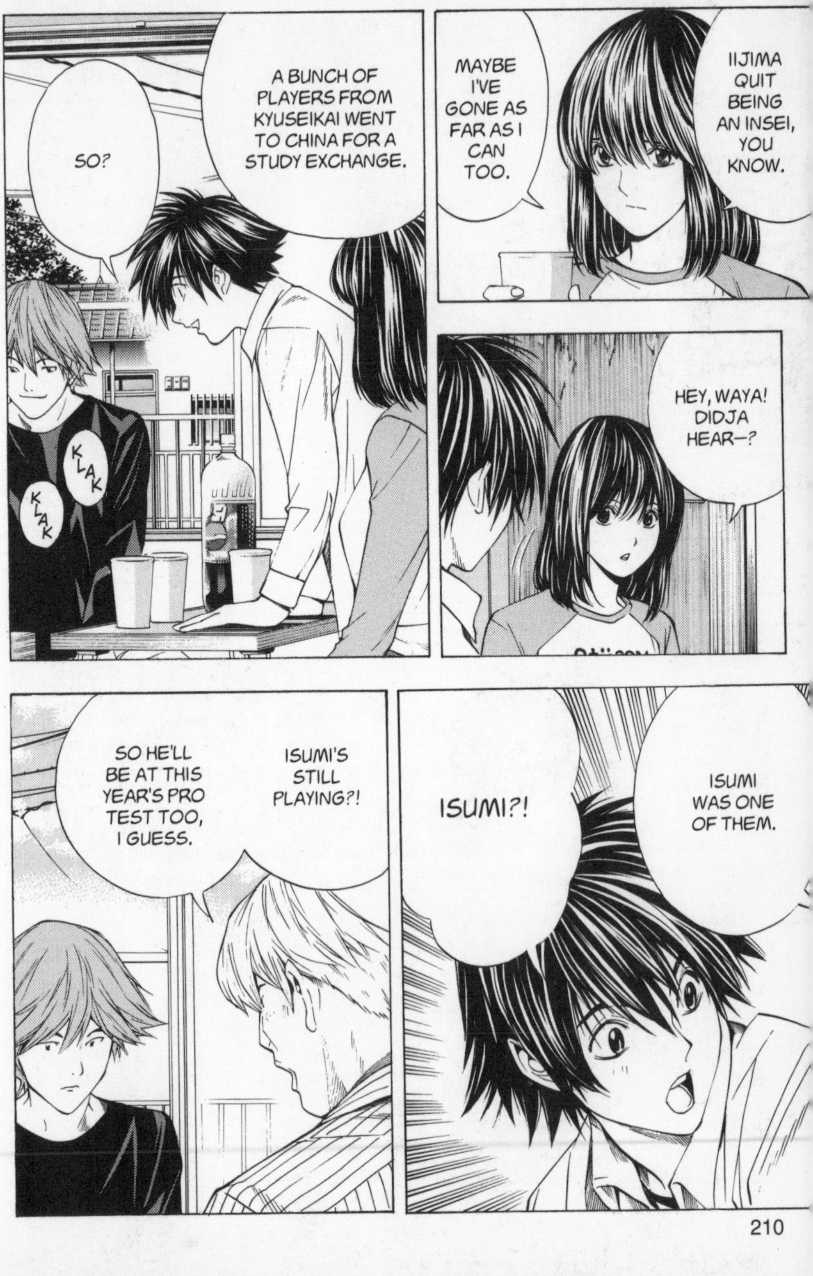
IIJIMA QUIT BEING AN INSEI, YOU KNOW.
MAYBE I'VE GONE AS FAR AS I CAN TOO.
HEY, WAYA! DIDJA HEAR—?
A BUNCH OF PLAYERS FROM KYUSEIKAI WENT TO CHINA FOR A STUDY EXCHANGE.
SO?
KLAK
KLAK
ISUMI WAS ONE OF THEM.
ISUMI?!
ISUMI'S STILL PLAYING?!
SO HE'LL BE AT THIS YEAR'S PRO TEST TOO, I GUESS.

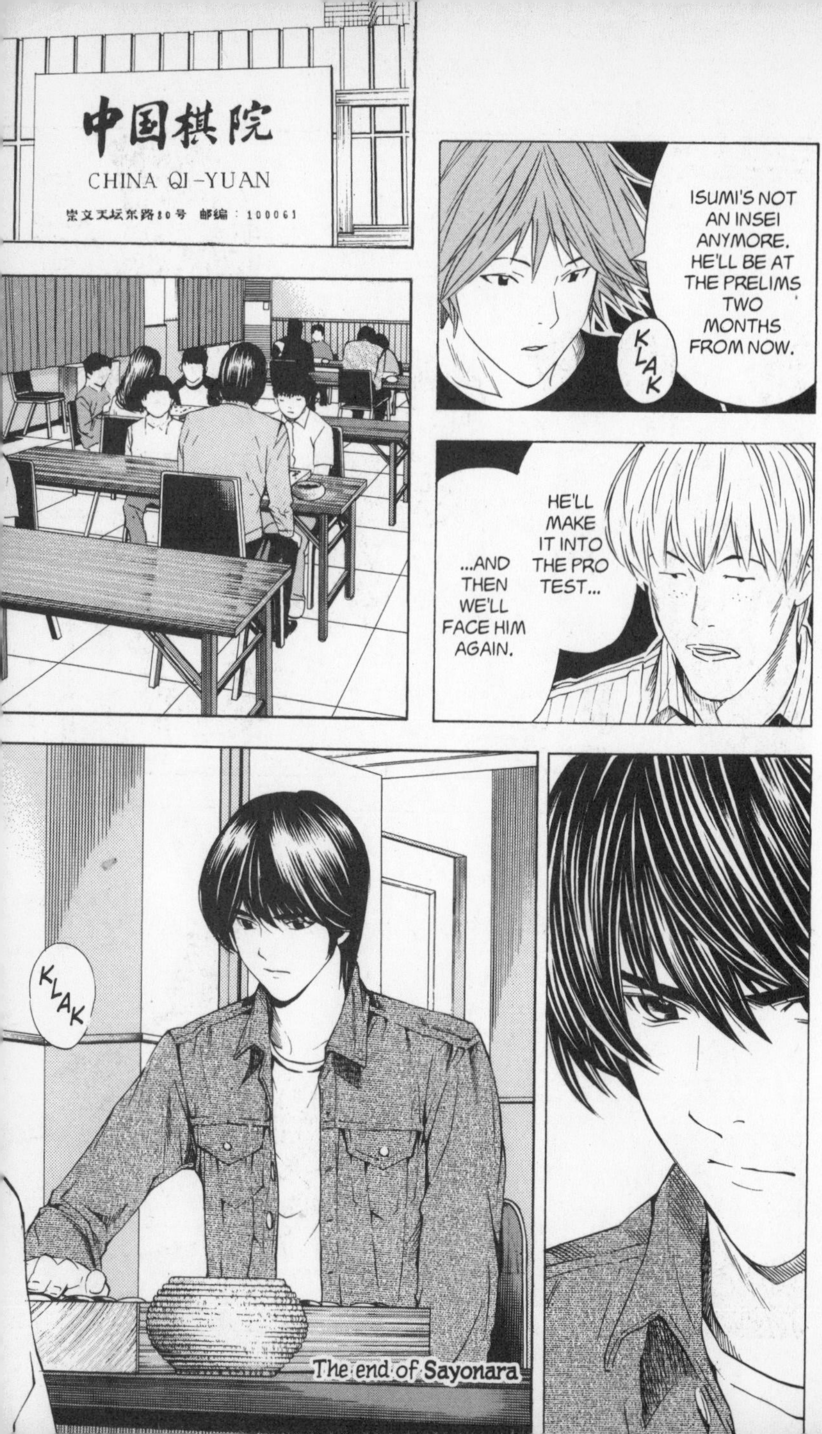
中国棋院
CHINA QI-YUAN
崇文天坛东路80号 邮编：100061
ISUMI'S NOT AN INSEI ANYMORE. HE'LL BE AT THE PRELIMS TWO MONTHS FROM NOW.
KLAK
HE'LL MAKE IT INTO THE PRO TEST...
...AND THEN WE'LL FACE HIM AGAIN.
KLAK
The end of Sayonara

Next Volume Preview

Since Sai's disappearance, Hikaru has given up go! Meanwhile, undefeated by his failure to pass the pro test, Isumi plays his heart out in China. His foreign training teaches him unique ways to handle the stress of mental challenges and competition. Upon his return, he asks Hikaru for a rematch! But how good will Hikaru's game be after such a long break—and without Sai...?

COMING AUGUST 2009

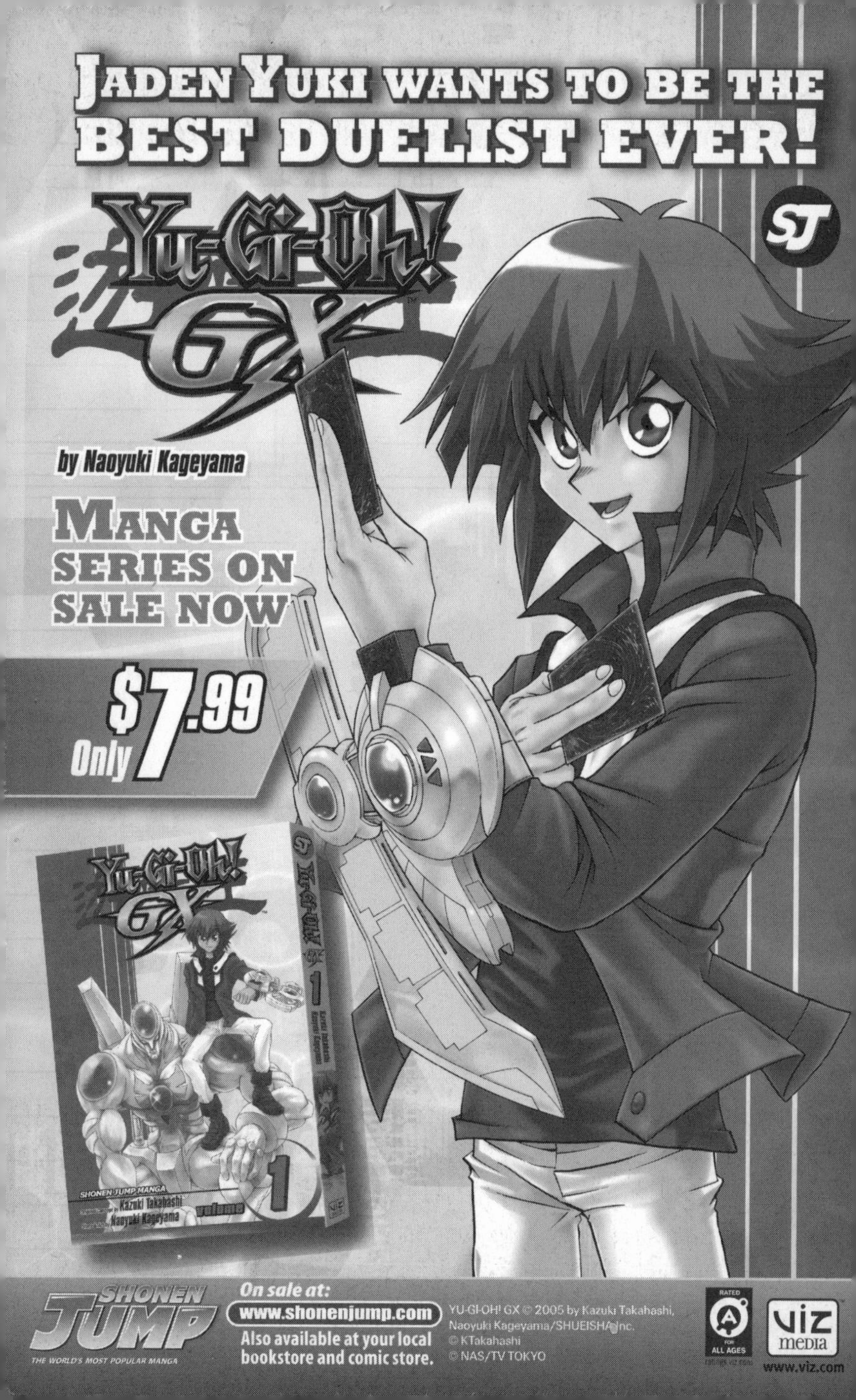
JADEN YUKI WANTS TO BE THE
BEST DUELIST EVER!
SJ
YU-GI-OH! GX
by Naoyuki Kageyama
MANGA
SERIES ON
SALE NOW
Only $7.99
YU-GI-OH! GX
1
SHONEN JUMP MANGA
Kazuki Takahashi
Naoyuki Kageyama
volume
1
SHONEN JUMP
THE WORLD'S MOST POPULAR MANGA
On sale at:
www.shonenjump.com
Also available at your local
bookstore and comic store.
YU-GI-OH! GX © 2005 by Kazuki Takahashi,
Naoyuki Kageyama/SHUEISHA Inc.
© KTakahashi
© NAS/TV TOKYO
RATED
A
FOR
ALL AGES
VIZ
media
www.viz.com